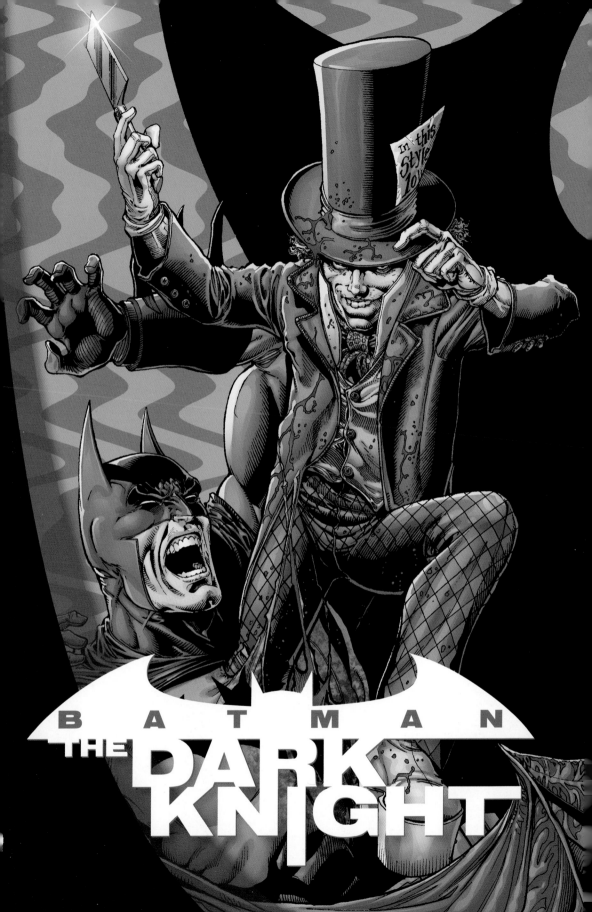

In this Style 10/6

# BATMAN
# THE DARK
# KNIGHT

VOLUME 3 **MAD**

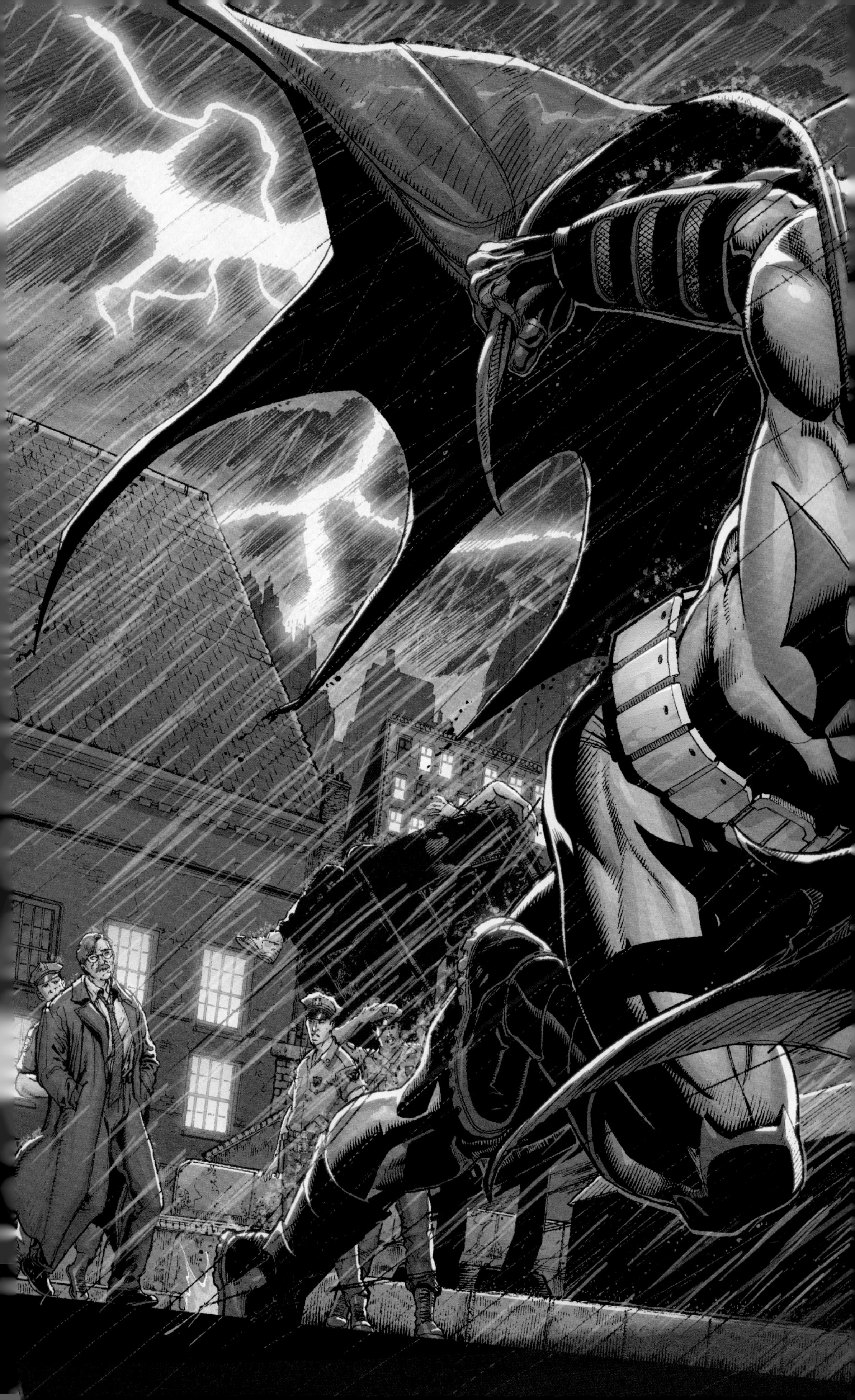

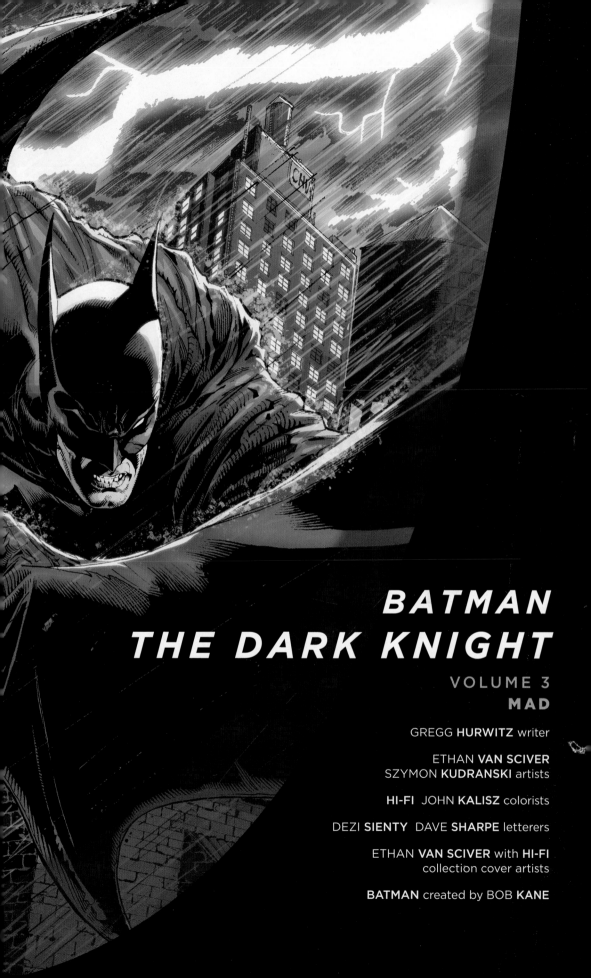

# BATMAN THE DARK KNIGHT

## VOLUME 3
### MAD

GREGG **HURWITZ** writer

ETHAN **VAN SCIVER**
SZYMON **KUDRANSKI** artists

**HI-FI** JOHN **KALISZ** colorists

DEZI **SIENTY** DAVE **SHARPE** letterers

ETHAN **VAN SCIVER** with **HI-FI**
collection cover artists

**BATMAN** created by BOB **KANE**

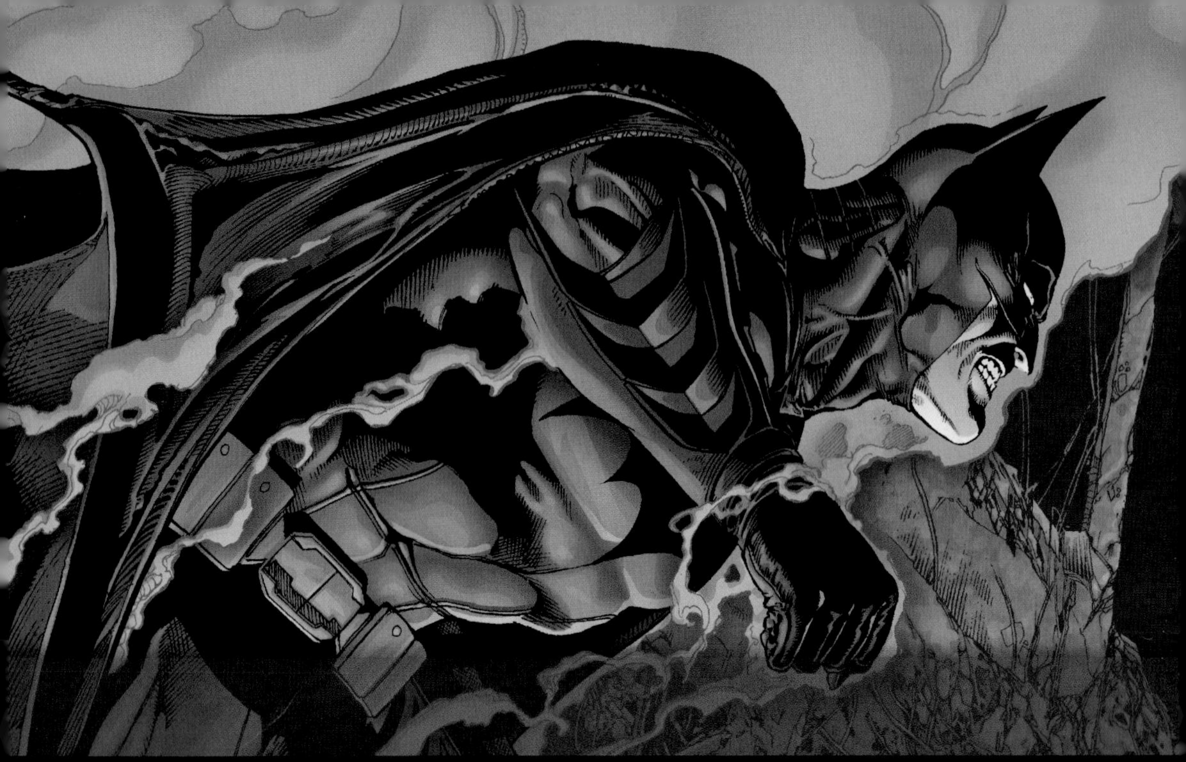

MIKE MARTS Editor – Original Series RICKEY PURDIN DARREN SHAN Assistant Editor – Original Series RACHEL PINNELAS Editor
ROBBIN BROSTERMAN Design Director – Books ROBBIE BIEDERMAN Publication Design

BOB HARRAS Senior VP – Editor-in-Chief, DC Comics

DIANE NELSON President DAN DIDIO and JIM LEE Co-Publishers
GEOFF JOHNS Chief Creative Officer
JOHN ROOD Executive VP – Sales, Marketing and Business Development
AMY GENKINS Senior VP – Business and Legal Affairs NAIRI GARDINER Senior VP – Finance
JEFF BOISON VP – Publishing Planning MARK CHIARELLO VP – Art Direction and Design
JOHN CUNNINGHAM VP – Marketing TERRI CUNNINGHAM VP – Editorial Administration
ALISON GILL Senior VP – Manufacturing and Operations HANK KANALZ Senior VP – Vertigo and Integrated Publishing
JAY KOGAN VP – Business and Legal Affairs, Publishing JACK MAHAN VP – Business Affairs, Talent
NICK NAPOLITANO VP – Manufacturing Administration SUE POHJA VP – Book Sales
COURTNEY SIMMONS Senior VP – Publicity BOB WAYNE Senior VP – Sales

BATMAN: THE DARK KNIGHT VOLUME 3: MAD



DC Comics, 1700 Broadway, New York, NY 10019
A Warner Bros. Entertainment Company.
Printed by RR Donnelley, Salem, VA, USA. 12/13/13. First Printing.

ISBN: 978-1-4012-4247-3

SUSTAINABLE FORESTRY INITIATIVE
Certified Chain of Custody
At Least 20% Certified Forest Content
www.sfiprogram.org
SFI-01042
APPLIES TO TEXT STOCK ONLY

Library of Congress Cataloging-in-Publication Data

Hurwitz, Gregg Andrew, author.
Batman, the Dark Knight. Volume 3, Mad / Gregg Hurwitz ; [illustrated by] Ethan Van Sciver.
pages cm. — (The New 52!)
ISBN 978-1-4012-4247-3 (hardback)
1. Graphic novels. I. Van Sciver, Ethan, illustrator. II. Title. III. Title: Mad.
PN6728.B36H84 2014
741.5'973—dc23
2013035966

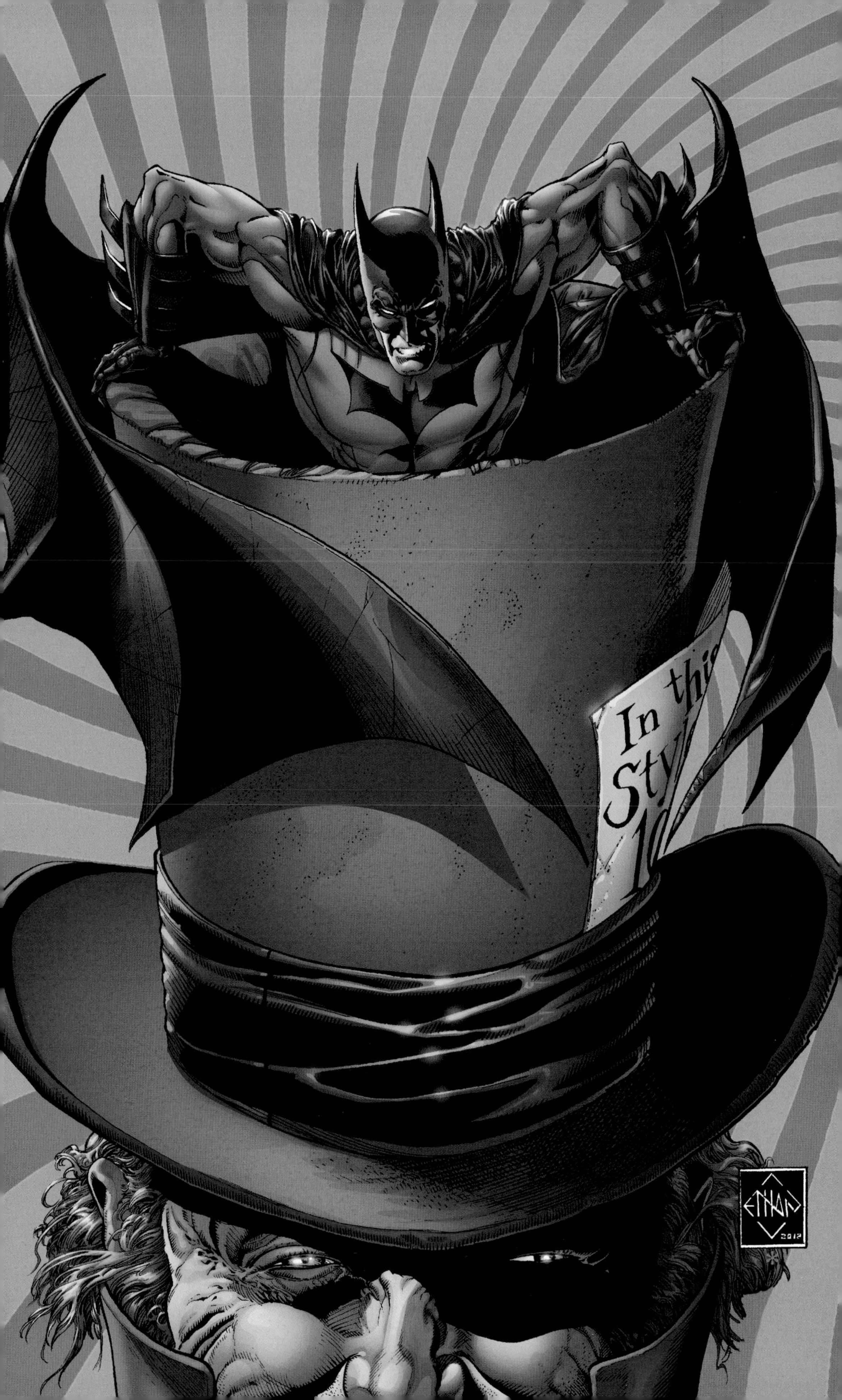
In thi
Sty
10

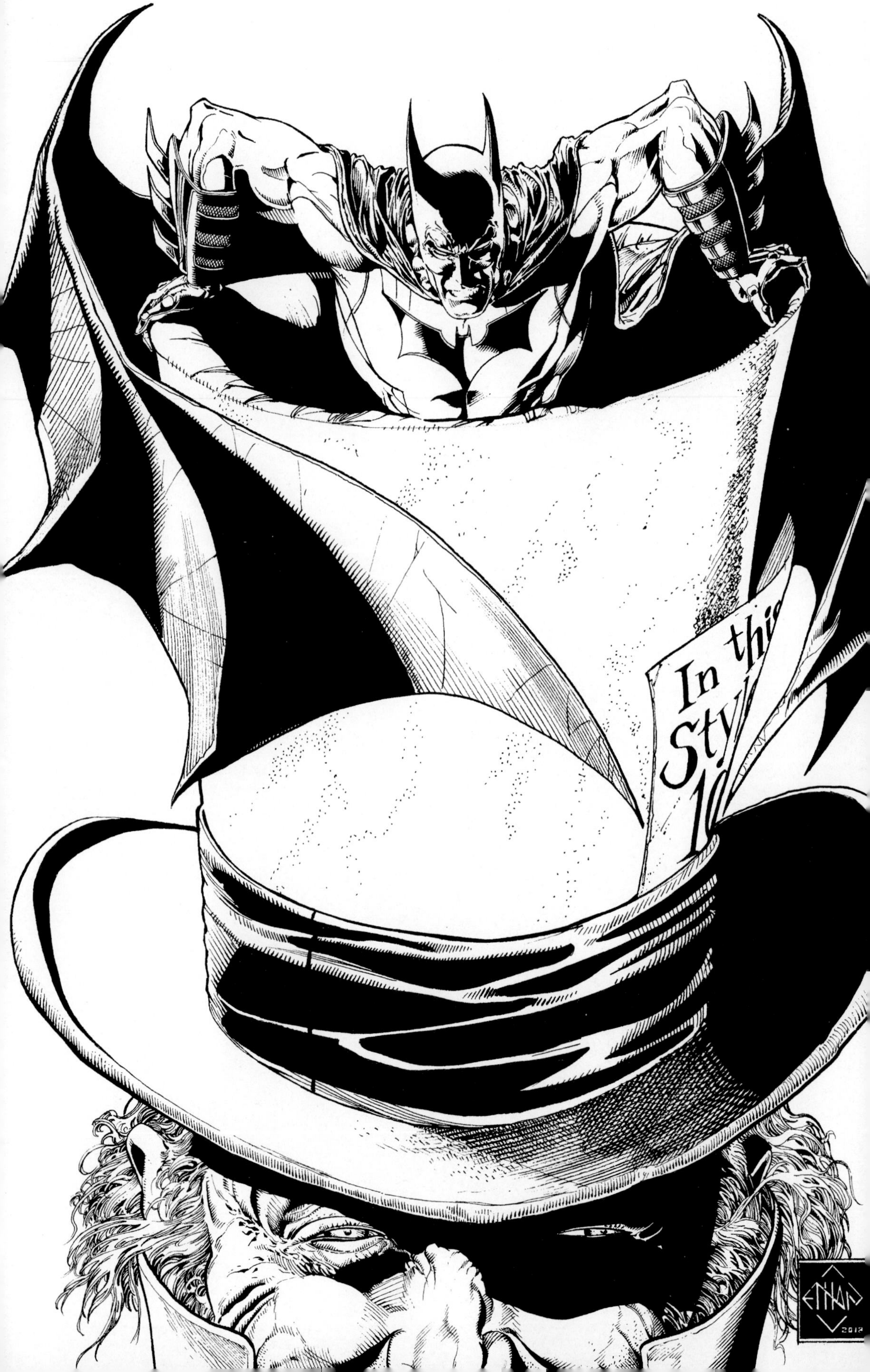

Gotham's coming apart at the seams.

Not the first time...

...but feels like it could be the last.

The citizens are panicked.

In the last week alone, there've been riots in Devil's Square, Old Town, and Robinson Park.

Can't blame them for being terrified...

...they're being taken.

A tidal wave of kidnappings. Every demographic, every age, every shape and size.

Some show up dead, some never show up at all.

There's no discernible pattern.

I prefer patterns.

MOTHER OF 3 DISAPPEARS

ISSING

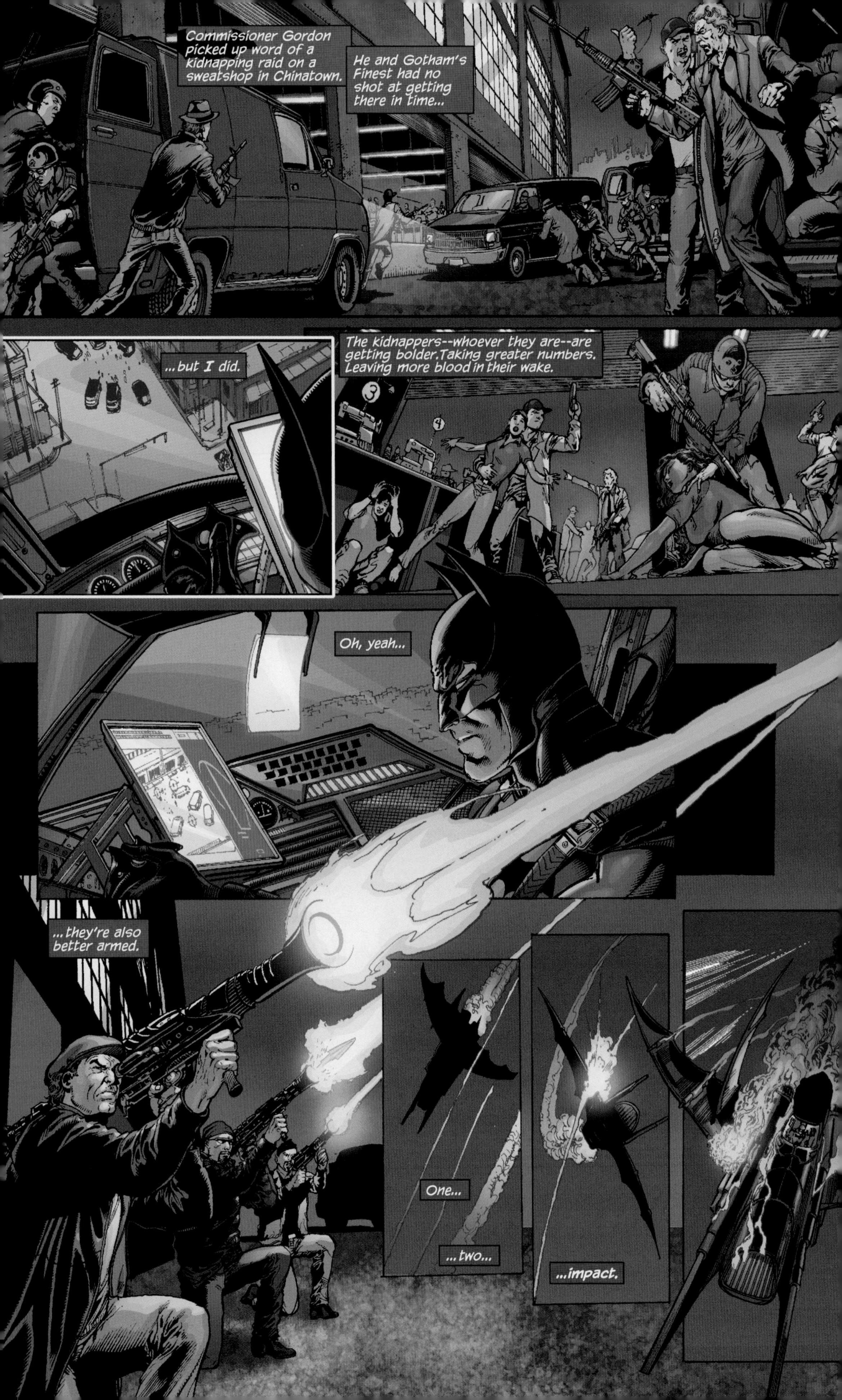
Commissioner Gordon picked up word of a kidnapping raid on a sweatshop in Chinatown.
He and Gotham's Finest had no shot at getting there in time...
...but I did.
The kidnappers--whoever they are--are getting bolder. Taking greater numbers. Leaving more blood in their wake.
Oh, yeah...
...they're also better armed.
One...
...two...
...impact.

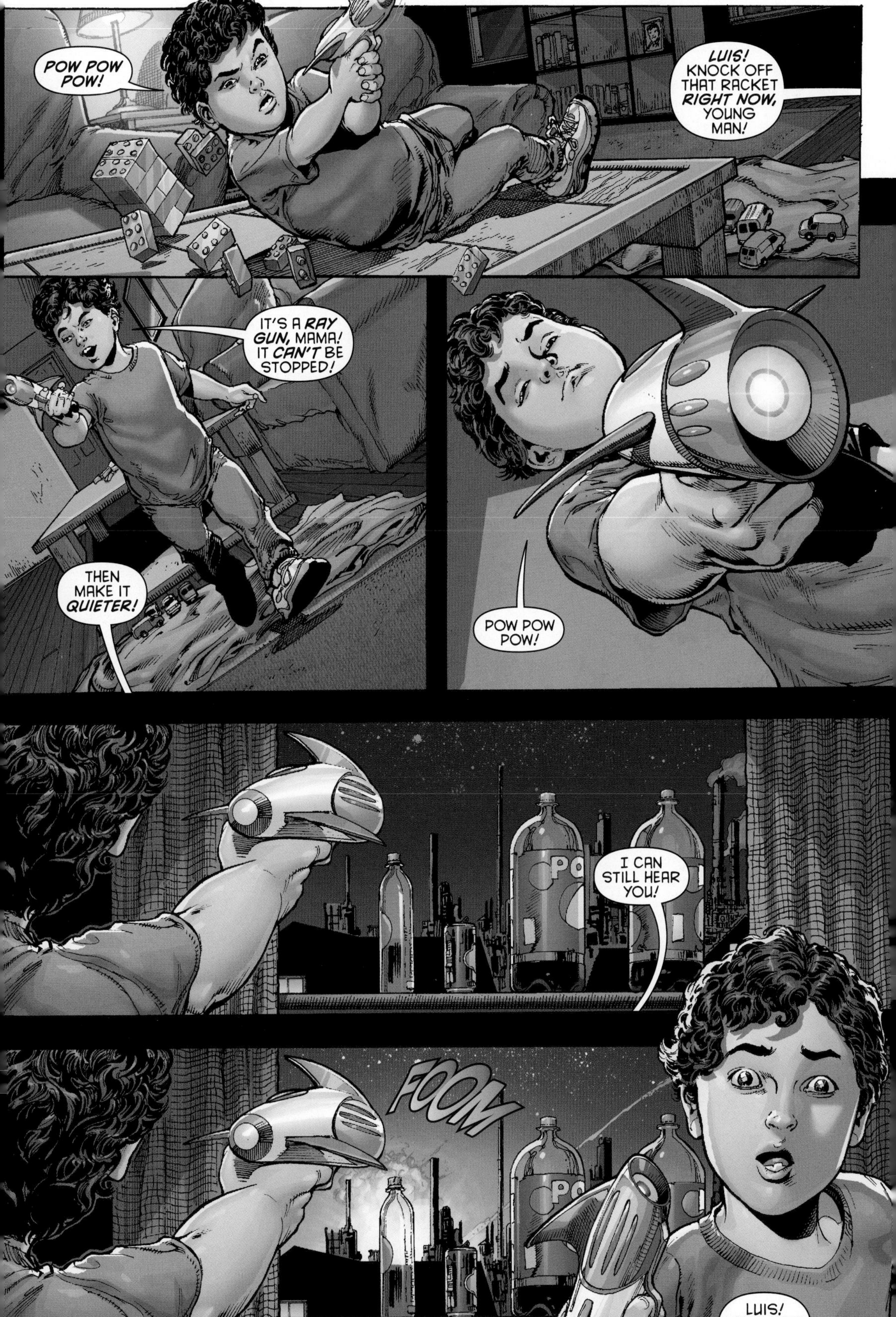
POW POW POW!
LUIS! KNOCK OFF THAT RACKET RIGHT NOW, YOUNG MAN!
IT'S A RAY GUN, MAMA! IT CAN'T BE STOPPED!
THEN MAKE IT QUIETER!
POW POW POW!
I CAN STILL HEAR YOU!
FOOM
LUIS! WHAT HAVE

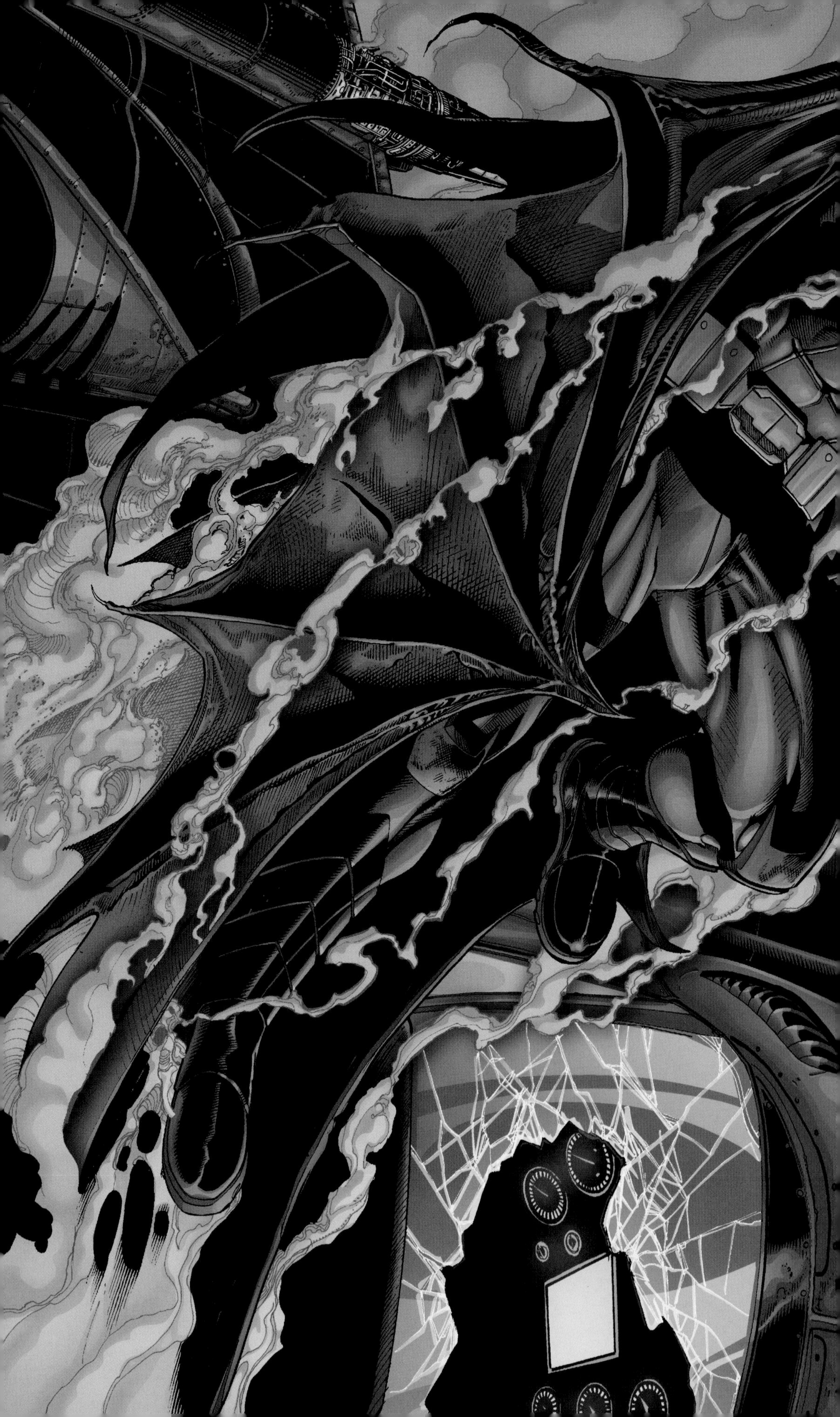

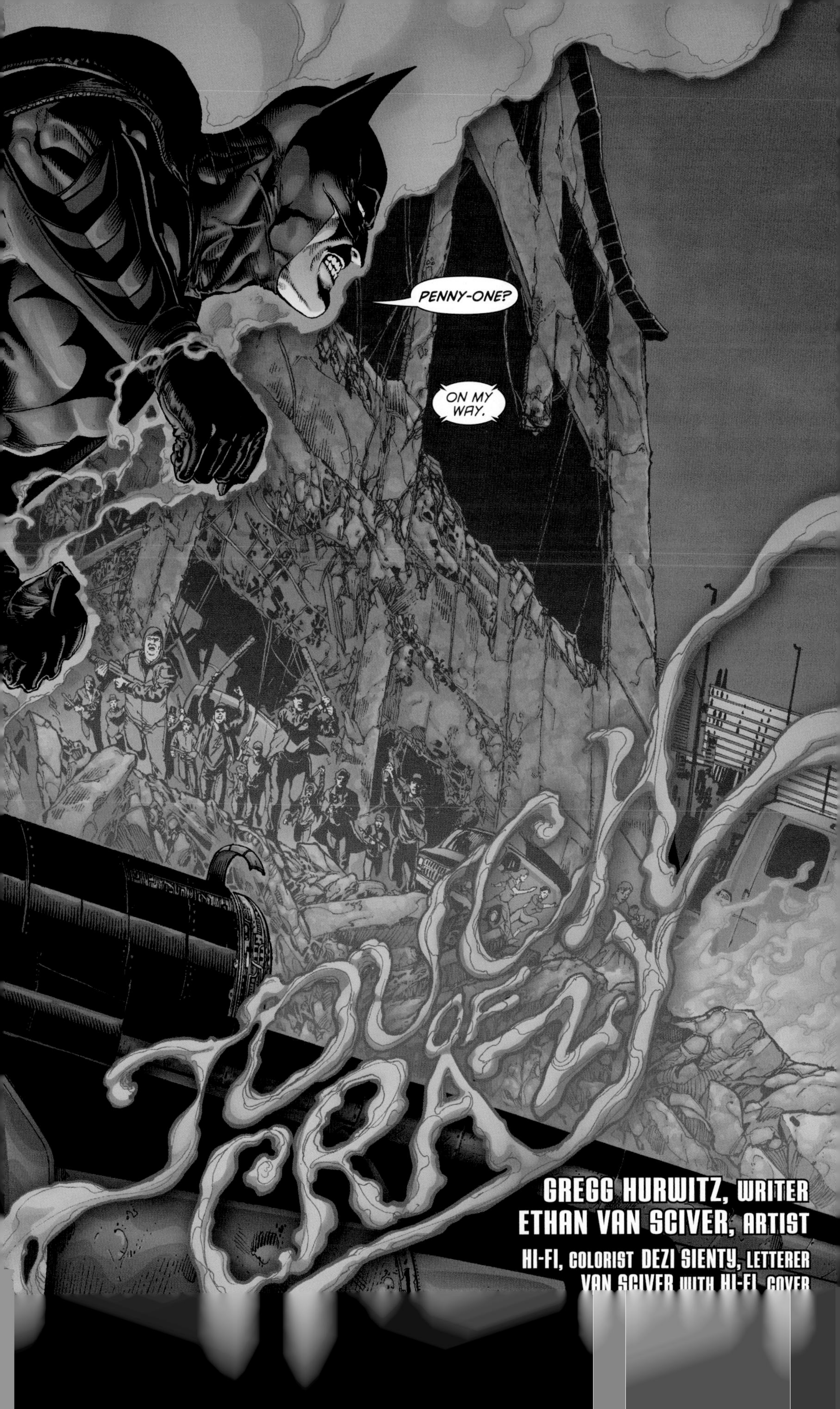
PENNY-ONE?
ON MY WAY.
GREGG HURWITZ, WRITER
ETHAN VAN SCIVER, ARTIST
HI-FI, COLORIST DEZI SIENTY, LETTERER
VAN SCIVER WITH HI-FI, COVER

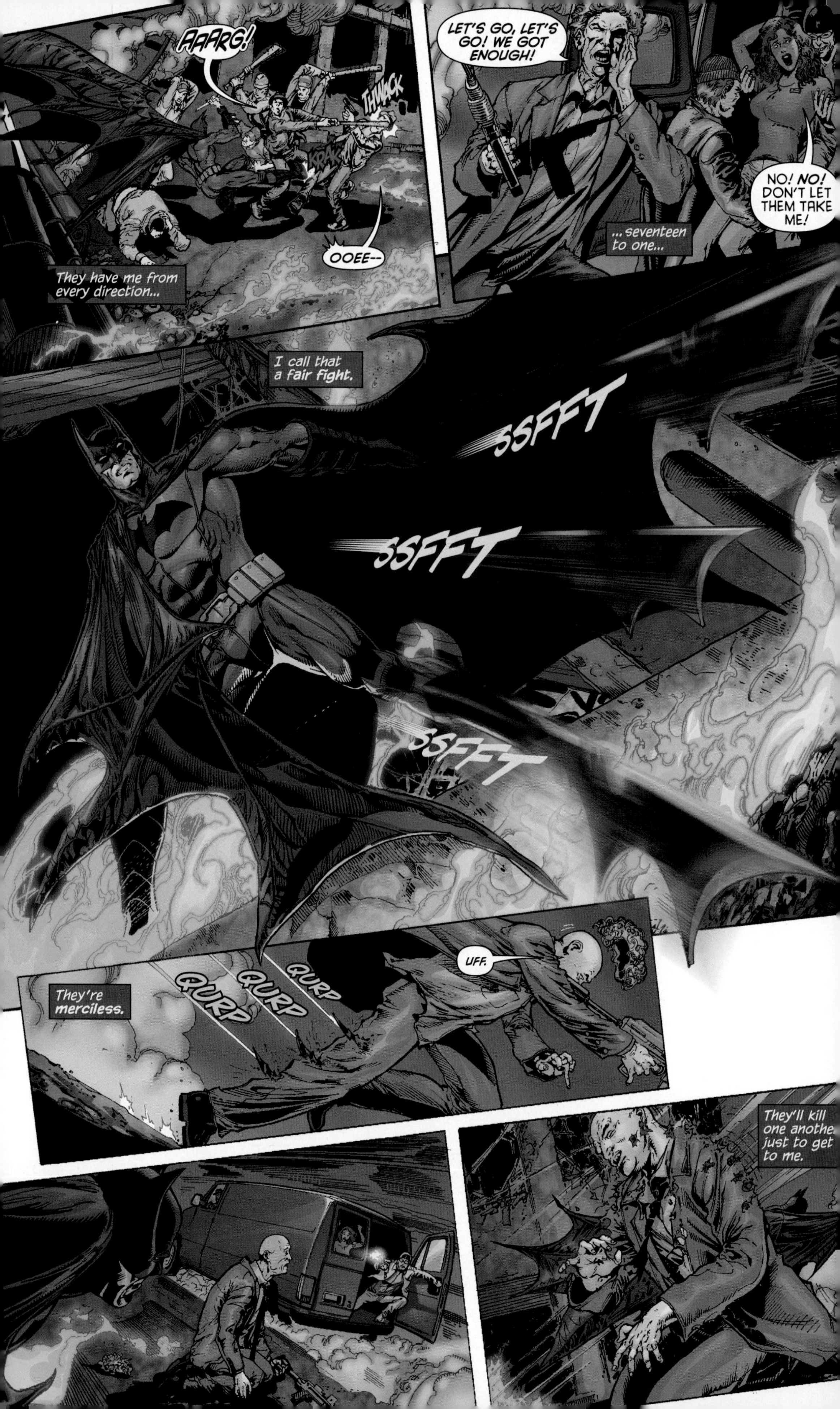
AAARG!
THWACK
KRAK
OOEE--
They have me from every direction...
LET'S GO, LET'S GO! WE GOT ENOUGH!
NO! NO! DON'T LET THEM TAKE ME!
...seventeen to one...
I call that a fair fight.
SSFFT
SSFFT
SSFFT
They're merciless.
QURP
QURP
QURP
UFF.
They'll kill one anothe just to get to me.

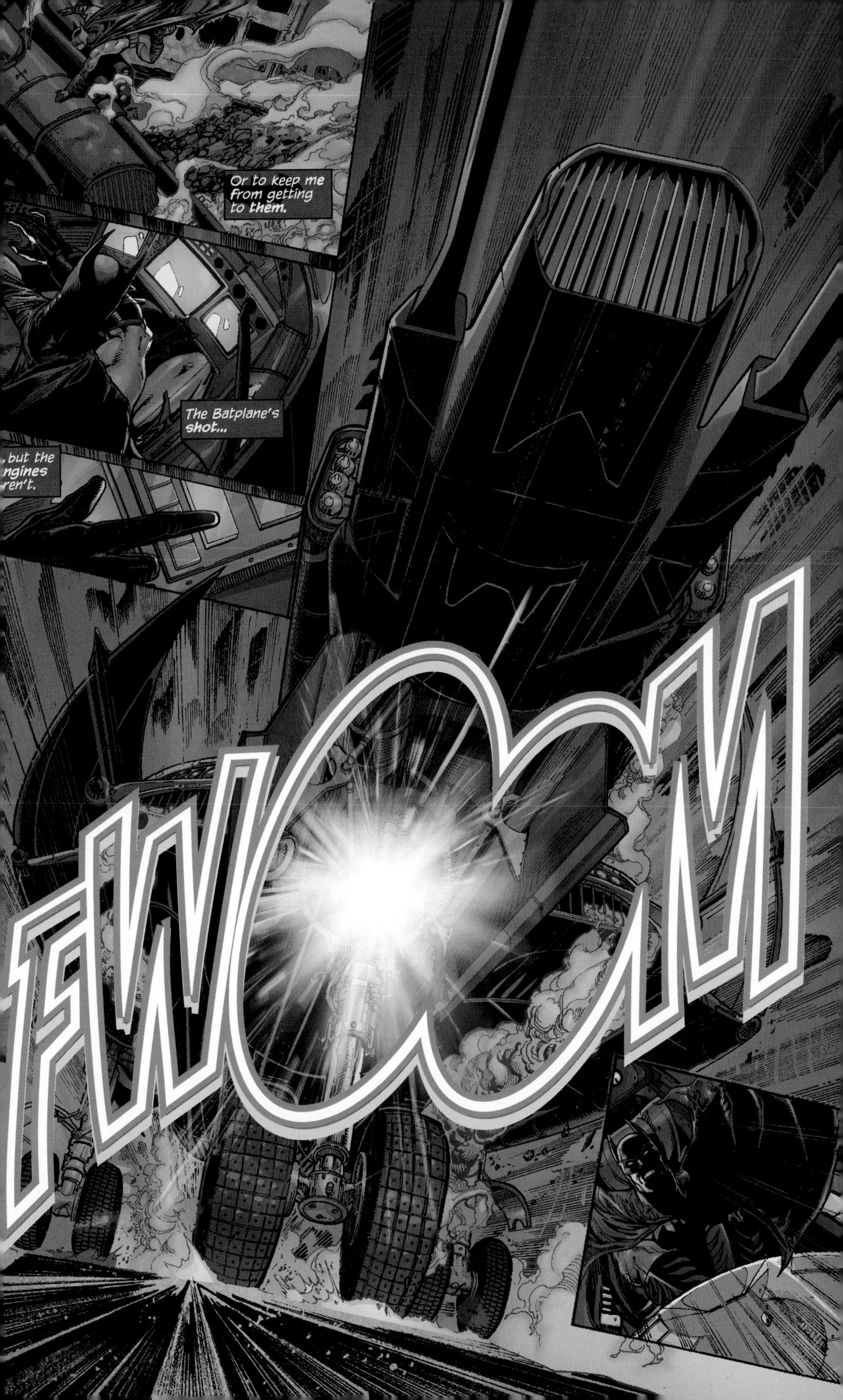
Or to keep me from getting to them.
The Batplane's shot...
, but the ngines ren't.
FWOOM

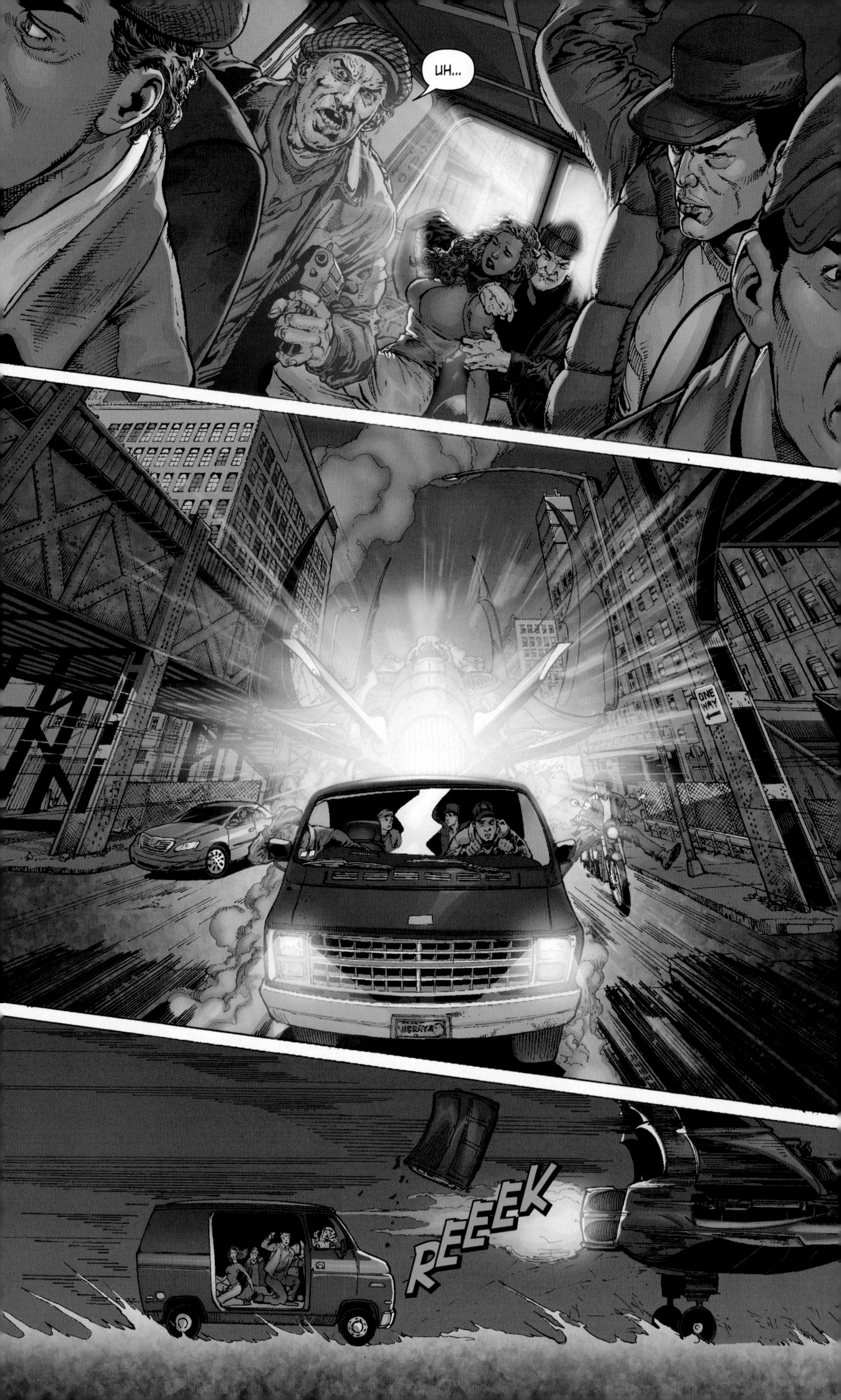

UH...
ONE WAY
REEEEK

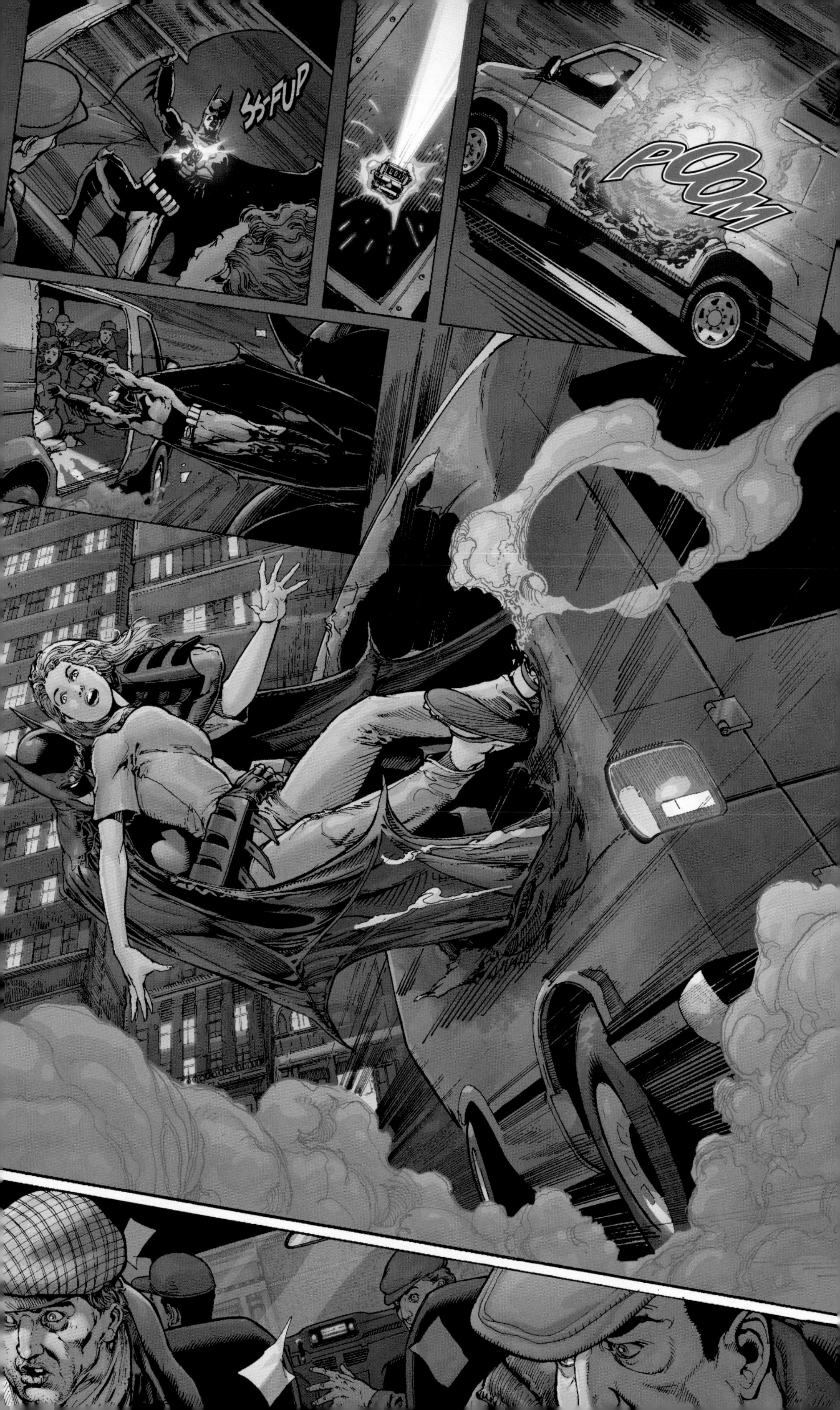
SS-FUP
POOM

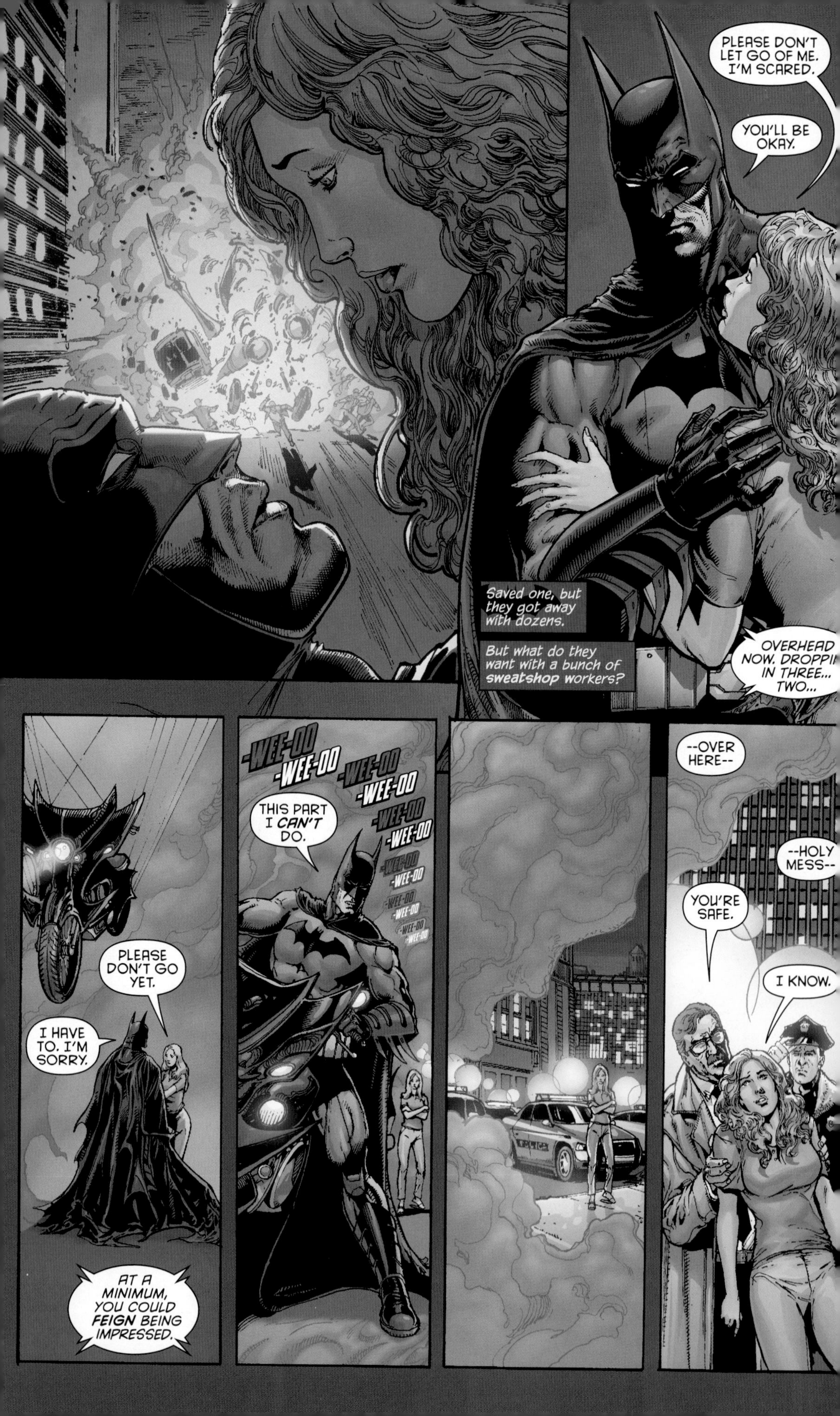
PLEASE DON'T LET GO OF ME. I'M SCARED.
YOU'LL BE OKAY.
Saved one, but they got away with dozens.
But what do they want with a bunch of **sweatshop** workers?
OVERHEAD NOW. DROPPI IN THREE... TWO...
PLEASE DON'T GO YET.
I HAVE TO. I'M SORRY.
AT A MINIMUM, YOU COULD **FEIGN** BEING IMPRESSED.
-WEE-OO -WEE-OO -WEE-OO -WEE-OO -WEE-OO -WEE-OO
THIS PART I *CAN'T* DO.
--OVER HERE--
--HOLY MESS--
YOU'RE SAFE.
I KNOW.

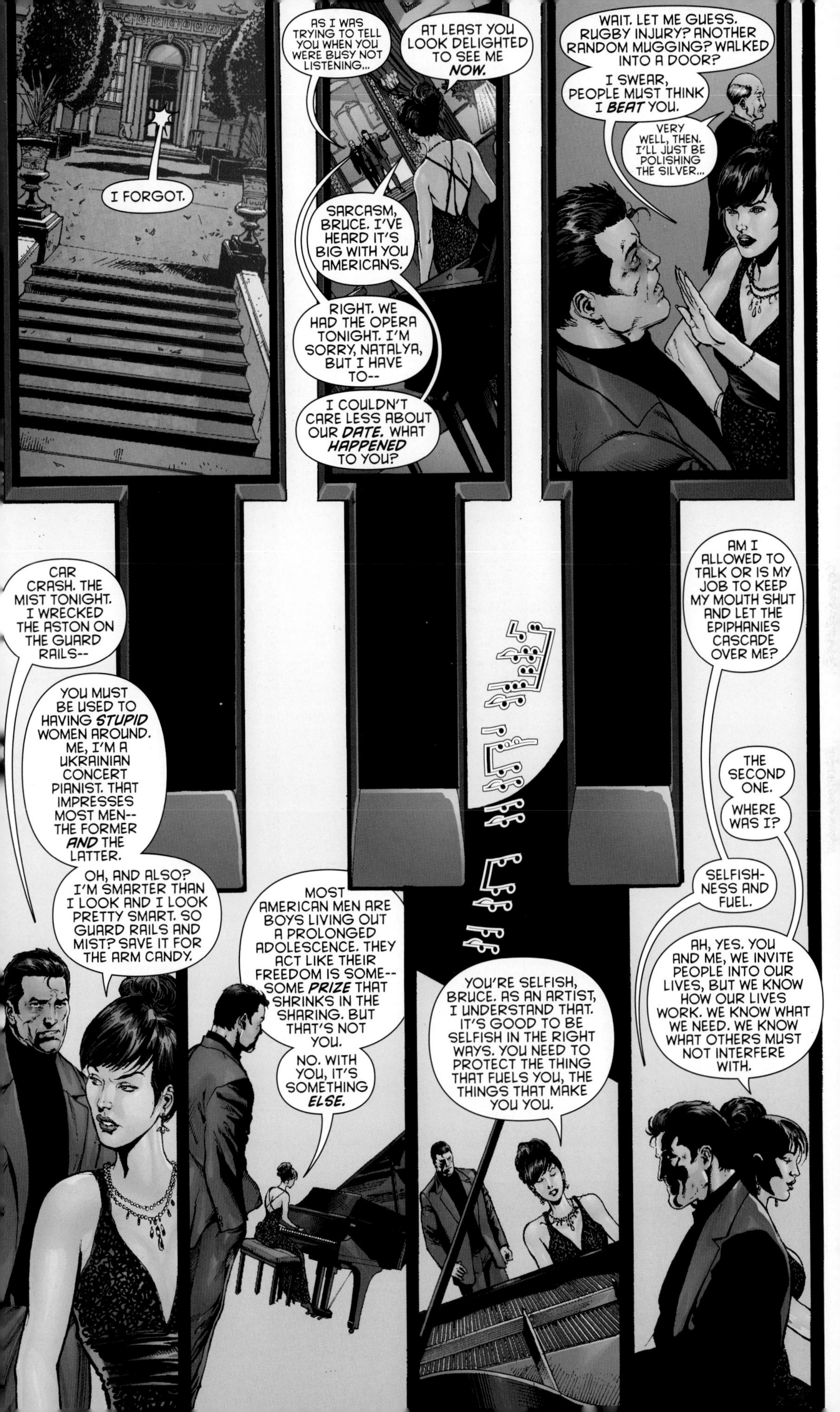
I FORGOT.
AS I WAS TRYING TO TELL YOU WHEN YOU WERE BUSY NOT LISTENING...
AT LEAST YOU LOOK DELIGHTED TO SEE ME NOW.
SARCASM, BRUCE. I'VE HEARD IT'S BIG WITH YOU AMERICANS.
RIGHT. WE HAD THE OPERA TONIGHT. I'M SORRY, NATALYA, BUT I HAVE TO--
I COULDN'T CARE LESS ABOUT OUR DATE. WHAT HAPPENED TO YOU?
WAIT. LET ME GUESS. RUGBY INJURY? ANOTHER RANDOM MUGGING? WALKED INTO A DOOR?
I SWEAR, PEOPLE MUST THINK I BEAT YOU.
VERY WELL, THEN. I'LL JUST BE POLISHING THE SILVER...
CAR CRASH. THE MIST TONIGHT. I WRECKED THE ASTON ON THE GUARD RAILS--
YOU MUST BE USED TO HAVING STUPID WOMEN AROUND. ME, I'M A UKRAINIAN CONCERT PIANIST. THAT IMPRESSES MOST MEN-- THE FORMER AND THE LATTER.
OH, AND ALSO? I'M SMARTER THAN I LOOK AND I LOOK PRETTY SMART. SO GUARD RAILS AND MIST? SAVE IT FOR THE ARM CANDY.
MOST AMERICAN MEN ARE BOYS LIVING OUT A PROLONGED ADOLESCENCE. THEY ACT LIKE THEIR FREEDOM IS SOME-- SOME PRIZE THAT SHRINKS IN THE SHARING. BUT THAT'S NOT YOU.
NO. WITH YOU, IT'S SOMETHING ELSE.
YOU'RE SELFISH, BRUCE. AS AN ARTIST, I UNDERSTAND THAT. IT'S GOOD TO BE SELFISH IN THE RIGHT WAYS. YOU NEED TO PROTECT THE THING THAT FUELS YOU, THE THINGS THAT MAKE YOU YOU.
AM I ALLOWED TO TALK OR IS MY JOB TO KEEP MY MOUTH SHUT AND LET THE EPIPHANIES CASCADE OVER ME?
THE SECOND ONE.
WHERE WAS I?
SELFISH-NESS AND FUEL.
AH, YES. YOU AND ME, WE INVITE PEOPLE INTO OUR LIVES, BUT WE KNOW HOW OUR LIVES WORK. WE KNOW WHAT WE NEED. WE KNOW WHAT OTHERS MUST NOT INTERFERE WITH.

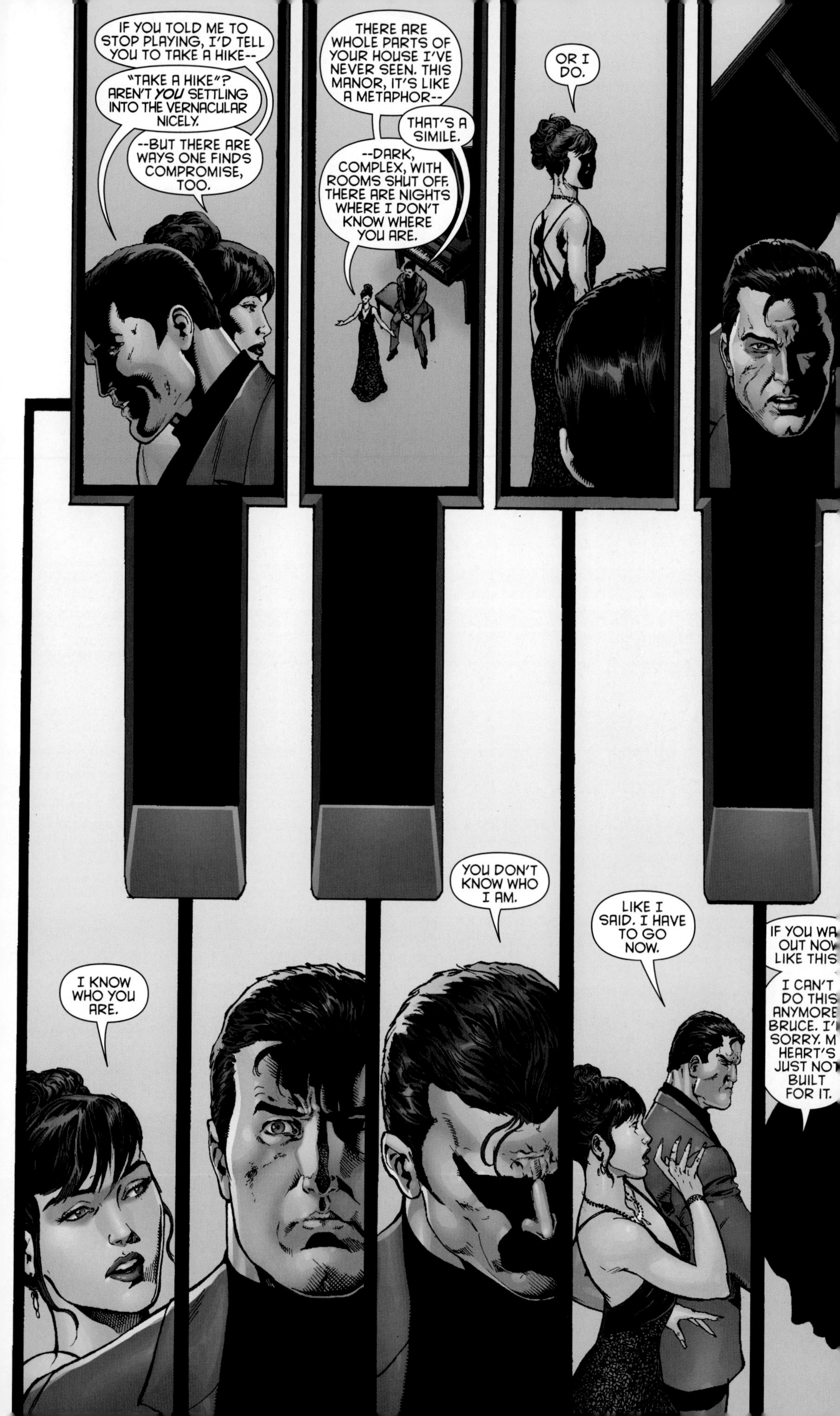
IF YOU TOLD ME TO STOP PLAYING, I'D TELL YOU TO TAKE A HIKE--
"TAKE A HIKE"? AREN'T *YOU* SETTLING INTO THE VERNACULAR NICELY.
--BUT THERE ARE WAYS ONE FINDS COMPROMISE, TOO.
THERE ARE WHOLE PARTS OF YOUR HOUSE I'VE NEVER SEEN. THIS MANOR, IT'S LIKE A METAPHOR--
THAT'S A SIMILE.
--DARK, COMPLEX, WITH ROOMS SHUT OFF. THERE ARE NIGHTS WHERE I DON'T KNOW WHERE YOU ARE.
OR I DO.
I KNOW WHO YOU ARE.
YOU DON'T KNOW WHO I AM.
LIKE I SAID. I HAVE TO GO NOW.
IF YOU WA OUT NOV LIKE THIS
I CAN'T DO THIS ANYMORE BRUCE. I' SORRY. M HEART'S JUST NOT BUILT FOR IT.

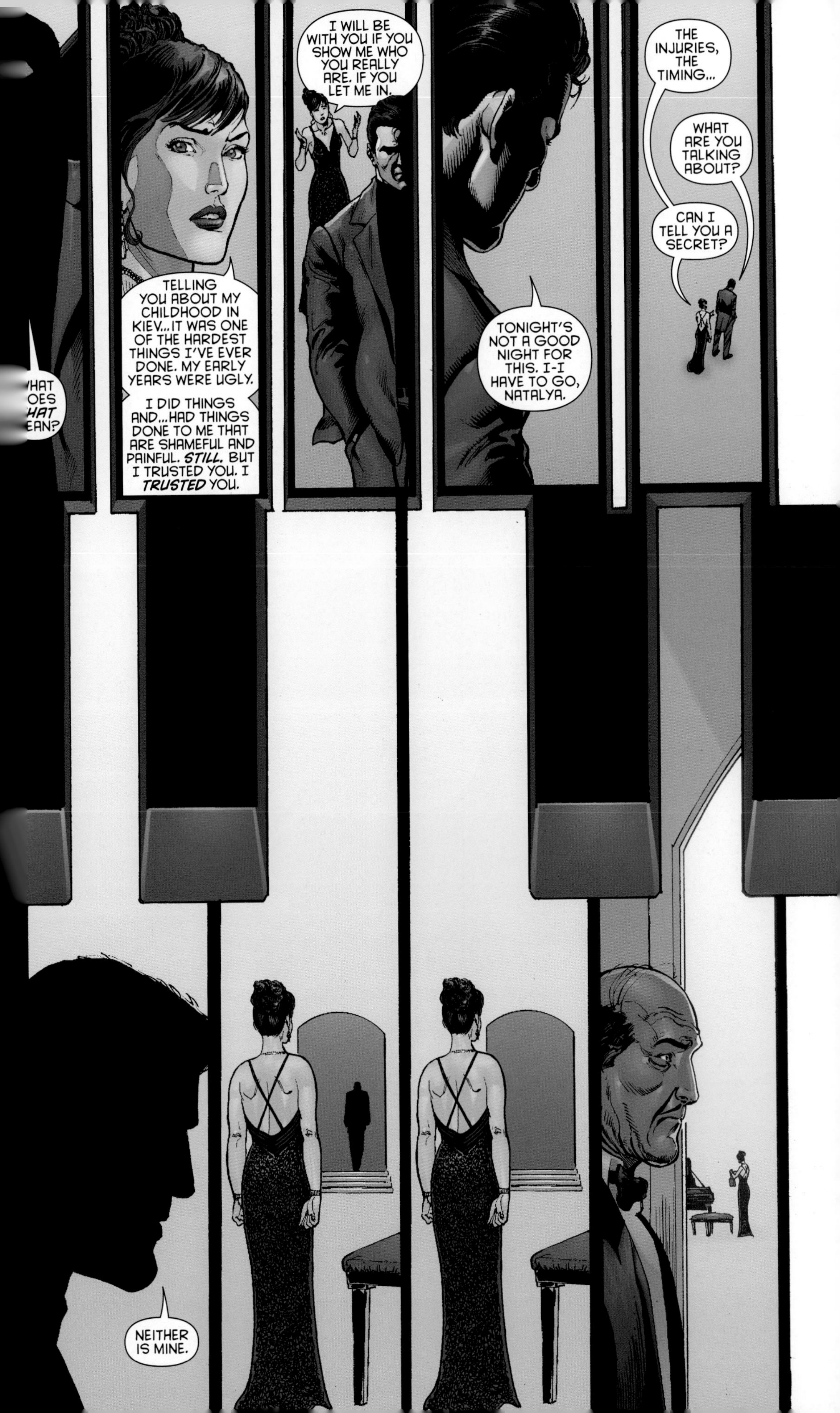

WHAT DOES THAT MEAN?
TELLING YOU ABOUT MY CHILDHOOD IN KIEV... IT WAS ONE OF THE HARDEST THINGS I'VE EVER DONE. MY EARLY YEARS WERE UGLY.
I DID THINGS AND... HAD THINGS DONE TO ME THAT ARE SHAMEFUL AND PAINFUL. STILL. BUT I TRUSTED YOU. I TRUSTED YOU.
I WILL BE WITH YOU IF YOU SHOW ME WHO YOU REALLY ARE. IF YOU LET ME IN.
TONIGHT'S NOT A GOOD NIGHT FOR THIS. I-I HAVE TO GO, NATALYA.
THE INJURIES, THE TIMING...
WHAT ARE YOU TALKING ABOUT?
CAN I TELL YOU A SECRET?
NEITHER IS MINE.

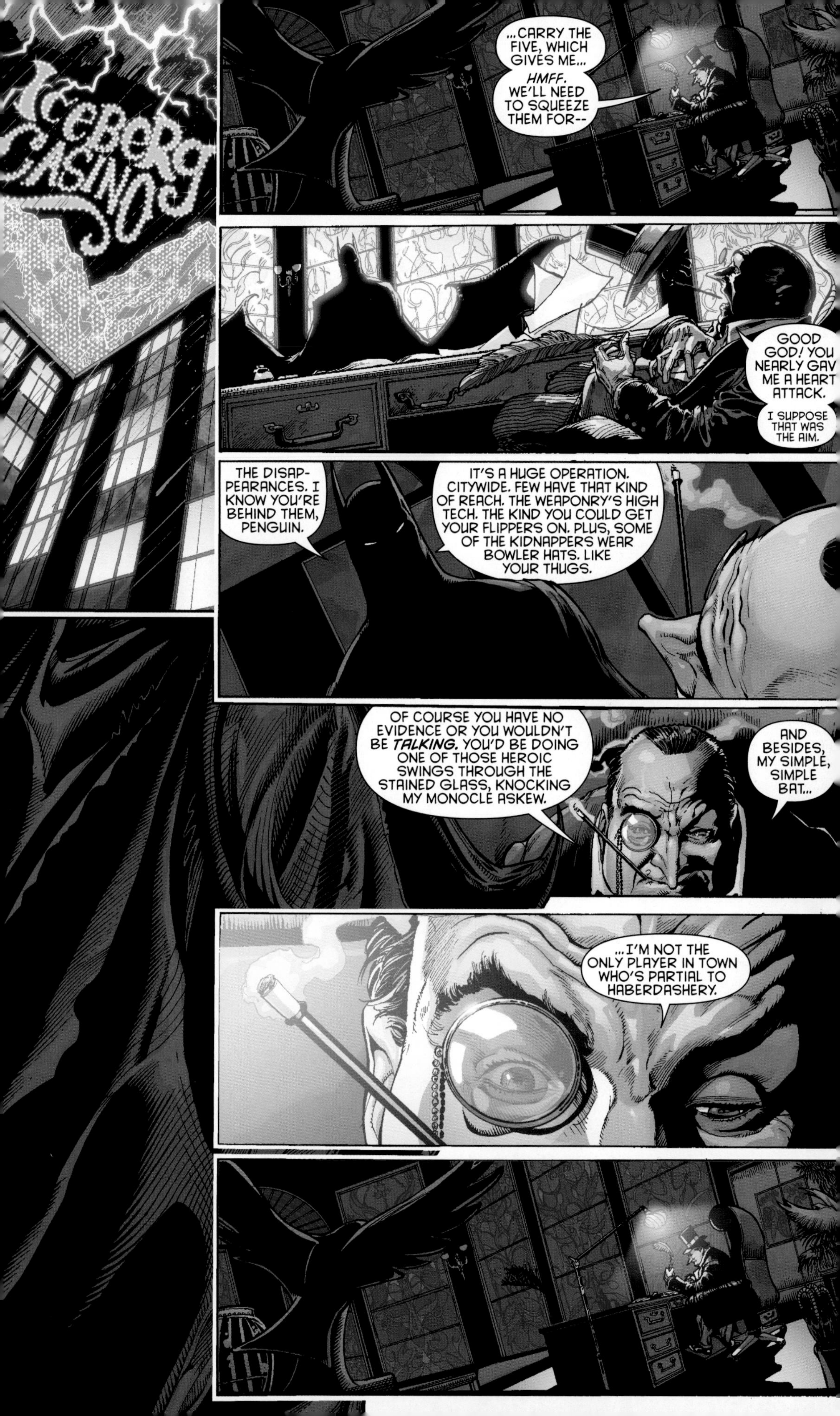

ICEBERG CASINO
...CARRY THE FIVE, WHICH GIVES ME... HMFF. WE'LL NEED TO SQUEEZE THEM FOR--
GOOD GOD! YOU NEARLY GAVE ME A HEART ATTACK.
I SUPPOSE THAT WAS THE AIM.
THE DISAP-PEARANCES. I KNOW YOU'RE BEHIND THEM, PENGUIN.
IT'S A HUGE OPERATION. CITYWIDE. FEW HAVE THAT KIND OF REACH. THE WEAPONRY'S HIGH TECH. THE KIND YOU COULD GET YOUR FLIPPERS ON. PLUS, SOME OF THE KIDNAPPERS WEAR BOWLER HATS. LIKE YOUR THUGS.
OF COURSE YOU HAVE NO EVIDENCE OR YOU WOULDN'T BE TALKING. YOU'D BE DOING ONE OF THOSE HEROIC SWINGS THROUGH THE STAINED GLASS, KNOCKING MY MONOCLE ASKEW.
AND BESIDES, MY SIMPLE, SIMPLE BAT...
...I'M NOT THE ONLY PLAYER IN TOWN WHO'S PARTIAL TO HABERDASHERY.

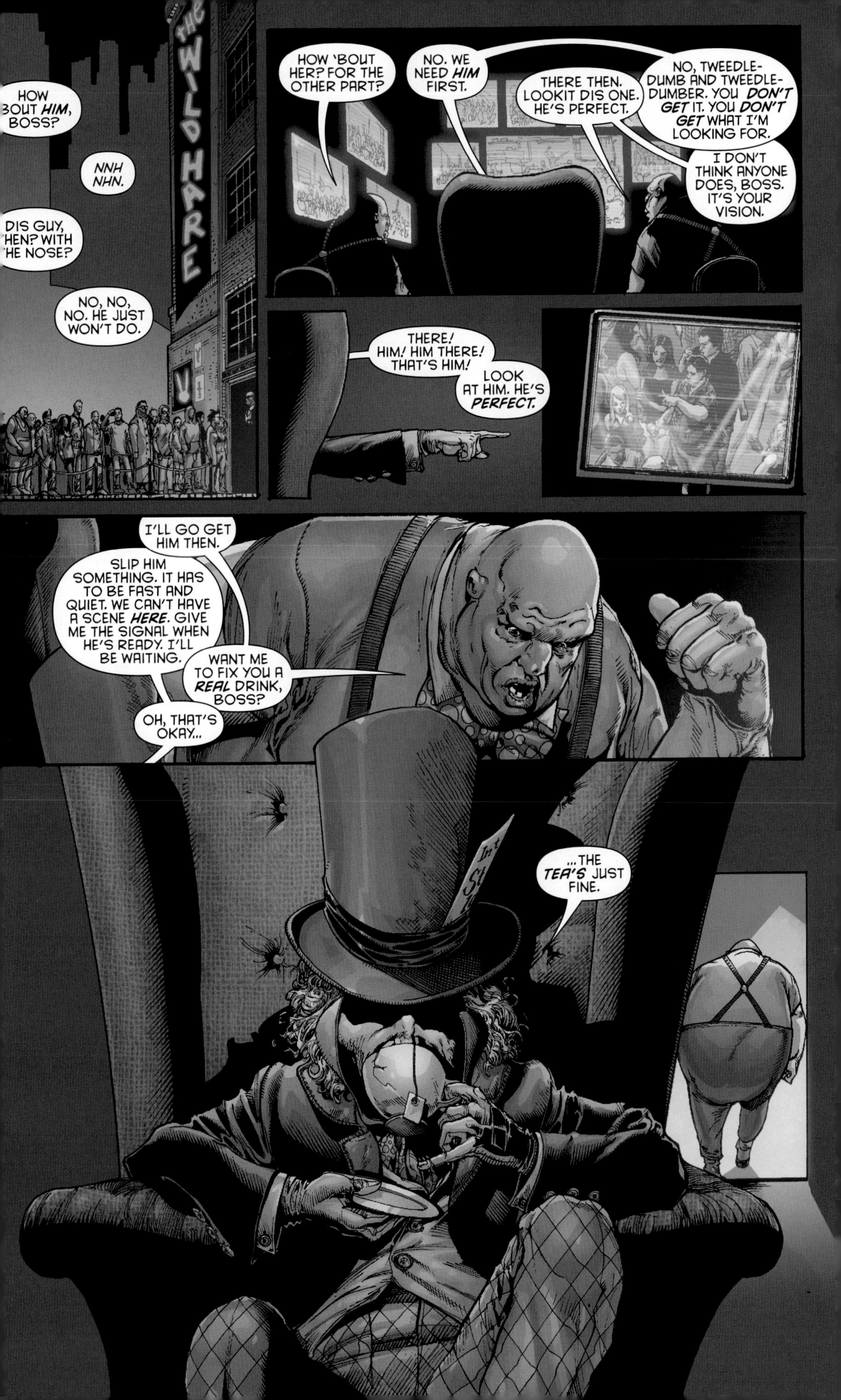
THE WILD HARE
HOW 'BOUT HIM, BOSS?
NNH NHN.
DIS GUY, THEN? WITH THE NOSE?
NO, NO, NO. HE JUST WON'T DO.
HOW 'BOUT HER? FOR THE OTHER PART?
NO. WE NEED HIM FIRST.
THERE THEN. LOOKIT DIS ONE. HE'S PERFECT.
NO, TWEEDLE-DUMB AND TWEEDLE-DUMBER. YOU DON'T GET IT. YOU DON'T GET WHAT I'M LOOKING FOR.
I DON'T THINK ANYONE DOES, BOSS. IT'S YOUR VISION.
THERE! HIM! HIM THERE! THAT'S HIM!
LOOK AT HIM. HE'S PERFECT.
I'LL GO GET HIM THEN.
SLIP HIM SOMETHING. IT HAS TO BE FAST AND QUIET. WE CAN'T HAVE A SCENE HERE. GIVE ME THE SIGNAL WHEN HE'S READY. I'LL BE WAITING.
WANT ME TO FIX YOU A REAL DRINK, BOSS?
OH, THAT'S OKAY...
...THE TEA'S JUST FINE.

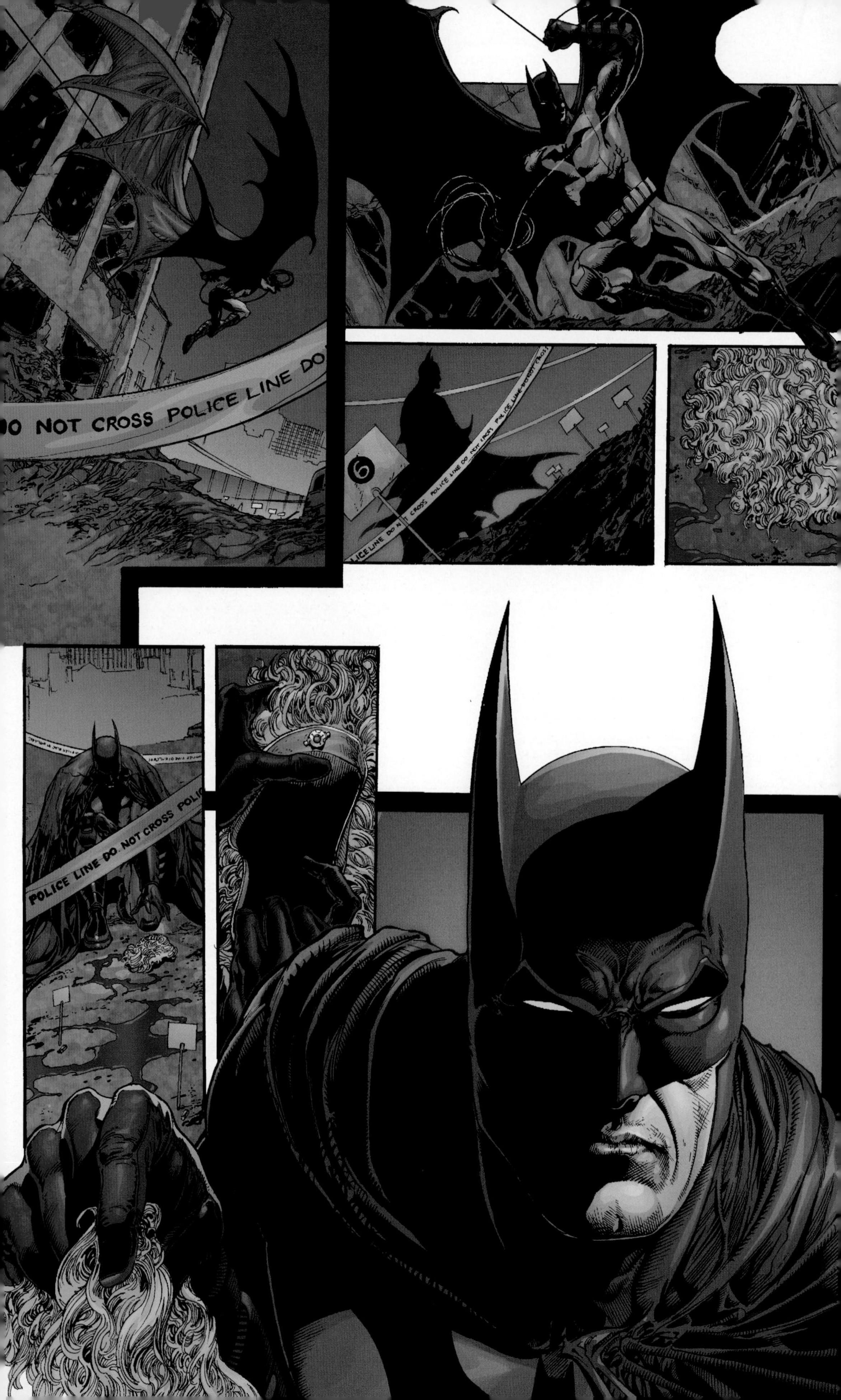

NOT CROSS POLICE LINE DO
POLICE LINE DO NOT CROSS

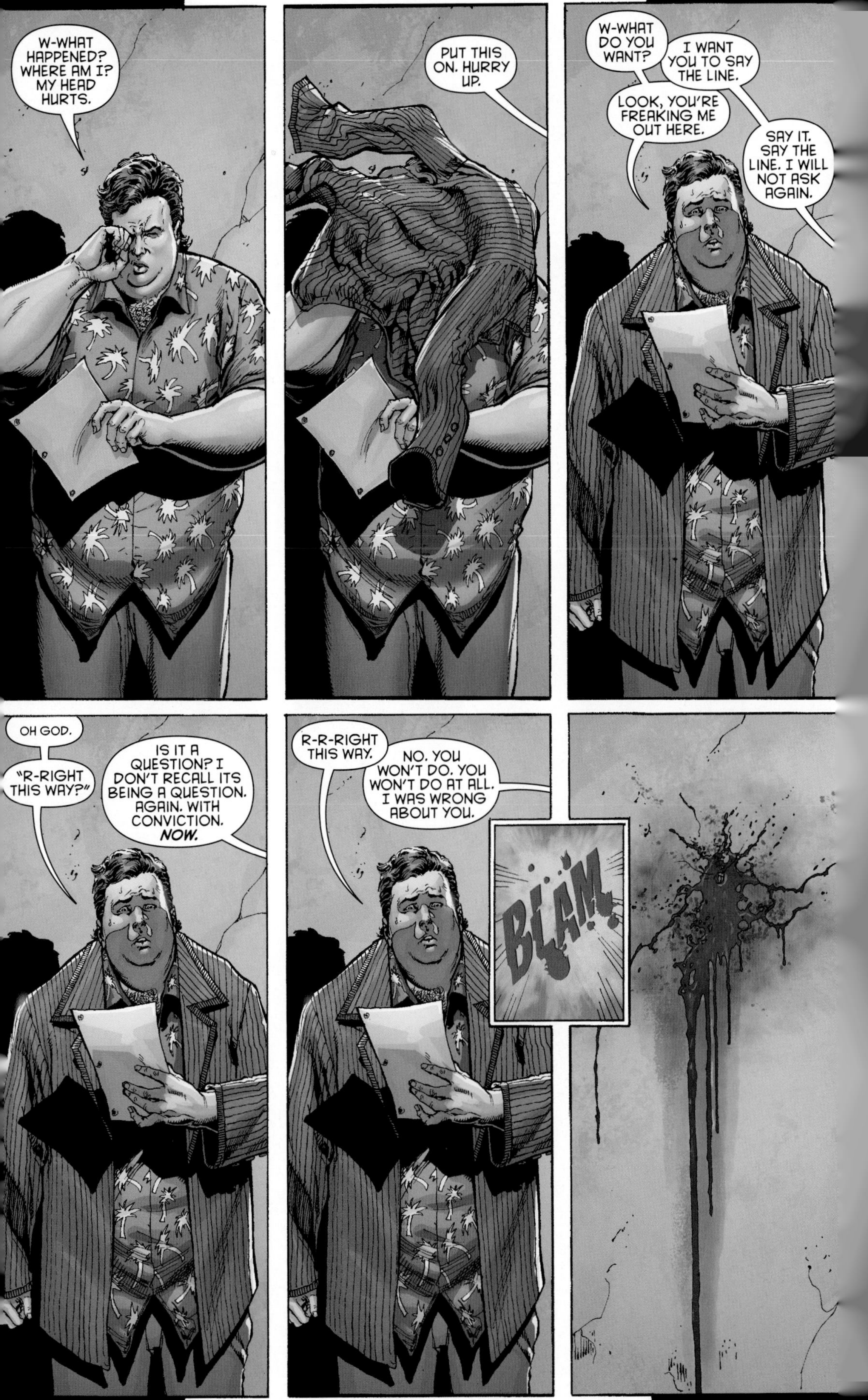
W-WHAT HAPPENED? WHERE AM I? MY HEAD HURTS.
PUT THIS ON. HURRY UP.
W-WHAT DO YOU WANT?
I WANT YOU TO SAY THE LINE.
LOOK, YOU'RE FREAKING ME OUT HERE.
SAY IT. SAY THE LINE. I WILL NOT ASK AGAIN.
OH GOD.
"R-RIGHT THIS WAY?"
IS IT A QUESTION? I DON'T RECALL ITS BEING A QUESTION. AGAIN. WITH CONVICTION. NOW.
R-R-RIGHT THIS WAY.
NO. YOU WON'T DO. YOU WON'T DO AT ALL. I WAS WRONG ABOUT YOU.
BLAM

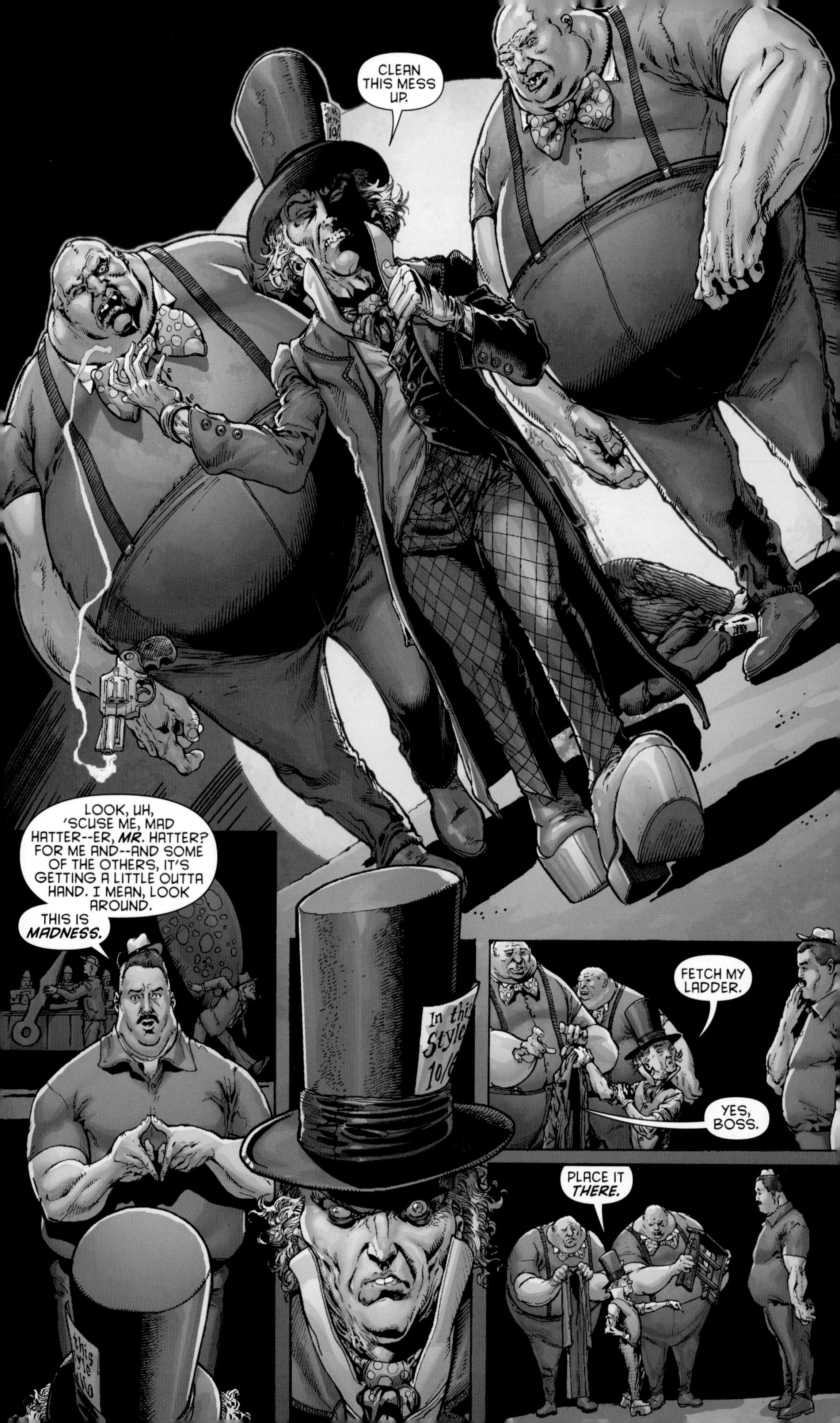

CLEAN THIS MESS UP.
LOOK, UH, 'SCUSE ME, MAD HATTER--ER, MR. HATTER? FOR ME AND--AND SOME OF THE OTHERS, IT'S GETTING A LITTLE OUTTA HAND. I MEAN, LOOK AROUND.
THIS IS MADNESS.
In this Style 10/6
FETCH MY LADDER.
YES, BOSS.
PLACE IT THERE.

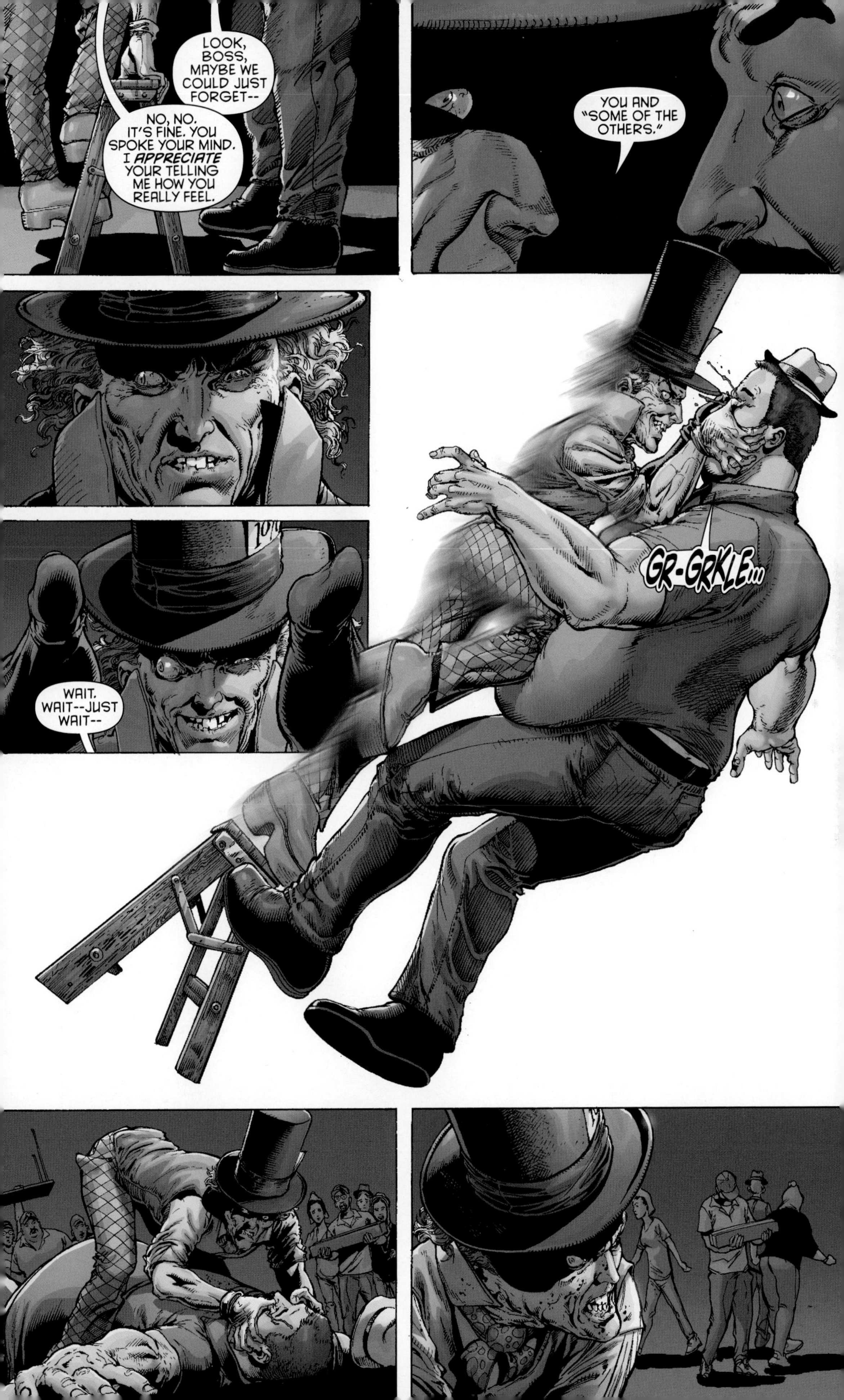
LOOK, BOSS, MAYBE WE COULD JUST FORGET--
NO, NO. IT'S FINE. YOU SPOKE YOUR MIND. I *APPRECIATE* YOUR TELLING ME HOW YOU REALLY FEEL.
YOU AND "SOME OF THE OTHERS."
WAIT. WAIT--JUST WAIT--
GR-GRKLE...

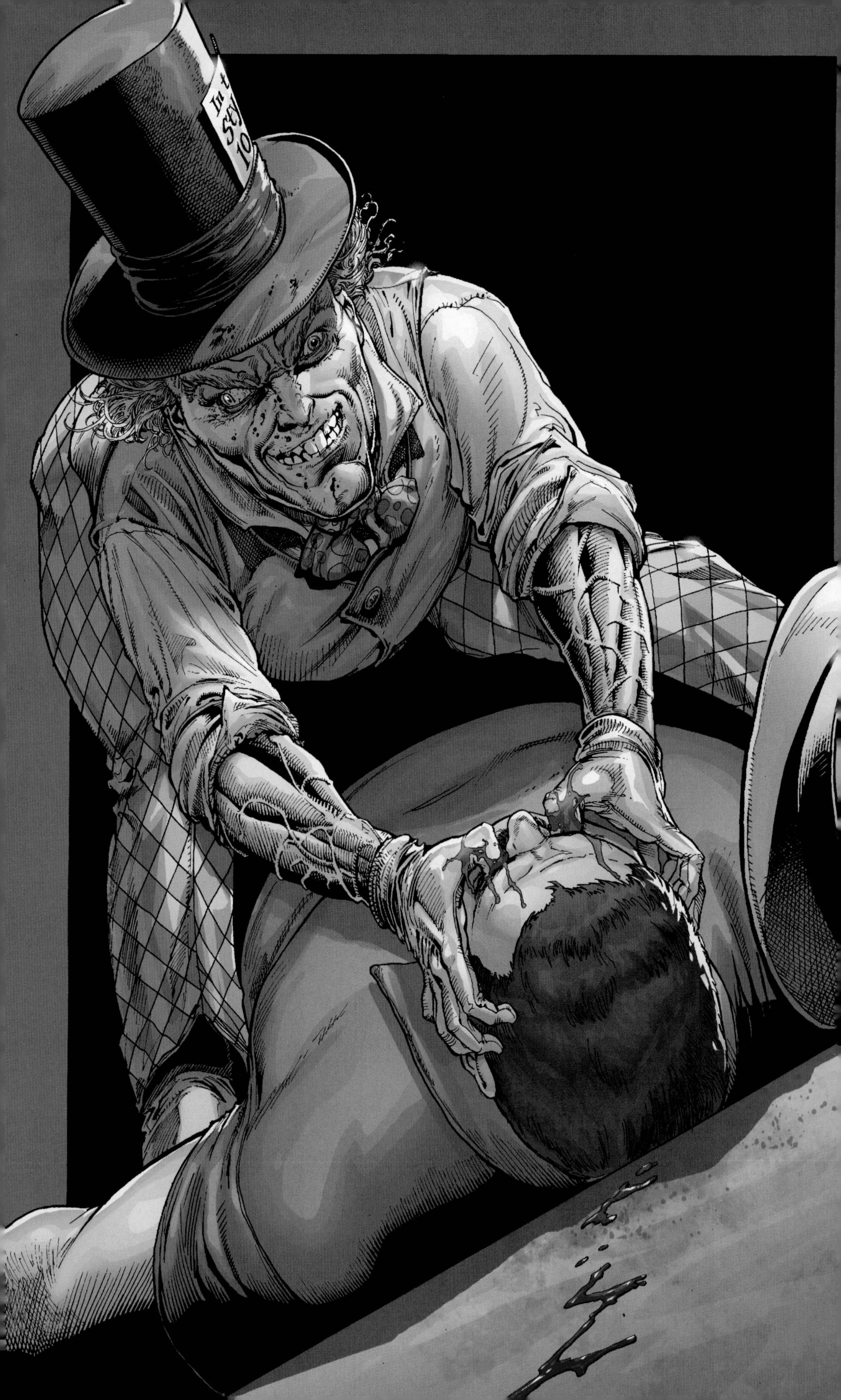

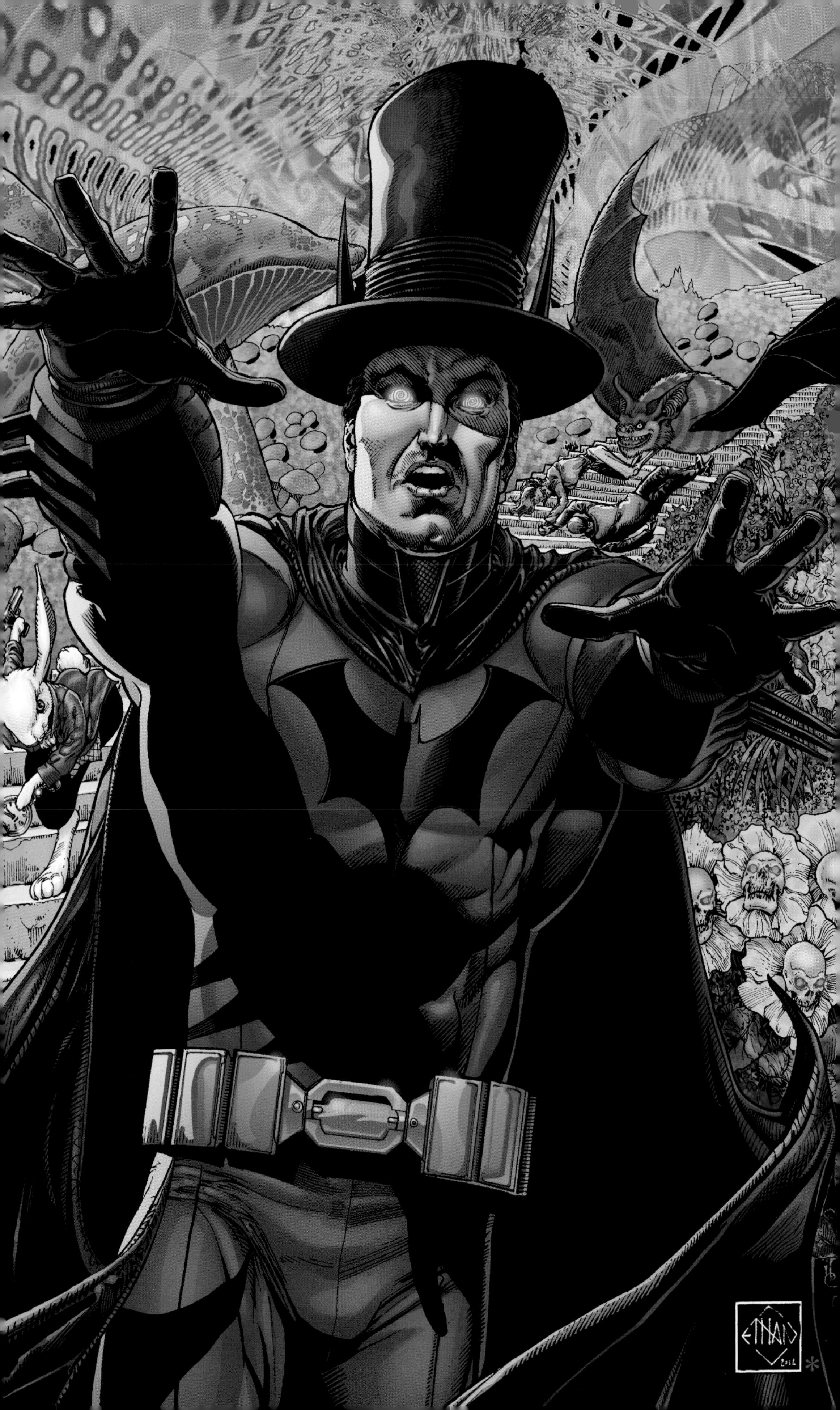

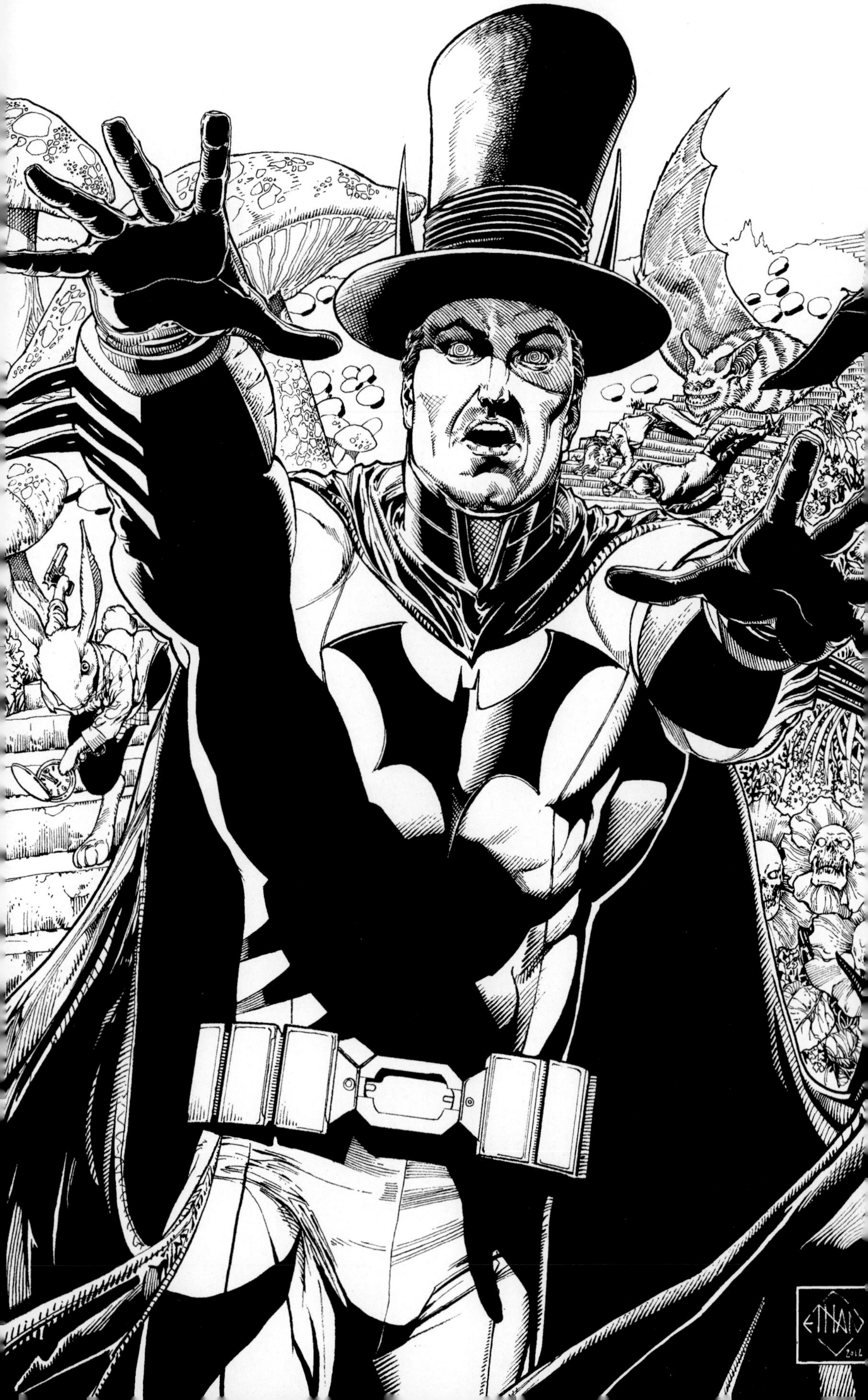

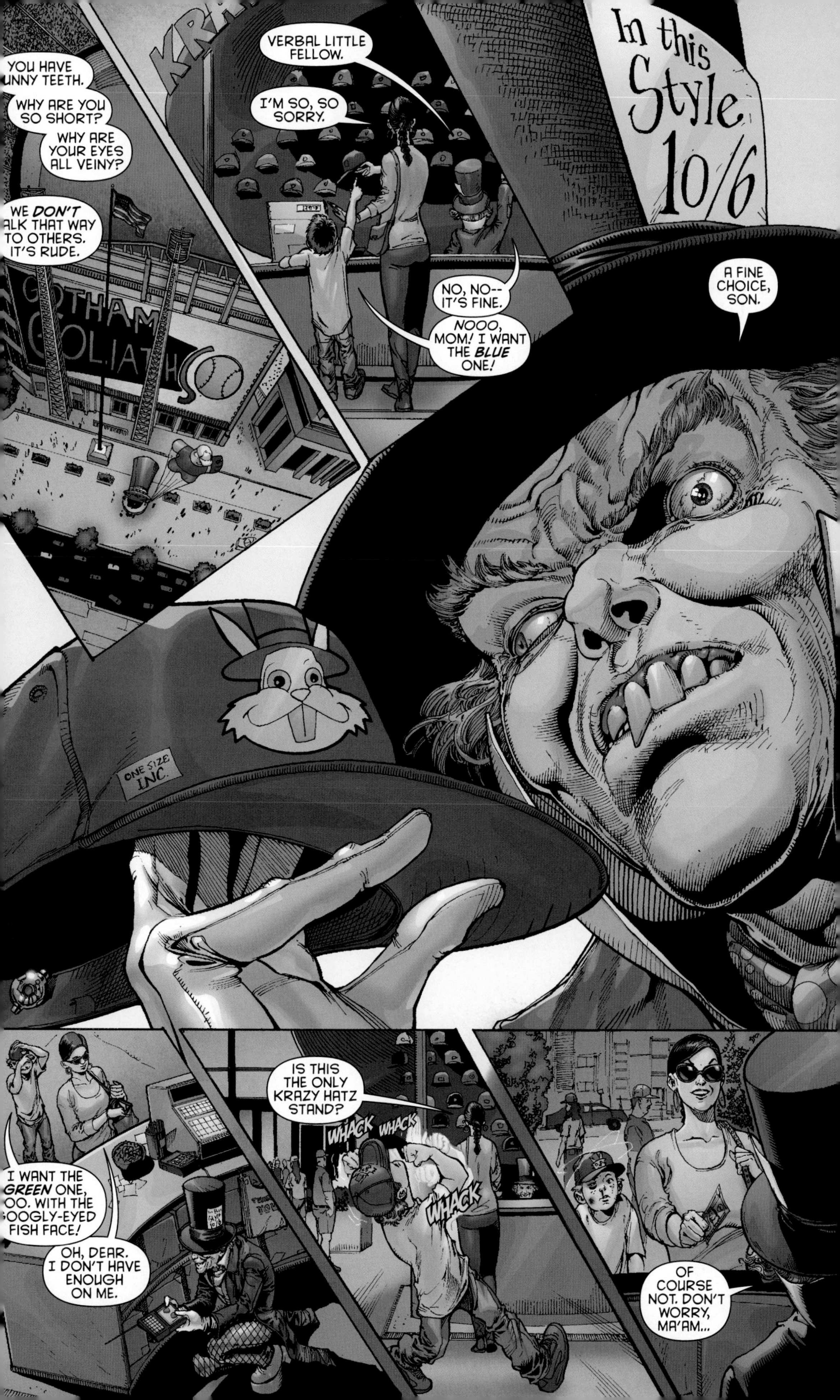

YOU HAVE
UNNY TEETH.
WHY ARE YOU SO SHORT?
WHY ARE YOUR EYES ALL VEINY?
WE DON'T ALK THAT WAY TO OTHERS. IT'S RUDE.
GOTHAM GOLIATHS
VERBAL LITTLE FELLOW.
I'M SO, SO SORRY.
NO, NO-- IT'S FINE.
NOOO, MOM! I WANT THE BLUE ONE!
In this Style 10/6
A FINE CHOICE, SON.
ONE SIZE INC.
I WANT THE GREEN ONE, OO. WITH THE OOGLY-EYED FISH FACE!
OH, DEAR. I DON'T HAVE ENOUGH ON ME.
IS THIS THE ONLY KRAZY HATZ STAND?
WHACK
WHACK
WHACK
OF COURSE NOT. DON'T WORRY, MA'AM...

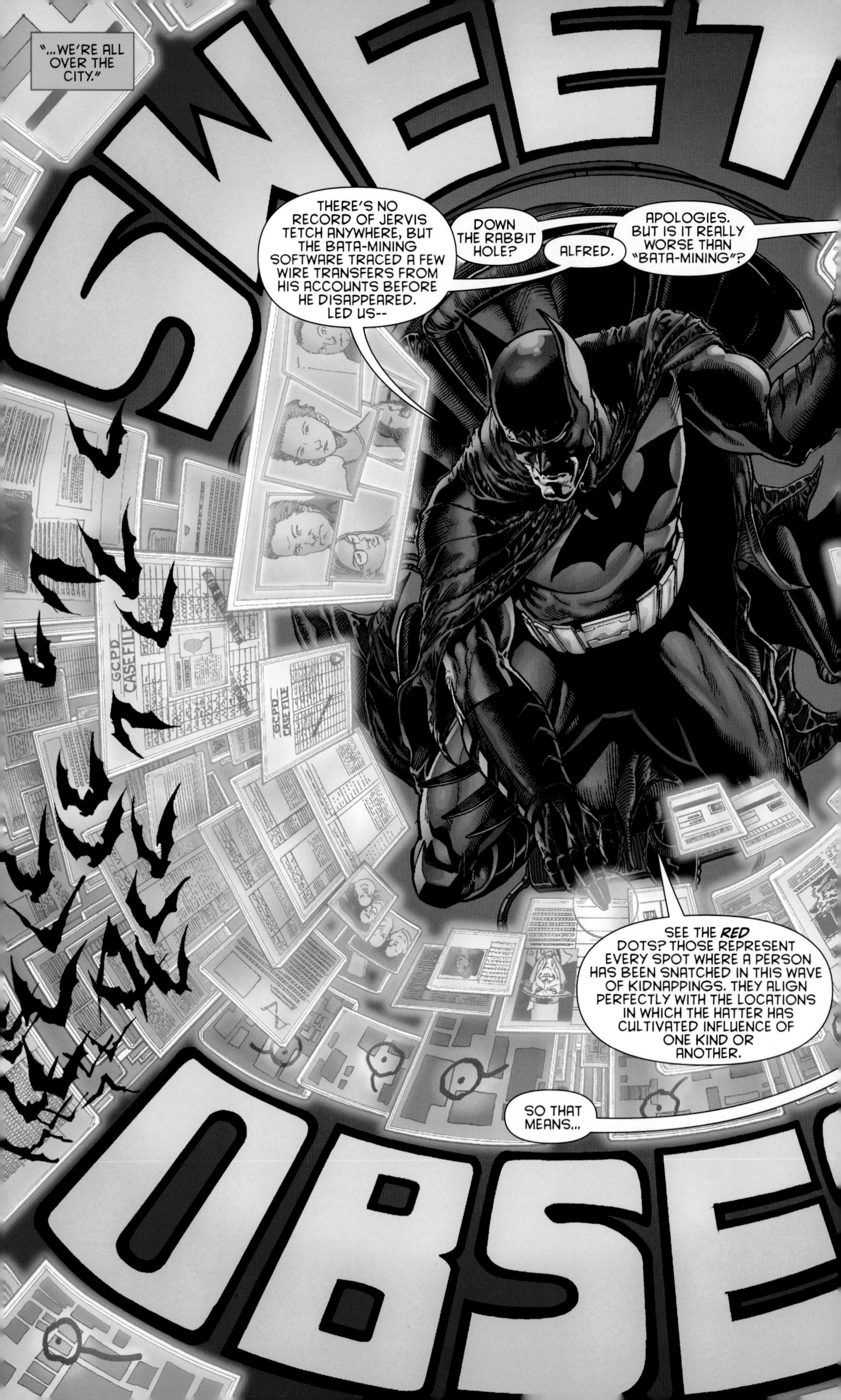
"...WE'RE ALL OVER THE CITY."
THERE'S NO RECORD OF JERVIS TETCH ANYWHERE, BUT THE BATA-MINING SOFTWARE TRACED A FEW WIRE TRANSFERS FROM HIS ACCOUNTS BEFORE HE DISAPPEARED. LED US--
DOWN THE RABBIT HOLE?
ALFRED.
APOLOGIES. BUT IS IT REALLY WORSE THAN "BATA-MINING"?
GCPD CASE FILE
GCPD CASE FILE
SEE THE *RED* DOTS? THOSE REPRESENT EVERY SPOT WHERE A PERSON HAS BEEN SNATCHED IN THIS WAVE OF KIDNAPPINGS. THEY ALIGN PERFECTLY WITH THE LOCATIONS IN WHICH THE HATTER HAS CULTIVATED INFLUENCE OF ONE KIND OR ANOTHER.
SO THAT MEANS...

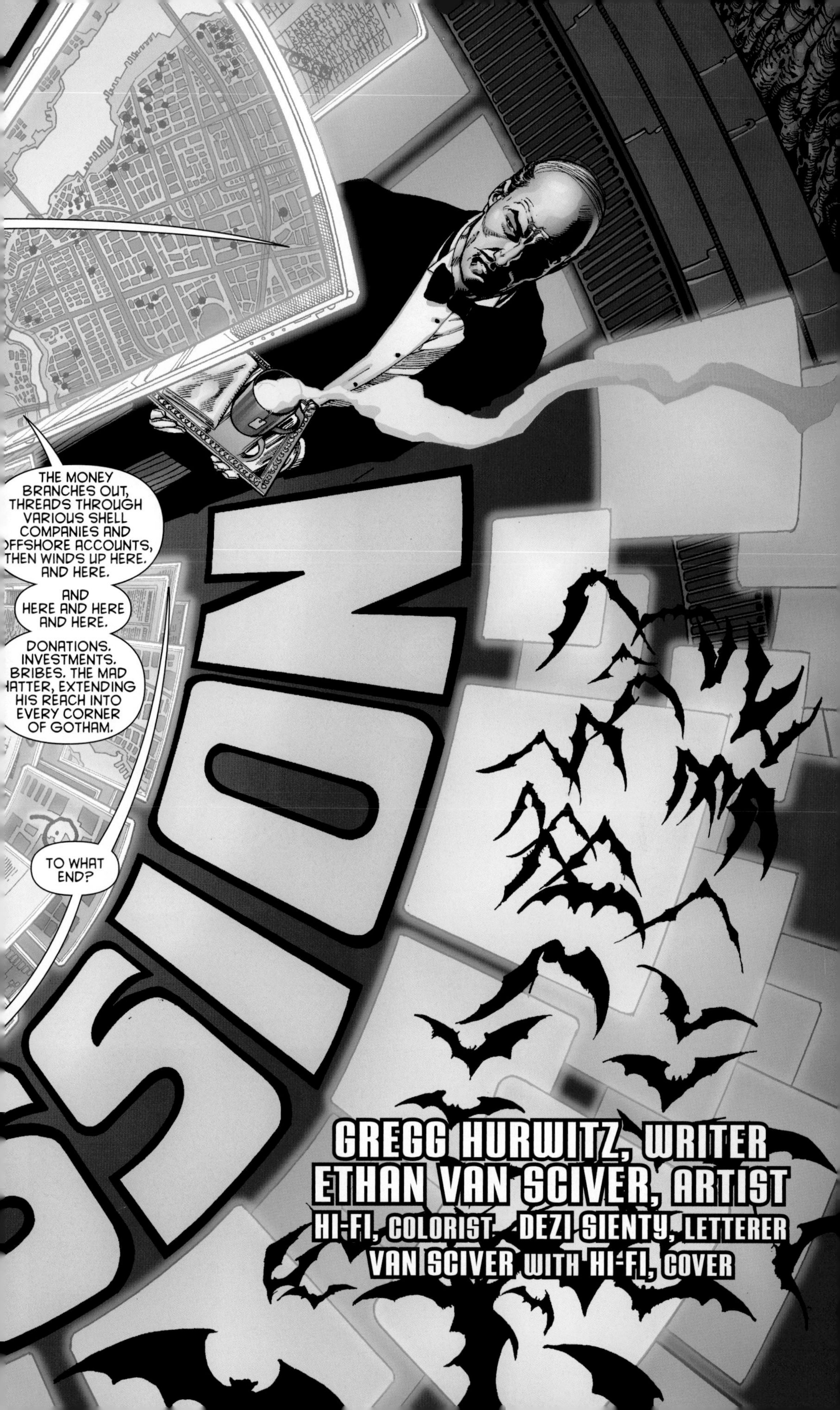
THE MONEY BRANCHES OUT, THREADS THROUGH VARIOUS SHELL COMPANIES AND FFSHORE ACCOUNTS, THEN WINDS UP HERE. AND HERE.
AND HERE AND HERE AND HERE.
DONATIONS. INVESTMENTS. BRIBES. THE MAD ATTER, EXTENDING HIS REACH INTO EVERY CORNER OF GOTHAM.
TO WHAT END?
GREGG HURWITZ, WRITER
ETHAN VAN SCIVER, ARTIST
HI-FI, COLORIST DEZI SIENTY, LETTERER
VAN SCIVER WITH HI-FI, COVER

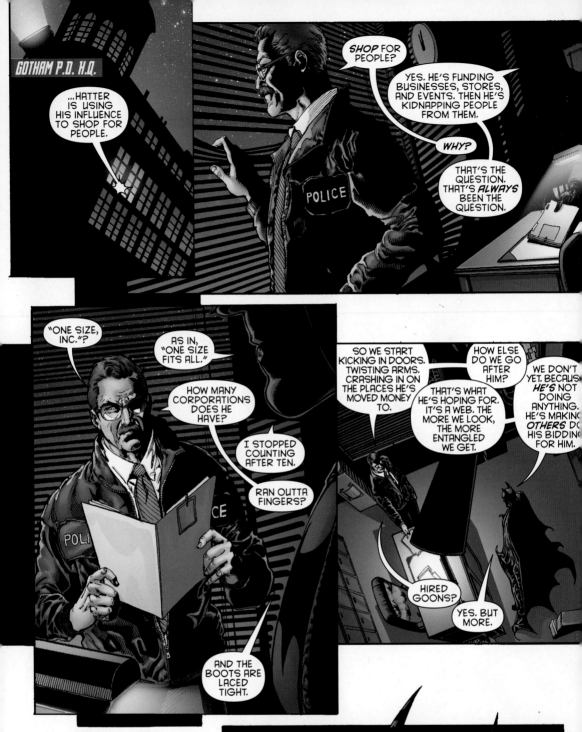

GOTHAM P.D. H.Q.

...HATTER IS USING HIS INFLUENCE TO SHOP FOR PEOPLE.

SHOP FOR PEOPLE?

YES. HE'S FUNDING BUSINESSES, STORES, AND EVENTS. THEN HE'S KIDNAPPING PEOPLE FROM THEM.

WHY?

THAT'S THE QUESTION. THAT'S ALWAYS BEEN THE QUESTION.

"ONE SIZE, INC."?

AS IN, "ONE SIZE FITS ALL."

HOW MANY CORPORATIONS DOES HE HAVE?

I STOPPED COUNTING AFTER TEN.

RAN OUTTA FINGERS?

AND THE BOOTS ARE LACED TIGHT.

SO WE START KICKING IN DOORS. TWISTING ARMS. CRASHING IN ON THE PLACES HE'S MOVED MONEY TO.

HOW ELSE DO WE GO AFTER HIM?

WE DON'T YET. BECAUSE HE'S NOT DOING ANYTHING. HE'S MAKING OTHERS DO HIS BIDDING FOR HIM.

THAT'S WHAT HE'S HOPING FOR. IT'S A WEB. THE MORE WE LOOK, THE MORE ENTANGLED WE GET.

HIRED GOONS?

YES. BUT MORE.

HE'S USING HIS HATS TO CONTROL PEOPLE, PUTTING MICROCHIPS IN THE LINING. DURING THE SWEATSHOP RAID, ONE OF THE KIDNAPPERS STUMBLED AND HIS WIG FELL OFF.

I SAW HIS EYES, RIGHT BEFORE THE HATTER'S THUGS SHOT HIM. HE WAS CONFUSED, LIKE HE DIDN'T KNOW WHY HE WAS THERE OR WHAT HE WAS DOING.

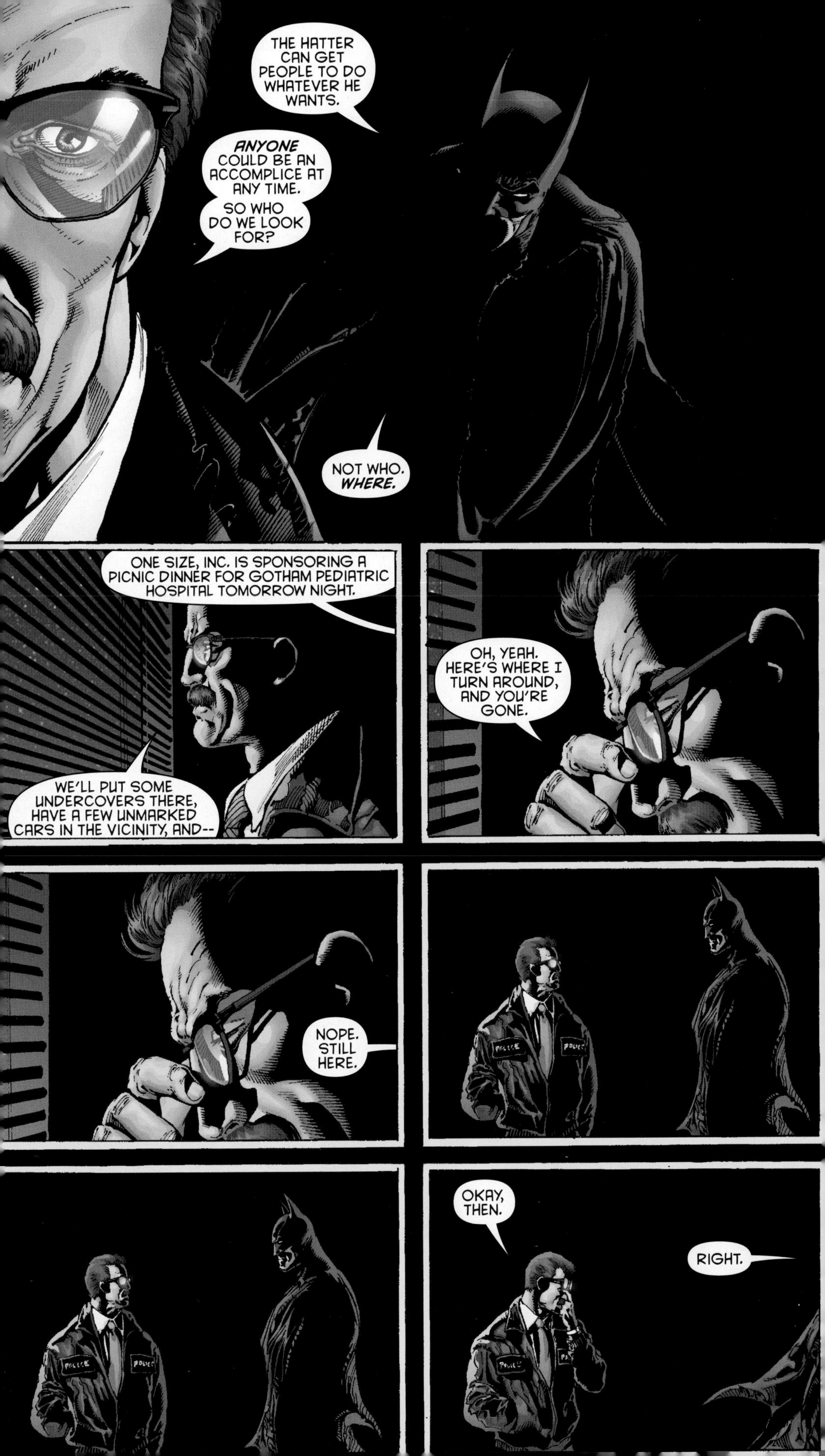
THE HATTER CAN GET PEOPLE TO DO WHATEVER HE WANTS.
ANYONE COULD BE AN ACCOMPLICE AT ANY TIME.
SO WHO DO WE LOOK FOR?
NOT WHO. WHERE.
ONE SIZE, INC. IS SPONSORING A PICNIC DINNER FOR GOTHAM PEDIATRIC HOSPITAL TOMORROW NIGHT.
WE'LL PUT SOME UNDERCOVERS THERE, HAVE A FEW UNMARKED CARS IN THE VICINITY, AND--
OH, YEAH. HERE'S WHERE I TURN AROUND, AND YOU'RE GONE.
NOPE. STILL HERE.
OKAY, THEN.
RIGHT.

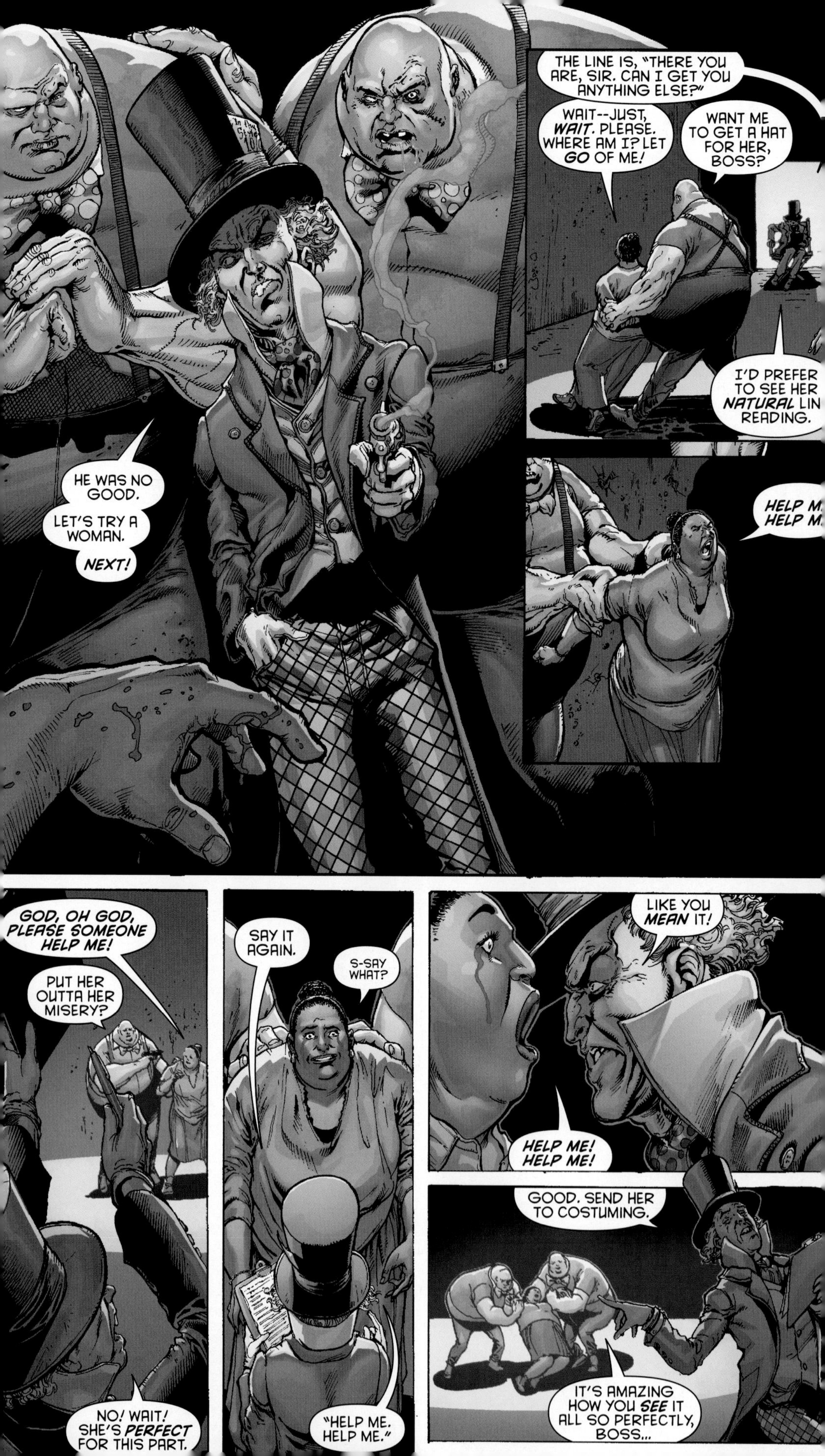
THE LINE IS, "THERE YOU ARE, SIR. CAN I GET YOU ANYTHING ELSE?"
WAIT--JUST, *WAIT*. PLEASE. WHERE AM I? LET *GO* OF ME!
WANT ME TO GET A HAT FOR HER, BOSS?
I'D PREFER TO SEE HER *NATURAL* LIN READING.
HE WAS NO GOOD.
LET'S TRY A WOMAN.
*NEXT!*
*HELP M. HELP M.*
*GOD, OH GOD, PLEASE SOMEONE HELP ME!*
PUT HER OUTTA HER MISERY?
NO! WAIT! SHE'S *PERFECT* FOR THIS PART.
SAY IT AGAIN.
S-SAY WHAT?
"HELP ME. HELP ME."
LIKE YOU *MEAN* IT!
*HELP ME! HELP ME!*
GOOD. SEND HER TO COSTUMING.
IT'S AMAZING HOW YOU *SEE* IT ALL SO PERFECTLY, BOSS...

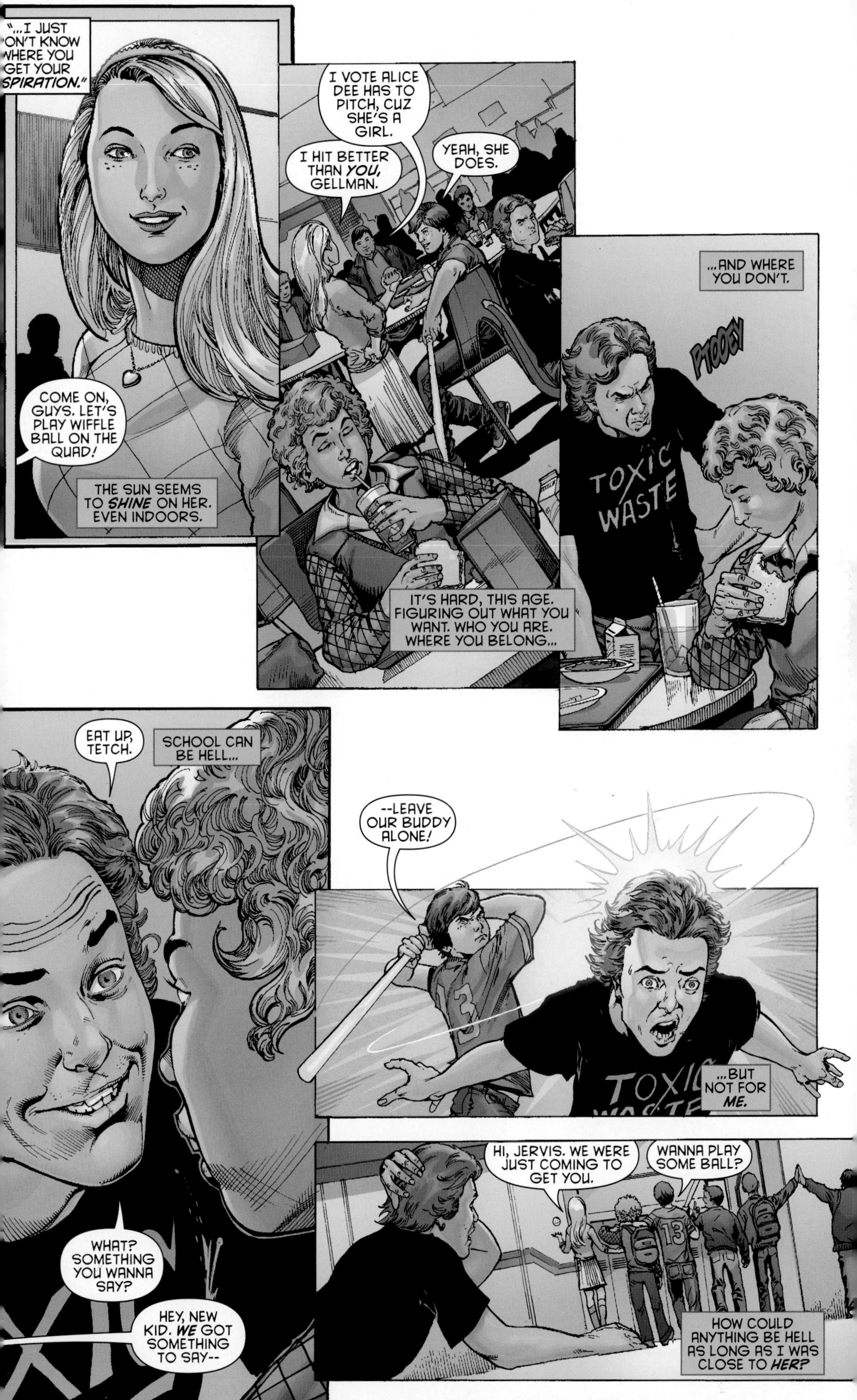
"...I JUST
ON'T KNOW
WHERE YOU
GET YOUR
SPIRATION."
COME ON, GUYS. LET'S PLAY WIFFLE BALL ON THE QUAD!
THE SUN SEEMS TO SHINE ON HER. EVEN INDOORS.
I VOTE ALICE DEE HAS TO PITCH, CUZ SHE'S A GIRL.
I HIT BETTER THAN YOU, GELLMAN.
YEAH, SHE DOES.
IT'S HARD, THIS AGE. FIGURING OUT WHAT YOU WANT. WHO YOU ARE. WHERE YOU BELONG...
...AND WHERE YOU DON'T.
PTOOEY
TOXIC WASTE
EAT UP, TETCH.
SCHOOL CAN BE HELL...
WHAT? SOMETHING YOU WANNA SAY?
HEY, NEW KID. WE GOT SOMETHING TO SAY--
--LEAVE OUR BUDDY ALONE!
...BUT NOT FOR ME.
HI, JERVIS. WE WERE JUST COMING TO GET YOU.
WANNA PLAY SOME BALL?
HOW COULD ANYTHING BE HELL AS LONG AS I WAS CLOSE TO HER?

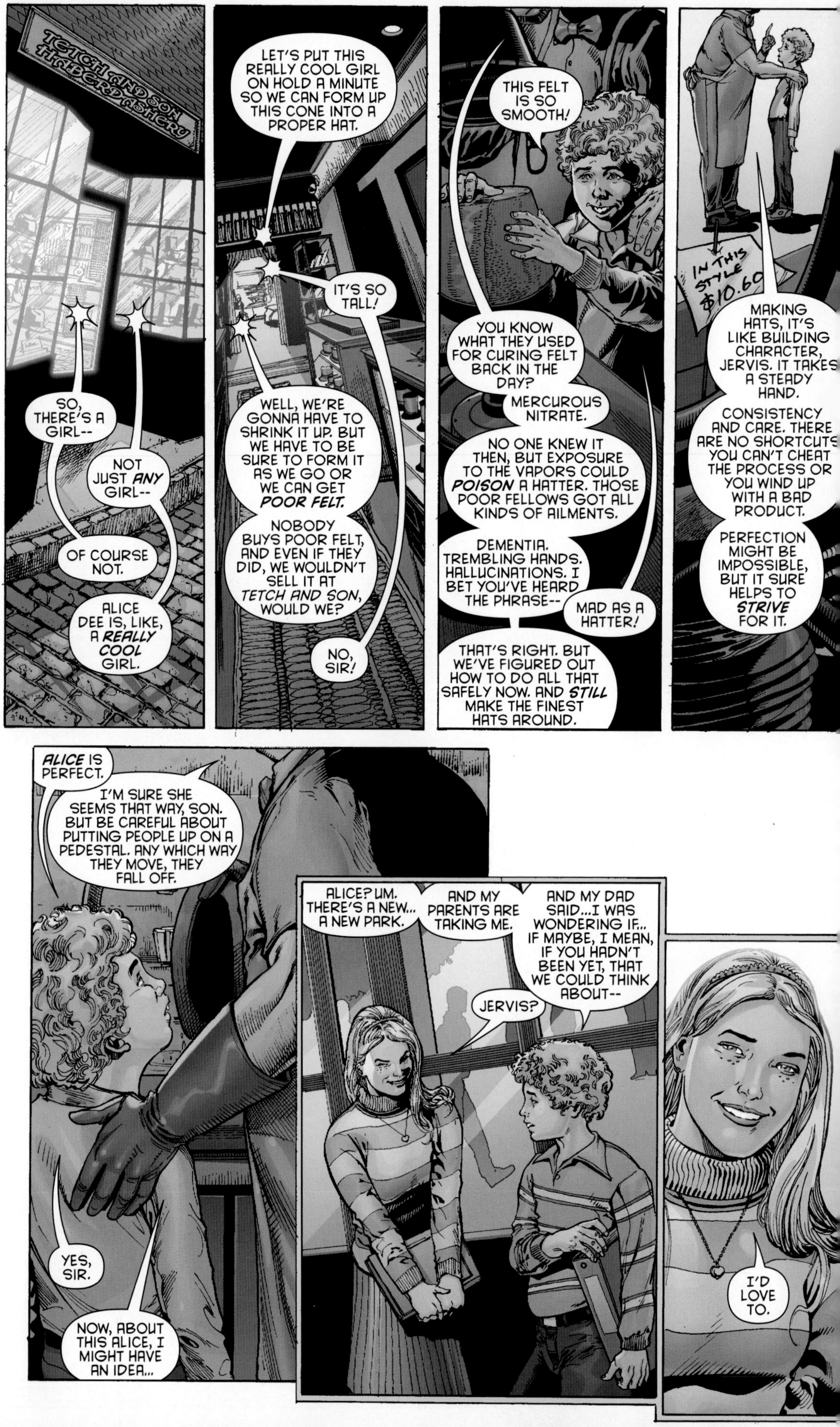
TETCH AND SON HABERDASHERY
SO, THERE'S A GIRL--
NOT JUST *ANY* GIRL--
OF COURSE NOT.
ALICE DEE IS, LIKE, A *REALLY COOL* GIRL.
LET'S PUT THIS REALLY COOL GIRL ON HOLD A MINUTE SO WE CAN FORM UP THIS CONE INTO A PROPER HAT.
IT'S SO TALL!
WELL, WE'RE GONNA HAVE TO SHRINK IT UP. BUT WE HAVE TO BE SURE TO FORM IT AS WE GO OR WE CAN GET *POOR FELT.*
NOBODY BUYS POOR FELT, AND EVEN IF THEY DID, WE WOULDN'T SELL IT AT *TETCH AND SON*, WOULD WE?
NO, SIR!
THIS FELT IS SO SMOOTH!
YOU KNOW WHAT THEY USED FOR CURING FELT BACK IN THE DAY?
MERCUROUS NITRATE.
NO ONE KNEW IT THEN, BUT EXPOSURE TO THE VAPORS COULD *POISON* A HATTER. THOSE POOR FELLOWS GOT ALL KINDS OF AILMENTS.
DEMENTIA. TREMBLING HANDS. HALLUCINATIONS. I BET YOU'VE HEARD THE PHRASE--
MAD AS A HATTER!
THAT'S RIGHT. BUT WE'VE FIGURED OUT HOW TO DO ALL THAT SAFELY NOW. AND *STILL* MAKE THE FINEST HATS AROUND.
IN THIS STYLE $10.60
MAKING HATS, IT'S LIKE BUILDING CHARACTER, JERVIS. IT TAKES A STEADY HAND.
CONSISTENCY AND CARE. THERE ARE NO SHORTCUTS. YOU CAN'T CHEAT THE PROCESS OR YOU WIND UP WITH A BAD PRODUCT.
PERFECTION MIGHT BE IMPOSSIBLE, BUT IT SURE HELPS TO *STRIVE* FOR IT.
*ALICE* IS PERFECT.
I'M SURE SHE SEEMS THAT WAY, SON. BUT BE CAREFUL ABOUT PUTTING PEOPLE UP ON A PEDESTAL. ANY WHICH WAY THEY MOVE, THEY FALL OFF.
YES, SIR.
NOW, ABOUT THIS ALICE, I MIGHT HAVE AN IDEA...
ALICE? UM. THERE'S A NEW... A NEW PARK.
AND MY PARENTS ARE TAKING ME.
AND MY DAD SAID...I WAS WONDERING IF... IF MAYBE, I MEAN, IF YOU HADN'T BEEN YET, THAT WE COULD THINK ABOUT--
JERVIS?
I'D LOVE TO.

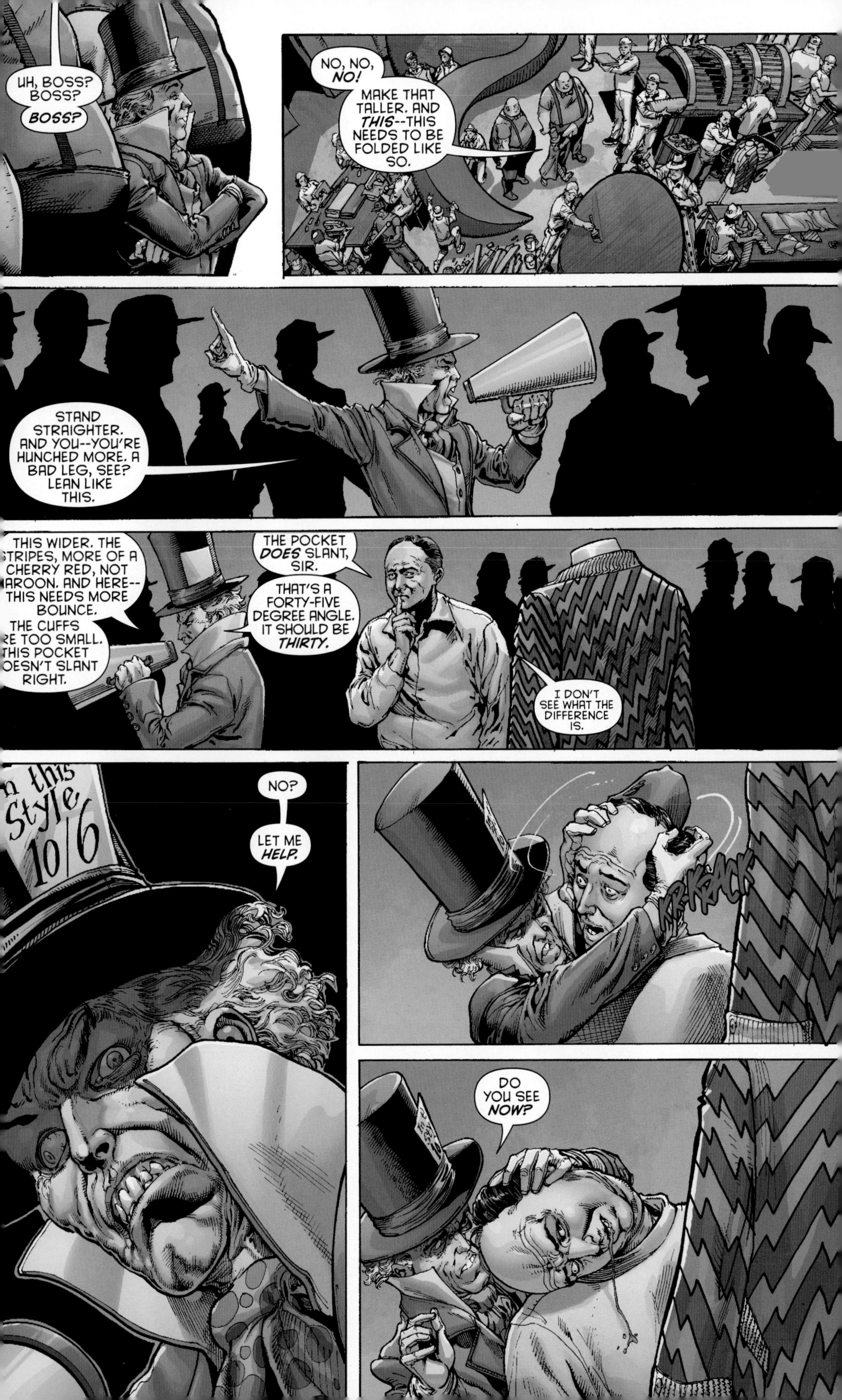
UH, BOSS? BOSS? BOSS?
NO, NO, NO!
MAKE THAT TALLER. AND THIS--THIS NEEDS TO BE FOLDED LIKE SO.
STAND STRAIGHTER. AND YOU--YOU'RE HUNCHED MORE. A BAD LEG, SEE? LEAN LIKE THIS.
THIS WIDER. THE STRIPES, MORE OF A CHERRY RED, NOT AROON. AND HERE--THIS NEEDS MORE BOUNCE.
THE CUFFS RE TOO SMALL. THIS POCKET OESN'T SLANT RIGHT.
THE POCKET DOES SLANT, SIR.
THAT'S A FORTY-FIVE DEGREE ANGLE. IT SHOULD BE THIRTY.
I DON'T SEE WHAT THE DIFFERENCE IS.
n this Style 10/6
NO?
LET ME HELP.
KR-KRACK
DO YOU SEE NOW?

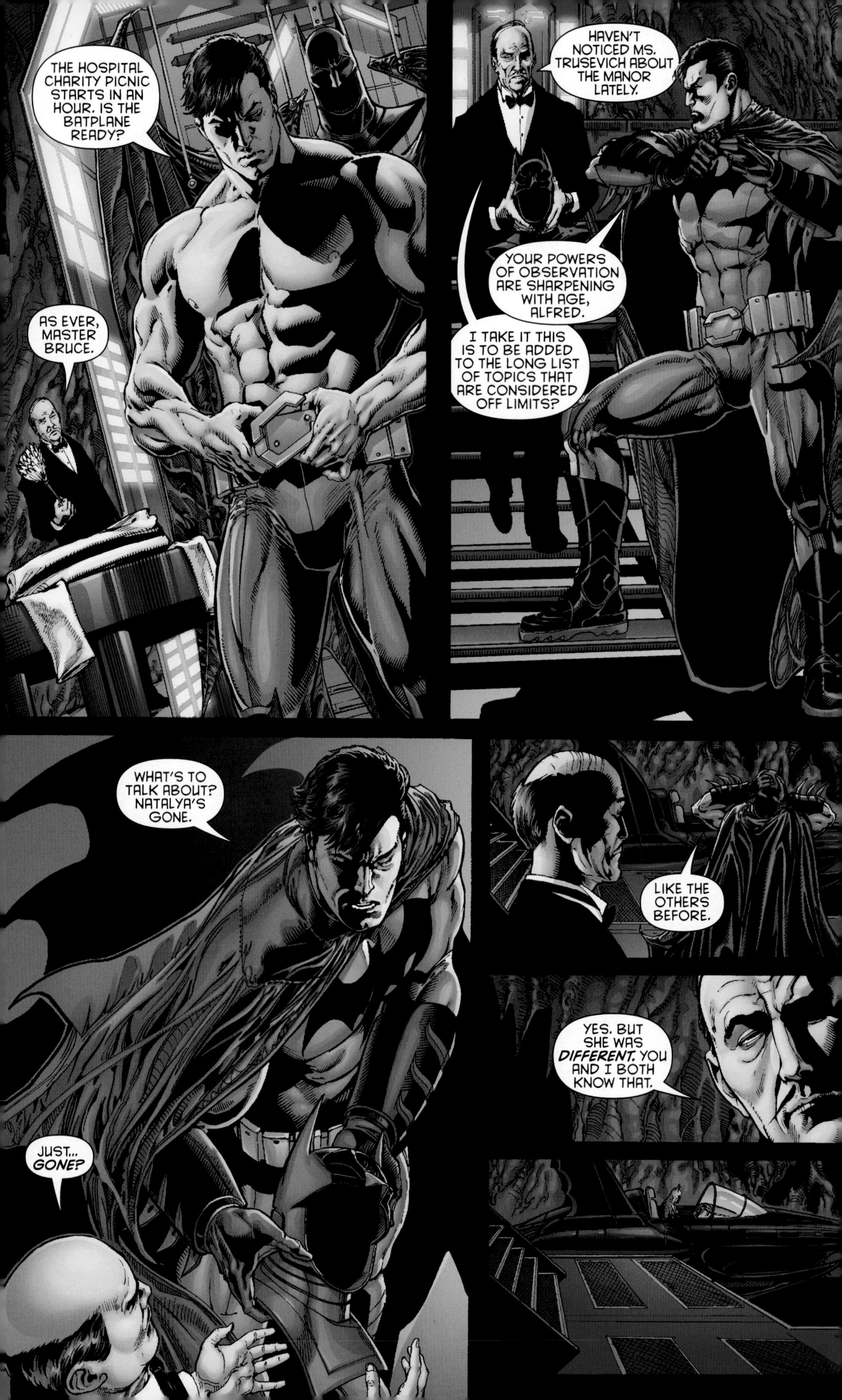
THE HOSPITAL CHARITY PICNIC STARTS IN AN HOUR. IS THE BATPLANE READY?
AS EVER, MASTER BRUCE.
HAVEN'T NOTICED MS. TRUSEVICH ABOUT THE MANOR LATELY.
YOUR POWERS OF OBSERVATION ARE SHARPENING WITH AGE, ALFRED.
I TAKE IT THIS IS TO BE ADDED TO THE LONG LIST OF TOPICS THAT ARE CONSIDERED OFF LIMITS?
WHAT'S TO TALK ABOUT? NATALYA'S GONE.
JUST... *GONE?*
LIKE THE OTHERS BEFORE.
YES. BUT SHE WAS *DIFFERENT.* YOU AND I BOTH KNOW THAT.

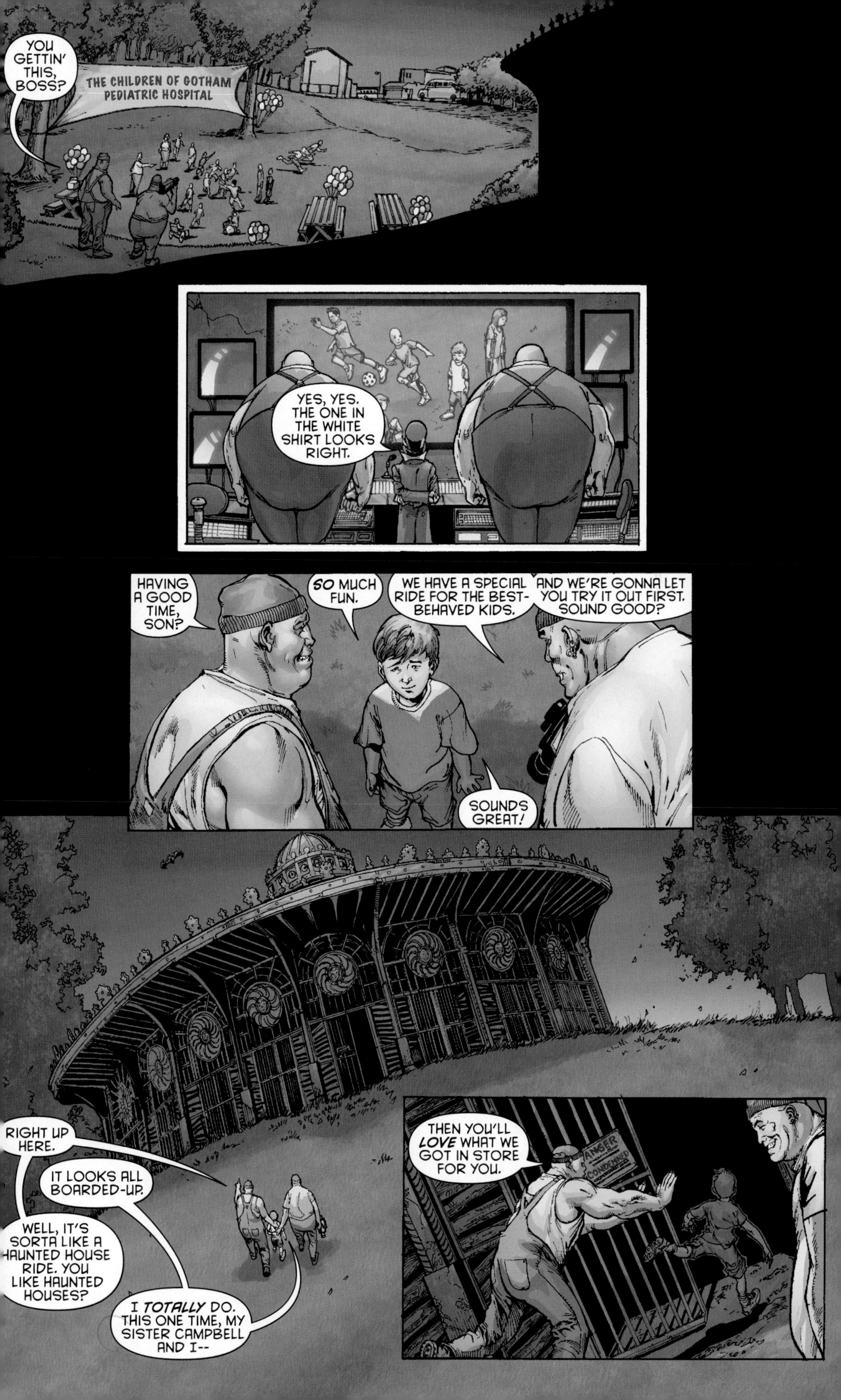

YOU GETTIN' THIS, BOSS?
THE CHILDREN OF GOTHAM PEDIATRIC HOSPITAL
YES, YES. THE ONE IN THE WHITE SHIRT LOOKS RIGHT.
HAVING A GOOD TIME, SON?
SO MUCH FUN.
WE HAVE A SPECIAL RIDE FOR THE BEST-BEHAVED KIDS.
AND WE'RE GONNA LET YOU TRY IT OUT FIRST. SOUND GOOD?
SOUNDS GREAT!
RIGHT UP HERE.
IT LOOKS ALL BOARDED-UP.
WELL, IT'S SORTA LIKE A HAUNTED HOUSE RIDE. YOU LIKE HAUNTED HOUSES?
I TOTALLY DO. THIS ONE TIME, MY SISTER CAMPBELL AND I--
THEN YOU'LL LOVE WHAT WE GOT IN STORE FOR YOU.

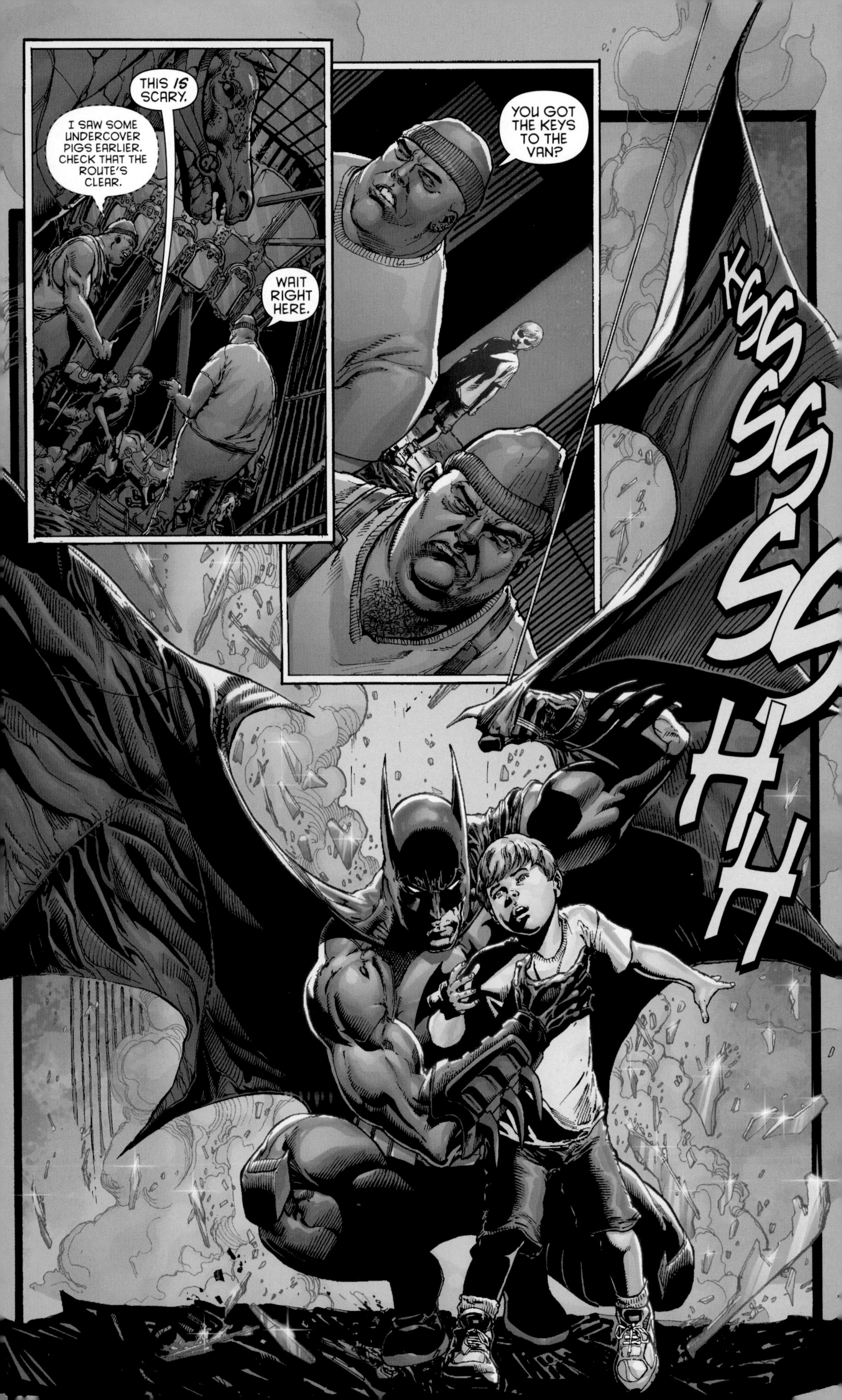

THIS *IS* SCARY.
I SAW SOME UNDERCOVER PIGS EARLIER. CHECK THAT THE ROUTE'S CLEAR.
WAIT RIGHT HERE.
YOU GOT THE KEYS TO THE VAN?
KSSSSSSSSHHH

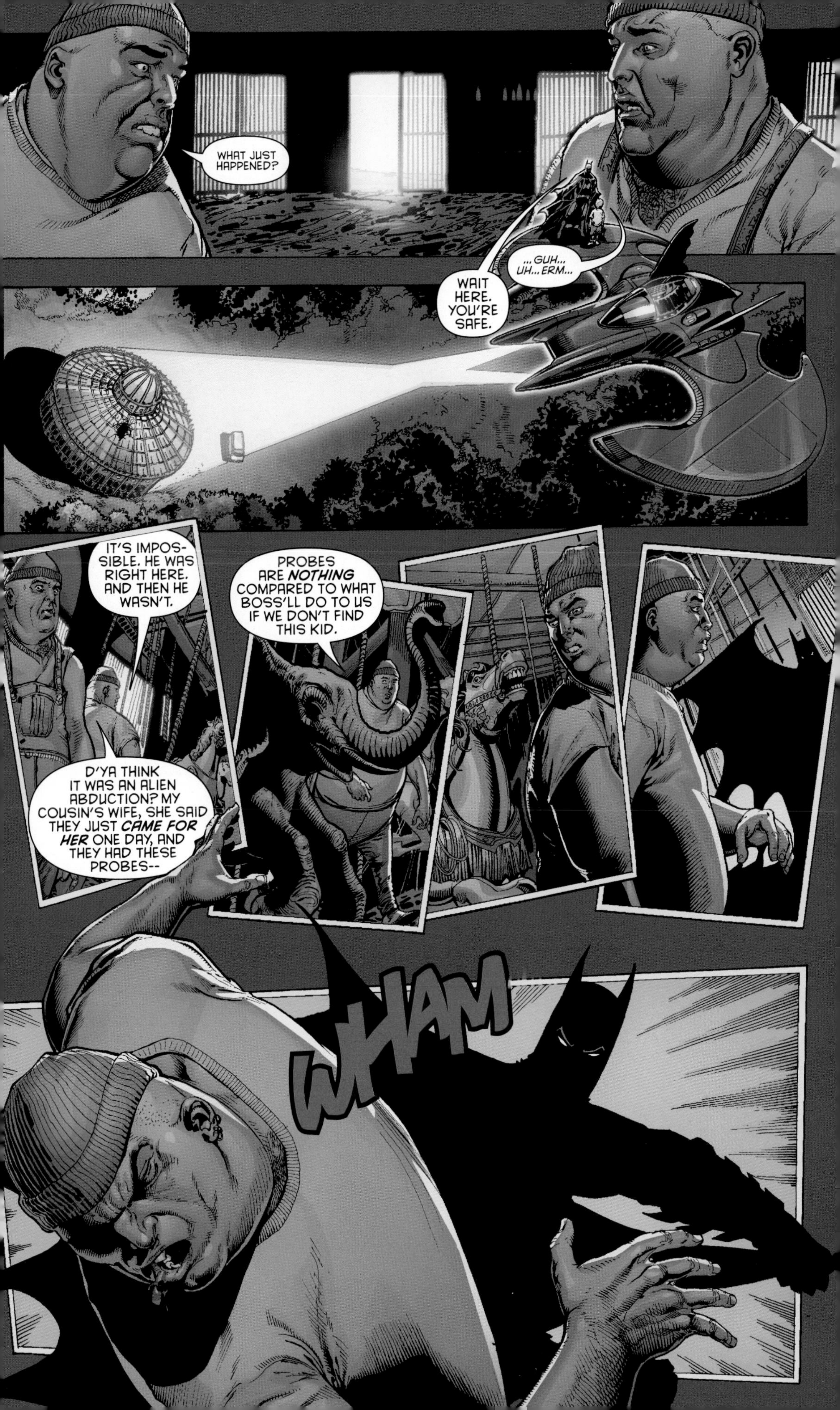
WHAT JUST HAPPENED?
...GUH... UH...ERM...
WAIT HERE. YOU'RE SAFE.
IT'S IMPOSSIBLE. HE WAS RIGHT HERE. AND THEN HE WASN'T.
PROBES ARE *NOTHING* COMPARED TO WHAT BOSS'LL DO TO US IF WE DON'T FIND THIS KID.
D'YA THINK IT WAS AN ALIEN ABDUCTION? MY COUSIN'S WIFE, SHE SAID THEY JUST *CAME FOR HER* ONE DAY, AND THEY HAD THESE PROBES--
WHAM

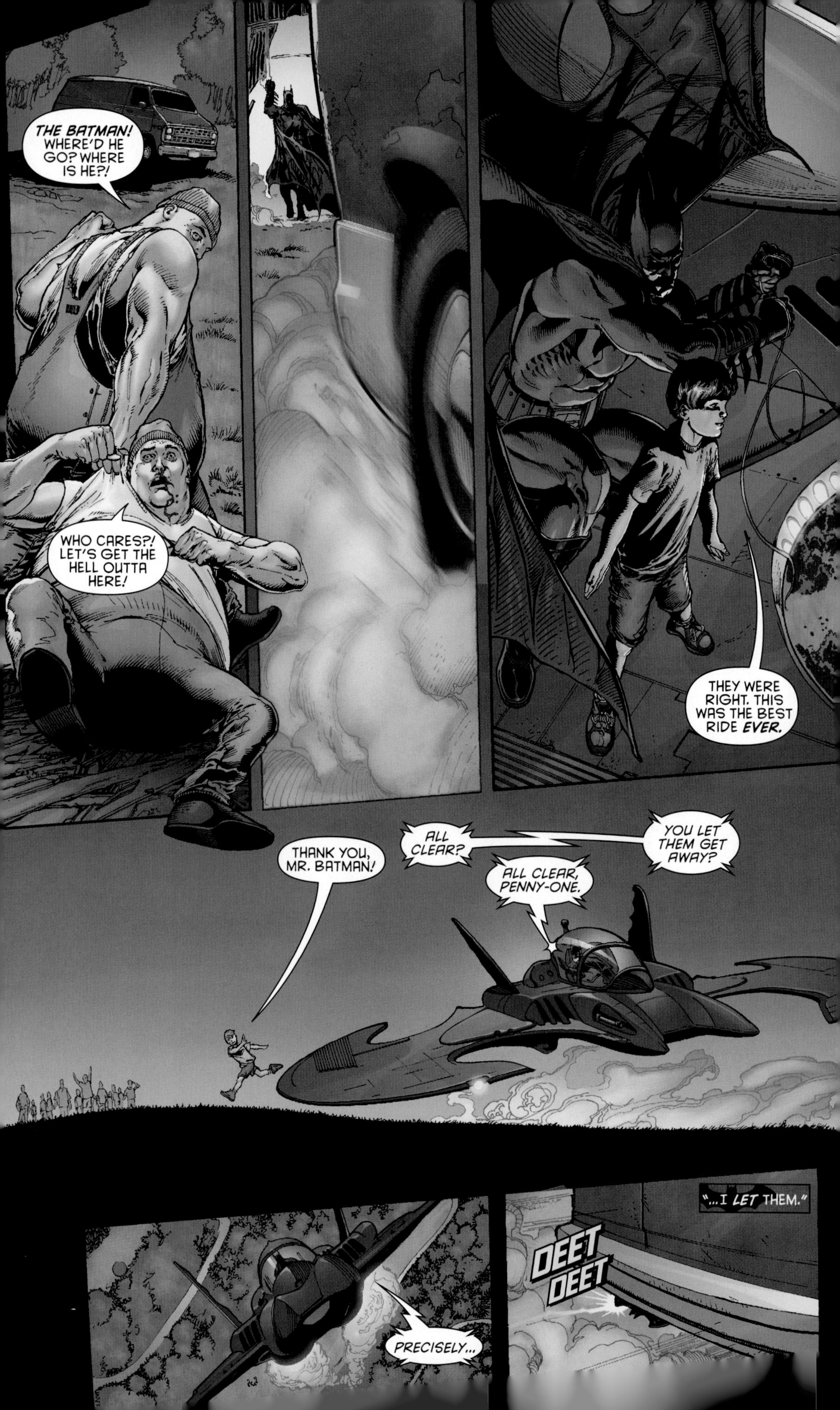
THE BATMAN! WHERE'D HE GO? WHERE IS HE?!
WHO CARES?! LET'S GET THE HELL OUTTA HERE!
THEY WERE RIGHT. THIS WAS THE BEST RIDE EVER.
THANK YOU, MR. BATMAN!
ALL CLEAR?
YOU LET THEM GET AWAY?
ALL CLEAR, PENNY-ONE.
"...I LET THEM."
DEET DEET
PRECISELY...

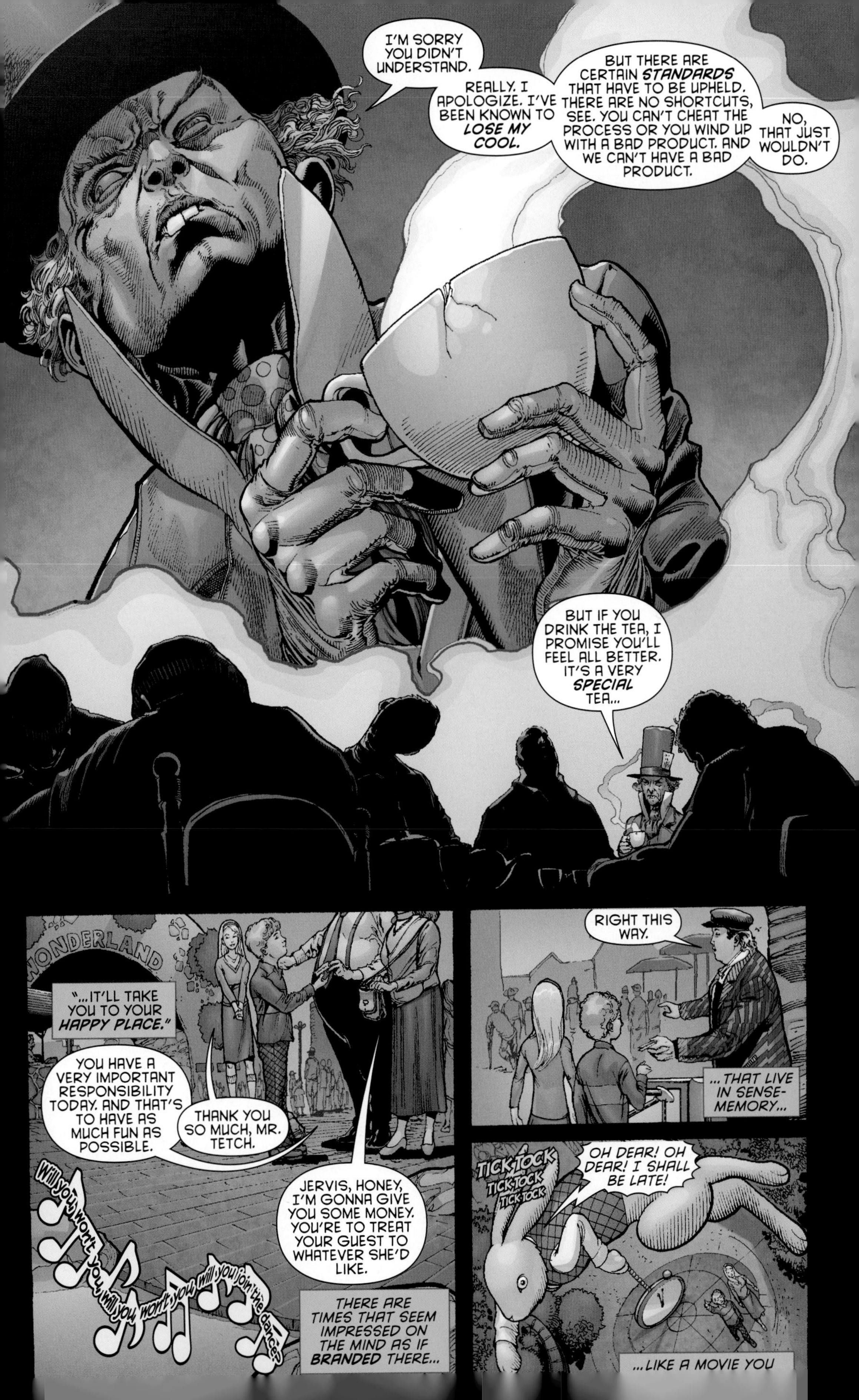
I'M SORRY YOU DIDN'T UNDERSTAND.
REALLY. I APOLOGIZE. I'VE BEEN KNOWN TO LOSE MY COOL.
BUT THERE ARE CERTAIN STANDARDS THAT HAVE TO BE UPHELD. THERE ARE NO SHORTCUTS, SEE. YOU CAN'T CHEAT THE PROCESS OR YOU WIND UP WITH A BAD PRODUCT. AND WE CAN'T HAVE A BAD PRODUCT.
NO, THAT JUST WOULDN'T DO.
BUT IF YOU DRINK THE TEA, I PROMISE YOU'LL FEEL ALL BETTER. IT'S A VERY SPECIAL TEA...
WONDERLAND
"...IT'LL TAKE YOU TO YOUR HAPPY PLACE."
YOU HAVE A VERY IMPORTANT RESPONSIBILITY TODAY. AND THAT'S TO HAVE AS MUCH FUN AS POSSIBLE.
THANK YOU SO MUCH, MR. TETCH.
JERVIS, HONEY, I'M GONNA GIVE YOU SOME MONEY. YOU'RE TO TREAT YOUR GUEST TO WHATEVER SHE'D LIKE.
Will you, won't you, will you, won't you, will you join the dance?
THERE ARE TIMES THAT SEEM IMPRESSED ON THE MIND AS IF BRANDED THERE...
RIGHT THIS WAY.
...THAT LIVE IN SENSE-MEMORY...
TICK-TOCK TICK-TOCK TICK-TOCK
OH DEAR! OH DEAR! I SHALL BE LATE!
...LIKE A MOVIE YOU

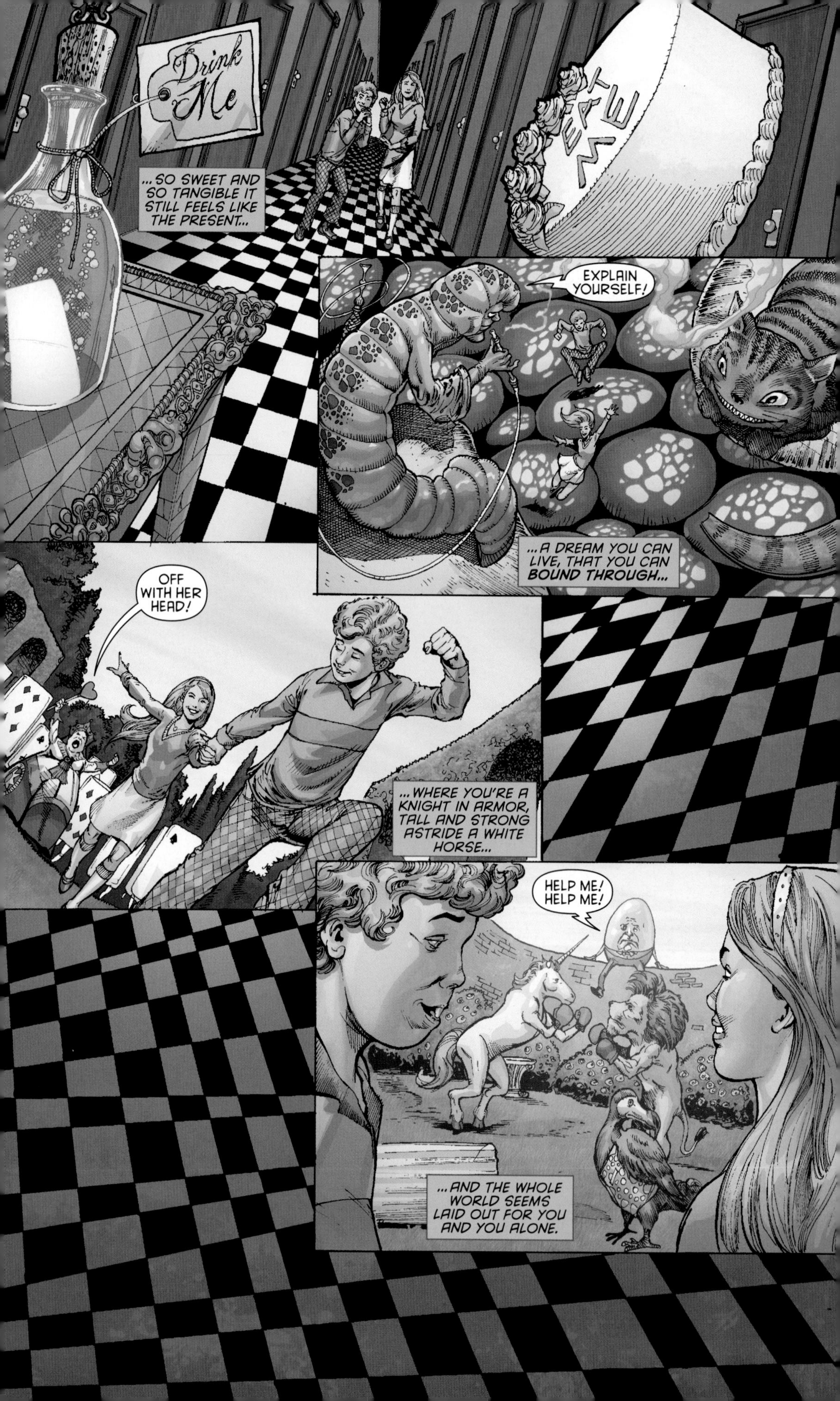
Drink Me
...SO SWEET AND SO TANGIBLE IT STILL FEELS LIKE THE PRESENT...
EAT ME
EXPLAIN YOURSELF!
...A DREAM YOU CAN LIVE, THAT YOU CAN BOUND THROUGH...
OFF WITH HER HEAD!
...WHERE YOU'RE A KNIGHT IN ARMOR, TALL AND STRONG ASTRIDE A WHITE HORSE...
HELP ME! HELP ME!
...AND THE WHOLE WORLD SEEMS LAID OUT FOR YOU AND YOU ALONE.

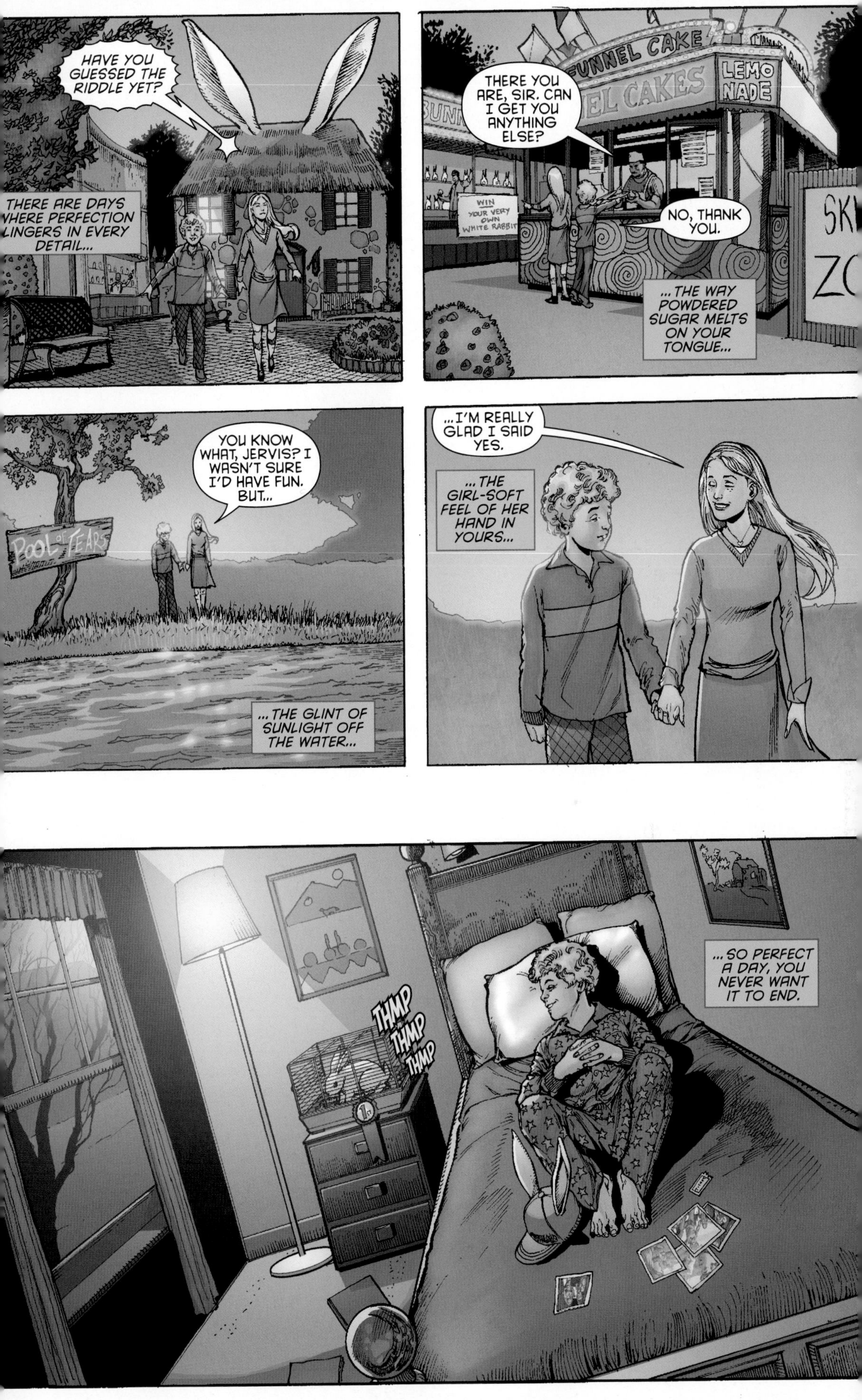
HAVE YOU GUESSED THE RIDDLE YET?
THERE ARE DAYS WHERE PERFECTION LINGERS IN EVERY DETAIL...
FUNNEL CAKE
EL CAKES
LEMO NADE
THERE YOU ARE, SIR. CAN I GET YOU ANYTHING ELSE?
WIN YOUR VERY OWN WHITE RABBIT
NO, THANK YOU.
...THE WAY POWDERED SUGAR MELTS ON YOUR TONGUE...
YOU KNOW WHAT, JERVIS? I WASN'T SURE I'D HAVE FUN. BUT...
POOL OF TEARS
...THE GLINT OF SUNLIGHT OFF THE WATER...
...I'M REALLY GLAD I SAID YES.
...THE GIRL-SOFT FEEL OF HER HAND IN YOURS...
...SO PERFECT A DAY, YOU NEVER WANT IT TO END.
THMP THMP THMP

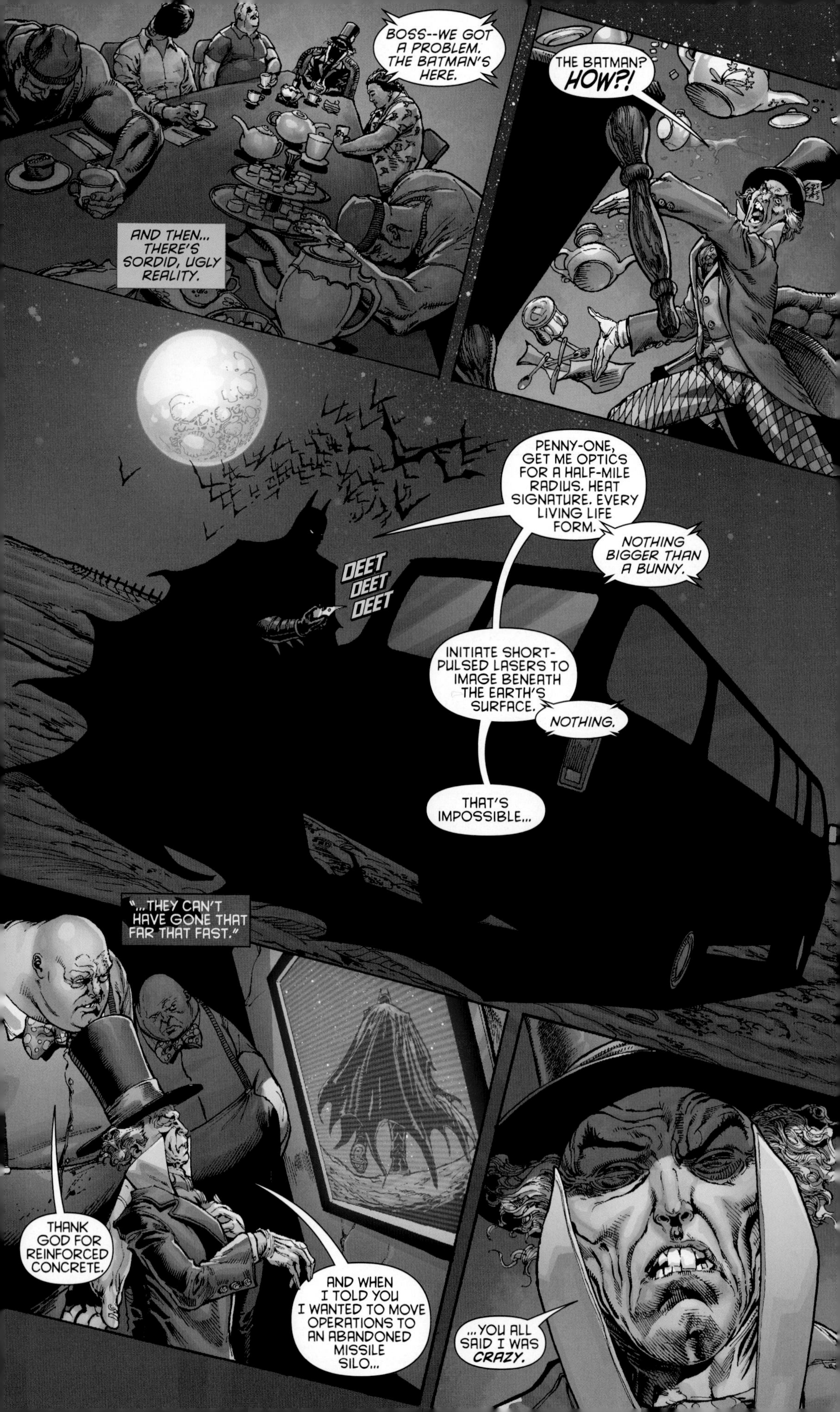
BOSS--WE GOT A PROBLEM. THE BATMAN'S HERE.
AND THEN... THERE'S SORDID, UGLY REALITY.
THE BATMAN? HOW?!
PENNY-ONE, GET ME OPTICS FOR A HALF-MILE RADIUS. HEAT SIGNATURE. EVERY LIVING LIFE FORM.
NOTHING BIGGER THAN A BUNNY.
DEET DEET DEET
INITIATE SHORT-PULSED LASERS TO IMAGE BENEATH THE EARTH'S SURFACE.
NOTHING.
THAT'S IMPOSSIBLE...
"...THEY CAN'T HAVE GONE THAT FAR THAT FAST."
THANK GOD FOR REINFORCED CONCRETE.
AND WHEN I TOLD YOU I WANTED TO MOVE OPERATIONS TO AN ABANDONED MISSILE SILO...
...YOU ALL SAID I WAS CRAZY.

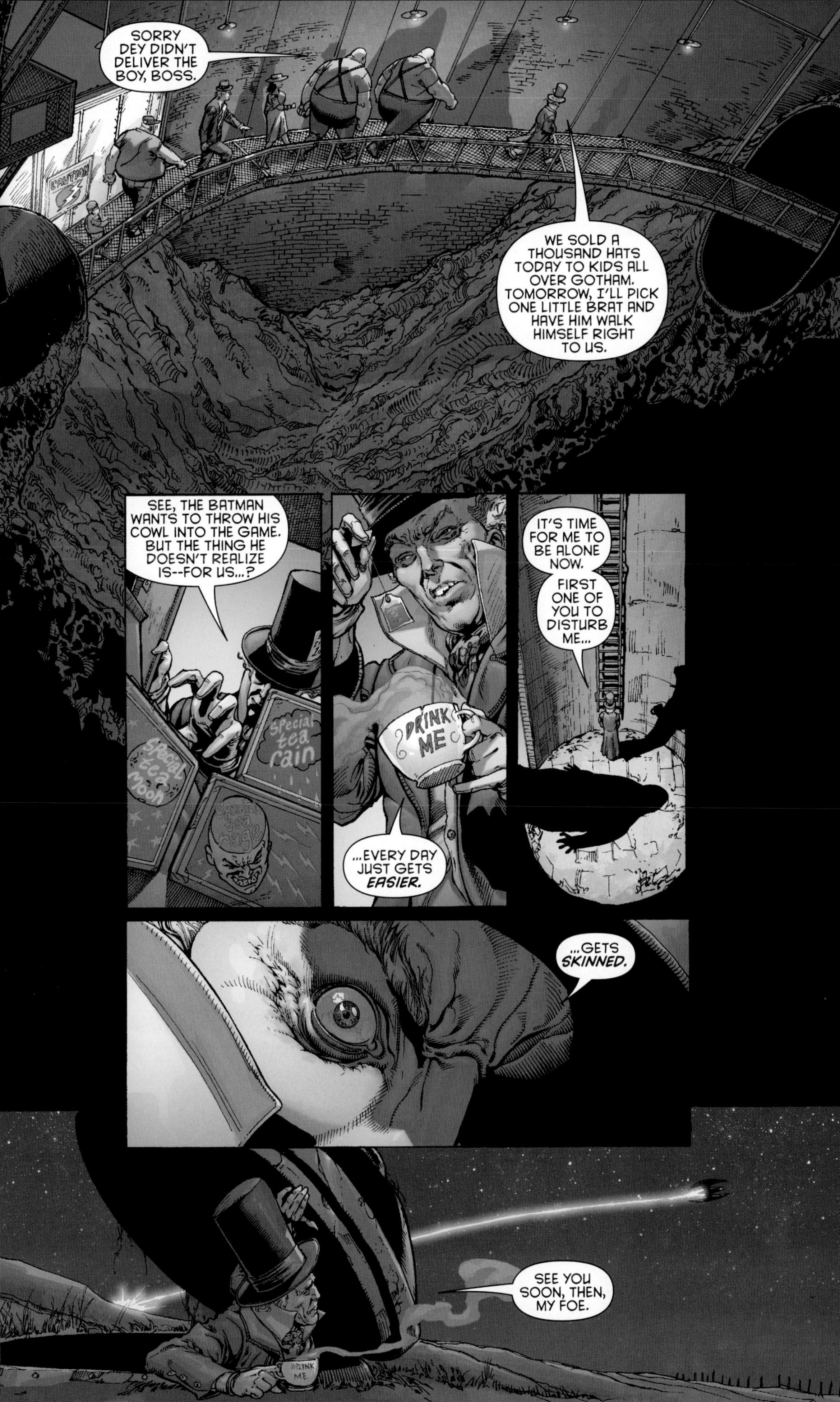
SORRY DEY DIDN'T DELIVER THE BOY, BOSS.
CAUTION
WE SOLD A THOUSAND HATS TODAY TO KIDS ALL OVER GOTHAM. TOMORROW, I'LL PICK ONE LITTLE BRAT AND HAVE HIM WALK HIMSELF RIGHT TO US.
SEE, THE BATMAN WANTS TO THROW HIS COWL INTO THE GAME. BUT THE THING HE DOESN'T REALIZE IS--FOR US...?
Special tea rain
Special tea moon
Special tea rage
DRINK ME
...EVERY DAY JUST GETS EASIER.
IT'S TIME FOR ME TO BE ALONE NOW.
FIRST ONE OF YOU TO DISTURB ME...
...GETS SKINNED.
SEE YOU SOON, THEN, MY FOE.

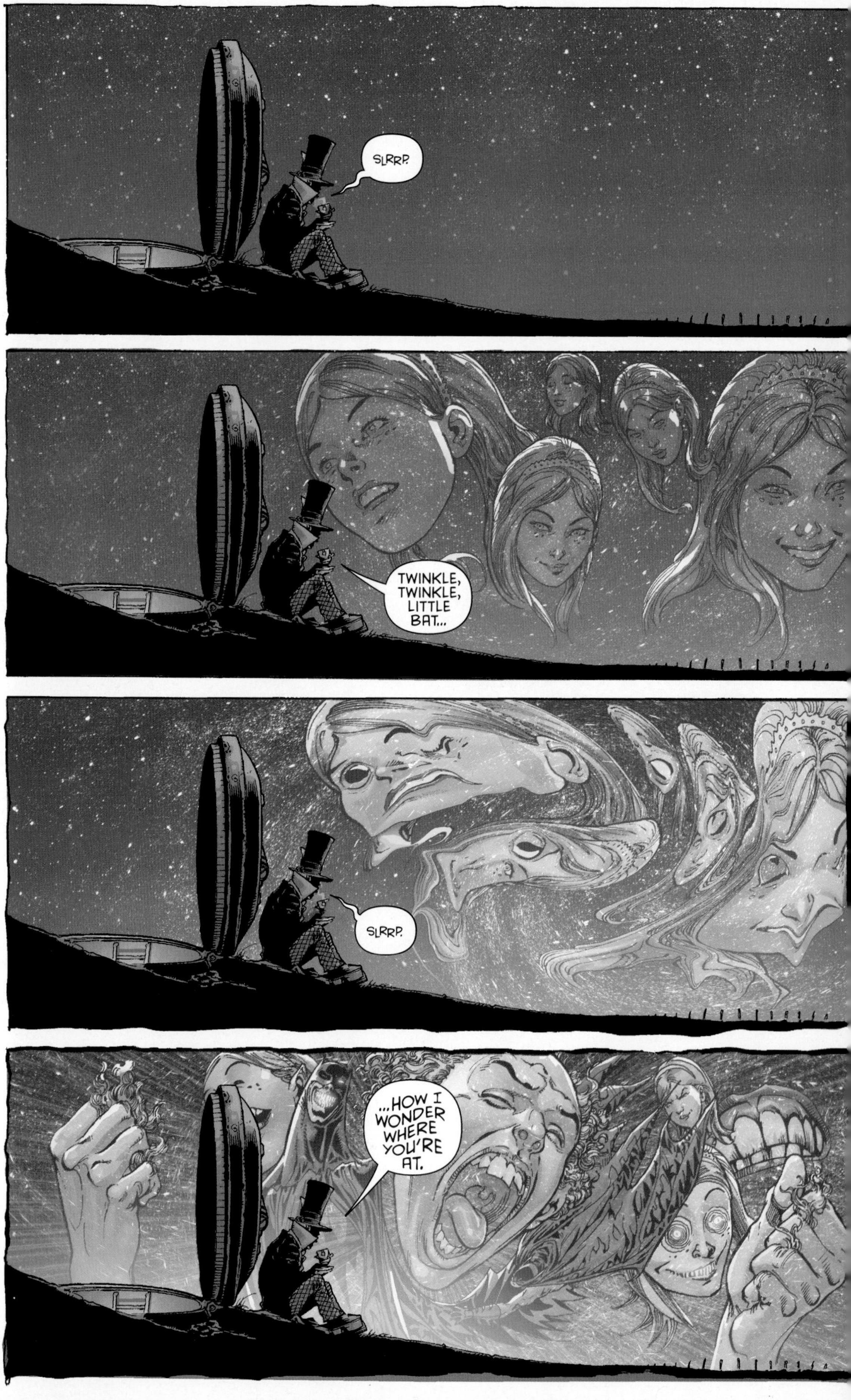
SLRRP.
TWINKLE, TWINKLE, LITTLE BAT...
SLRRP.
...HOW I WONDER WHERE YOU'RE AT.

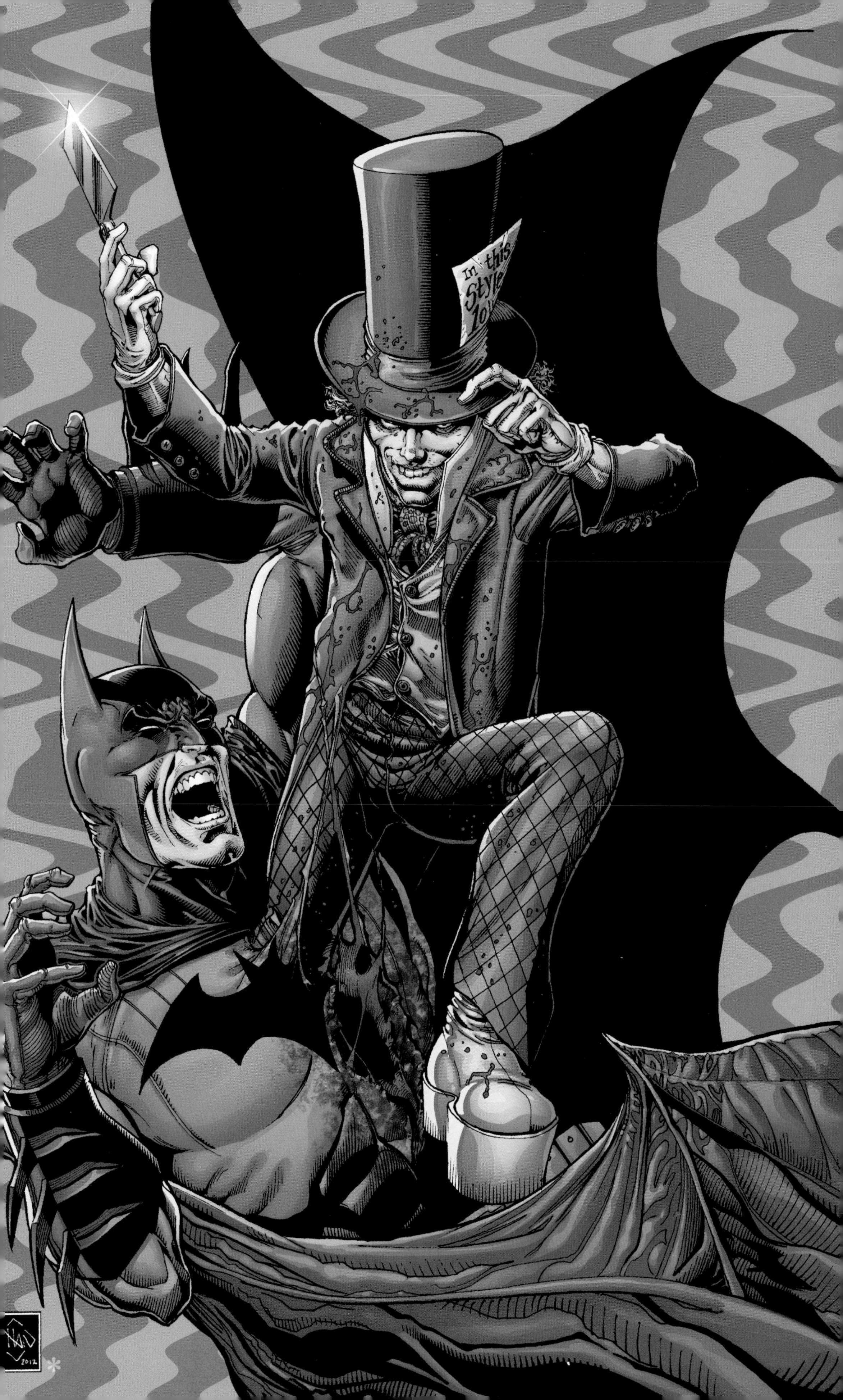
In this Style

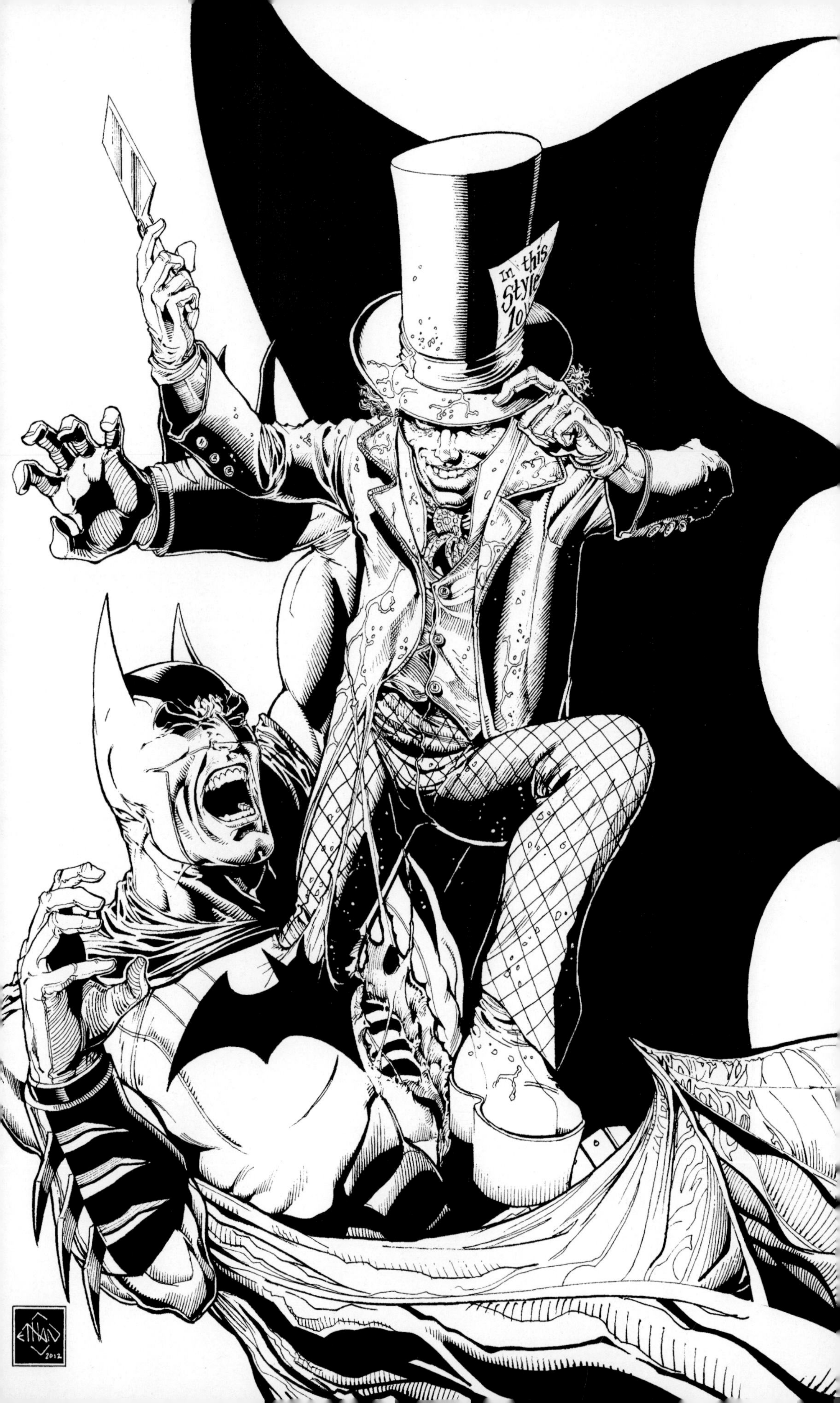
In this
Style
2012

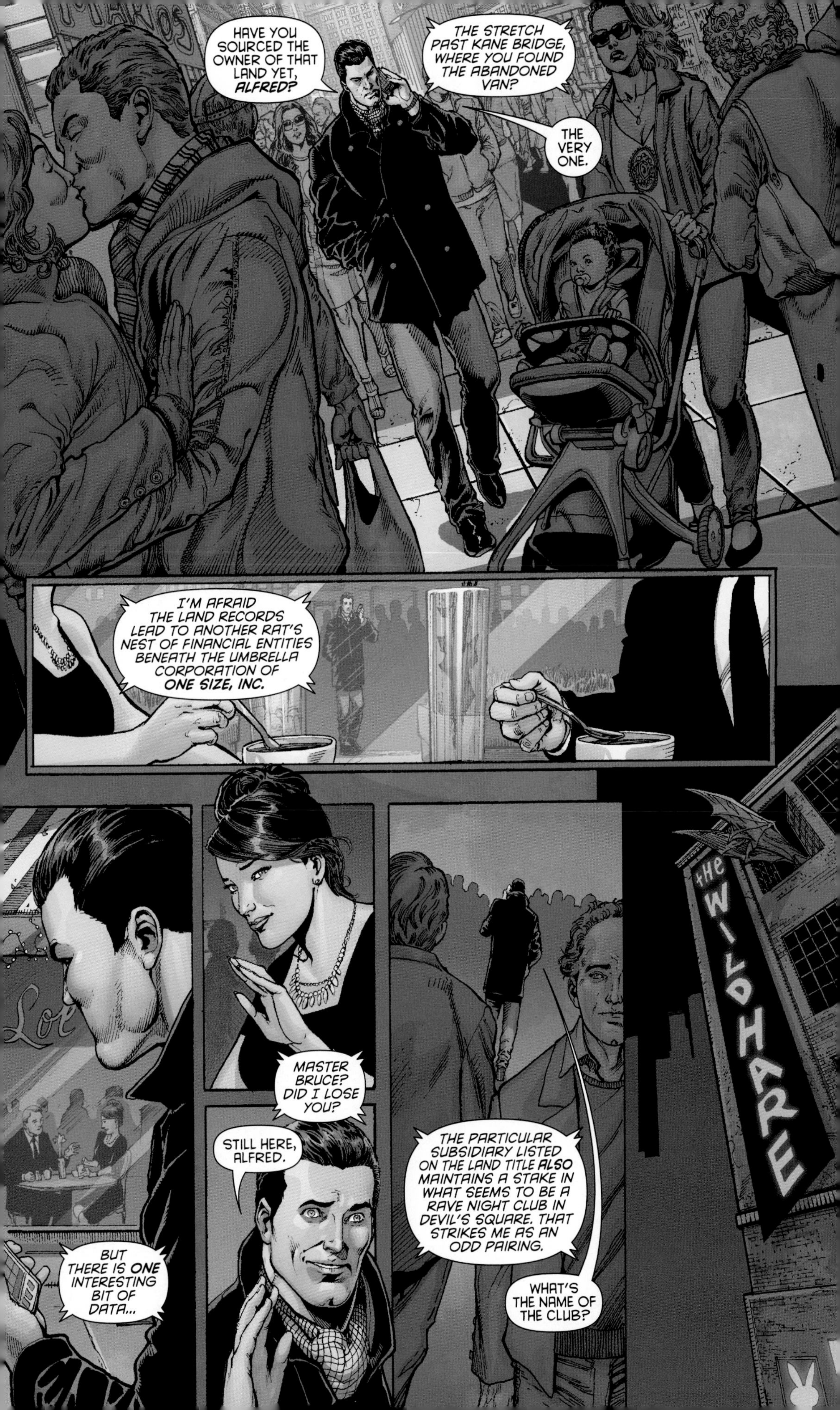
HAVE YOU SOURCED THE OWNER OF THAT LAND YET, ALFRED?
THE STRETCH PAST KANE BRIDGE, WHERE YOU FOUND THE ABANDONED VAN?
THE VERY ONE.
I'M AFRAID THE LAND RECORDS LEAD TO ANOTHER RAT'S NEST OF FINANCIAL ENTITIES BENEATH THE UMBRELLA CORPORATION OF ONE SIZE, INC.
BUT THERE IS ONE INTERESTING BIT OF DATA...
MASTER BRUCE? DID I LOSE YOU?
STILL HERE, ALFRED.
THE PARTICULAR SUBSIDIARY LISTED ON THE LAND TITLE ALSO MAINTAINS A STAKE IN WHAT SEEMS TO BE A RAVE NIGHT CLUB IN DEVIL'S SQUARE. THAT STRIKES ME AS AN ODD PAIRING.
WHAT'S THE NAME OF THE CLUB?
THE WILDHARE

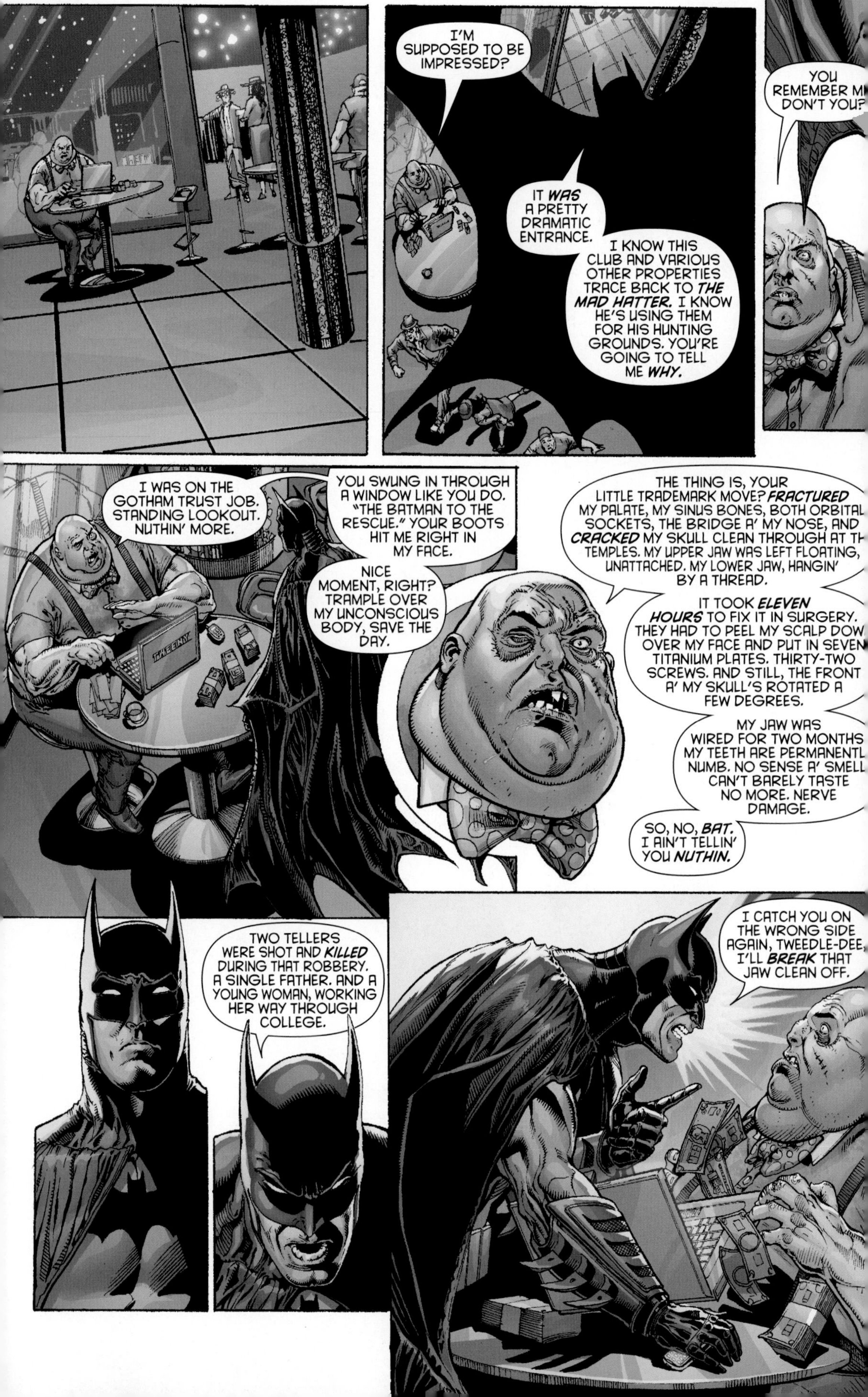
I'M SUPPOSED TO BE IMPRESSED?
IT WAS A PRETTY DRAMATIC ENTRANCE.
I KNOW THIS CLUB AND VARIOUS OTHER PROPERTIES TRACE BACK TO THE MAD HATTER. I KNOW HE'S USING THEM FOR HIS HUNTING GROUNDS. YOU'RE GOING TO TELL ME WHY.
YOU REMEMBER M DON'T YOU?
I WAS ON THE GOTHAM TRUST JOB. STANDING LOOKOUT. NUTHIN' MORE.
YOU SWUNG IN THROUGH A WINDOW LIKE YOU DO. "THE BATMAN TO THE RESCUE." YOUR BOOTS HIT ME RIGHT IN MY FACE.
NICE MOMENT, RIGHT? TRAMPLE OVER MY UNCONSCIOUS BODY, SAVE THE DAY.
THE THING IS, YOUR LITTLE TRADEMARK MOVE? FRACTURED MY PALATE, MY SINUS BONES, BOTH ORBITAL SOCKETS, THE BRIDGE A' MY NOSE, AND CRACKED MY SKULL CLEAN THROUGH AT TH TEMPLES. MY UPPER JAW WAS LEFT FLOATING, UNATTACHED. MY LOWER JAW, HANGIN' BY A THREAD.
IT TOOK ELEVEN HOURS TO FIX IT IN SURGERY. THEY HAD TO PEEL MY SCALP DOW OVER MY FACE AND PUT IN SEVEN TITANIUM PLATES. THIRTY-TWO SCREWS. AND STILL, THE FRONT A' MY SKULL'S ROTATED A FEW DEGREES.
MY JAW WAS WIRED FOR TWO MONTHS MY TEETH ARE PERMANENTL NUMB. NO SENSE A' SMELL CAN'T BARELY TASTE NO MORE. NERVE DAMAGE.
SO, NO, BAT. I AIN'T TELLIN' YOU NUTHIN.
TWO TELLERS WERE SHOT AND KILLED DURING THAT ROBBERY. A SINGLE FATHER. AND A YOUNG WOMAN, WORKING HER WAY THROUGH COLLEGE.
I CATCH YOU ON THE WRONG SIDE AGAIN, TWEEDLE-DEE, I'LL BREAK THAT JAW CLEAN OFF.

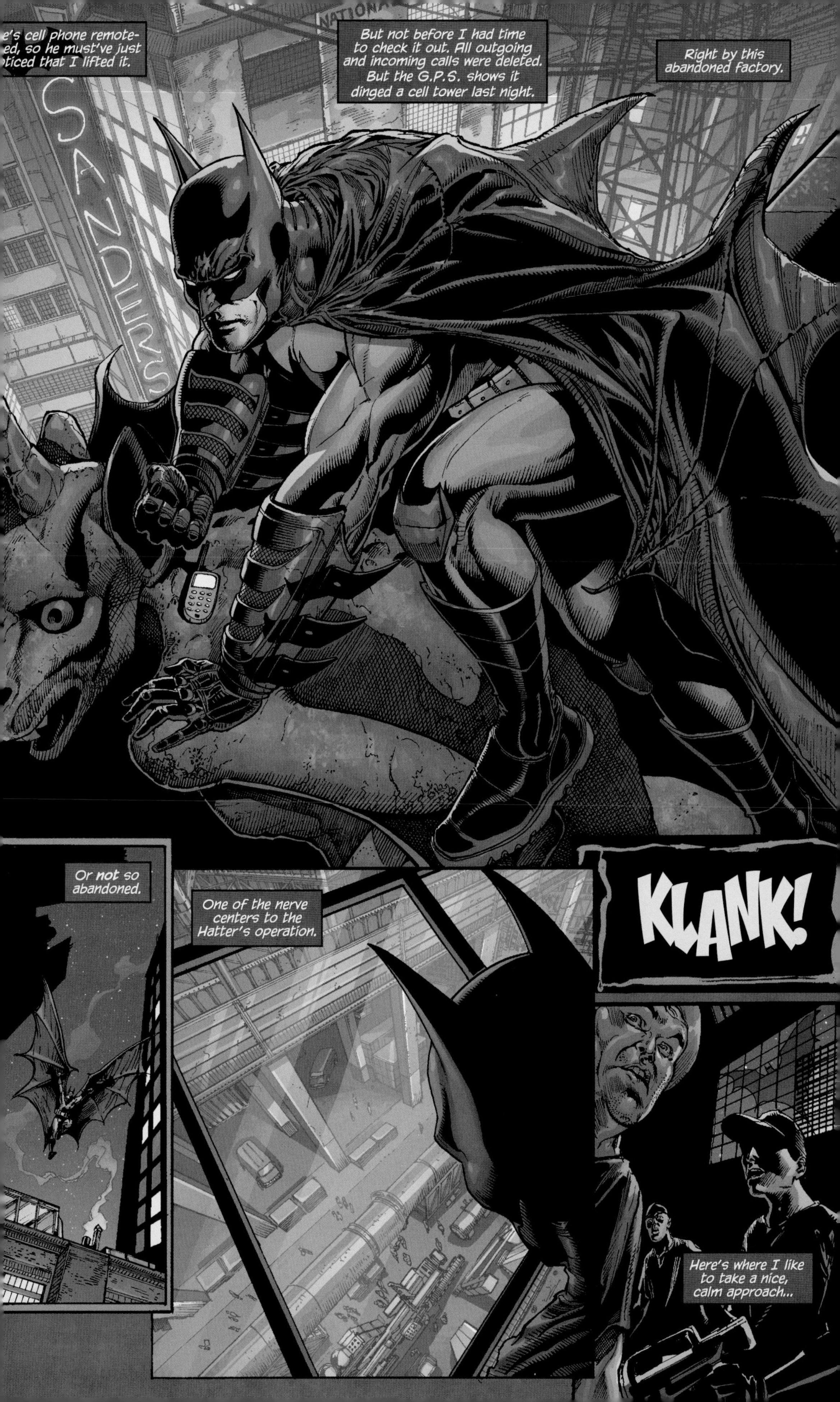

e's cell phone remote-
ed, so he must've just
ticed that I lifted it.
But not before I had time to check it out. All outgoing and incoming calls were deleted. But the G.P.S. shows it dinged a cell tower last night.
Right by this abandoned factory.
SANDERS
Or not so abandoned.
One of the nerve centers to the Hatter's operation.
KLANK!
Here's where I like to take a nice, calm approach...

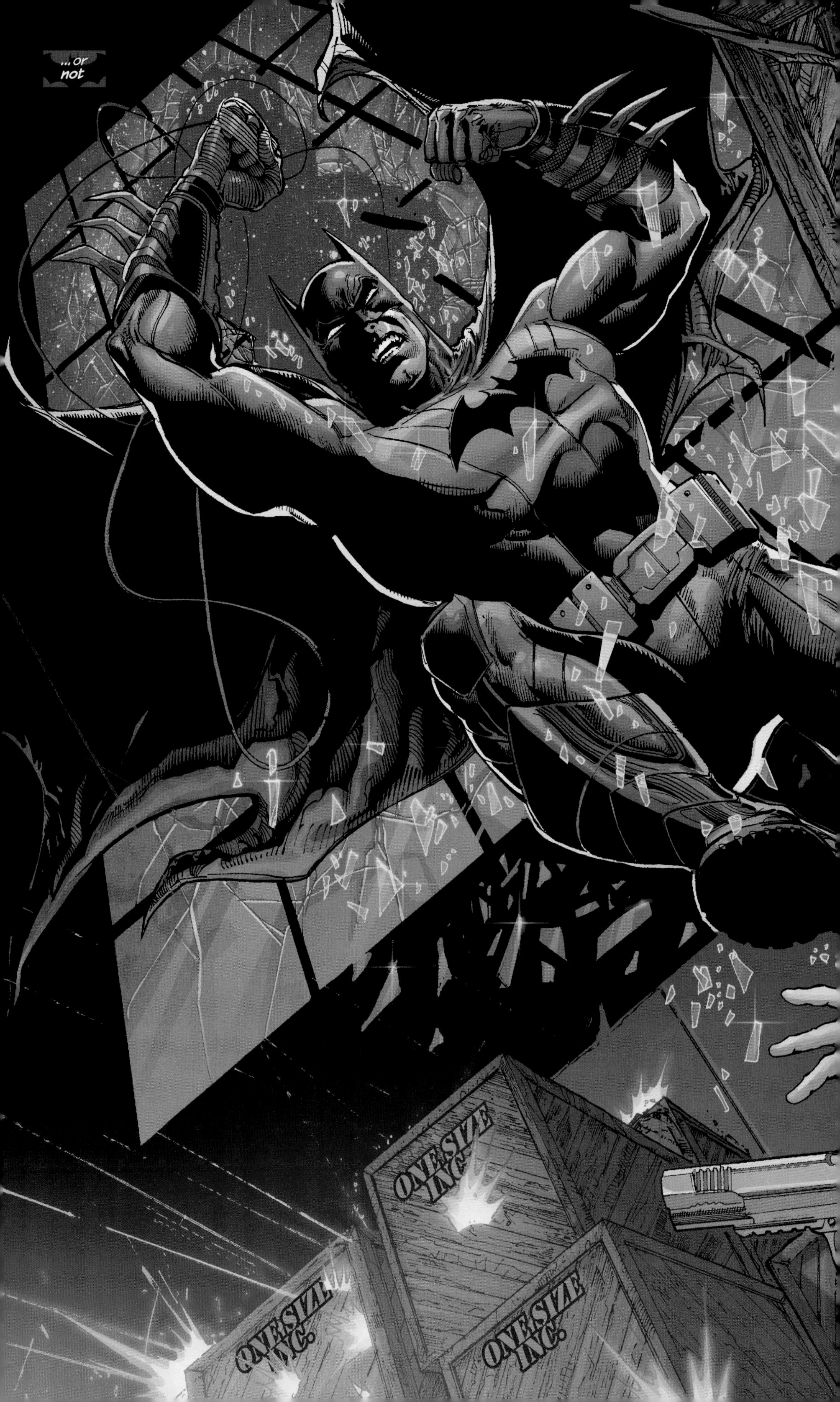
...or not
ONE SIZE INC.
ONE SIZE INC.
ONE SIZE INC.

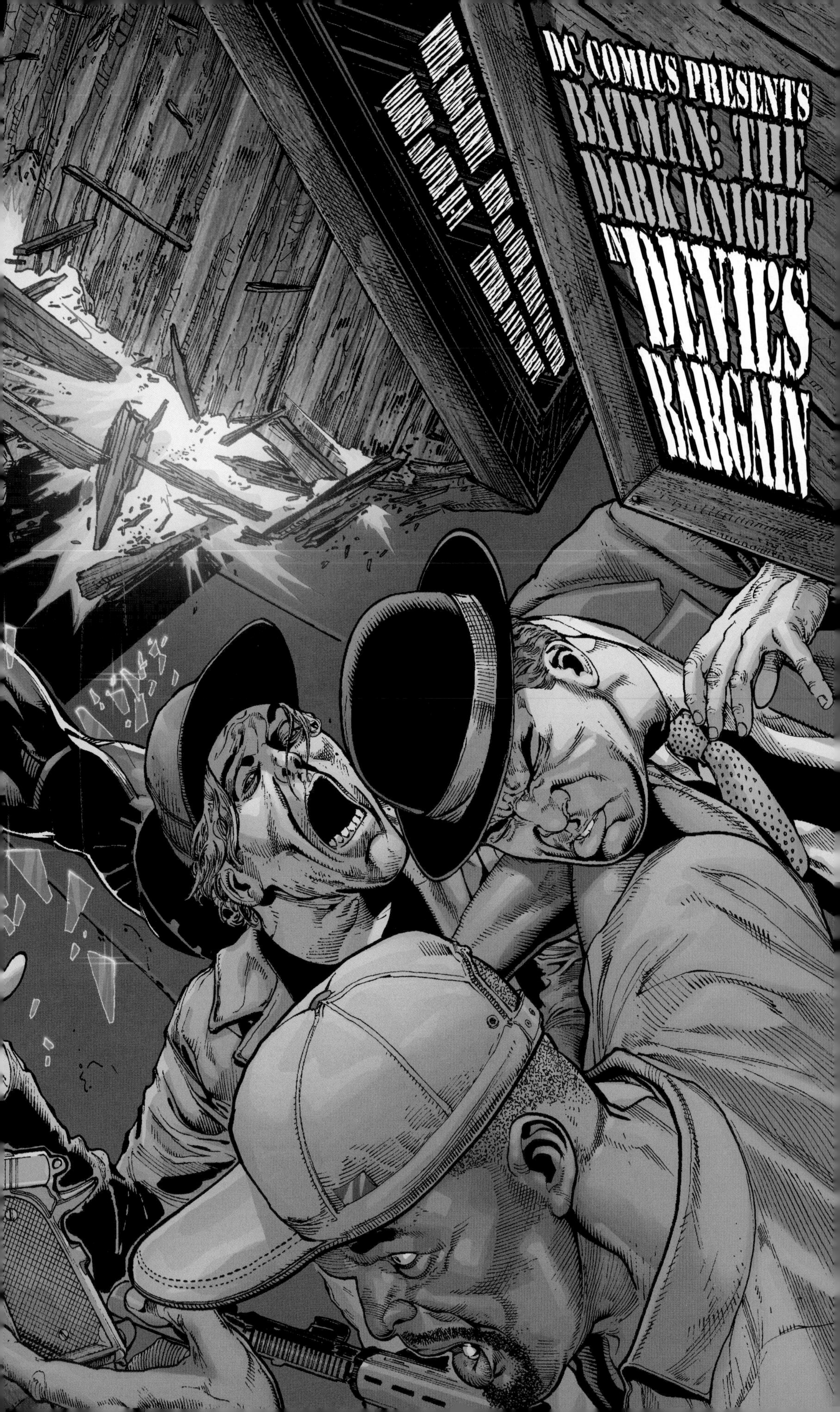
DC COMICS PRESENTS
BATMAN: THE DARK KNIGHT
IN "DEVIL'S BARGAIN"

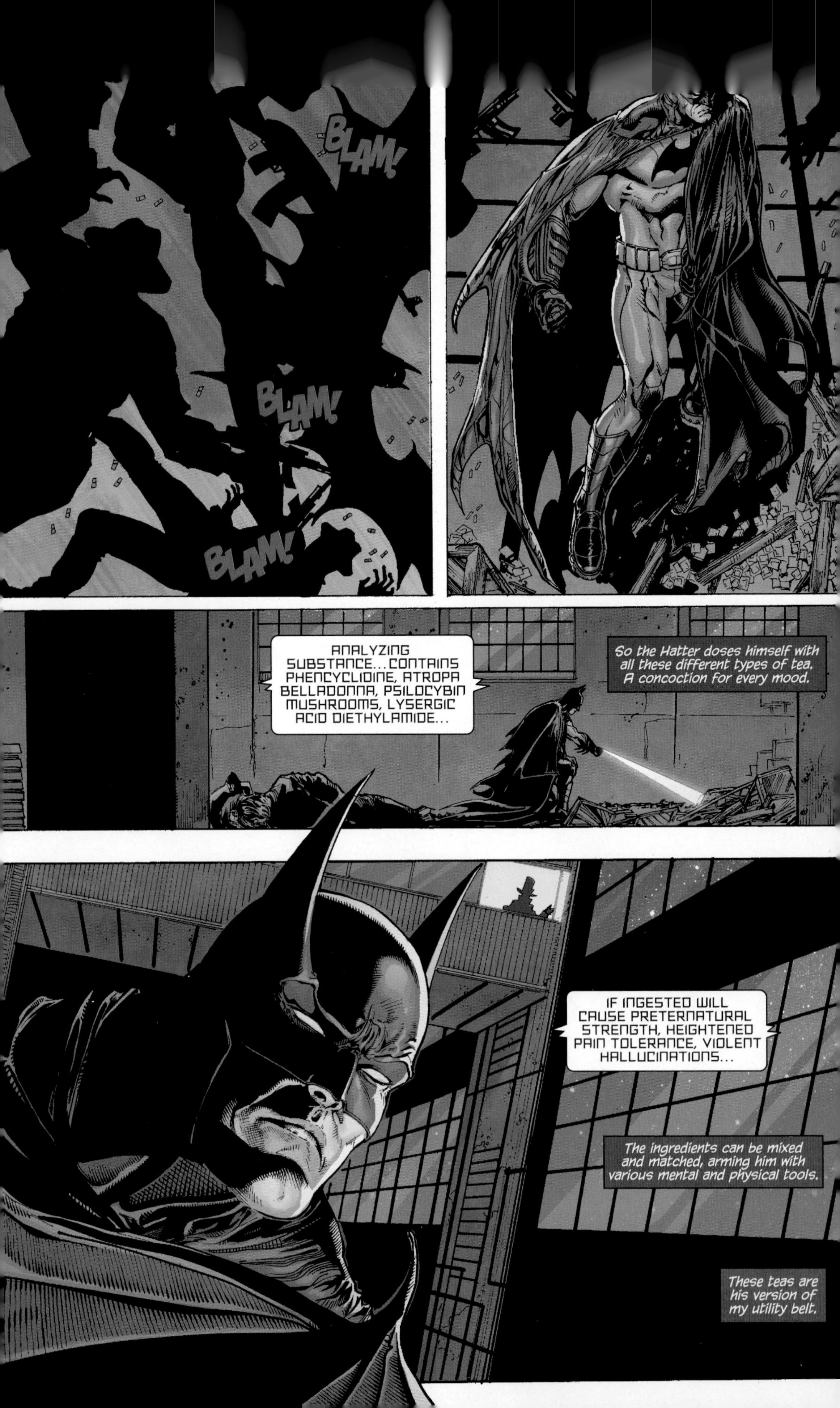
BLAM!
BLAM!
BLAM!
ANALYZING SUBSTANCE... CONTAINS PHENCYCLIDINE, ATROPA BELLADONNA, PSILOCYBIN MUSHROOMS, LYSERGIC ACID DIETHYLAMIDE...
So the Hatter doses himself with all these different types of tea. A concoction for every mood.
IF INGESTED WILL CAUSE PRETERNATURAL STRENGTH, HEIGHTENED PAIN TOLERANCE, VIOLENT HALLUCINATIONS...
The ingredients can be mixed and matched, arming him with various mental and physical tools.
These teas are his version of my utility belt.

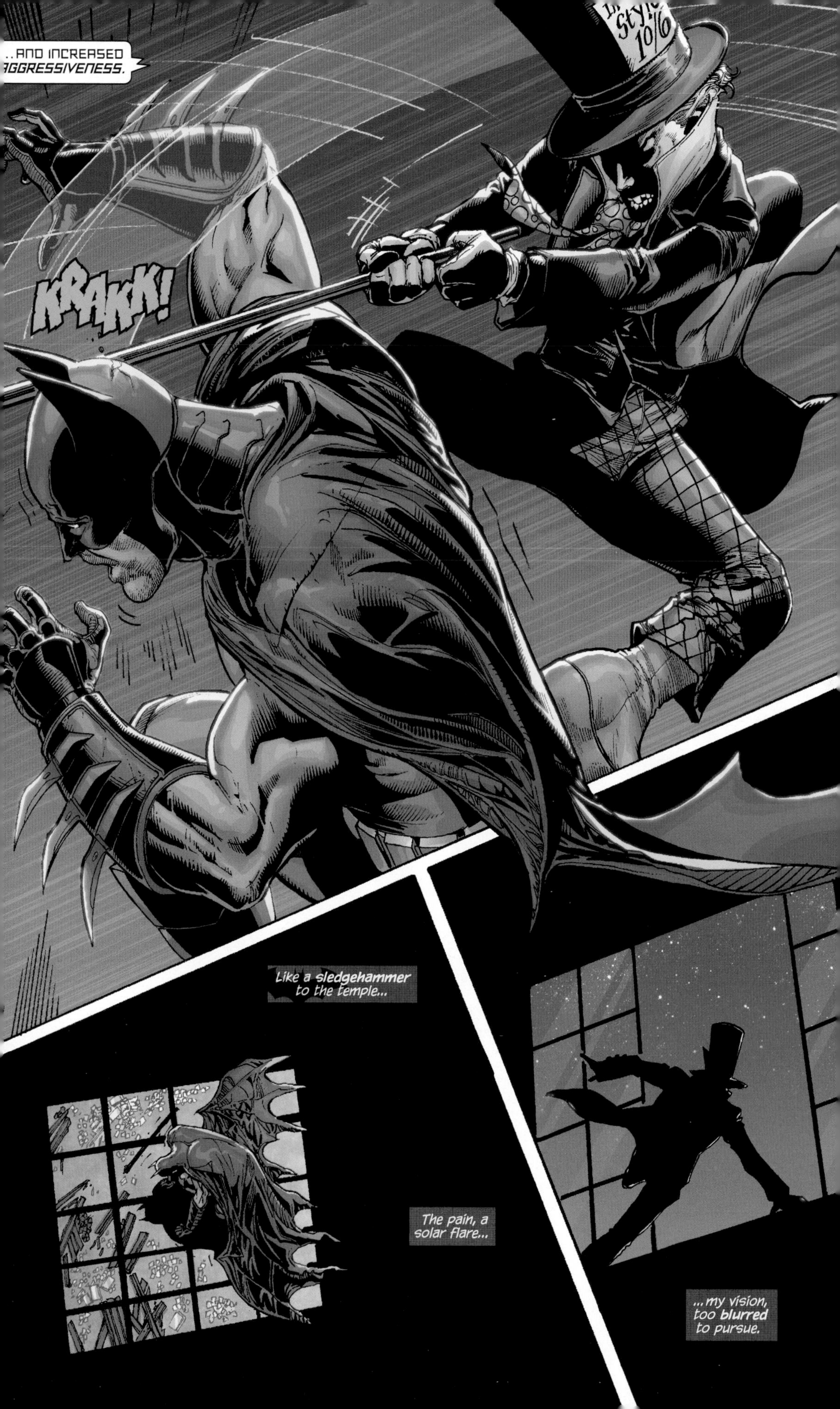

..AND INCREASED AGGRESSIVENESS.
KRAKK!
Like a sledgehammer to the temple...
The pain, a solar flare...
...my vision, too blurred to pursue.

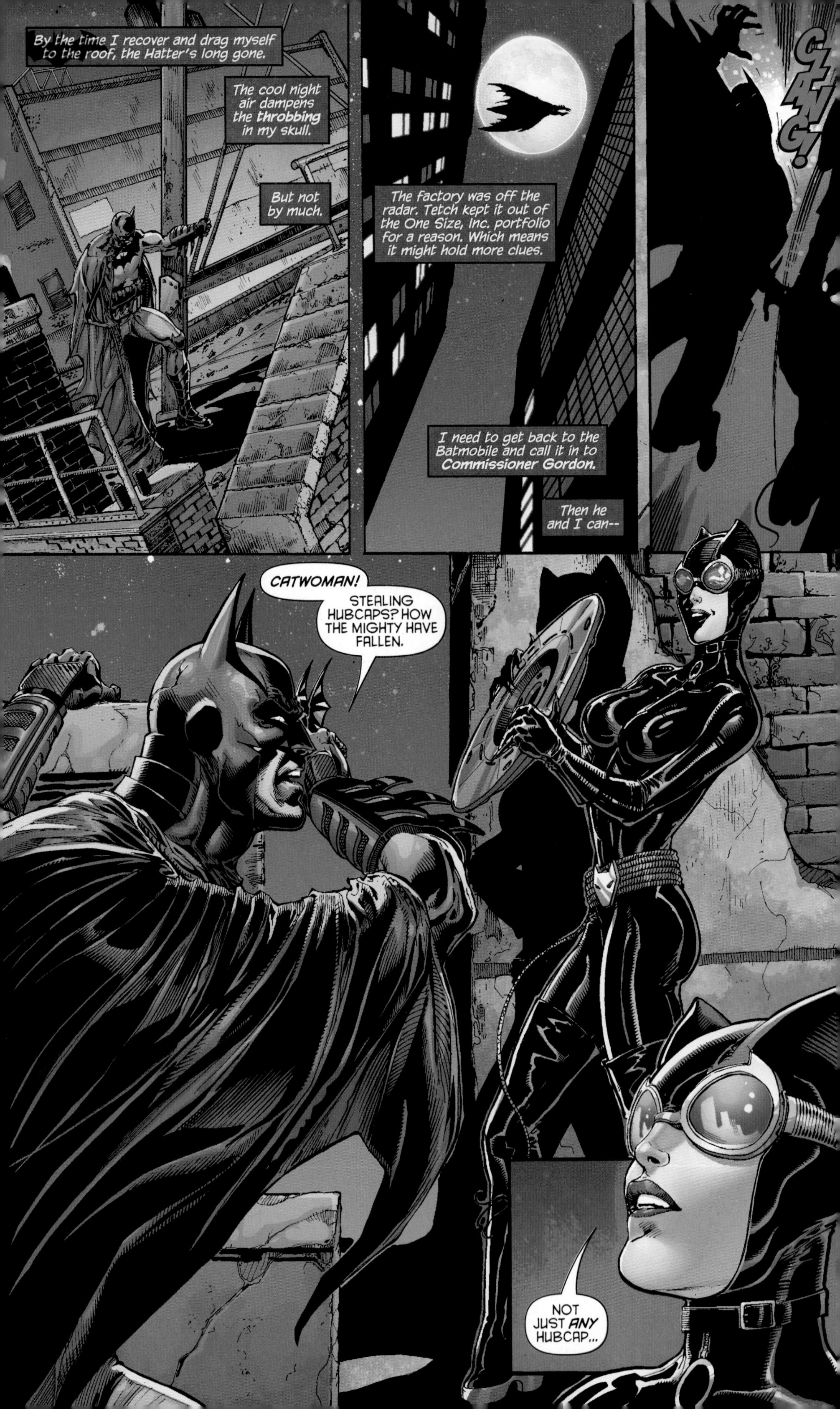

By the time I recover and drag myself to the roof, the Hatter's long gone.
The cool night air dampens the **throbbing** in my skull.
But not by much.
The factory was off the radar. Tetch kept it out of the One Size, Inc. portfolio for a reason. Which means it might hold more clues.
I need to get back to the Batmobile and call it in to **Commissioner Gordon.**
Then he and I can--
CLANG!
CATWOMAN!
STEALING HUBCAPS? HOW THE MIGHTY HAVE FALLEN.
NOT JUST *ANY* HUBCAP...

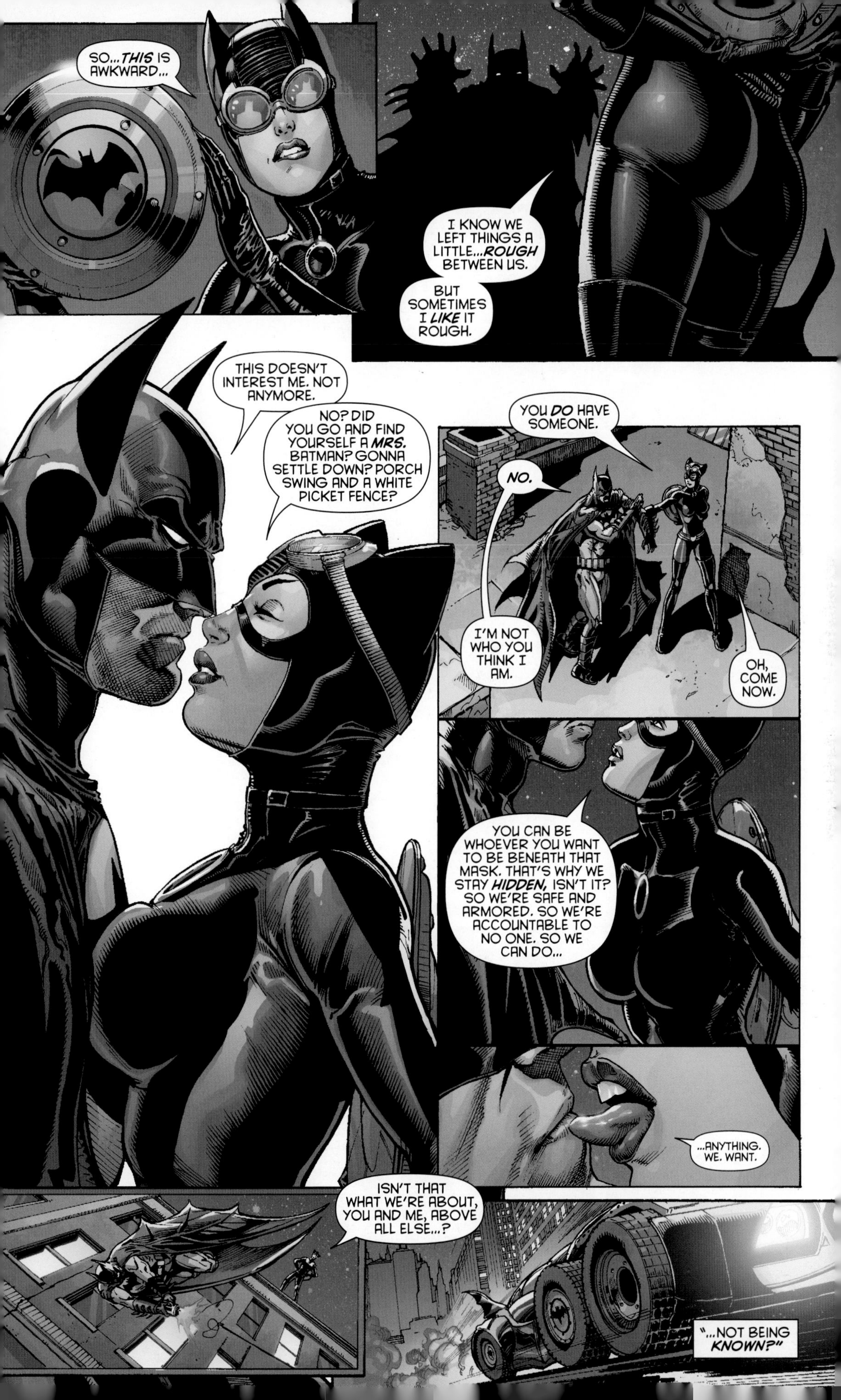

SO...THIS IS AWKWARD...
I KNOW WE LEFT THINGS A LITTLE...ROUGH BETWEEN US.
BUT SOMETIMES I LIKE IT ROUGH.
THIS DOESN'T INTEREST ME. NOT ANYMORE.
NO? DID YOU GO AND FIND YOURSELF A MRS. BATMAN? GONNA SETTLE DOWN? PORCH SWING AND A WHITE PICKET FENCE?
YOU DO HAVE SOMEONE.
NO.
I'M NOT WHO YOU THINK I AM.
OH, COME NOW.
YOU CAN BE WHOEVER YOU WANT TO BE BENEATH THAT MASK. THAT'S WHY WE STAY HIDDEN, ISN'T IT? SO WE'RE SAFE AND ARMORED. SO WE'RE ACCOUNTABLE TO NO ONE. SO WE CAN DO...
...ANYTHING. WE. WANT.
ISN'T THAT WHAT WE'RE ABOUT, YOU AND ME, ABOVE ALL ELSE...?
"...NOT BEING KNOWN?"

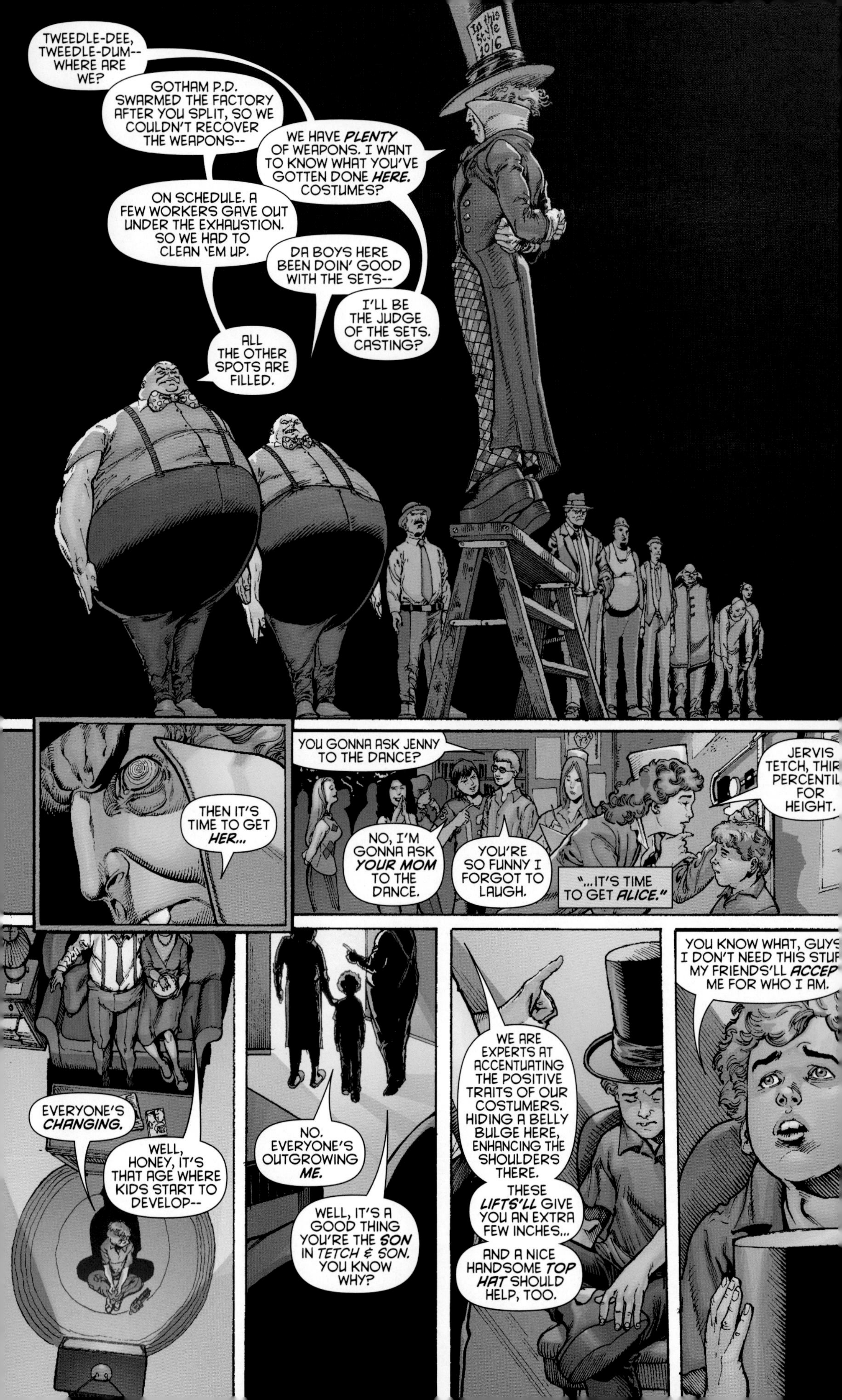

TWEEDLE-DEE, TWEEDLE-DUM-- WHERE ARE WE?
GOTHAM P.D. SWARMED THE FACTORY AFTER YOU SPLIT, SO WE COULDN'T RECOVER THE WEAPONS--
WE HAVE *PLENTY* OF WEAPONS. I WANT TO KNOW WHAT YOU'VE GOTTEN DONE *HERE.* COSTUMES?
ON SCHEDULE. A FEW WORKERS GAVE OUT UNDER THE EXHAUSTION. SO WE HAD TO CLEAN 'EM UP.
DA BOYS HERE BEEN DOIN' GOOD WITH THE SETS--
I'LL BE THE JUDGE OF THE SETS. CASTING?
ALL THE OTHER SPOTS ARE FILLED.
THEN IT'S TIME TO GET *HER...*
YOU GONNA ASK JENNY TO THE DANCE?
NO, I'M GONNA ASK *YOUR MOM* TO THE DANCE.
YOU'RE SO FUNNY I FORGOT TO LAUGH.
"...IT'S TIME TO GET *ALICE.*"
JERVIS TETCH, THIR PERCENTIL FOR HEIGHT.
EVERYONE'S *CHANGING.*
WELL, HONEY, IT'S THAT AGE WHERE KIDS START TO DEVELOP--
NO. EVERYONE'S OUTGROWING *ME.*
WELL, IT'S A GOOD THING YOU'RE THE *SON* IN *TETCH & SON.* YOU KNOW WHY?
WE ARE EXPERTS AT ACCENTUATING THE POSITIVE TRAITS OF OUR COSTUMERS. HIDING A BELLY BULGE HERE, ENHANCING THE SHOULDERS THERE.
THESE *LIFTS'LL* GIVE YOU AN EXTRA FEW INCHES...
AND A NICE HANDSOME *TOP HAT* SHOULD HELP, TOO.
YOU KNOW WHAT, GUYS I DON'T NEED THIS STUF MY FRIENDS'LL *ACCEP* ME FOR WHO I AM.

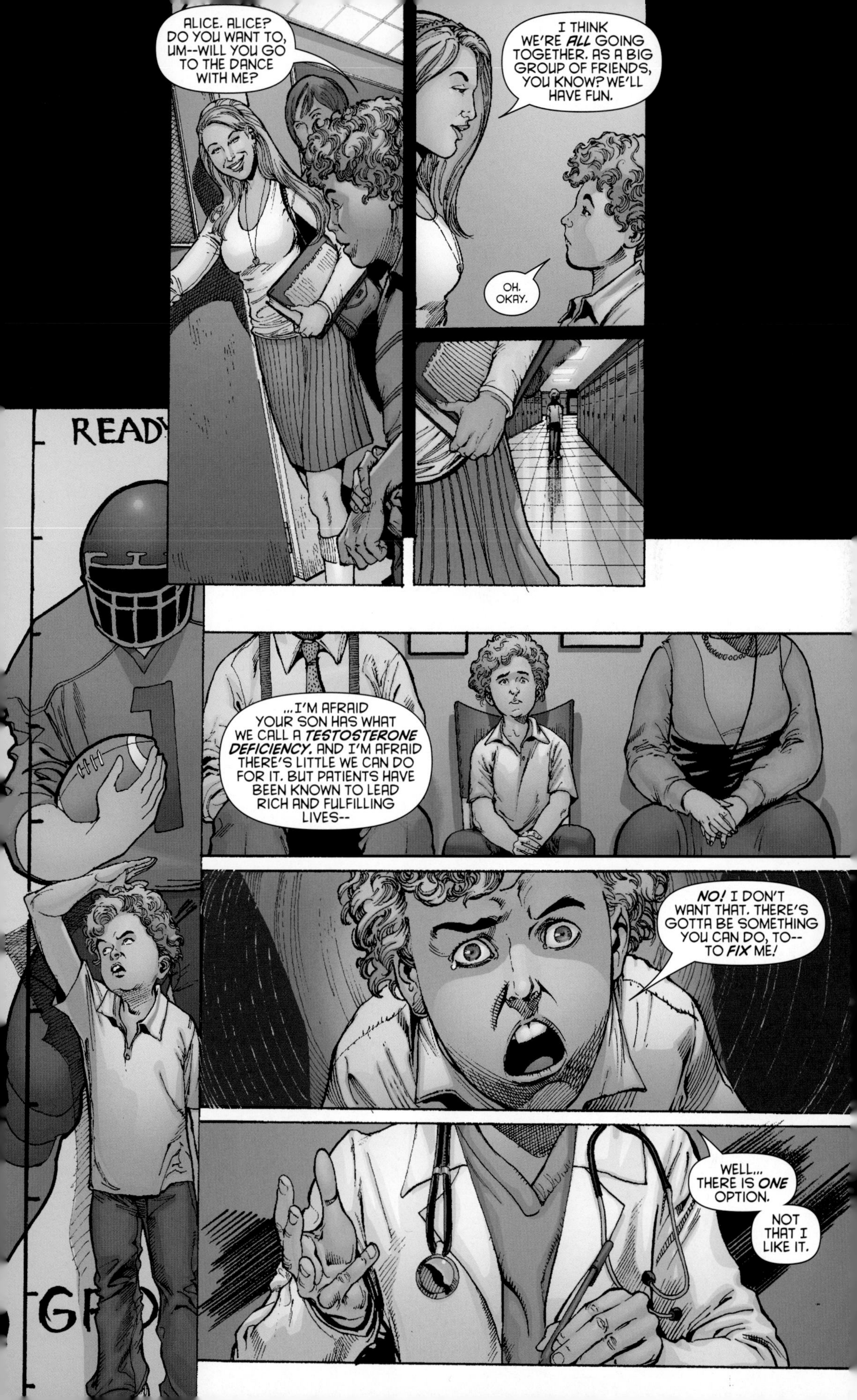
ALICE. ALICE? DO YOU WANT TO, UM--WILL YOU GO TO THE DANCE WITH ME?
I THINK WE'RE *ALL* GOING TOGETHER. AS A BIG GROUP OF FRIENDS, YOU KNOW? WE'LL HAVE FUN.
OH. OKAY.
READY
GRO
...I'M AFRAID YOUR SON HAS WHAT WE CALL A ***TESTOSTERONE DEFICIENCY.*** AND I'M AFRAID THERE'S LITTLE WE CAN DO FOR IT. BUT PATIENTS HAVE BEEN KNOWN TO LEAD RICH AND FULFILLING LIVES--
*NO!* I DON'T WANT THAT. THERE'S GOTTA BE SOMETHING YOU CAN DO, TO-- TO *FIX* ME!
WELL... THERE IS *ONE* OPTION.
NOT THAT I LIKE IT.

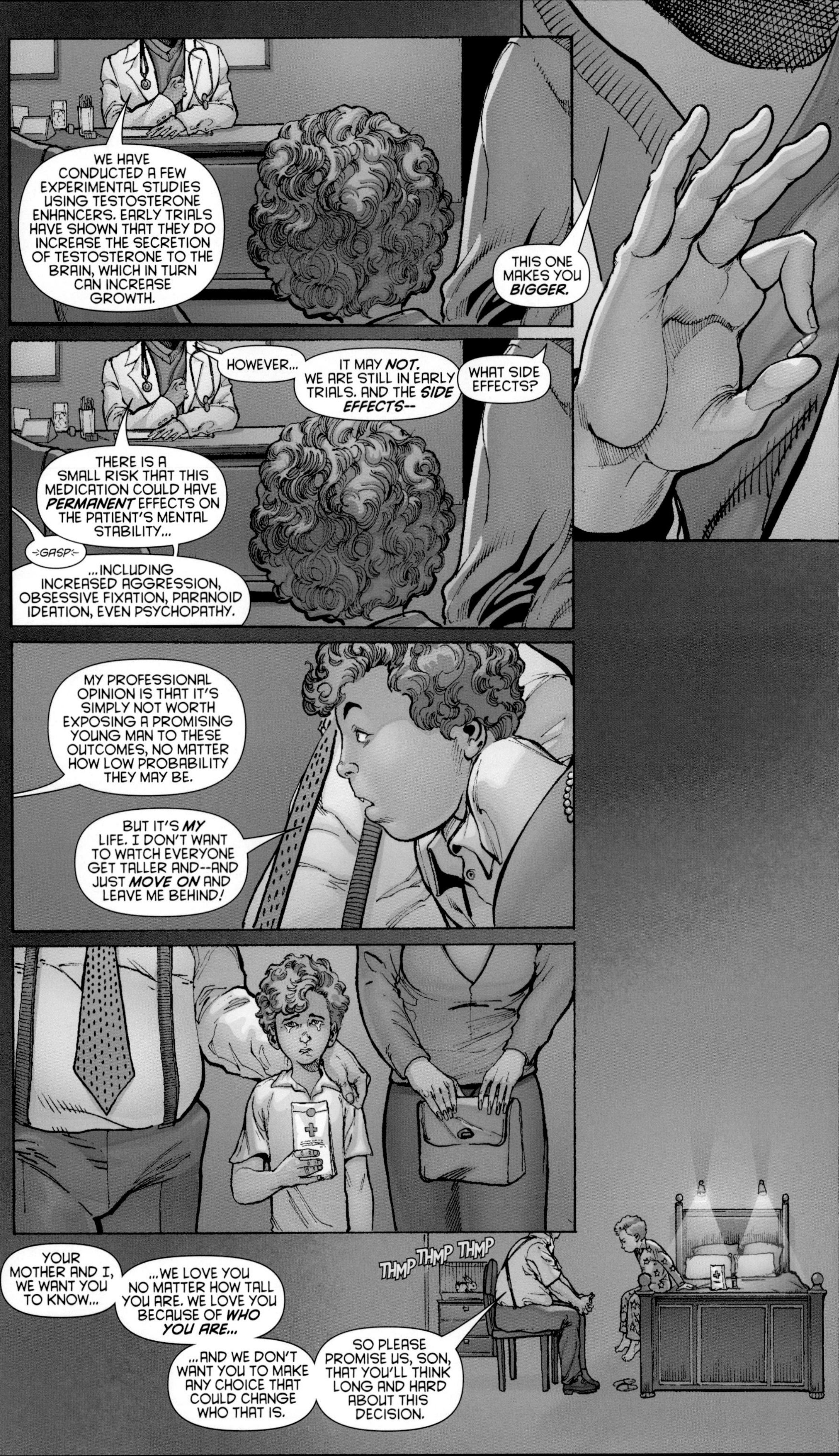
WE HAVE CONDUCTED A FEW EXPERIMENTAL STUDIES USING TESTOSTERONE ENHANCERS. EARLY TRIALS HAVE SHOWN THAT THEY DO INCREASE THE SECRETION OF TESTOSTERONE TO THE BRAIN, WHICH IN TURN CAN INCREASE GROWTH.
THIS ONE MAKES YOU BIGGER.
HOWEVER...
IT MAY NOT. WE ARE STILL IN EARLY TRIALS. AND THE SIDE EFFECTS--
WHAT SIDE EFFECTS?
THERE IS A SMALL RISK THAT THIS MEDICATION COULD HAVE PERMANENT EFFECTS ON THE PATIENT'S MENTAL STABILITY...
GASP
...INCLUDING INCREASED AGGRESSION, OBSESSIVE FIXATION, PARANOID IDEATION, EVEN PSYCHOPATHY.
MY PROFESSIONAL OPINION IS THAT IT'S SIMPLY NOT WORTH EXPOSING A PROMISING YOUNG MAN TO THESE OUTCOMES, NO MATTER HOW LOW PROBABILITY THEY MAY BE.
BUT IT'S MY LIFE. I DON'T WANT TO WATCH EVERYONE GET TALLER AND--AND JUST MOVE ON AND LEAVE ME BEHIND!
YOUR MOTHER AND I, WE WANT YOU TO KNOW...
...WE LOVE YOU NO MATTER HOW TALL YOU ARE. WE LOVE YOU BECAUSE OF WHO YOU ARE...
...AND WE DON'T WANT YOU TO MAKE ANY CHOICE THAT COULD CHANGE WHO THAT IS.
THMP THMP THMP
SO PLEASE PROMISE US, SON, THAT YOU'LL THINK LONG AND HARD ABOUT THIS DECISION.

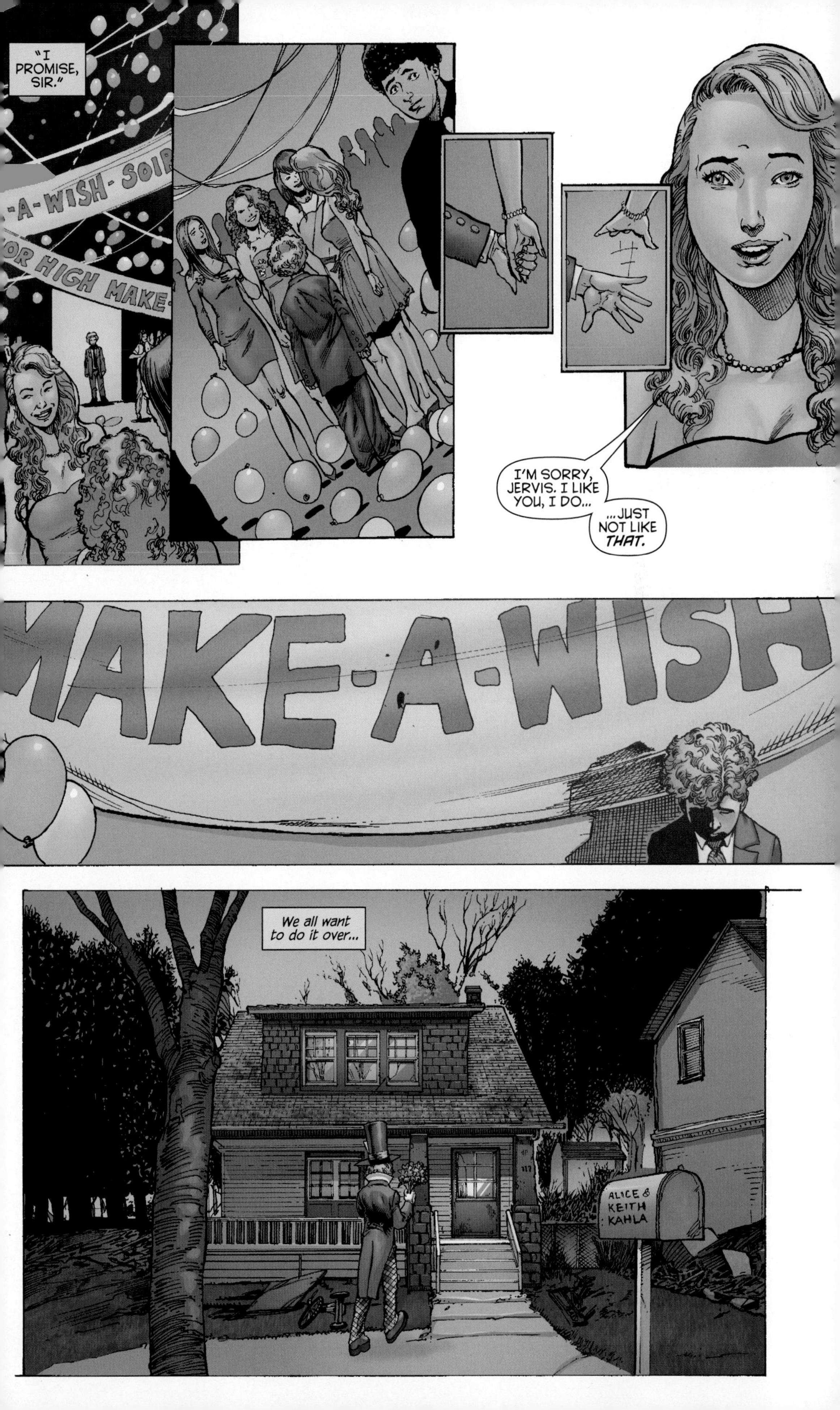
"I PROMISE, SIR."
-A-WISH-SOIR
OR HIGH MAKE-
I'M SORRY, JERVIS. I LIKE YOU, I DO...
...JUST NOT LIKE *THAT.*
MAKE-A-WISH
We all want to do it over...
ALICE & KEITH KAHLA

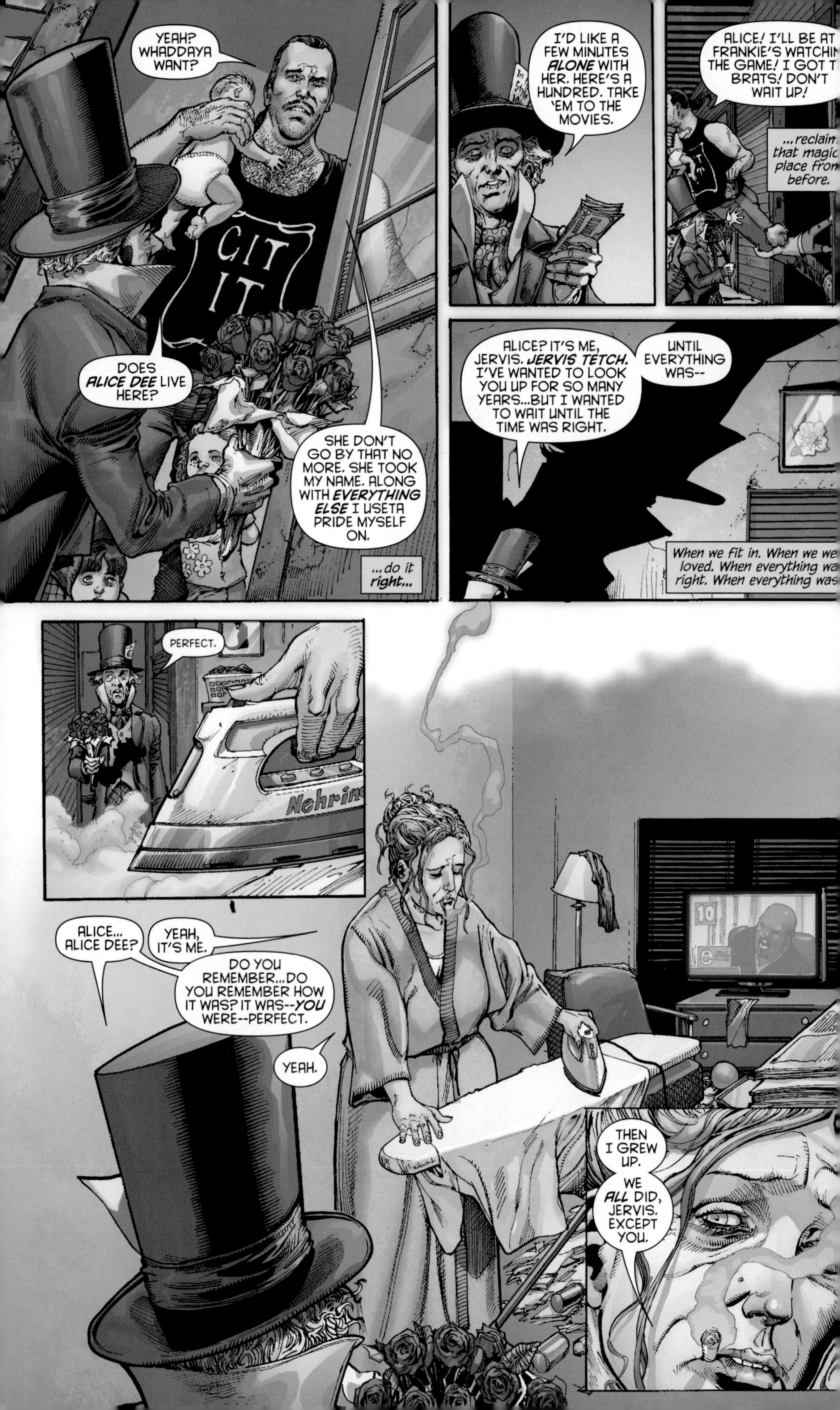
YEAH? WHADDAYA WANT?
DOES ALICE DEE LIVE HERE?
SHE DON'T GO BY THAT NO MORE. SHE TOOK MY NAME. ALONG WITH EVERYTHING ELSE I USETA PRIDE MYSELF ON.
...do it right...
I'D LIKE A FEW MINUTES ALONE WITH HER. HERE'S A HUNDRED. TAKE 'EM TO THE MOVIES.
ALICE! I'LL BE AT FRANKIE'S WATCHIN THE GAME! I GOT T BRATS! DON'T WAIT UP!
...reclaim that magic place from before.
ALICE? IT'S ME, JERVIS. JERVIS TETCH. I'VE WANTED TO LOOK YOU UP FOR SO MANY YEARS...BUT I WANTED TO WAIT UNTIL THE TIME WAS RIGHT.
UNTIL EVERYTHING WAS--
When we fit in. When we we loved. When everything wa right. When everything was
PERFECT.
Nehrin
ALICE... ALICE DEE?
YEAH, IT'S ME.
DO YOU REMEMBER...DO YOU REMEMBER HOW IT WAS? IT WAS--YOU WERE--PERFECT.
YEAH.
THEN I GREW UP.
WE ALL DID, JERVIS. EXCEPT YOU.

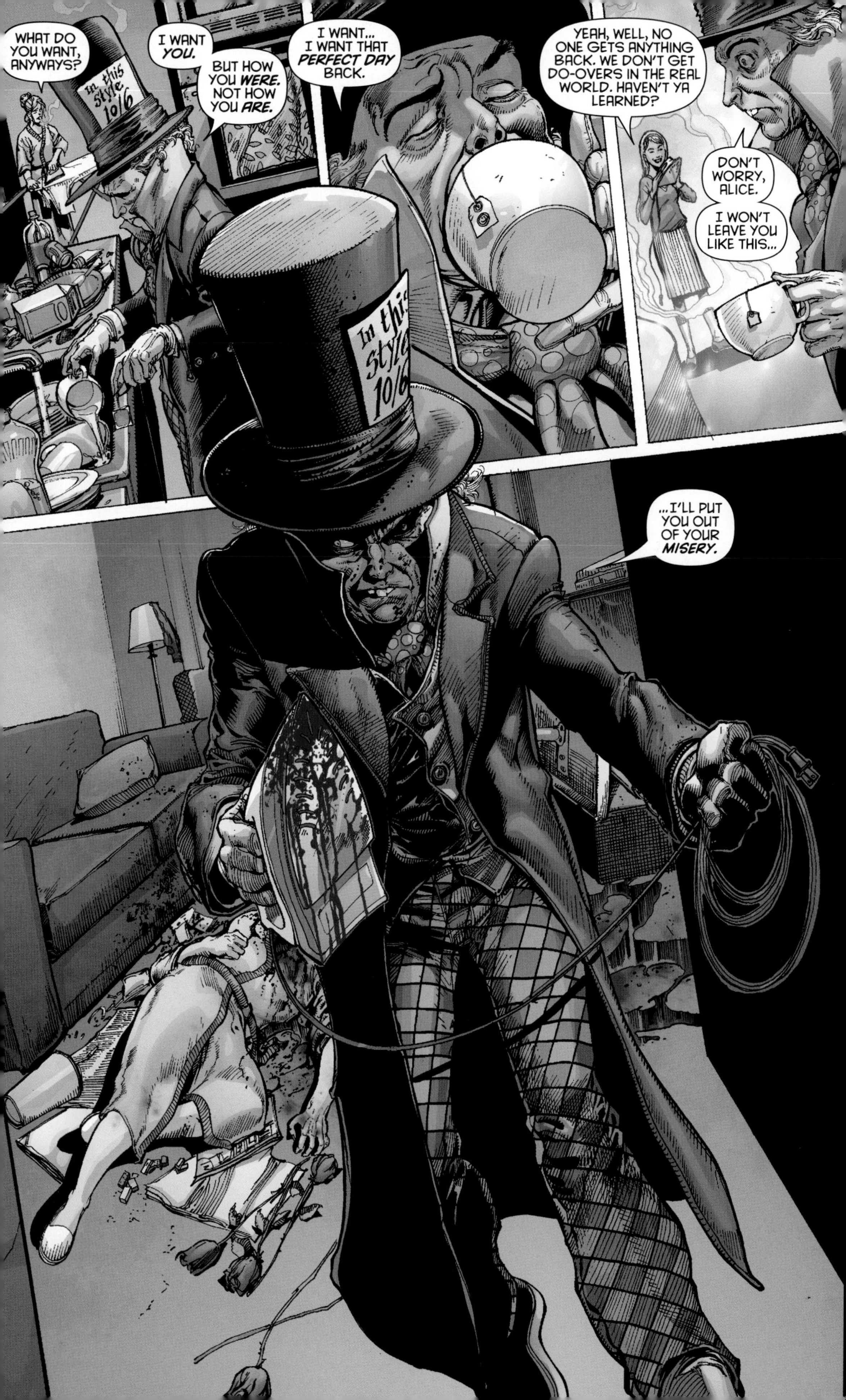
WHAT DO YOU WANT, ANYWAYS?
I WANT *YOU.*
BUT HOW YOU *WERE.* NOT HOW YOU *ARE.*
I WANT... I WANT THAT *PERFECT DAY* BACK.
YEAH, WELL, NO ONE GETS ANYTHING BACK. WE DON'T GET DO-OVERS IN THE REAL WORLD. HAVEN'T YA LEARNED?
DON'T WORRY, ALICE.
I WON'T LEAVE YOU LIKE THIS...
...I'LL PUT YOU OUT OF YOUR *MISERY.*
In this Style 10/6

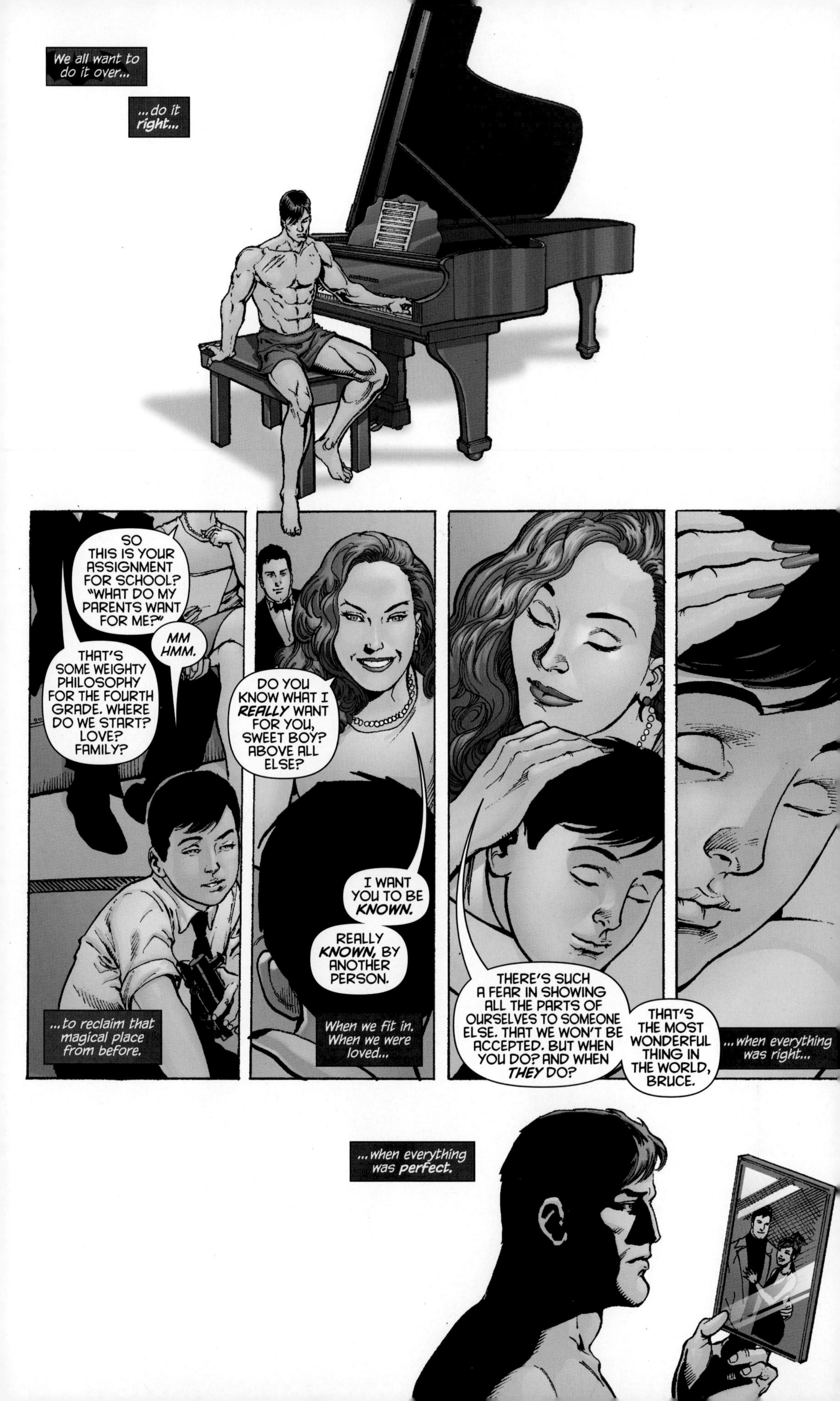
We all want to do it over...
...do it right...
SO THIS IS YOUR ASSIGNMENT FOR SCHOOL? "WHAT DO MY PARENTS WANT FOR ME?"
MM HMM.
THAT'S SOME WEIGHTY PHILOSOPHY FOR THE FOURTH GRADE. WHERE DO WE START? LOVE? FAMILY?
...to reclaim that magical place from before.
DO YOU KNOW WHAT I REALLY WANT FOR YOU, SWEET BOY? ABOVE ALL ELSE?
I WANT YOU TO BE KNOWN.
REALLY KNOWN, BY ANOTHER PERSON.
When we fit in. When we were loved...
THERE'S SUCH A FEAR IN SHOWING ALL THE PARTS OF OURSELVES TO SOMEONE ELSE. THAT WE WON'T BE ACCEPTED. BUT WHEN YOU DO? AND WHEN THEY DO?
THAT'S THE MOST WONDERFUL THING IN THE WORLD, BRUCE.
...when everything was right...
...when everything was perfect.

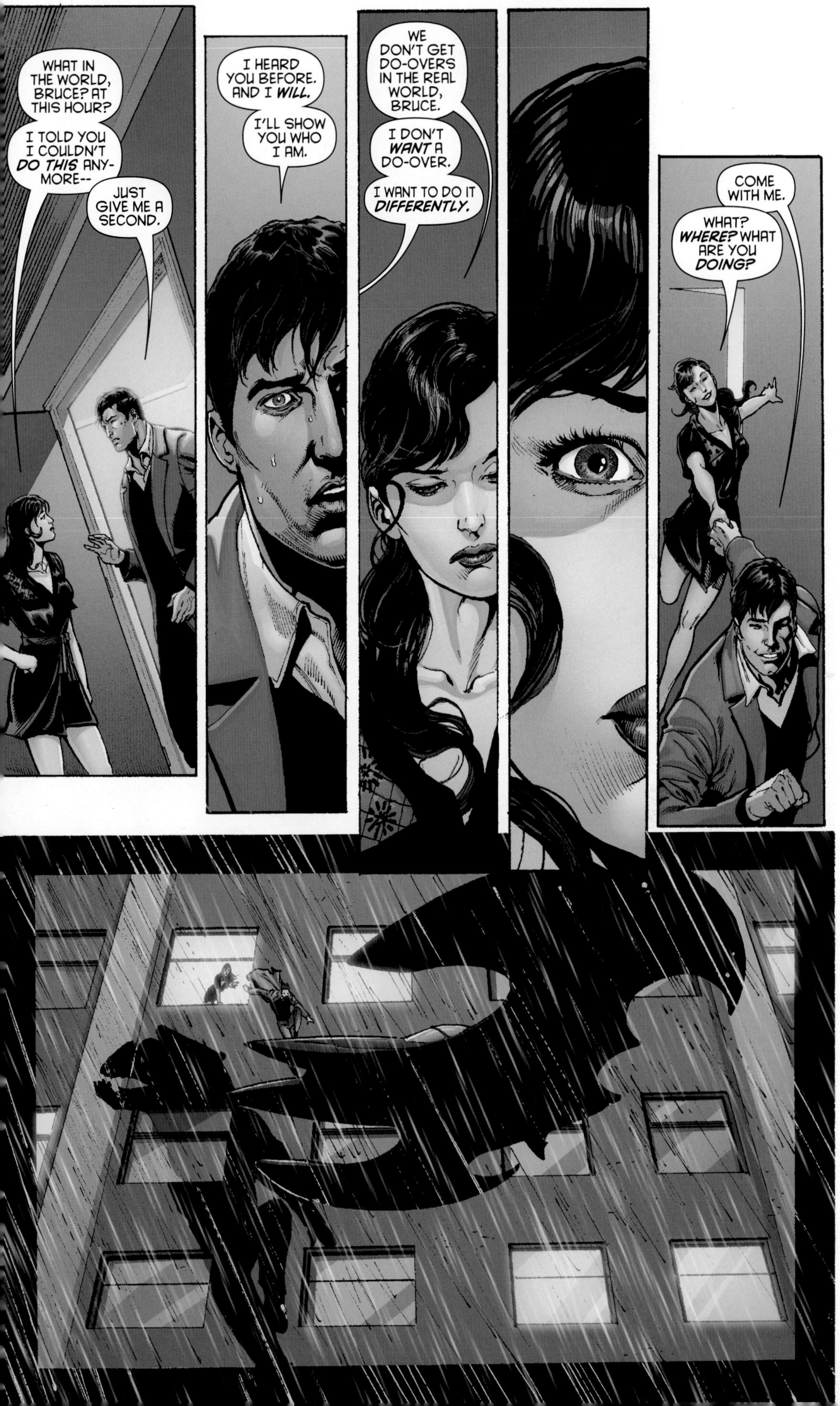
WHAT IN THE WORLD, BRUCE? AT THIS HOUR?
I TOLD YOU I COULDN'T DO THIS ANY-MORE--
JUST GIVE ME A SECOND.
I HEARD YOU BEFORE. AND I WILL.
I'LL SHOW YOU WHO I AM.
WE DON'T GET DO-OVERS IN THE REAL WORLD, BRUCE.
I DON'T WANT A DO-OVER.
I WANT TO DO IT DIFFERENTLY.
COME WITH ME.
WHAT? WHERE? WHAT ARE YOU DOING?

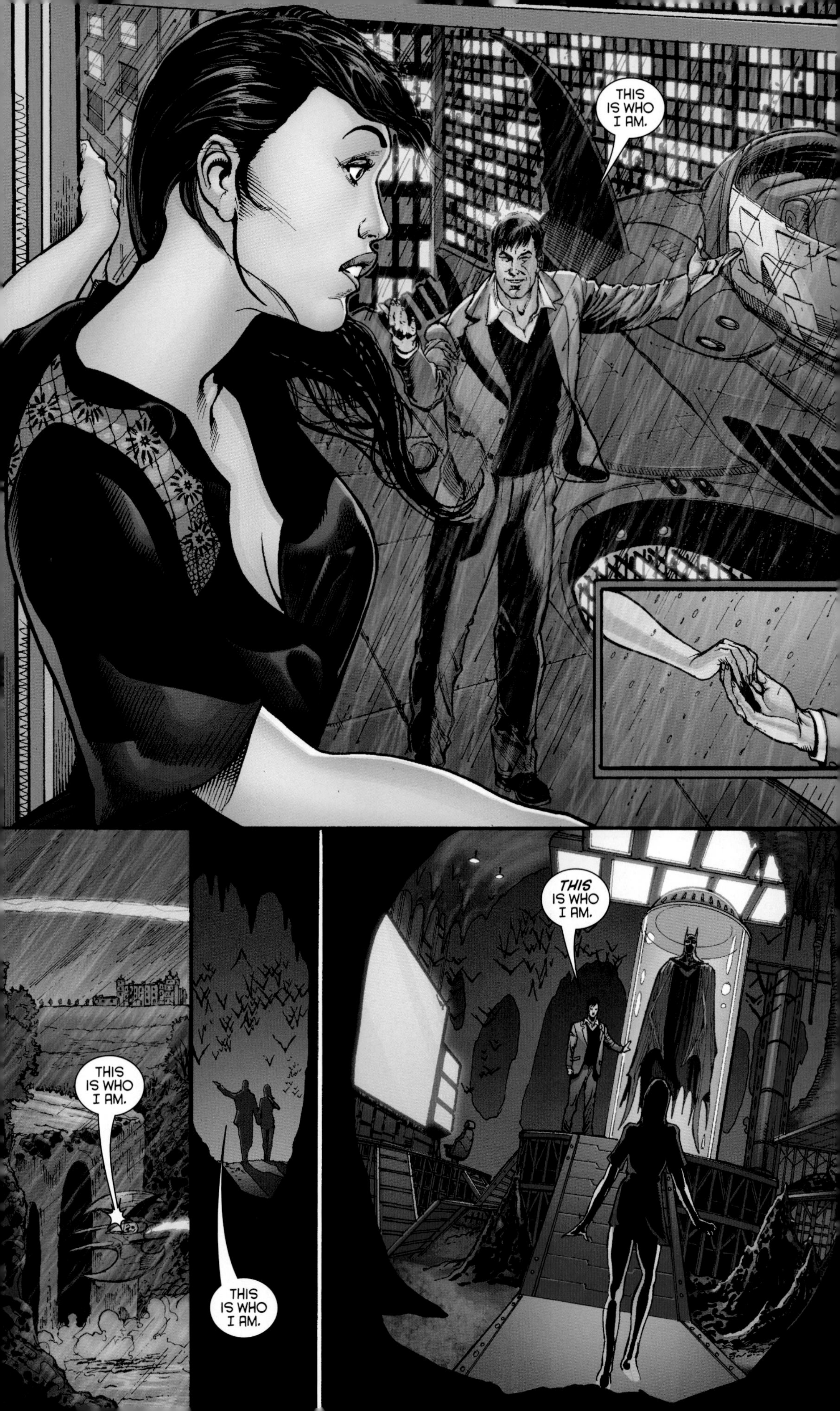
THIS IS WHO I AM.
THIS IS WHO I AM.
THIS IS WHO I AM.
*THIS* IS WHO I AM.

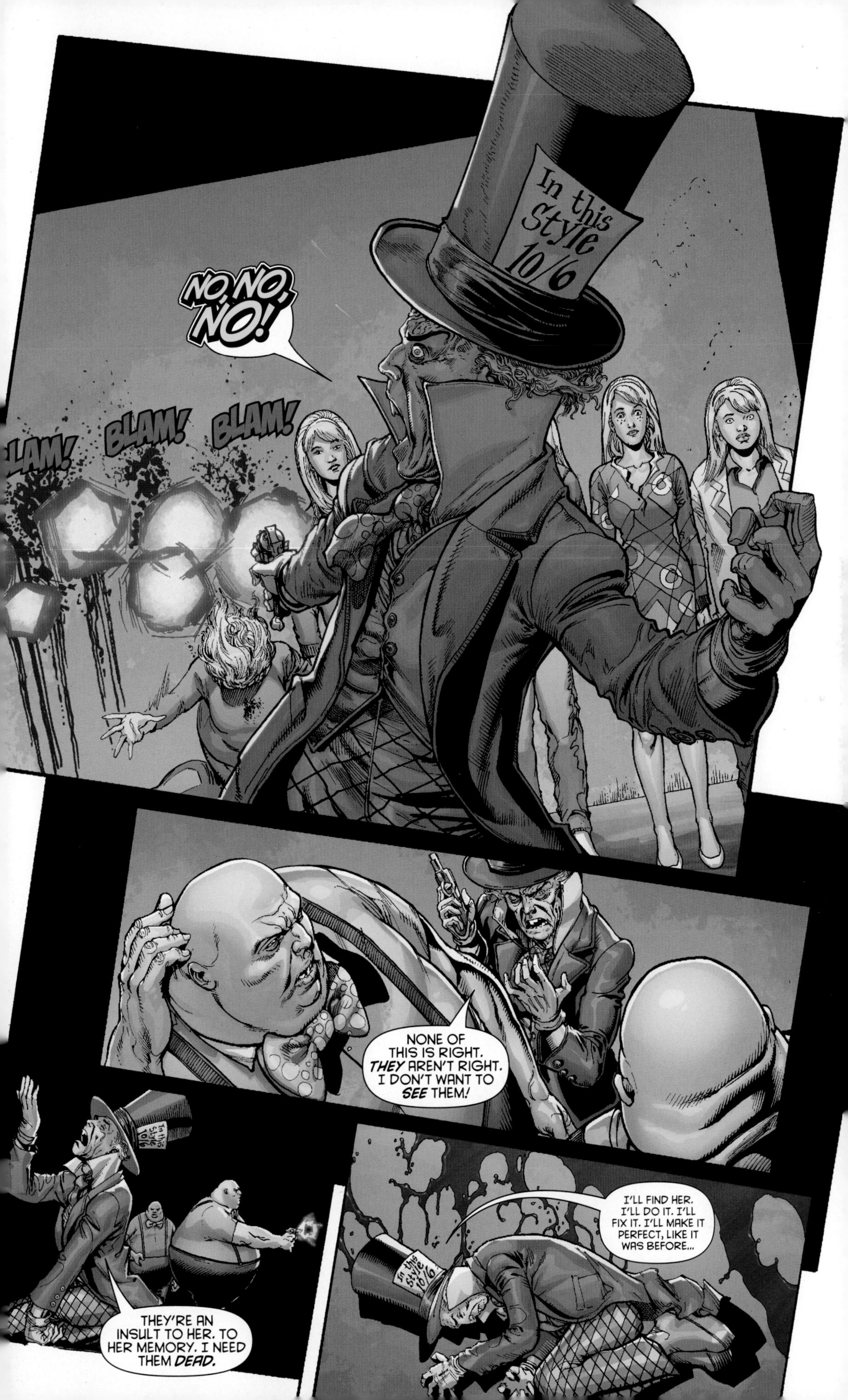
NO, NO, NO!
BLAM! BLAM! BLAM!
In this Style 10/6
NONE OF THIS IS RIGHT. *THEY* AREN'T RIGHT. I DON'T WANT TO *SEE* THEM!
THEY'RE AN INSULT TO HER. TO HER MEMORY. I NEED THEM *DEAD.*
I'LL FIND HER. I'LL DO IT. I'LL FIX IT. I'LL MAKE IT PERFECT, LIKE IT WAS BEFORE...

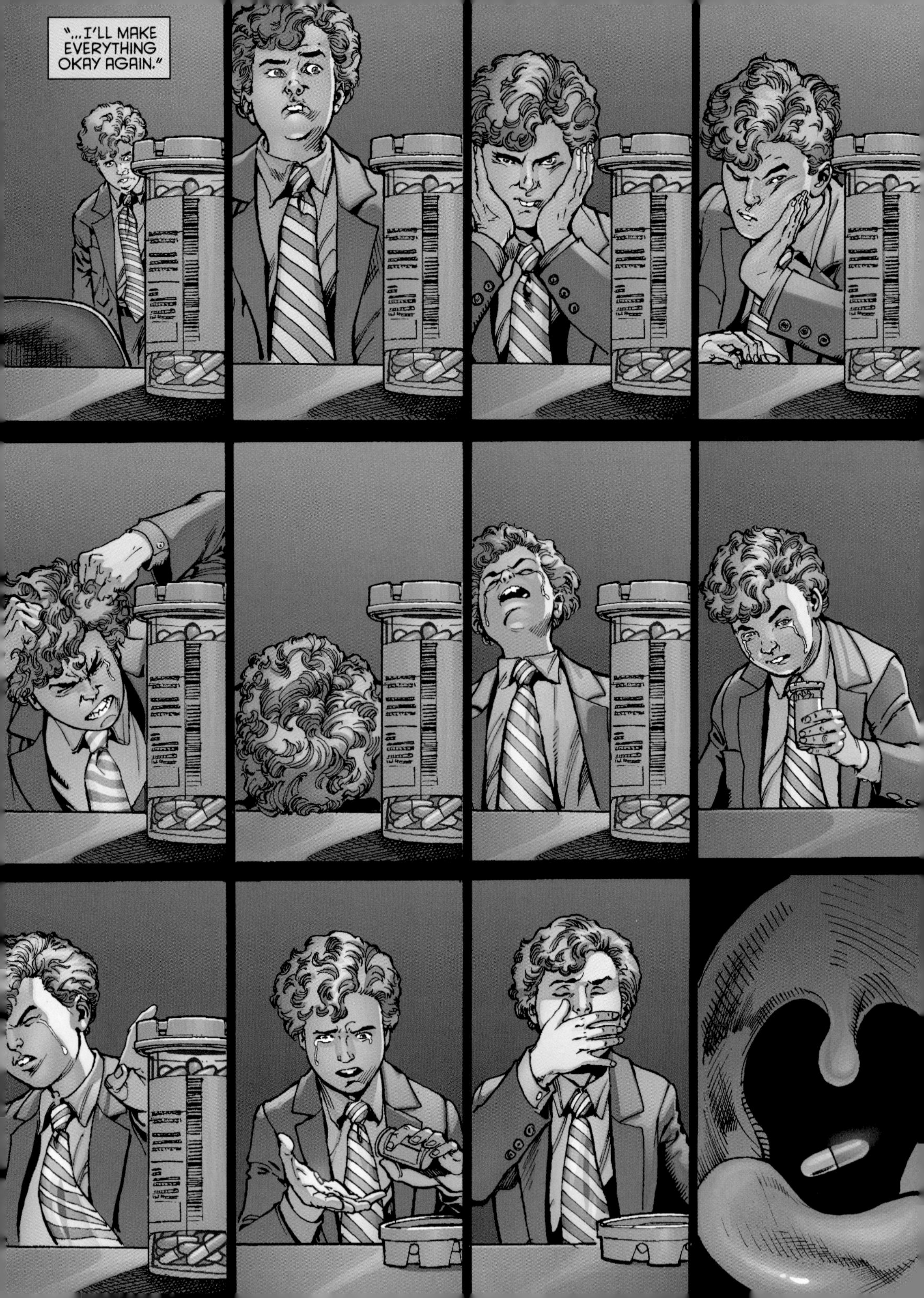
"...I'LL MAKE EVERYTHING OKAY AGAIN."

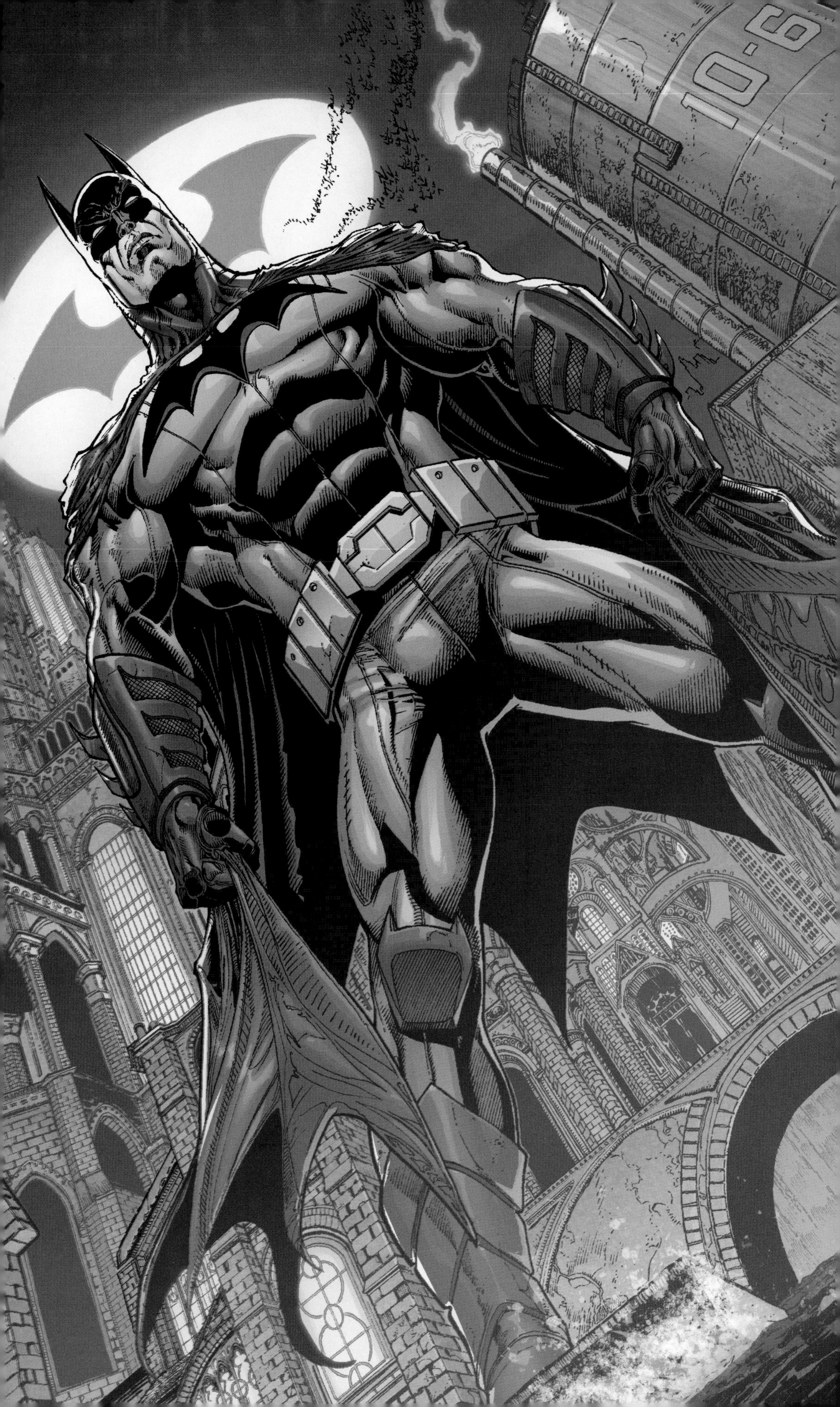

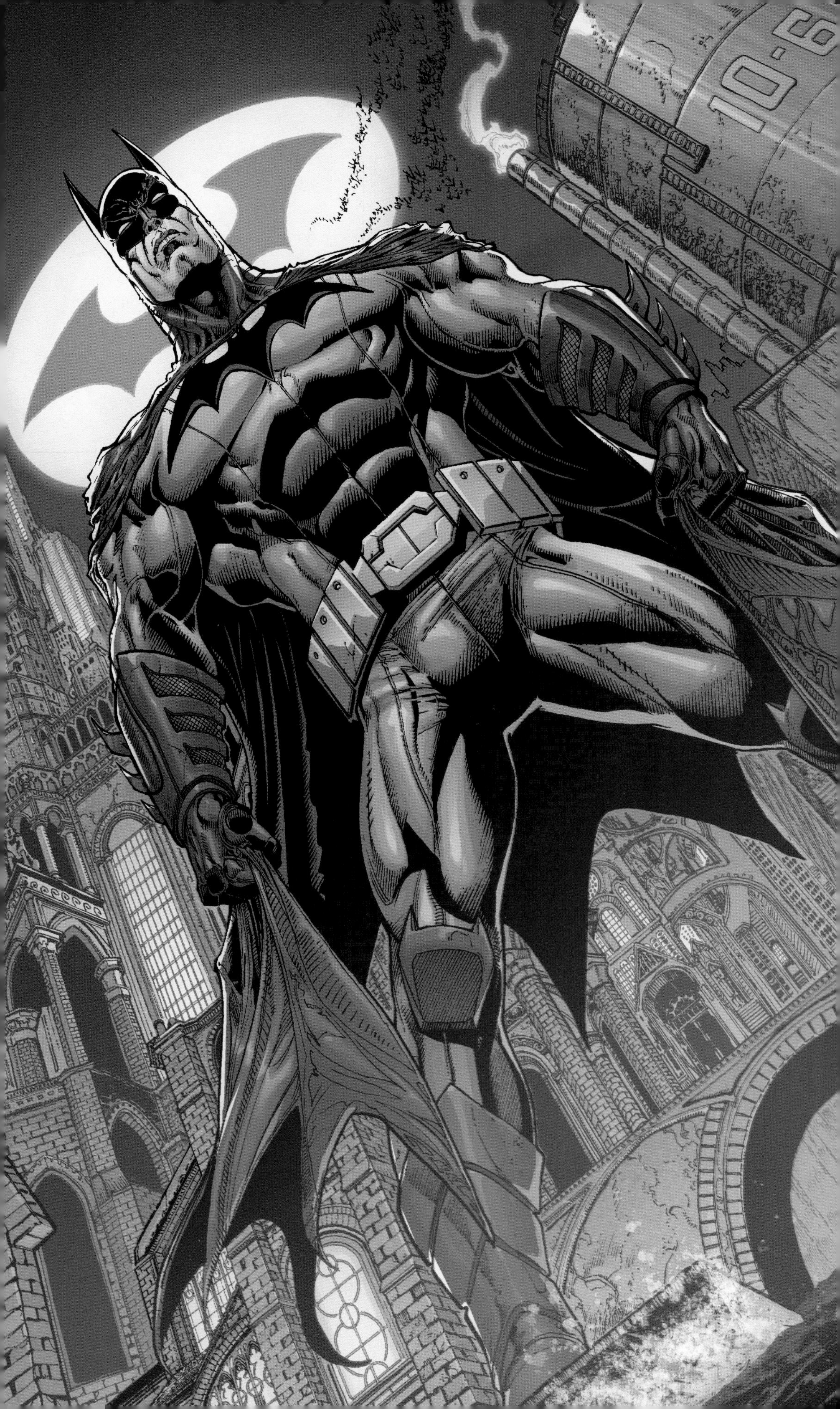

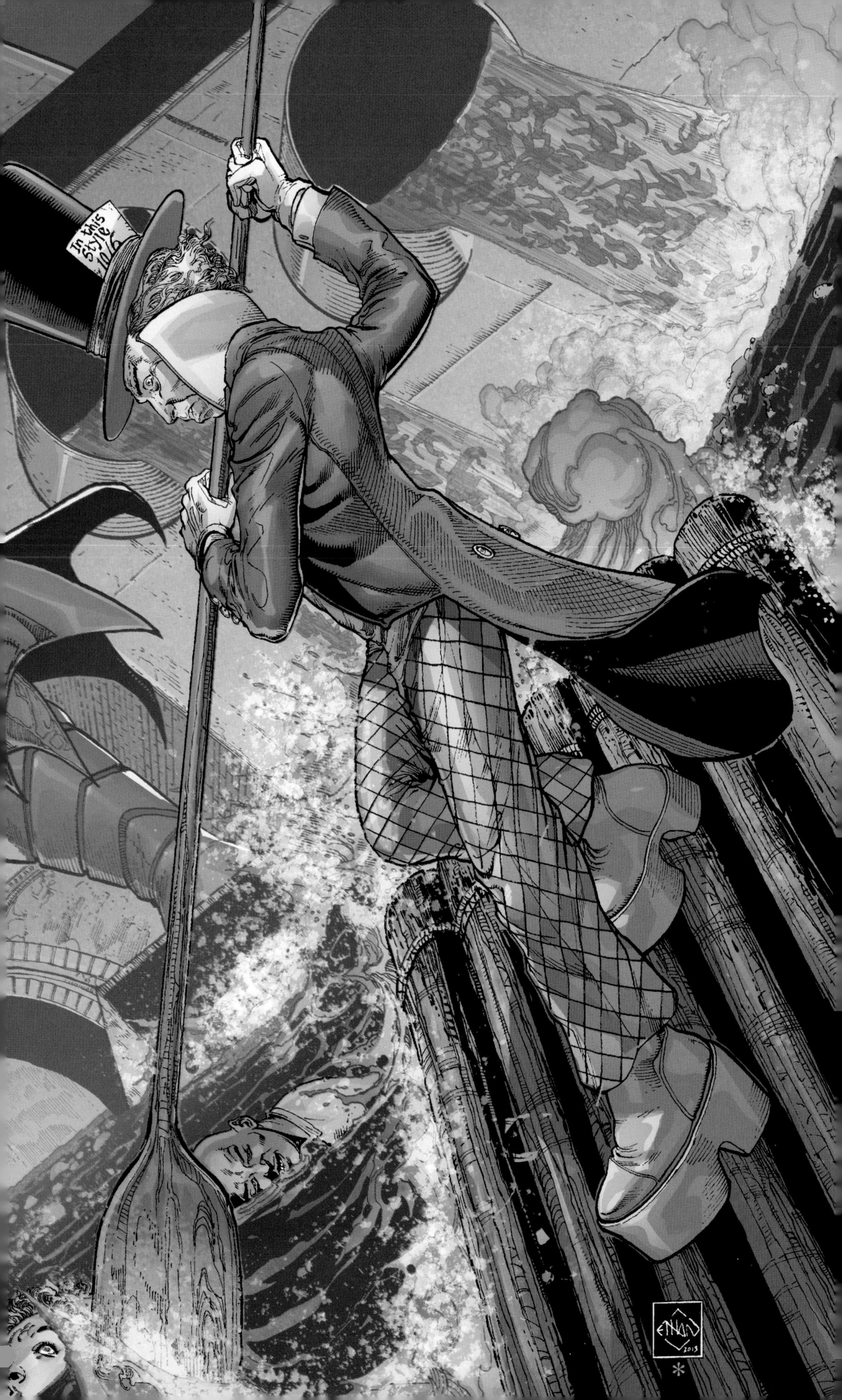
In this Style 10/6

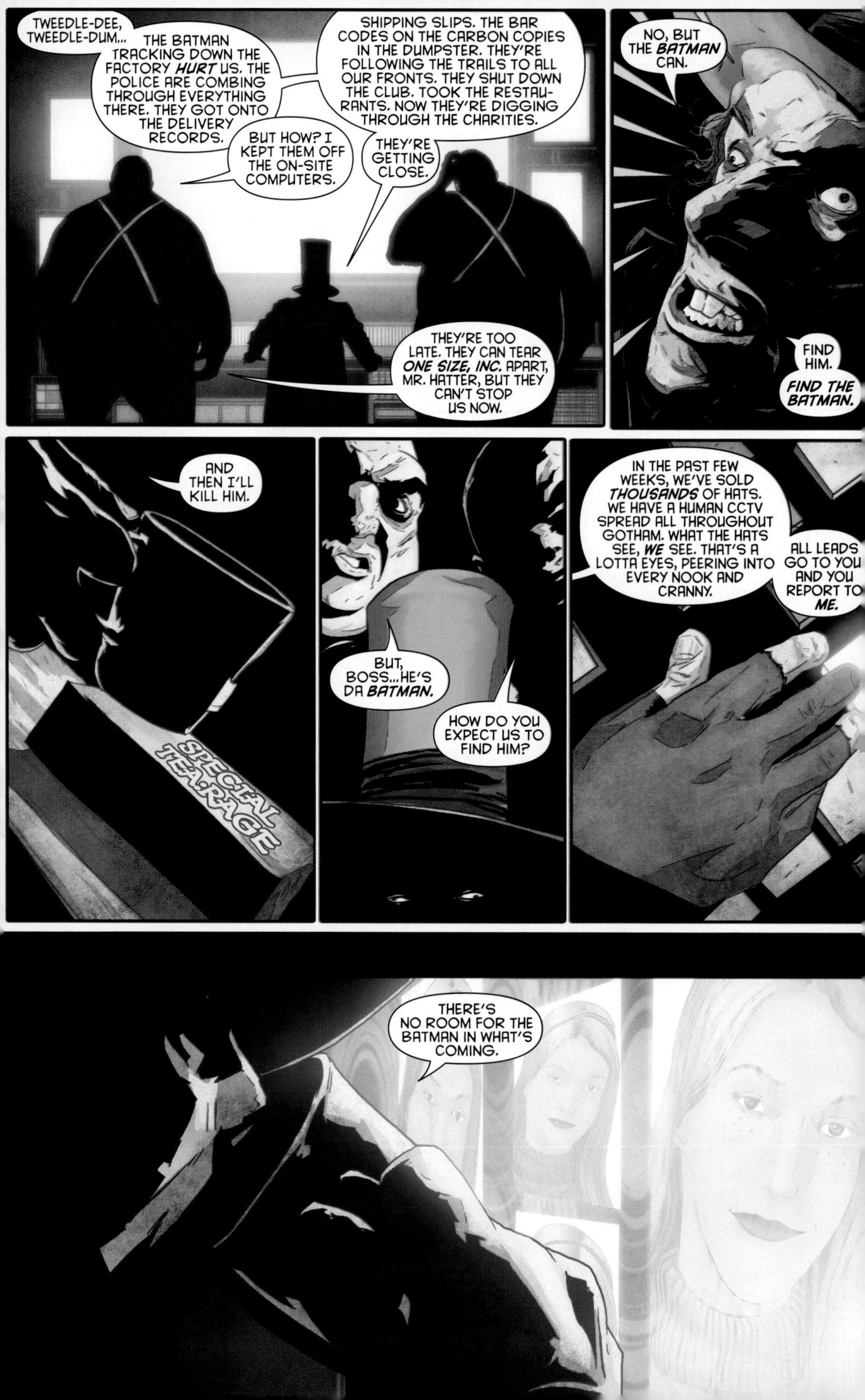
TWEEDLE-DEE, TWEEDLE-DUM...
THE BATMAN TRACKING DOWN THE FACTORY HURT US. THE POLICE ARE COMBING THROUGH EVERYTHING THERE. THEY GOT ONTO THE DELIVERY RECORDS.
BUT HOW? I KEPT THEM OFF THE ON-SITE COMPUTERS.
SHIPPING SLIPS. THE BAR CODES ON THE CARBON COPIES IN THE DUMPSTER. THEY'RE FOLLOWING THE TRAILS TO ALL OUR FRONTS. THEY SHUT DOWN THE CLUB. TOOK THE RESTAU-RANTS. NOW THEY'RE DIGGING THROUGH THE CHARITIES.
THEY'RE GETTING CLOSE.
THEY'RE TOO LATE. THEY CAN TEAR ONE SIZE, INC. APART, MR. HATTER, BUT THEY CAN'T STOP US NOW.
NO, BUT THE BATMAN CAN.
FIND HIM.
FIND THE BATMAN.
AND THEN I'LL KILL HIM.
SPECIAL TEA-RAGE
BUT, BOSS...HE'S DA BATMAN.
HOW DO YOU EXPECT US TO FIND HIM?
IN THE PAST FEW WEEKS, WE'VE SOLD THOUSANDS OF HATS. WE HAVE A HUMAN CCTV SPREAD ALL THROUGHOUT GOTHAM. WHAT THE HATS SEE, WE SEE. THAT'S A LOTTA EYES, PEERING INTO EVERY NOOK AND CRANNY.
ALL LEADS GO TO YOU AND YOU REPORT TO ME.
THERE'S NO ROOM FOR THE BATMAN IN WHAT'S COMING.

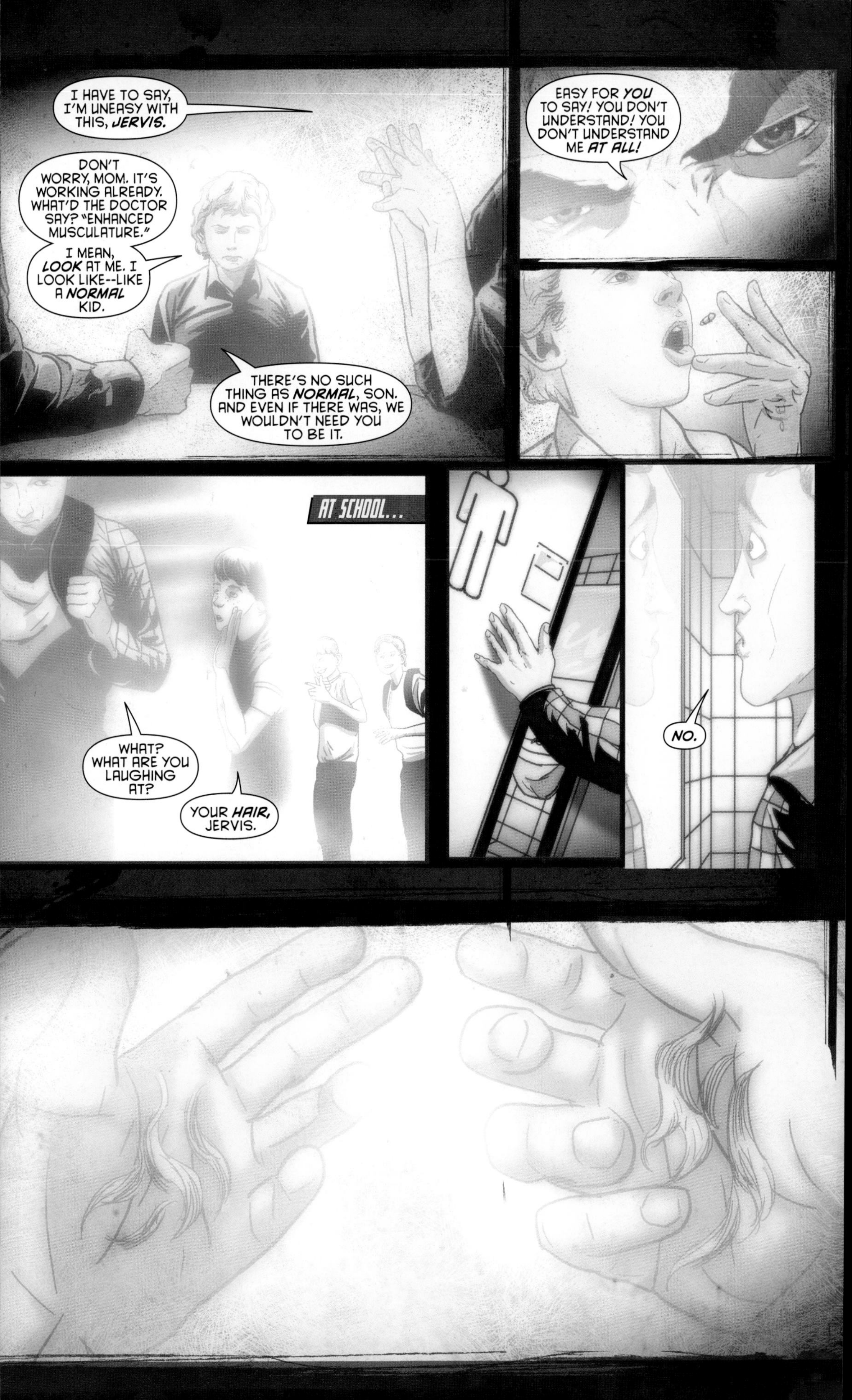
I HAVE TO SAY, I'M UNEASY WITH THIS, JERVIS.
DON'T WORRY, MOM. IT'S WORKING ALREADY. WHAT'D THE DOCTOR SAY? "ENHANCED MUSCULATURE."
I MEAN, LOOK AT ME. I LOOK LIKE--LIKE A NORMAL KID.
THERE'S NO SUCH THING AS NORMAL, SON. AND EVEN IF THERE WAS, WE WOULDN'T NEED YOU TO BE IT.
EASY FOR YOU TO SAY! YOU DON'T UNDERSTAND! YOU DON'T UNDERSTAND ME AT ALL!
AT SCHOOL...
WHAT? WHAT ARE YOU LAUGHING AT?
YOUR HAIR, JERVIS.
NO.

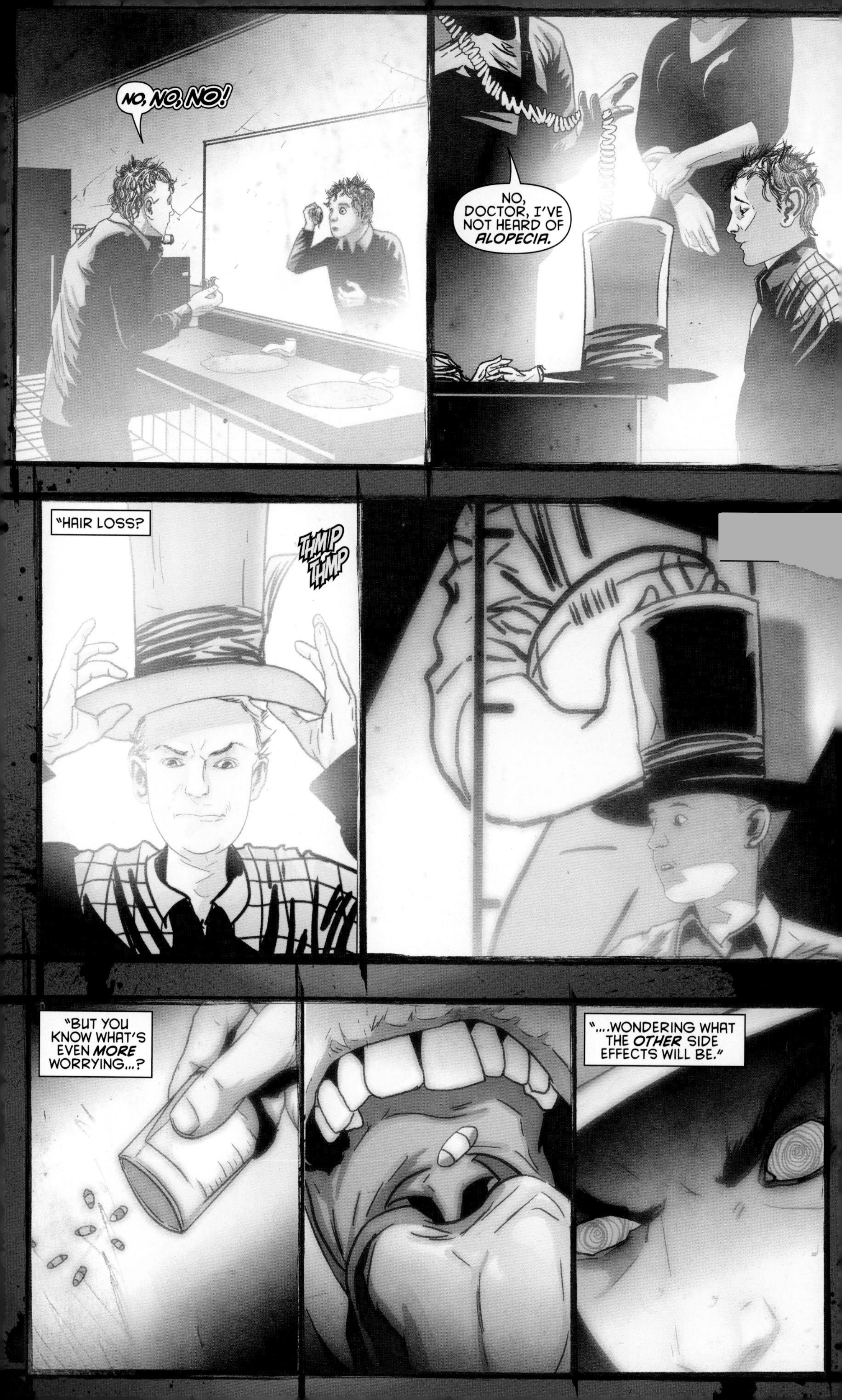
NO, NO, NO!
NO, DOCTOR, I'VE NOT HEARD OF *ALOPECIA.*
"HAIR LOSS?
THMP THMP
"BUT YOU KNOW WHAT'S EVEN *MORE* WORRYING...?
"....WONDERING WHAT THE *OTHER* SIDE EFFECTS WILL BE."

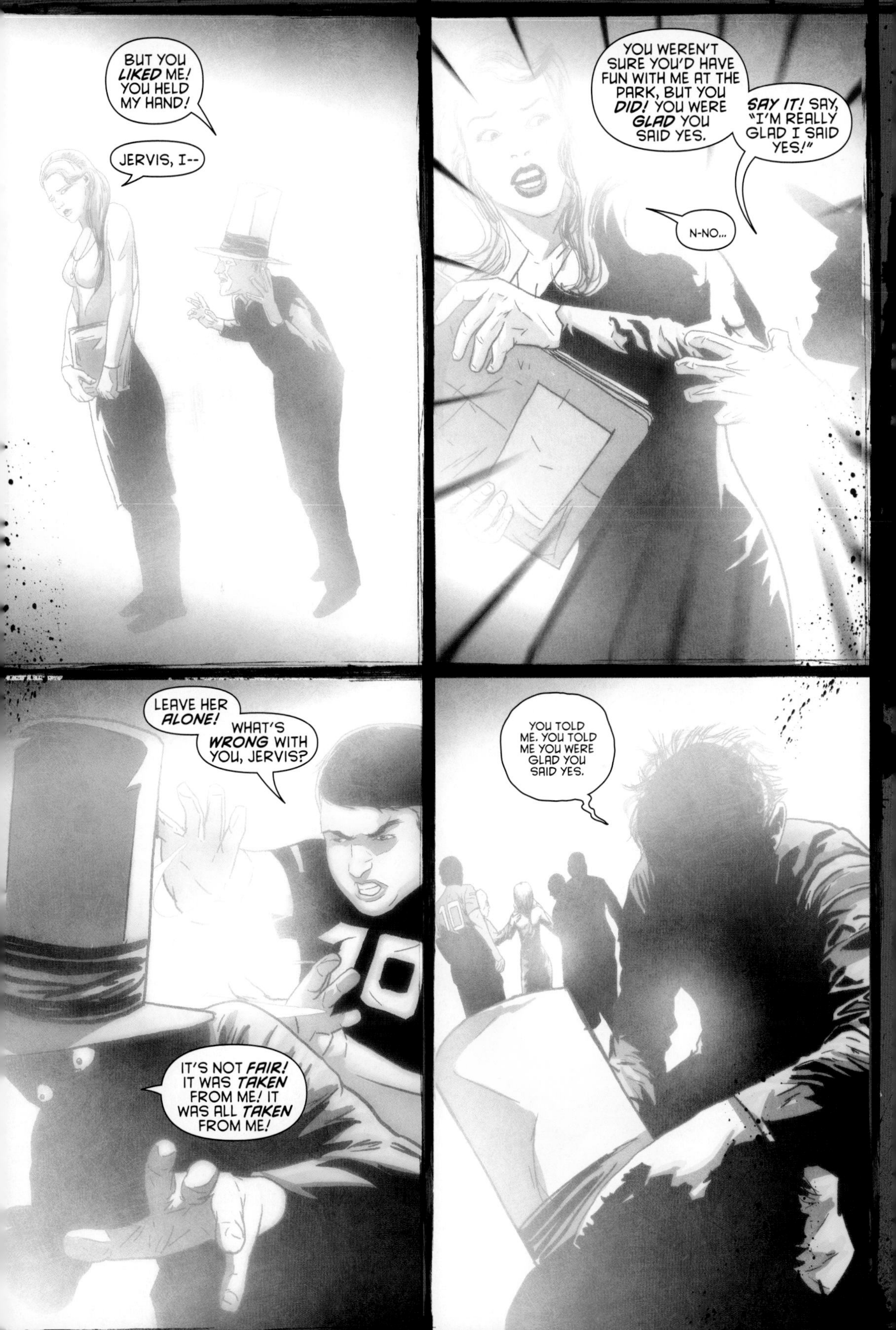
BUT YOU LIKED ME! YOU HELD MY HAND!
JERVIS, I--
YOU WEREN'T SURE YOU'D HAVE FUN WITH ME AT THE PARK, BUT YOU DID! YOU WERE GLAD YOU SAID YES.
SAY IT! SAY, "I'M REALLY GLAD I SAID YES!"
N-NO...
LEAVE HER ALONE!
WHAT'S WRONG WITH YOU, JERVIS?
IT'S NOT FAIR! IT WAS TAKEN FROM ME! IT WAS ALL TAKEN FROM ME!
YOU TOLD ME. YOU TOLD ME YOU WERE GLAD YOU SAID YES.

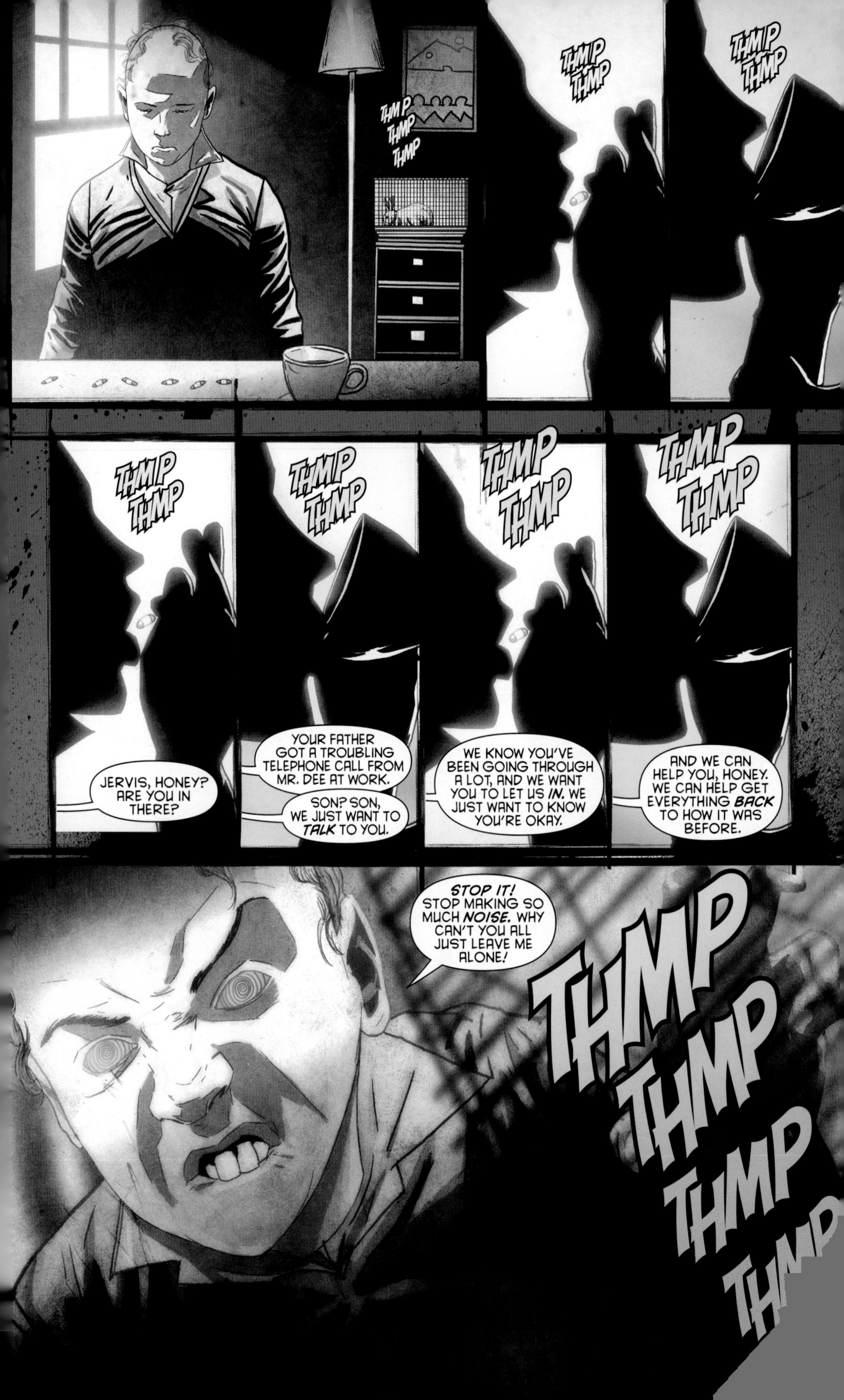
THMP THMP THMP
THMP THMP
THMP THMP
THMP THMP
JERVIS, HONEY? ARE YOU IN THERE?
THMP THMP
YOUR FATHER GOT A TROUBLING TELEPHONE CALL FROM MR. DEE AT WORK.
SON? SON, WE JUST WANT TO TALK TO YOU.
THMP THMP
WE KNOW YOU'VE BEEN GOING THROUGH A LOT, AND WE WANT YOU TO LET US IN. WE JUST WANT TO KNOW YOU'RE OKAY.
THMP THMP
AND WE CAN HELP YOU, HONEY. WE CAN HELP GET EVERYTHING BACK TO HOW IT WAS BEFORE.
STOP IT! STOP MAKING SO MUCH NOISE. WHY CAN'T YOU ALL JUST LEAVE ME ALONE!
THMP THMP THMP

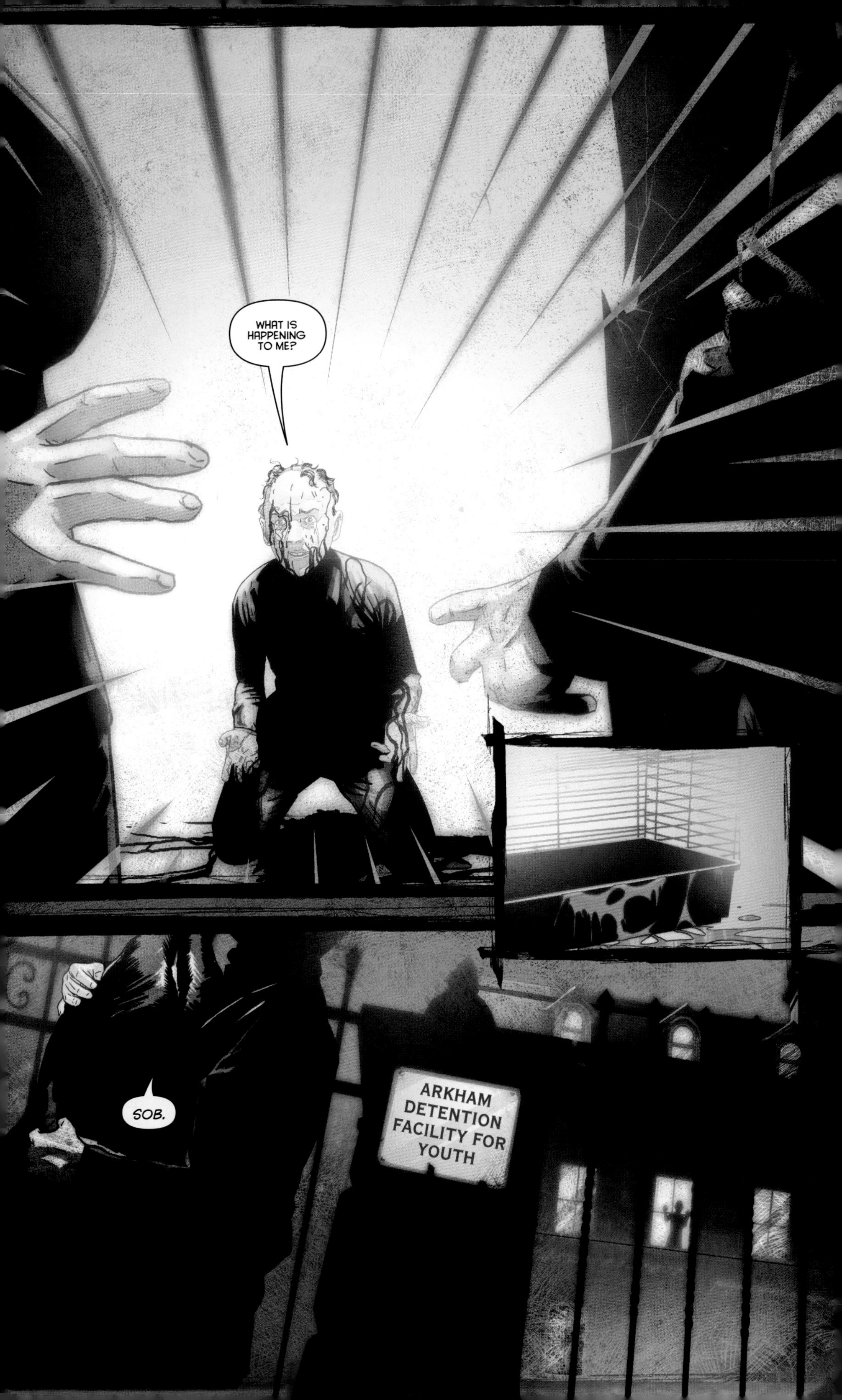
WHAT IS HAPPENING TO ME?
SOB.
ARKHAM DETENTION FACILITY FOR YOUTH

Commissioner Gordon has half the force running down leads from the factory.

It's heavy slogging, a lot of desk work, but he has the manpower.

Gordon thinks he's getting close.

In the meantime, there's not much to do but wait for that light to call me to action.

BRUCE?

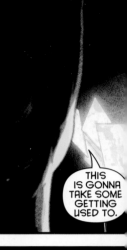

THIS IS GONNA TAKE SOME GETTING USED TO.

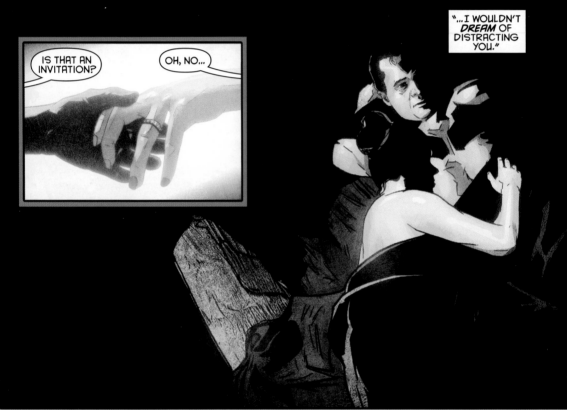

IS THAT AN INVITATION?

OH, NO...

"...I WOULDN'T *DREAM* OF DISTRACTING YOU."

"...IT'S ONE OF THE *PERKS* OF THE JOB."

WATCH YOUR STEP.

CAN NEVER BE TOO CAREFUL.

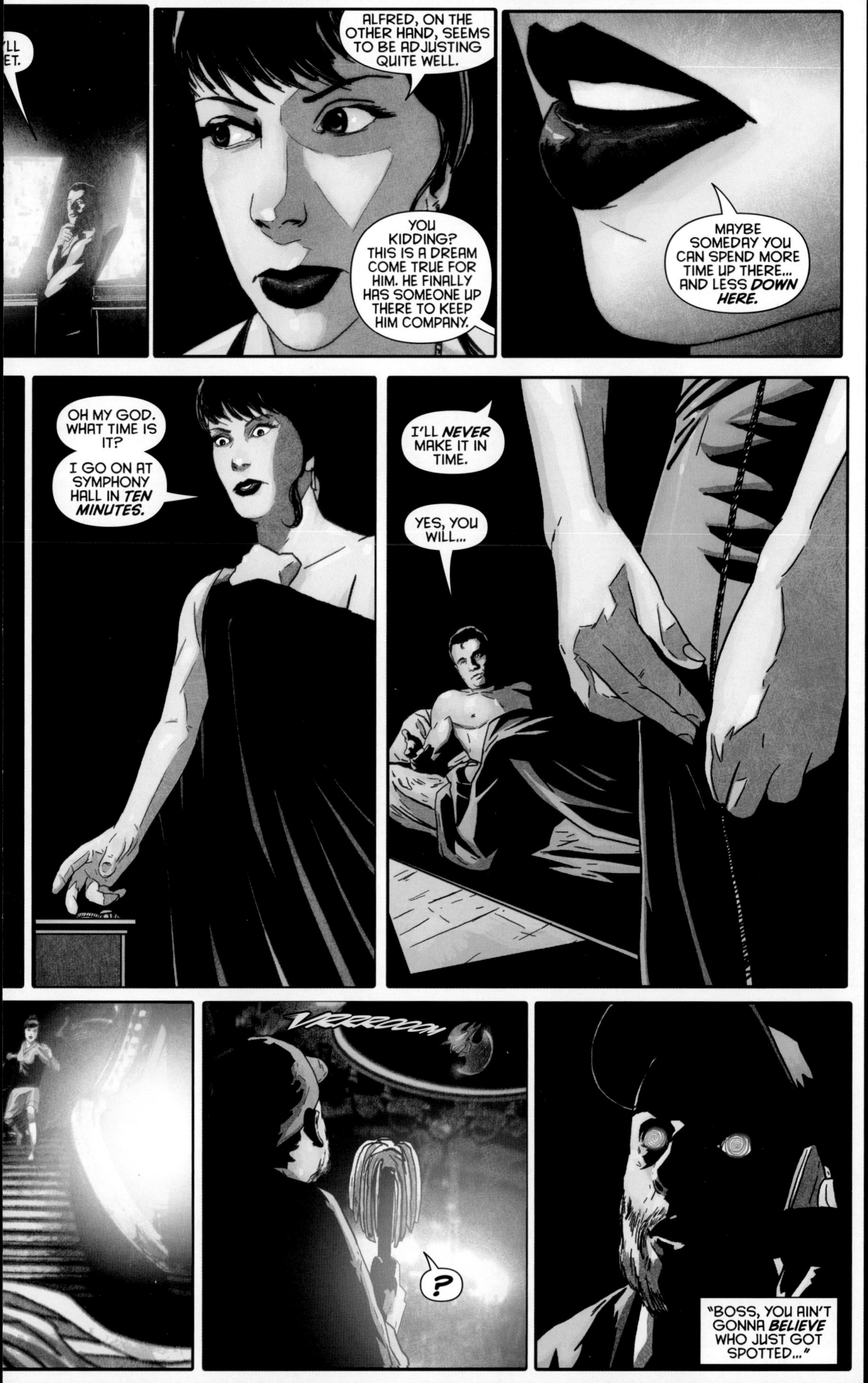
...'LL
...ET.
ALFRED, ON THE OTHER HAND, SEEMS TO BE ADJUSTING QUITE WELL.
YOU KIDDING? THIS IS A DREAM COME TRUE FOR HIM. HE FINALLY HAS SOMEONE UP THERE TO KEEP HIM COMPANY.
MAYBE SOMEDAY YOU CAN SPEND MORE TIME UP THERE... AND LESS DOWN HERE.
OH MY GOD. WHAT TIME IS IT?
I GO ON AT SYMPHONY HALL IN TEN MINUTES.
I'LL NEVER MAKE IT IN TIME.
YES, YOU WILL...
VRRROOOM
?
"BOSS, YOU AIN'T GONNA BELIEVE WHO JUST GOT SPOTTED..."

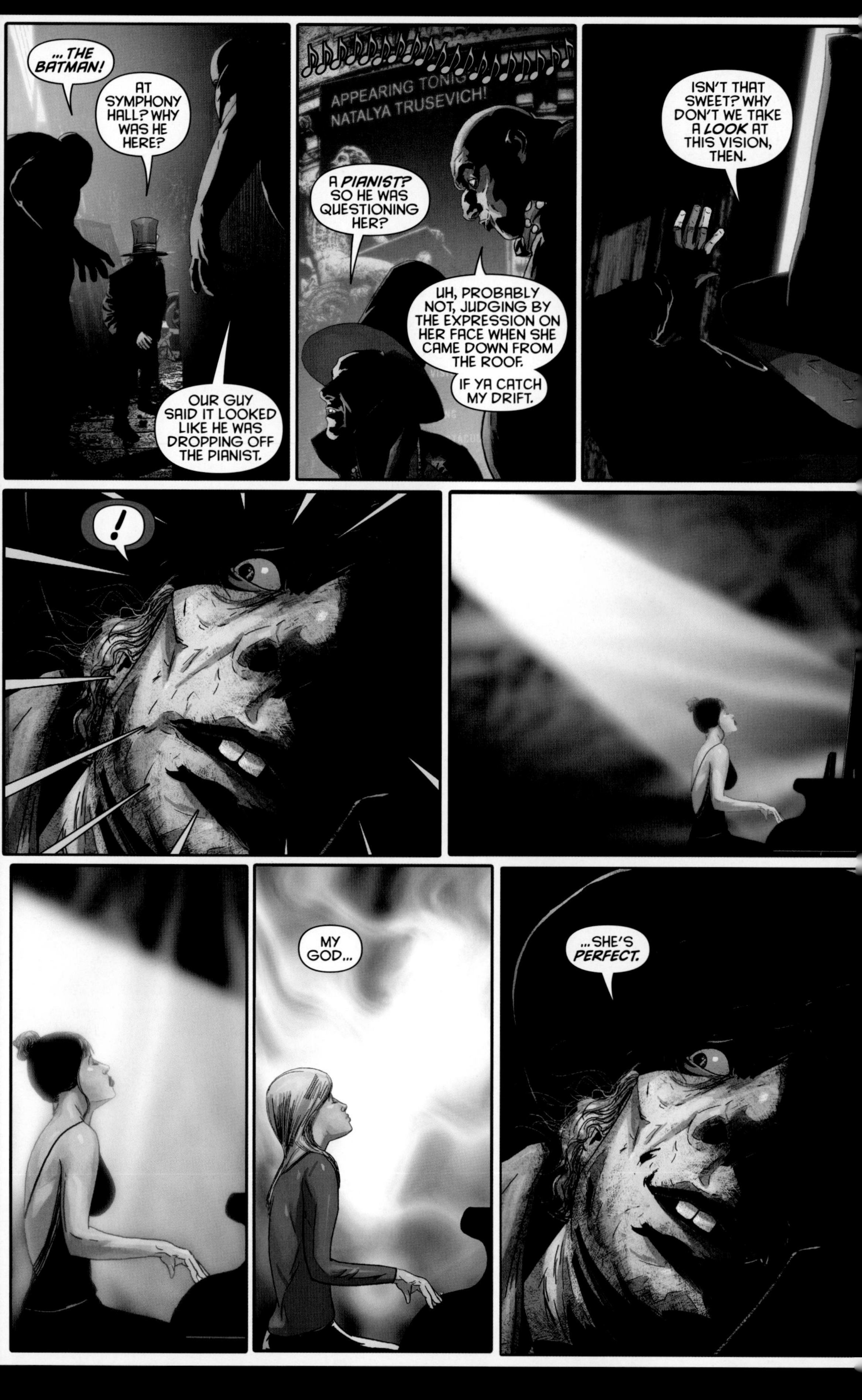
...THE BATMAN!
AT SYMPHONY HALL? WHY WAS HE HERE?
OUR GUY SAID IT LOOKED LIKE HE WAS DROPPING OFF THE PIANIST.
APPEARING TONIG
NATALYA TRUSEVICH!
A PIANIST? SO HE WAS QUESTIONING HER?
UH, PROBABLY NOT, JUDGING BY THE EXPRESSION ON HER FACE WHEN SHE CAME DOWN FROM THE ROOF.
IF YA CATCH MY DRIFT.
ISN'T THAT SWEET? WHY DON'T WE TAKE A LOOK AT THIS VISION, THEN.
!
MY GOD...
...SHE'S PERFECT.

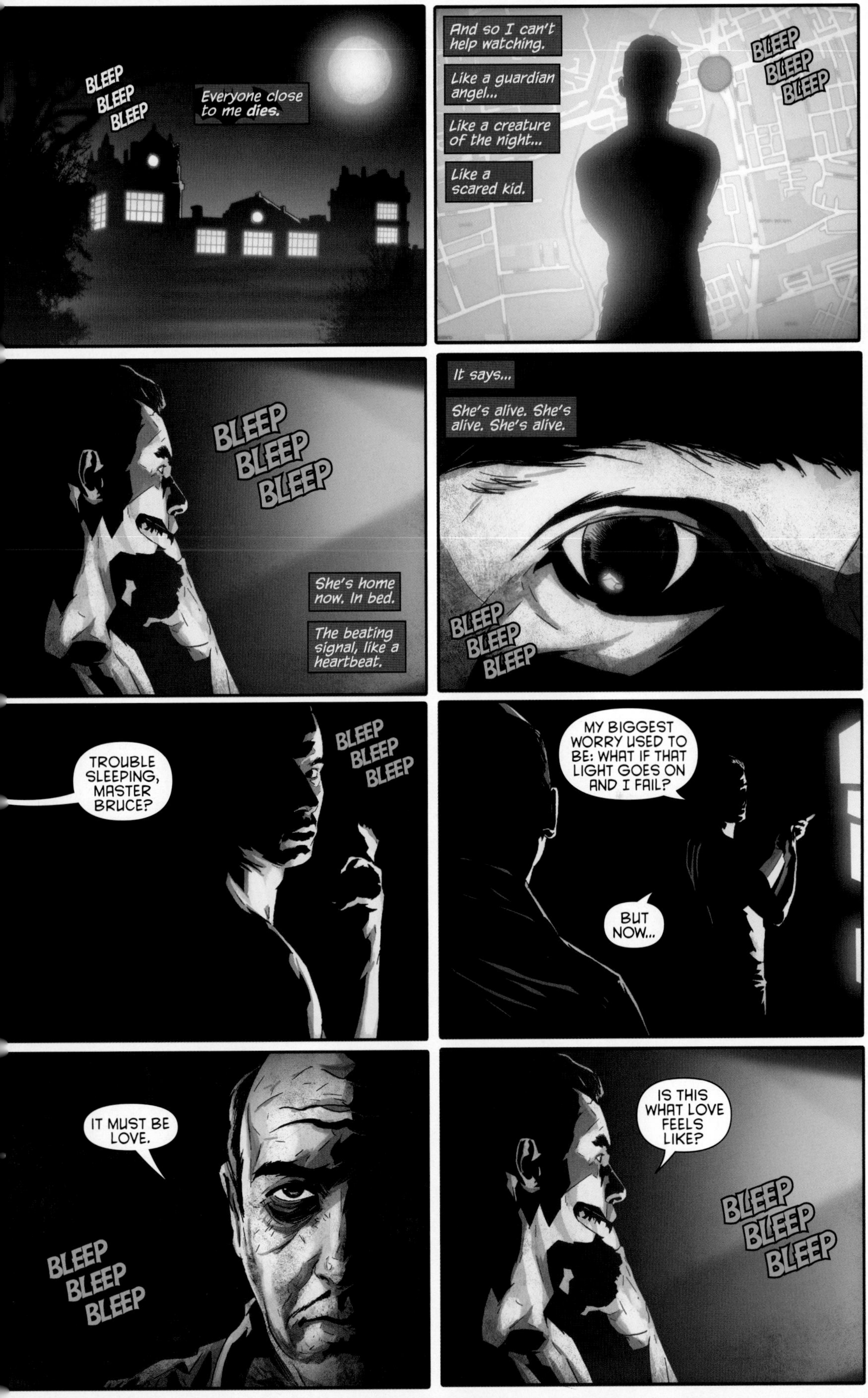
BLEEP
BLEEP
BLEEP
Everyone close to me dies.
And so I can't help watching.
Like a guardian angel...
Like a creature of the night...
Like a scared kid.
BLEEP
BLEEP
BLEEP
BLEEP
BLEEP
BLEEP
She's home now. In bed.
The beating signal, like a heartbeat.
It says...
She's alive. She's alive. She's alive.
BLEEP
BLEEP
BLEEP
TROUBLE SLEEPING, MASTER BRUCE?
BLEEP
BLEEP
BLEEP
MY BIGGEST WORRY USED TO BE: WHAT IF THAT LIGHT GOES ON AND I FAIL?
BUT NOW...
IT MUST BE LOVE.
BLEEP
BLEEP
BLEEP
IS THIS WHAT LOVE FEELS LIKE?
BLEEP
BLEEP
BLEEP

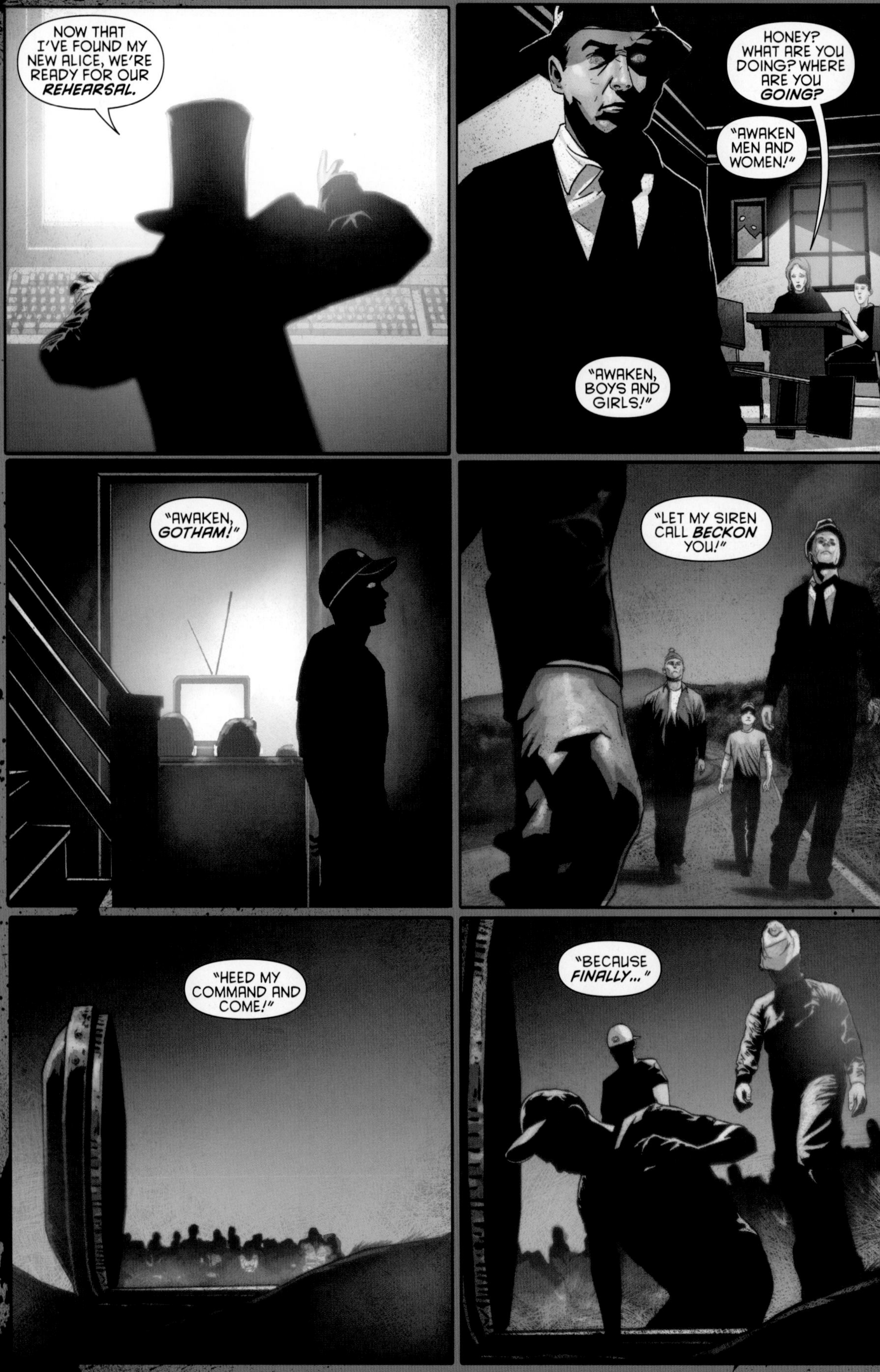
NOW THAT I'VE FOUND MY NEW ALICE, WE'RE READY FOR OUR REHEARSAL.
HONEY? WHAT ARE YOU DOING? WHERE ARE YOU GOING?
"AWAKEN MEN AND WOMEN!"
"AWAKEN, BOYS AND GIRLS!"
"AWAKEN, GOTHAM!"
"LET MY SIREN CALL BECKON YOU!"
"HEED MY COMMAND AND COME!"
"BECAUSE FINALLY..."

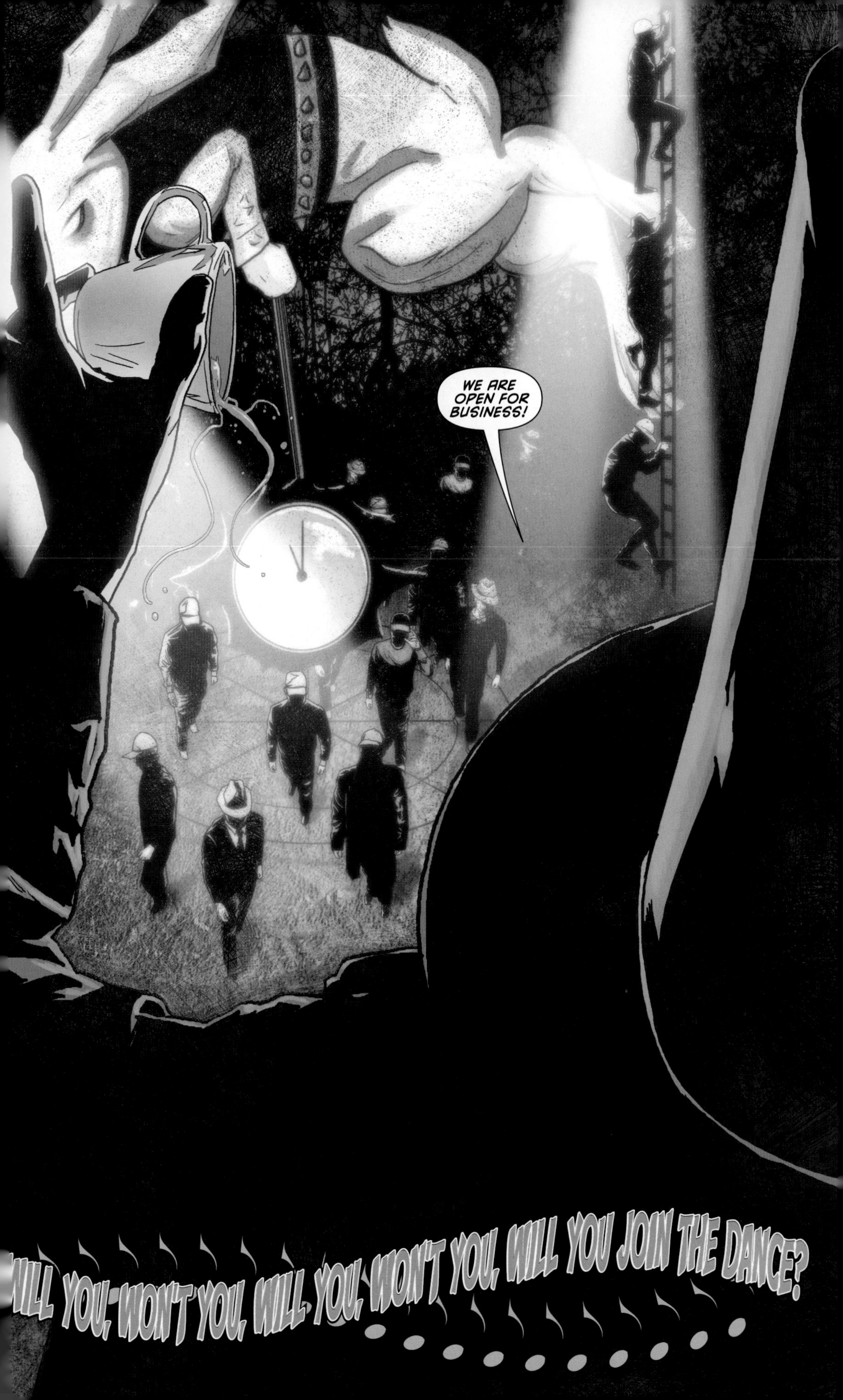
WE ARE OPEN FOR BUSINESS!
WILL YOU, WON'T YOU, WILL YOU, WON'T YOU, WILL YOU JOIN THE DANCE?

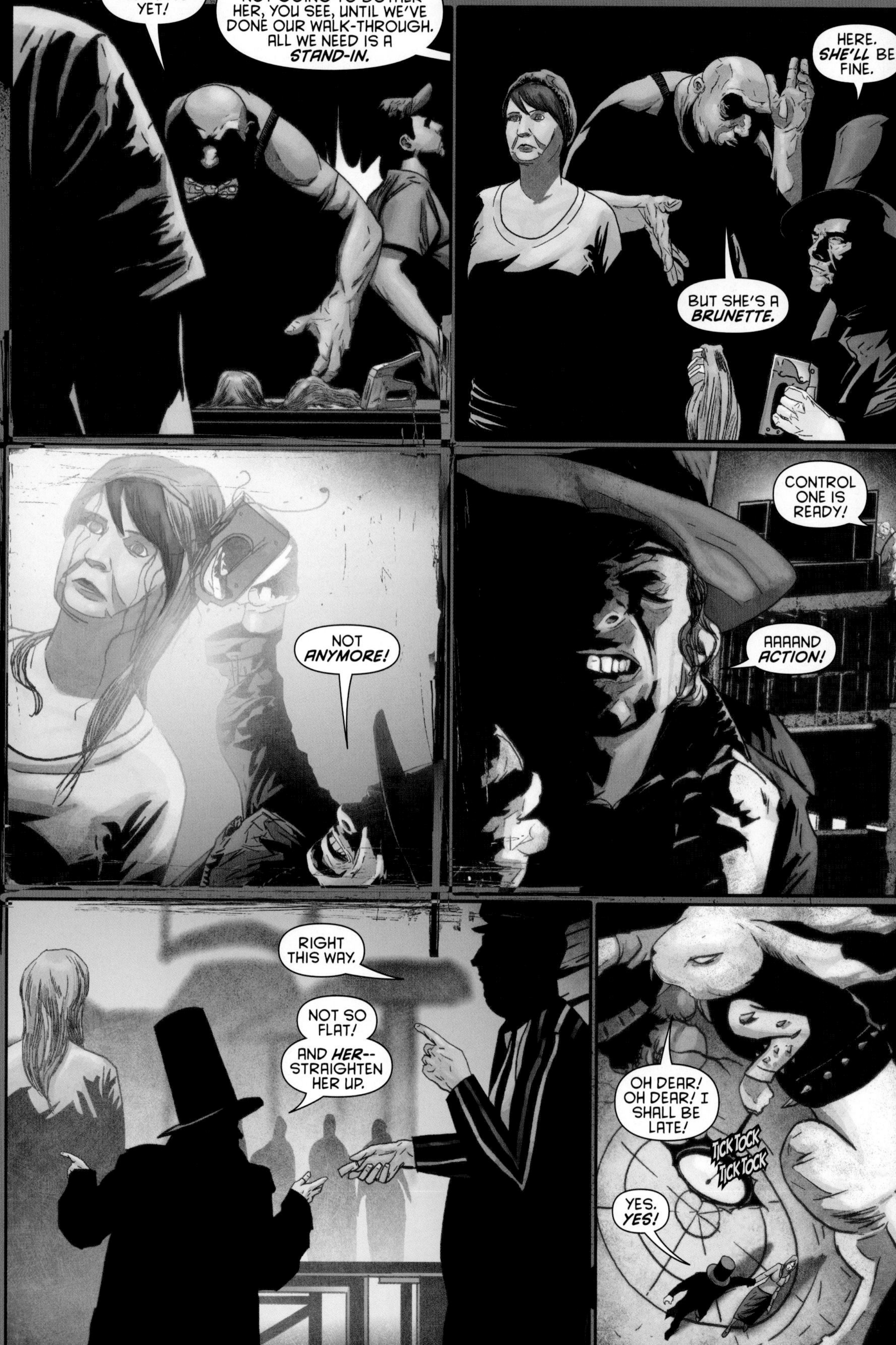
WAIT! YOU DON'T HAVE YER ALICE YET!
IT'S A REHEARSAL, DUM. WE'RE NOT GOING TO BOTHER HER, YOU SEE, UNTIL WE'VE DONE OUR WALK-THROUGH. ALL WE NEED IS A STAND-IN.
HERE. SHE'LL BE FINE.
BUT SHE'S A BRUNETTE.
NOT ANYMORE!
CONTROL ONE IS READY!
AAAAND ACTION!
RIGHT THIS WAY.
NOT SO FLAT!
AND HER-- STRAIGHTEN HER UP.
OH DEAR! OH DEAR! I SHALL BE LATE!
TICK TOCK TICK TOCK
YES. YES!

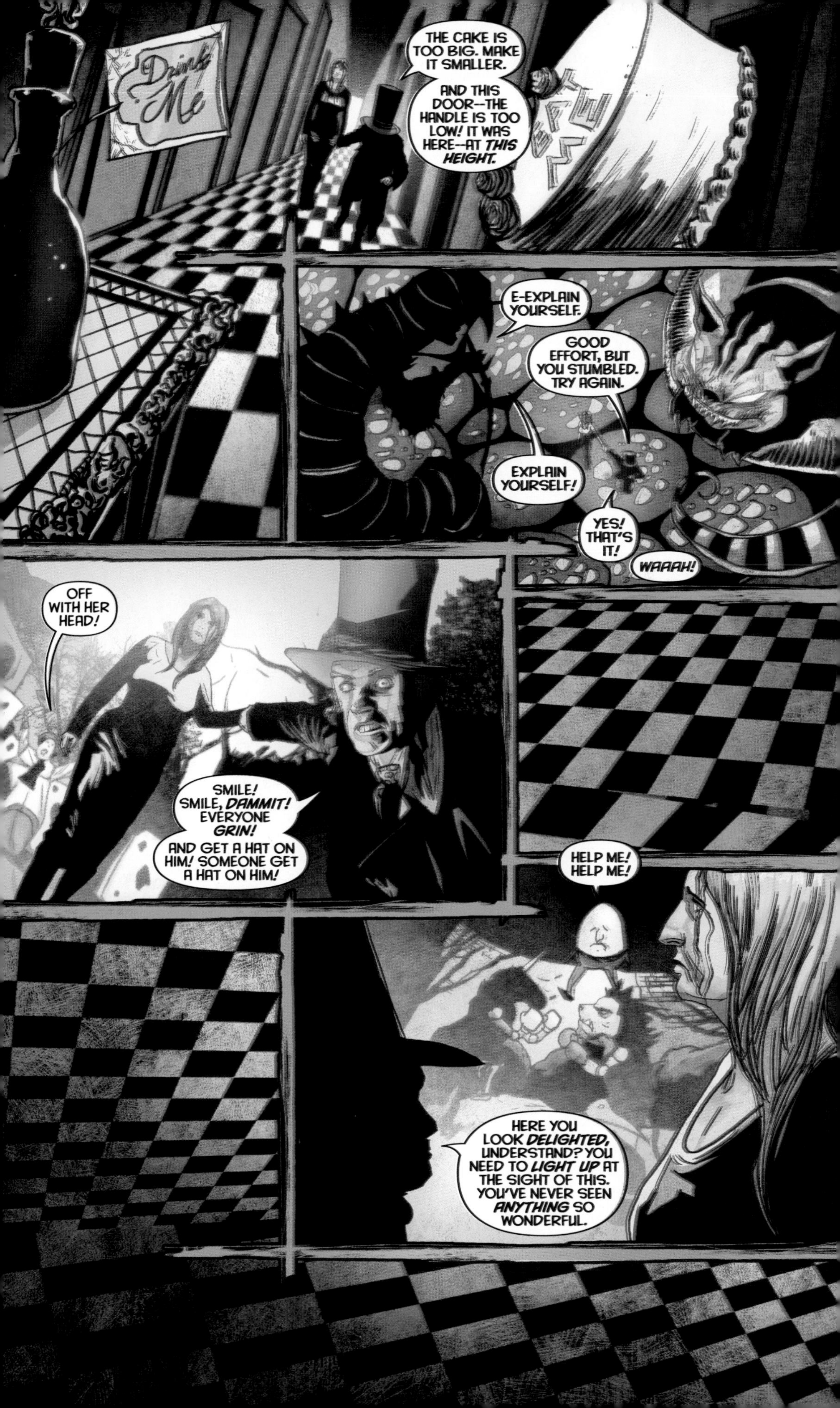

Drink Me
THE CAKE IS TOO BIG. MAKE IT SMALLER.
AND THIS DOOR--THE HANDLE IS TOO LOW! IT WAS HERE--AT THIS HEIGHT.
E-EXPLAIN YOURSELF.
GOOD EFFORT, BUT YOU STUMBLED. TRY AGAIN.
EXPLAIN YOURSELF!
YES! THAT'S IT!
WAAAH!
OFF WITH HER HEAD!
SMILE! SMILE, DAMMIT! EVERYONE GRIN!
AND GET A HAT ON HIM! SOMEONE GET A HAT ON HIM!
HELP ME! HELP ME!
HERE YOU LOOK DELIGHTED, UNDERSTAND? YOU NEED TO LIGHT UP AT THE SIGHT OF THIS. YOU'VE NEVER SEEN ANYTHING SO WONDERFUL.

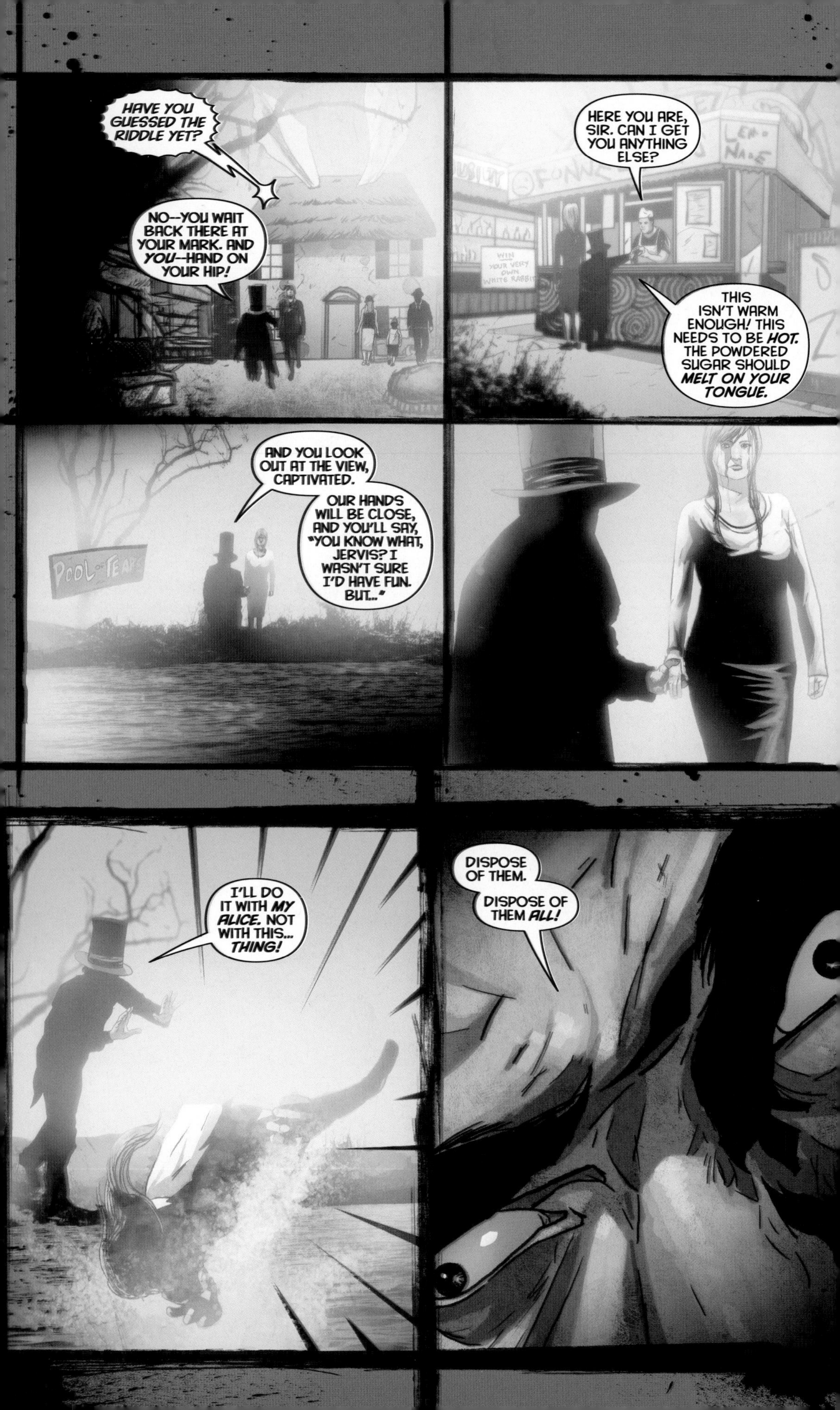
HAVE YOU GUESSED THE RIDDLE YET?
NO--YOU WAIT BACK THERE AT YOUR MARK. AND YOU--HAND ON YOUR HIP!
HERE YOU ARE, SIR. CAN I GET YOU ANYTHING ELSE?
WIN YOUR VERY OWN WHITE RABBIT
THIS ISN'T WARM ENOUGH! THIS NEEDS TO BE HOT. THE POWDERED SUGAR SHOULD MELT ON YOUR TONGUE.
AND YOU LOOK OUT AT THE VIEW, CAPTIVATED.
OUR HANDS WILL BE CLOSE, AND YOU'LL SAY, "YOU KNOW WHAT, JERVIS? I WASN'T SURE I'D HAVE FUN. BUT..."
POOL OF TEARS
I'LL DO IT WITH MY ALICE. NOT WITH THIS... THING!
DISPOSE OF THEM.
DISPOSE OF THEM ALL!

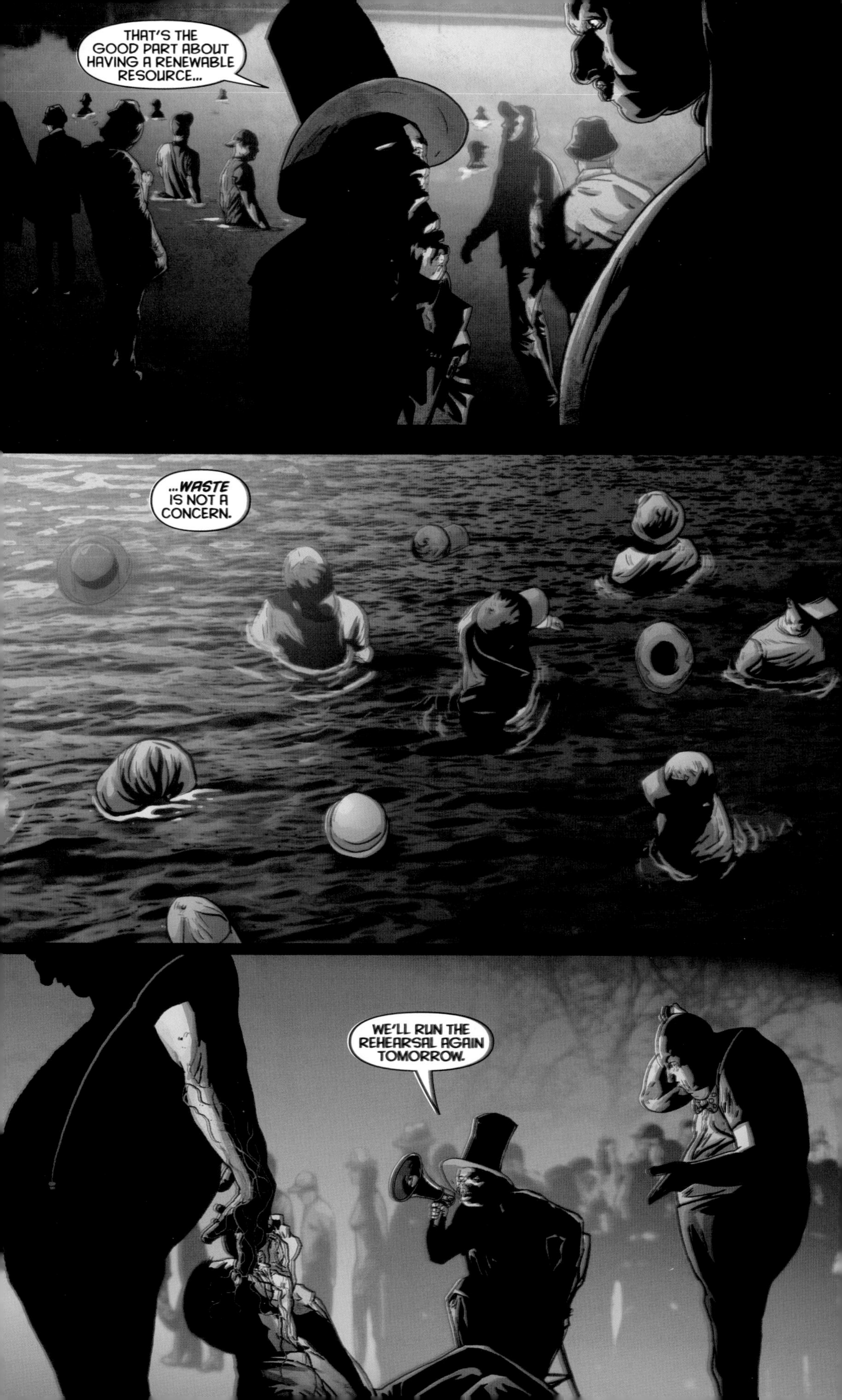
THAT'S THE GOOD PART ABOUT HAVING A RENEWABLE RESOURCE...
...WASTE IS NOT A CONCERN.
WE'LL RUN THE REHEARSAL AGAIN TOMORROW.

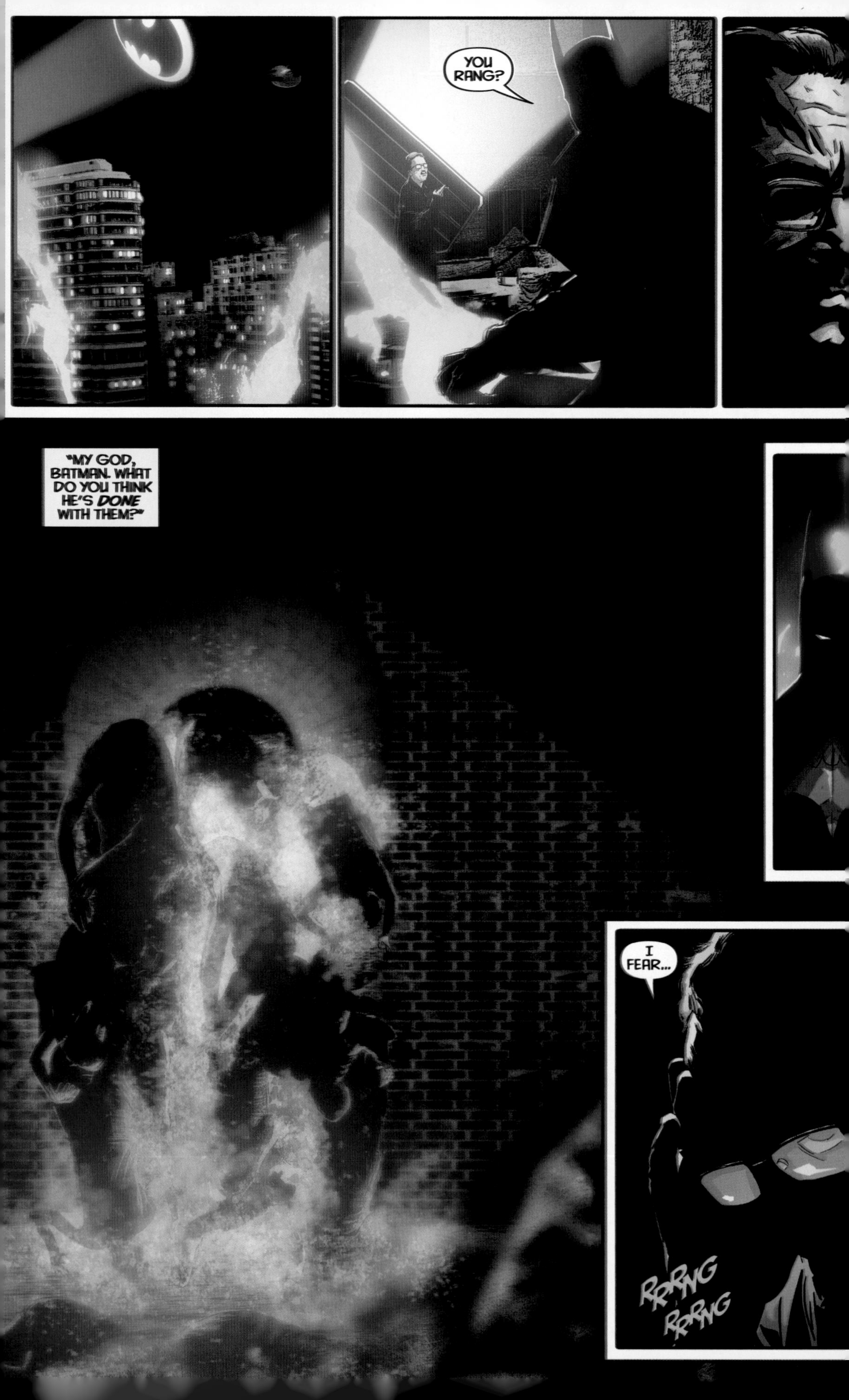
YOU RANG?
"MY GOD, BATMAN. WHAT DO YOU THINK HE'S *DONE* WITH THEM?"
I FEAR...
RRRRNG
RRRRNG

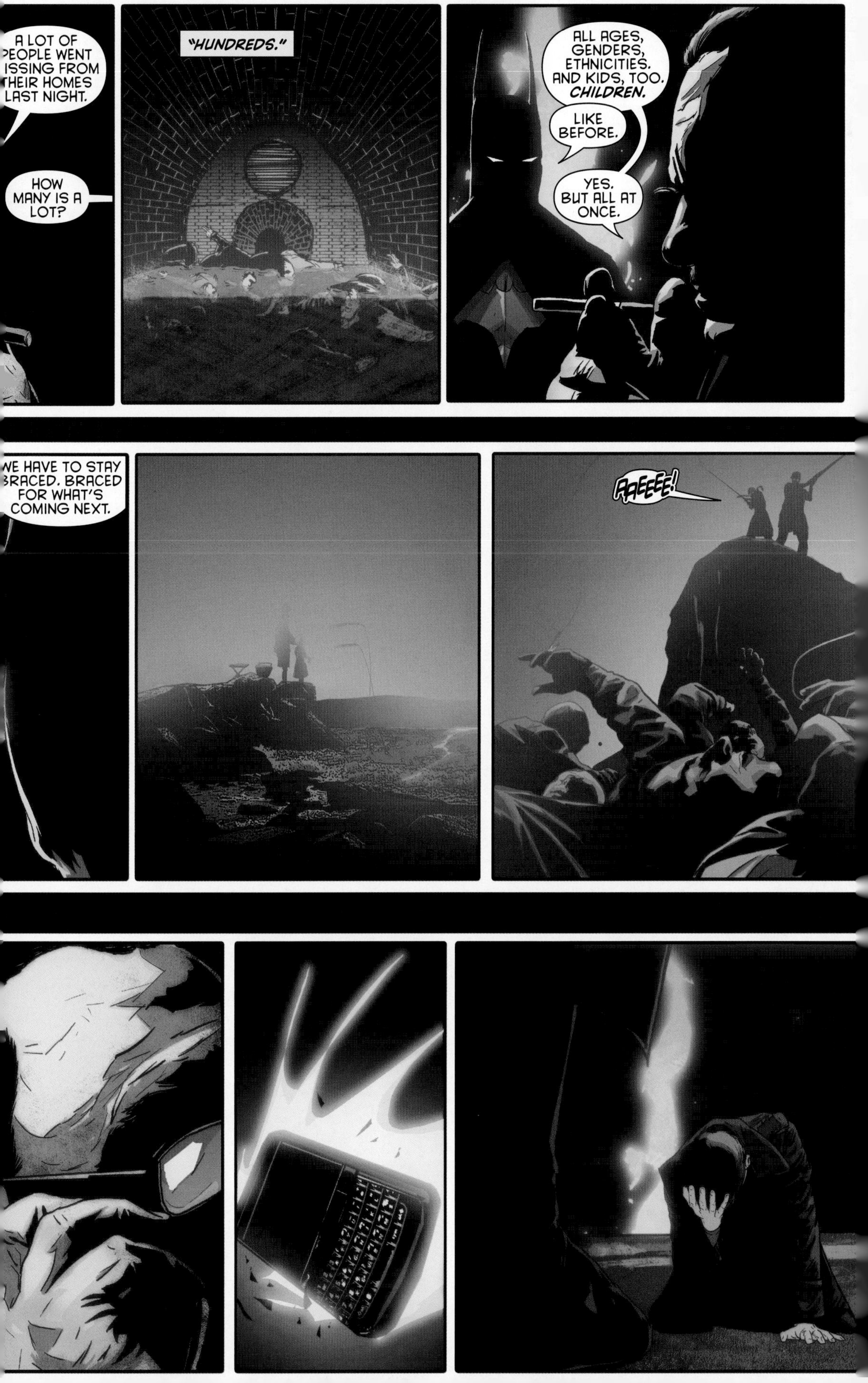

A LOT OF
PEOPLE WENT
ISSING FROM
THEIR HOMES
LAST NIGHT.
HOW MANY IS A LOT?
"HUNDREDS."
ALL AGES, GENDERS, ETHNICITIES. AND KIDS, TOO. *CHILDREN.*
LIKE BEFORE.
YES. BUT ALL AT ONCE.
WE HAVE TO STAY BRACED. BRACED FOR WHAT'S COMING NEXT.
AAEEEE!

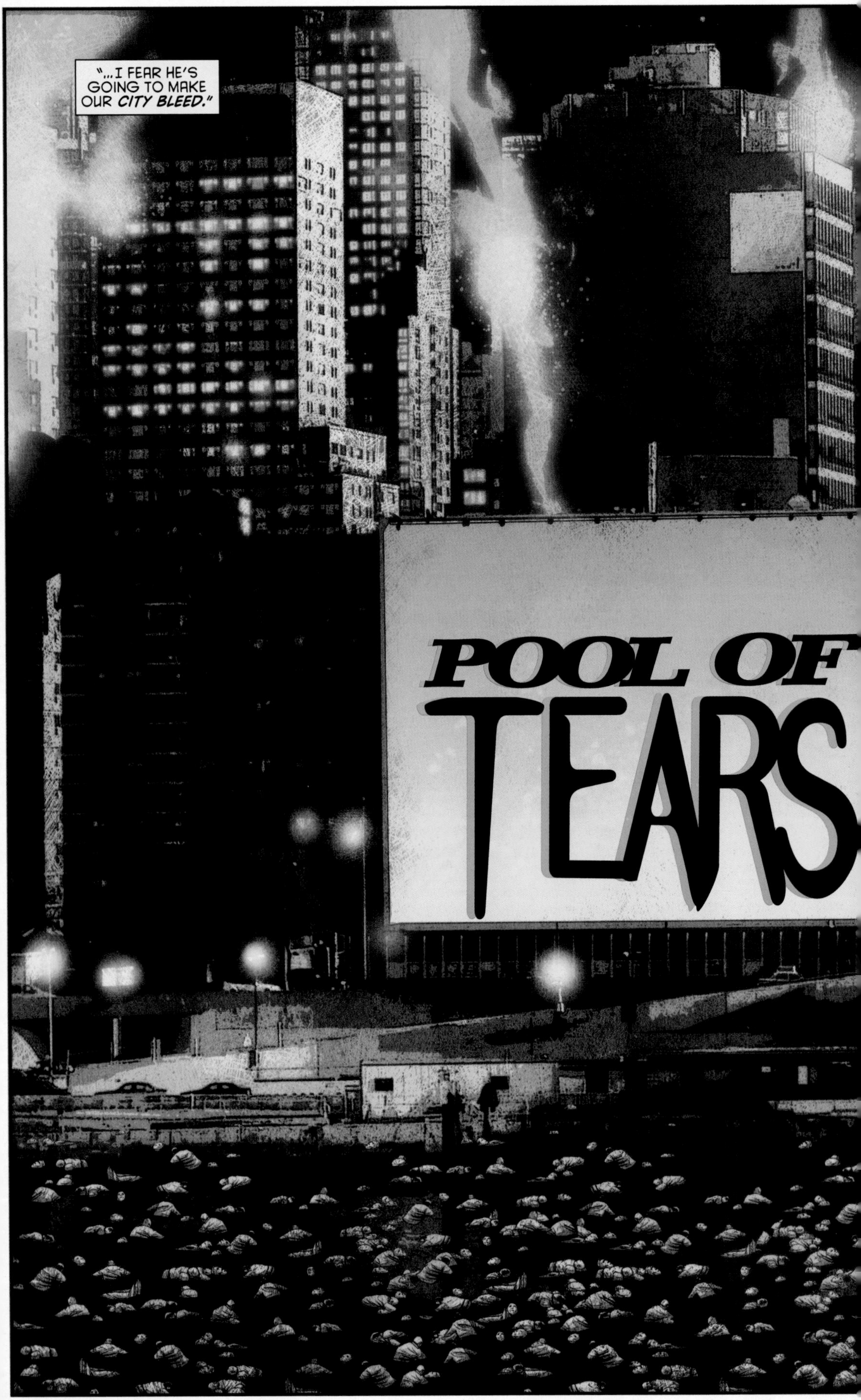
"...I FEAR HE'S GOING TO MAKE OUR *CITY BLEED.*"
POOL OF
TEARS

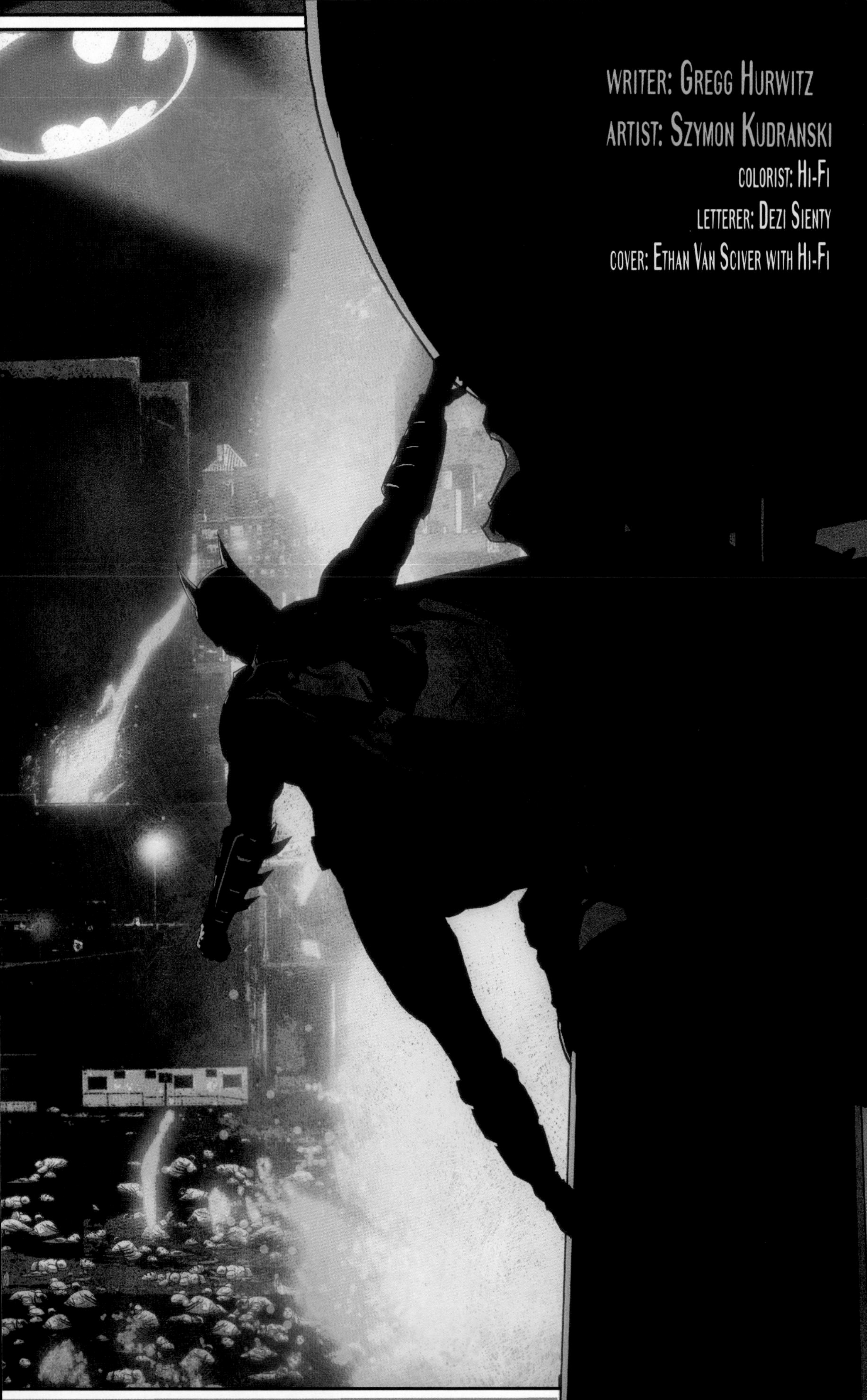
WRITER: GREGG HURWITZ
ARTIST: SZYMON KUDRANSKI
COLORIST: HI-FI
LETTERER: DEZI SIENTY
COVER: ETHAN VAN SCIVER WITH HI-FI

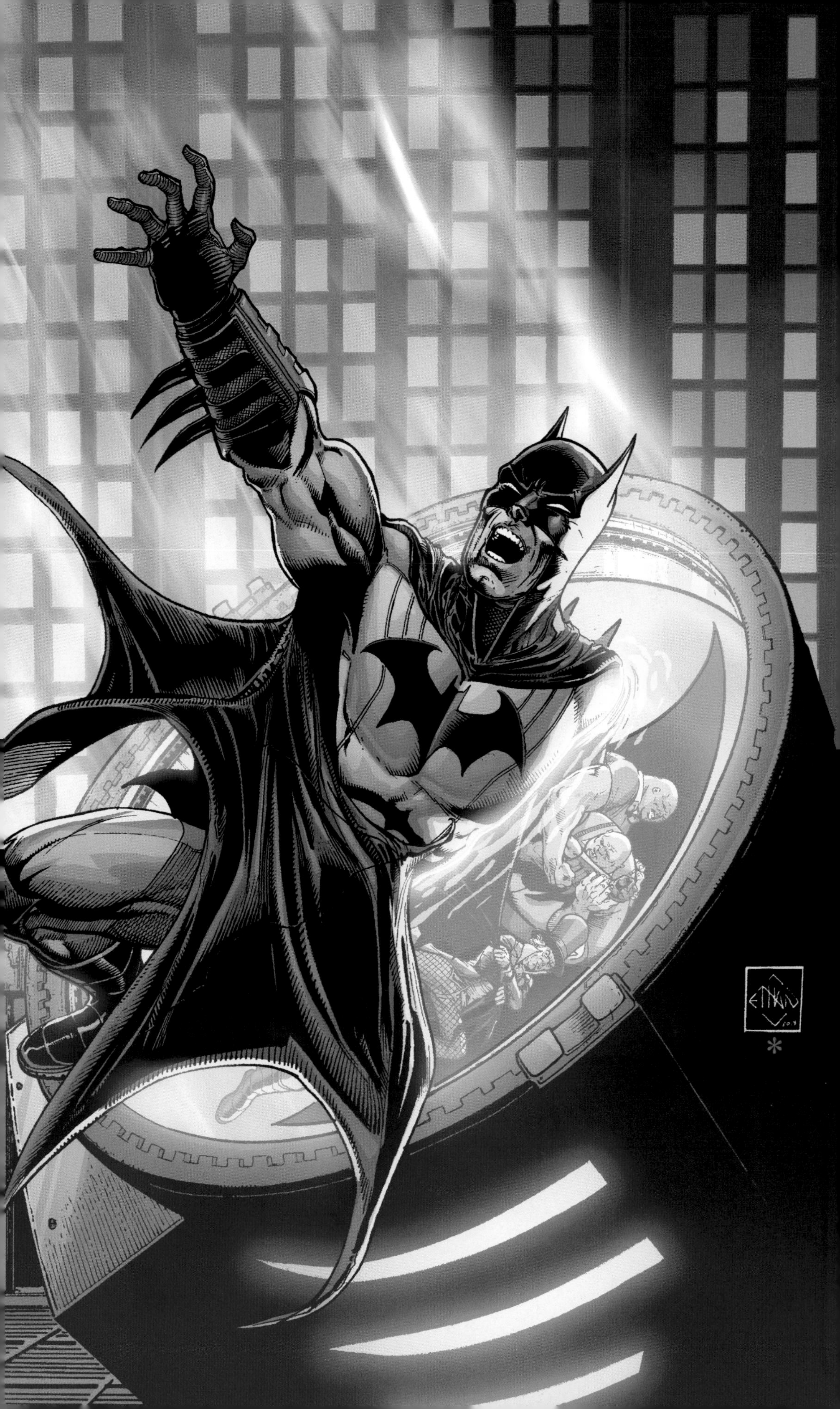

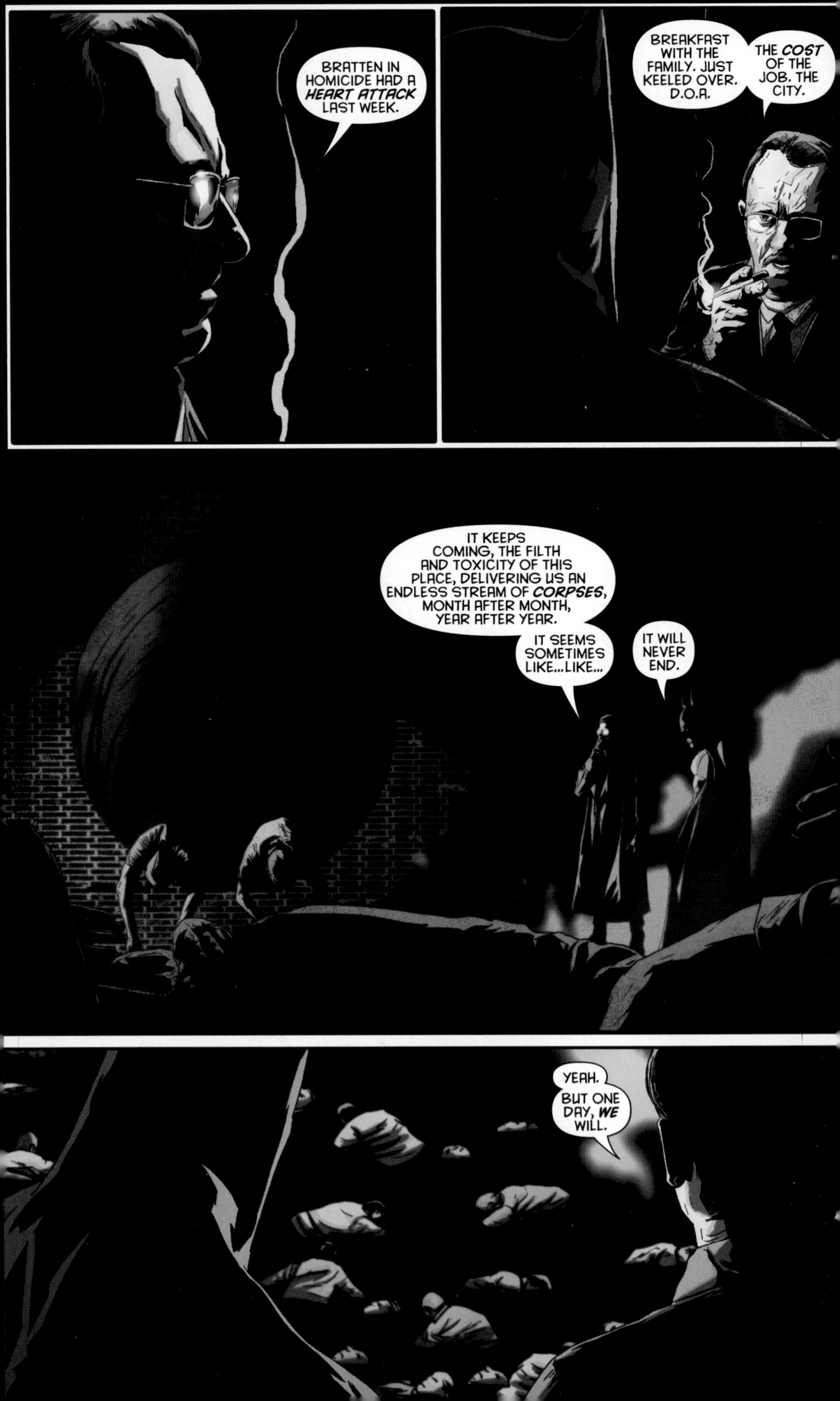
BRATTEN IN HOMICIDE HAD A HEART ATTACK LAST WEEK.
BREAKFAST WITH THE FAMILY. JUST KEELED OVER. D.O.A.
THE COST OF THE JOB. THE CITY.
IT KEEPS COMING, THE FILTH AND TOXICITY OF THIS PLACE, DELIVERING US AN ENDLESS STREAM OF CORPSES, MONTH AFTER MONTH, YEAR AFTER YEAR.
IT SEEMS SOMETIMES LIKE...LIKE...
IT WILL NEVER END.
YEAH.
BUT ONE DAY, WE WILL.

...WANT TO ASSURE YOU THAT THE FINE MEN AND WOMEN OF GOTHAM P.D. WILL WORK WITHOUT REST UNTIL WE HAVE IDENTIFIED EVERY LAST BODY AND SERVED NOTICE TO THE SUFFERING FAMILIES.

I MUST MAKE A PRESSING ANNOUNCEMENT NOW. WE HAVE SUCCEEDED IN TRACING THE SOURCE OF THIS MASS HYPNOSIS BACK TO THE *KRAZY HATZ STANDS* ALL OVER THE CITY....

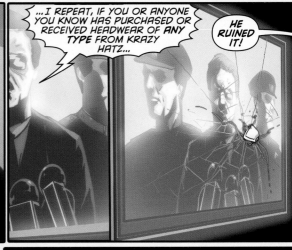

...I REPEAT, IF YOU OR ANYONE YOU KNOW HAS PURCHASED OR RECEIVED HEADWEAR OF *ANY TYPE* FROM KRAZY HATZ...

HE RUINED IT!

THE BATMAN RUINED *EVERY-THING!*

NOW THERE WON'T BE THRONGS OF PATRONS AT MY *WONDERLAND.*

IS IT...IS IT OVER, MR. HATTER?

OF COURSE NOT, TWEEDLE-DIPSTICK. IT'S *NEVER* OVER. NOT SO LONG AS I HAVE MY *ALICE.*

SHE AND I CAN STILL HAVE OUR *PERFECT DAY* AGAIN.

ALL THE WORKERS WILL BE IN PLACE, BUT THE PARK WILL BE OPEN *JUST FOR US.*

IT'LL BE A CAST AND CREW PERFORMANCE.

...ouled, or walled-up.

There are entire networks that are defunct, others that rush with sea water when high tide rolls in.

Some passageways have caved in, some have eroded through to vast chambers beneath.

STILL WITH ME, PENNY ONE?

BZZT-ON YOUR GPS.

It's a mess, as unpredictable and labyrinthine as the city above.

--SEEMS TO BE A GREAT DEAL OF INTERFERENCE-- BZZT--SIGNAL IS--BZZT--

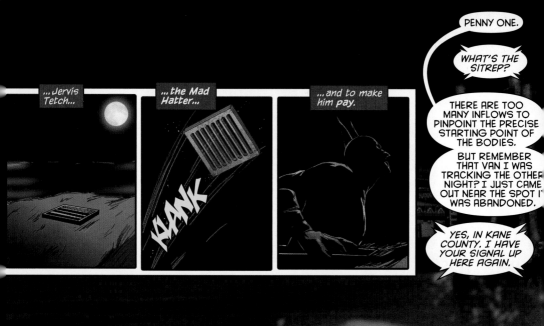

...Jervis Tetch...

...the Mad Hatter...

KLANK

...and to make him pay.

PENNY ONE.

WHAT'S THE SITREP?

THERE ARE TOO MANY INFLOWS TO PINPOINT THE PRECISE STARTING POINT OF THE BODIES.

BUT REMEMBER THAT VAN I WAS TRACKING THE OTHER NIGHT? I JUST CAME OUT NEAR THE SPOT IT WAS ABANDONED.

YES, IN KANE COUNTY. I HAVE YOUR SIGNAL UP HERE AGAIN.

BREAK IN. GET THEM.

I'LL START THE PORT SCANNERS NOW TO DETECT VULNERABILITIES...

...BUT IT WILL TAKE TIME, SO WE'LL REQUIRE YOU TO MAKE USE OF YOUR RENOWNED PATIENCE

JUST DO IT. OVER--ZZZP.

THREE... AND

PENNY ONE?

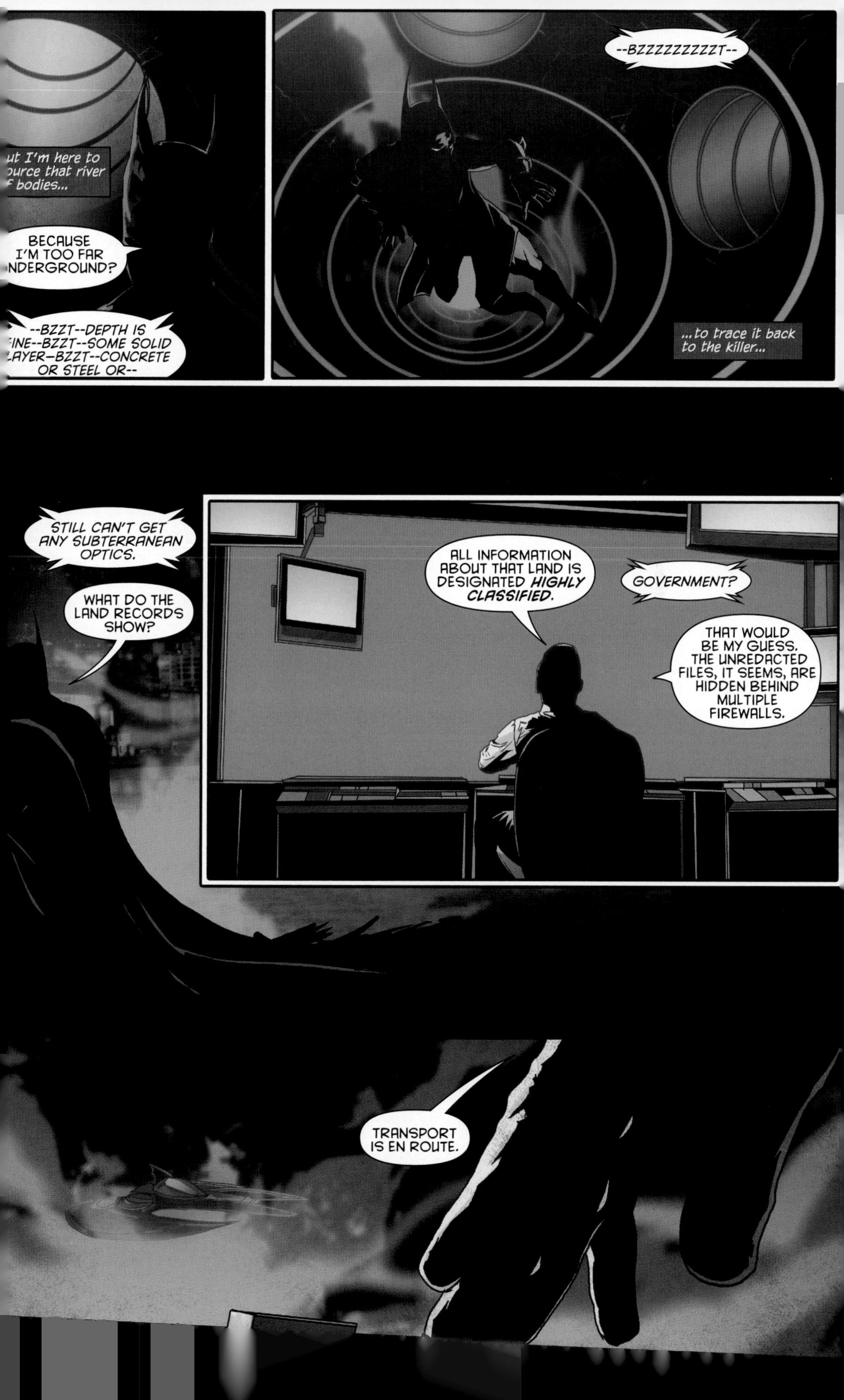
ut I'm here to ource that river f bodies...
BECAUSE I'M TOO FAR NDERGROUND?
--BZZT--DEPTH IS INE--BZZT--SOME SOLID AYER--BZZT--CONCRETE OR STEEL OR--
--BZZZZZZZZZT--
...to trace it back to the killer...
STILL CAN'T GET ANY SUBTERRANEAN OPTICS.
WHAT DO THE LAND RECORDS SHOW?
ALL INFORMATION ABOUT THAT LAND IS DESIGNATED HIGHLY CLASSIFIED.
GOVERNMENT?
THAT WOULD BE MY GUESS. THE UNREDACTED FILES, IT SEEMS, ARE HIDDEN BEHIND MULTIPLE FIREWALLS.
TRANSPORT IS EN ROUTE.

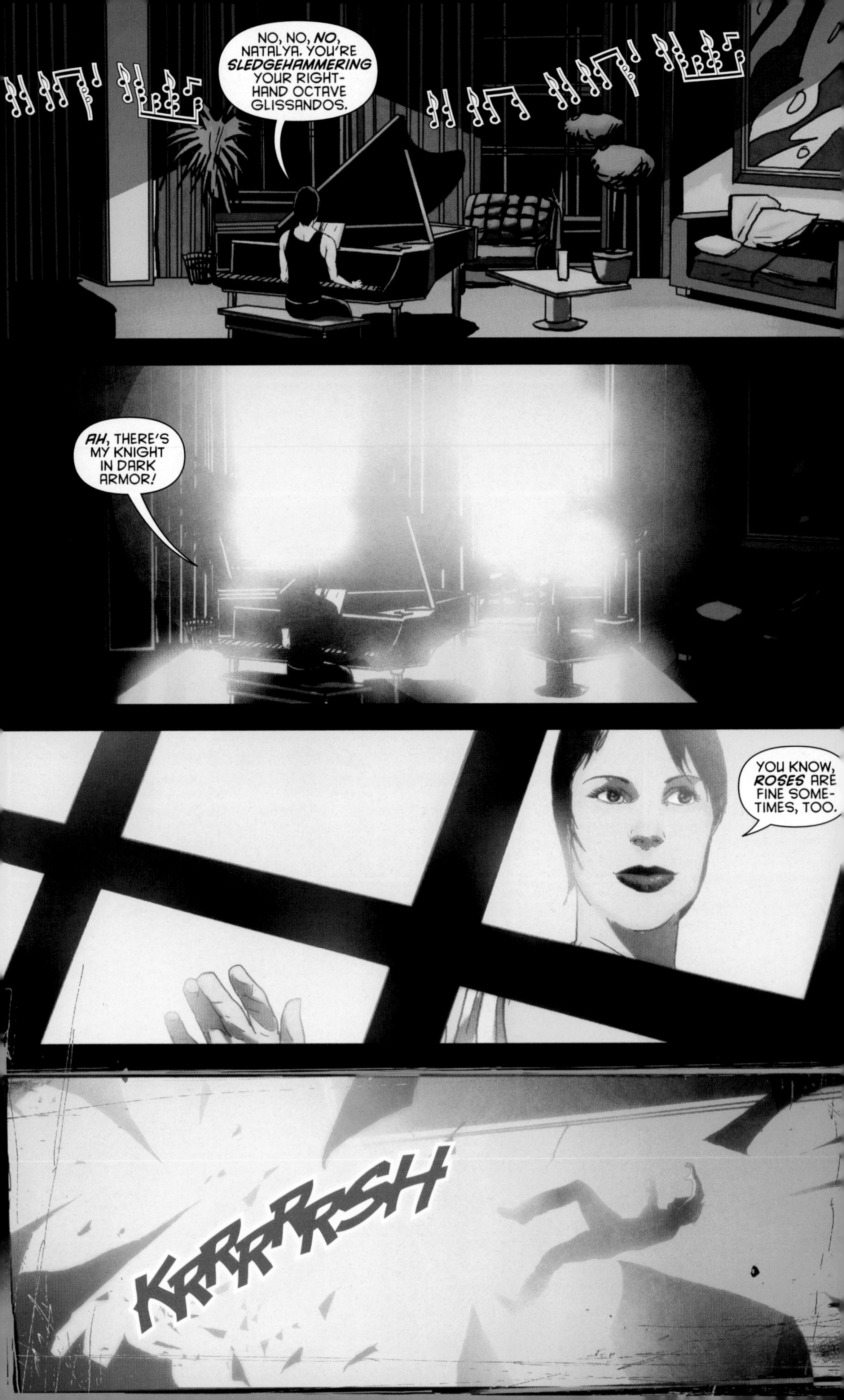
NO, NO, NO, NATALYA. YOU'RE SLEDGEHAMMERING YOUR RIGHT-HAND OCTAVE GLISSANDOS.
AH, THERE'S MY KNIGHT IN DARK ARMOR!
YOU KNOW, ROSES ARE FINE SOMETIMES, TOO.
KRRRRRSH

Some nights, a chill creeps over Wayne Manor...

...and it feels like a *tomb.*

On these nights, I wonder how many more years I can stay here...

KLK

...with the memories of the *dead.*

MASTER BRUCE?

I CAN'T STOP THINKING ABOUT HIM.

I THINK WE HAVE MS. TRUSEVICH TO THANK FOR OPENING YOU UP TO *LIFE* AGAIN...

...WHICH ALSO OPENS YOU TO *DEATH.*

I'M WORRIED I'LL LOSE HER LIKE I LOST DAMIAN. IT SEEMS LIKE THAT'S THE COST PEOPLE PAY BECAUSE OF ME.

NOT BECAUSE OF *YOU.* BECAUSE OF *THIS.*

I FEAR SOMETIMES, DEAR BOY, THAT IF YOU DON'T GIVE THIS UP, YOU'LL HAVE NOTHING.

YOU CAN'T HAVE DARKNESS AND LIGHT AT THE SAME TIME, MASTER BRUCE....

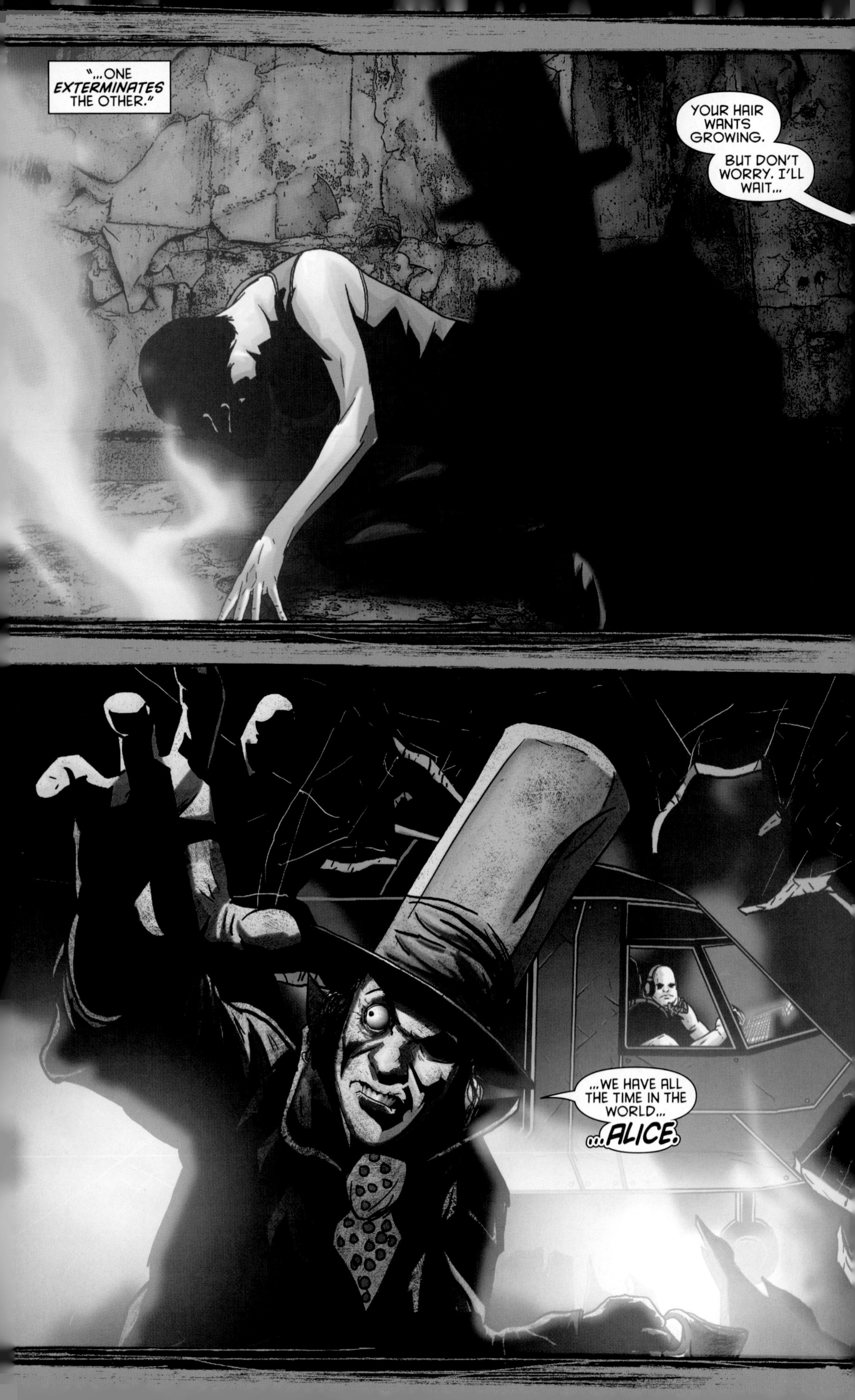
"...ONE EXTERMINATES THE OTHER."
YOUR HAIR WANTS GROWING.
BUT DON'T WORRY. I'LL WAIT...
...WE HAVE ALL THE TIME IN THE WORLD...
...ALICE.

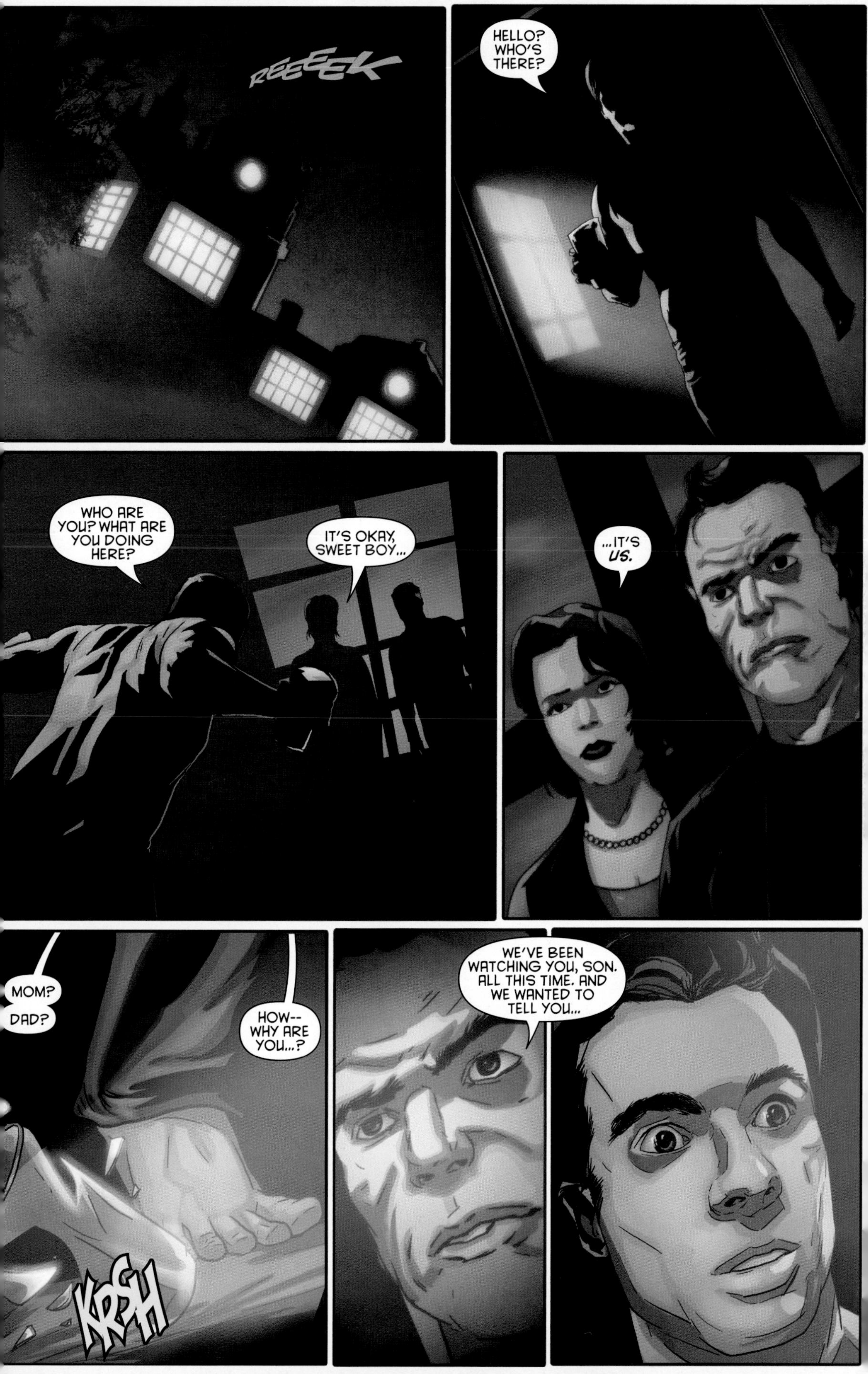
REEEEK
HELLO? WHO'S THERE?
WHO ARE YOU? WHAT ARE YOU DOING HERE?
IT'S OKAY, SWEET BOY...
...IT'S US.
MOM?
DAD?
HOW-- WHY ARE YOU...?
WE'VE BEEN WATCHING YOU, SON. ALL THIS TIME. AND WE WANTED TO TELL YOU...
KRSH

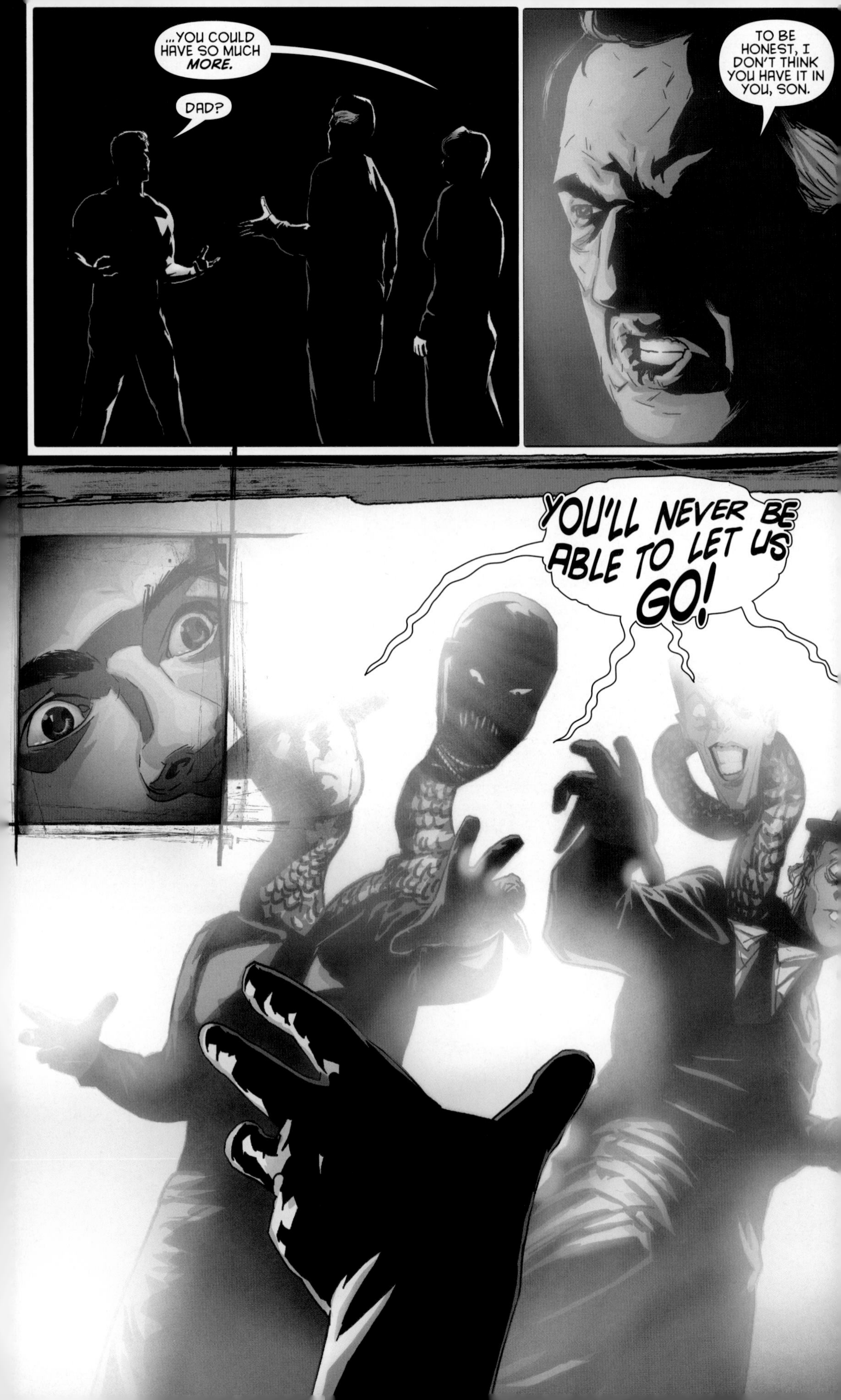
...YOU COULD HAVE SO MUCH MORE.
DAD?
TO BE HONEST, I DON'T THINK YOU HAVE IT IN YOU, SON.
YOU'LL NEVER BE ABLE TO LET US GO!

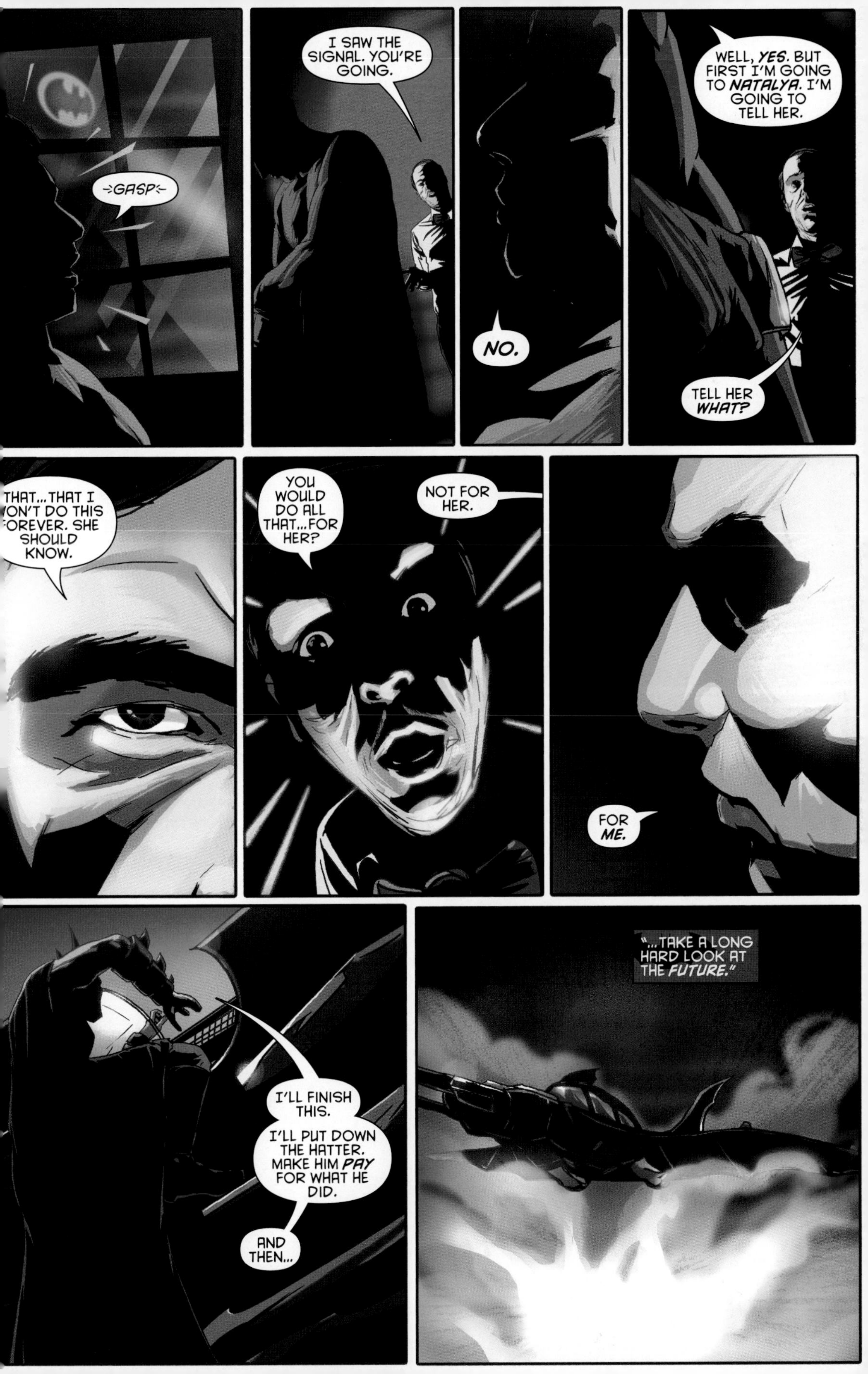

-GASP-
I SAW THE SIGNAL. YOU'RE GOING.
NO.
WELL, YES. BUT FIRST I'M GOING TO NATALYA. I'M GOING TO TELL HER.
TELL HER WHAT?
THAT... THAT I WON'T DO THIS FOREVER. SHE SHOULD KNOW.
YOU WOULD DO ALL THAT... FOR HER?
NOT FOR HER.
FOR ME.
I'LL FINISH THIS.
I'LL PUT DOWN THE HATTER. MAKE HIM PAY FOR WHAT HE DID.
AND THEN...
"...TAKE A LONG HARD LOOK AT THE FUTURE."

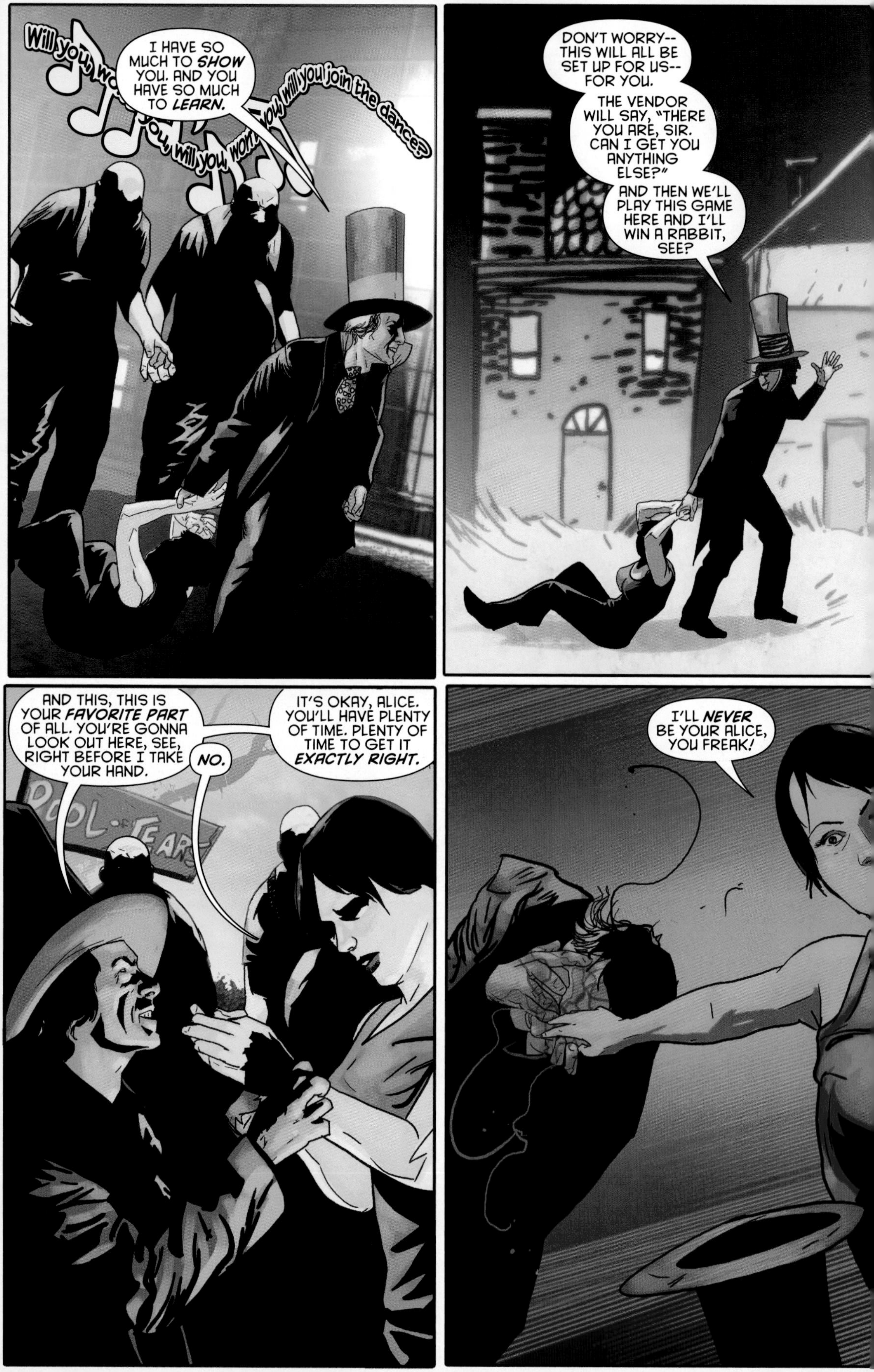
Will you, won't you, will you, won't you, will you join the dance?
I HAVE SO MUCH TO *SHOW* YOU. AND YOU HAVE SO MUCH TO *LEARN.*
DON'T WORRY-- THIS WILL ALL BE SET UP FOR US-- FOR YOU.
THE VENDOR WILL SAY, "THERE YOU ARE, SIR. CAN I GET YOU ANYTHING ELSE?"
AND THEN WE'LL PLAY THIS GAME HERE AND I'LL WIN A RABBIT, SEE?
AND THIS, THIS IS YOUR *FAVORITE PART* OF ALL. YOU'RE GONNA LOOK OUT HERE, SEE, RIGHT BEFORE I TAKE YOUR HAND.
*NO.*
IT'S OKAY, ALICE. YOU'LL HAVE PLENTY OF TIME. PLENTY OF TIME TO GET IT *EXACTLY RIGHT.*
I'LL *NEVER* BE YOUR ALICE, YOU FREAK!

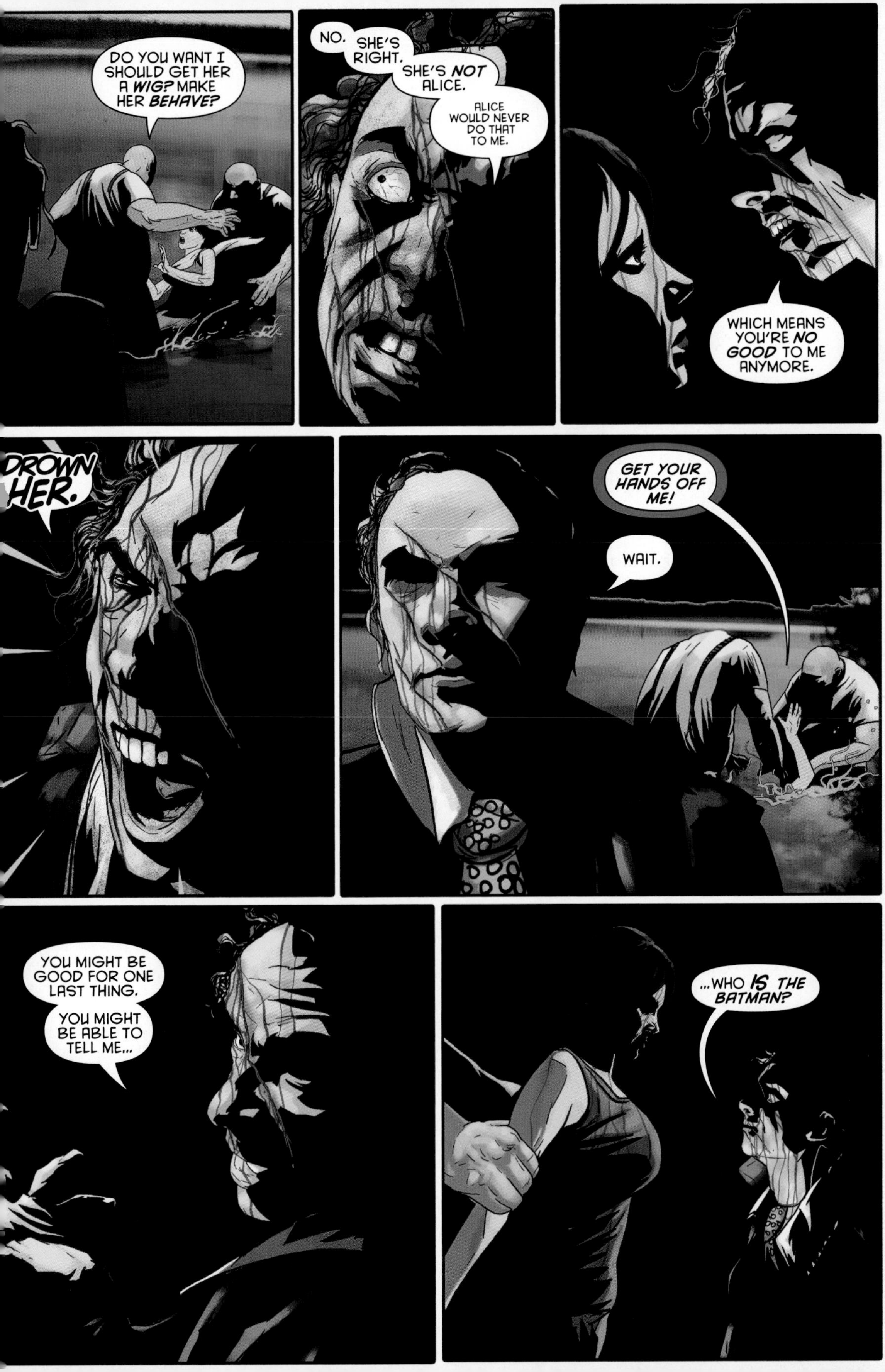
DO YOU WANT I SHOULD GET HER A WIG? MAKE HER BEHAVE?
NO.
SHE'S RIGHT.
SHE'S NOT ALICE.
ALICE WOULD NEVER DO THAT TO ME.
WHICH MEANS YOU'RE NO GOOD TO ME ANYMORE.
DROWN HER.
GET YOUR HANDS OFF ME!
WAIT.
YOU MIGHT BE GOOD FOR ONE LAST THING.
YOU MIGHT BE ABLE TO TELL ME...
...WHO IS THE BATMAN?

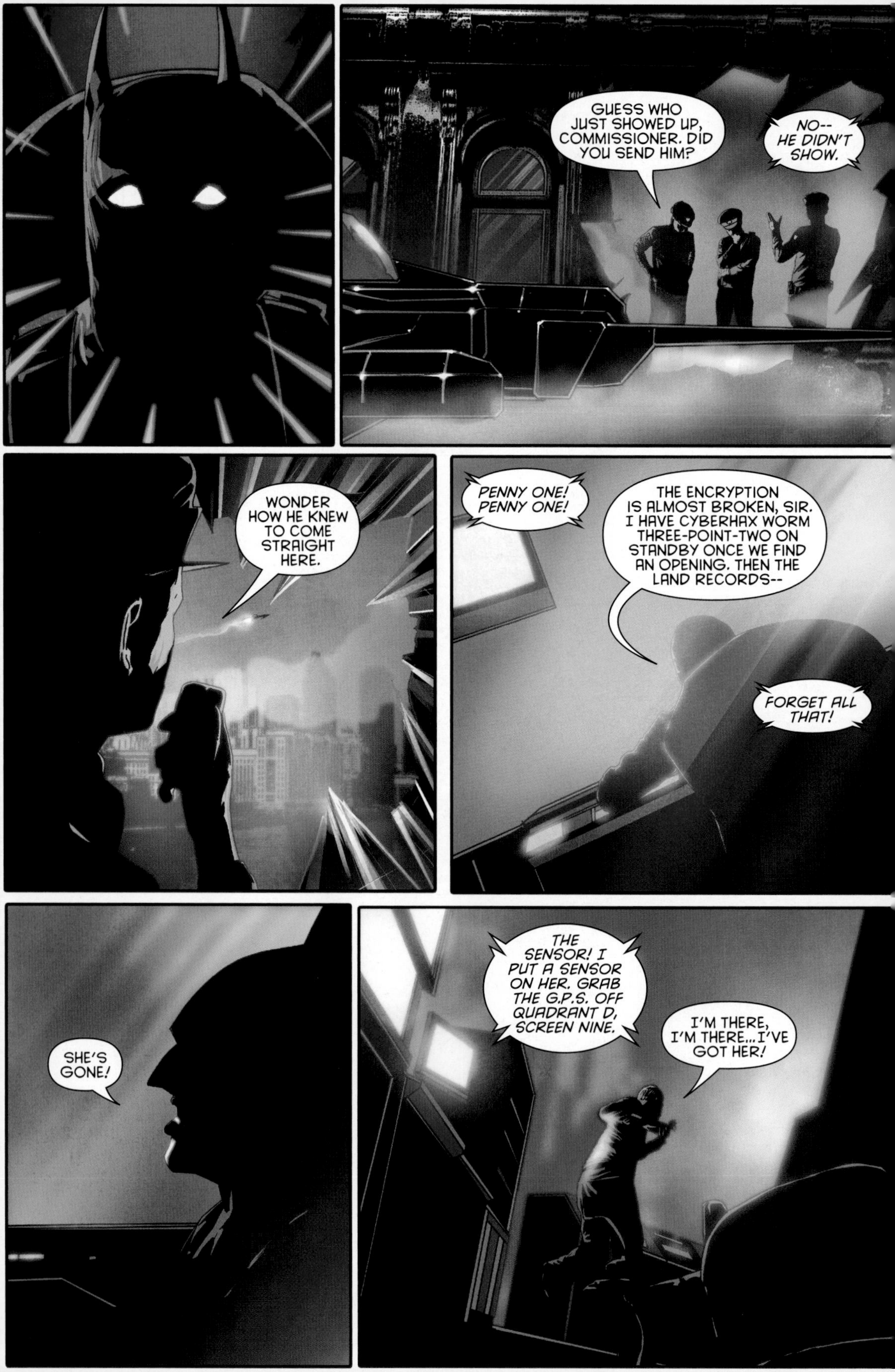
GUESS WHO JUST SHOWED UP, COMMISSIONER. DID YOU SEND HIM?
NO-- HE DIDN'T SHOW.
WONDER HOW HE KNEW TO COME STRAIGHT HERE.
PENNY ONE! PENNY ONE!
THE ENCRYPTION IS ALMOST BROKEN, SIR. I HAVE CYBERHAX WORM THREE-POINT-TWO ON STANDBY ONCE WE FIND AN OPENING. THEN THE LAND RECORDS--
FORGET ALL THAT!
SHE'S GONE!
THE SENSOR! I PUT A SENSOR ON HER. GRAB THE G.P.S. OFF QUADRANT D, SCREEN NINE.
I'M THERE, I'M THERE... I'VE GOT HER!

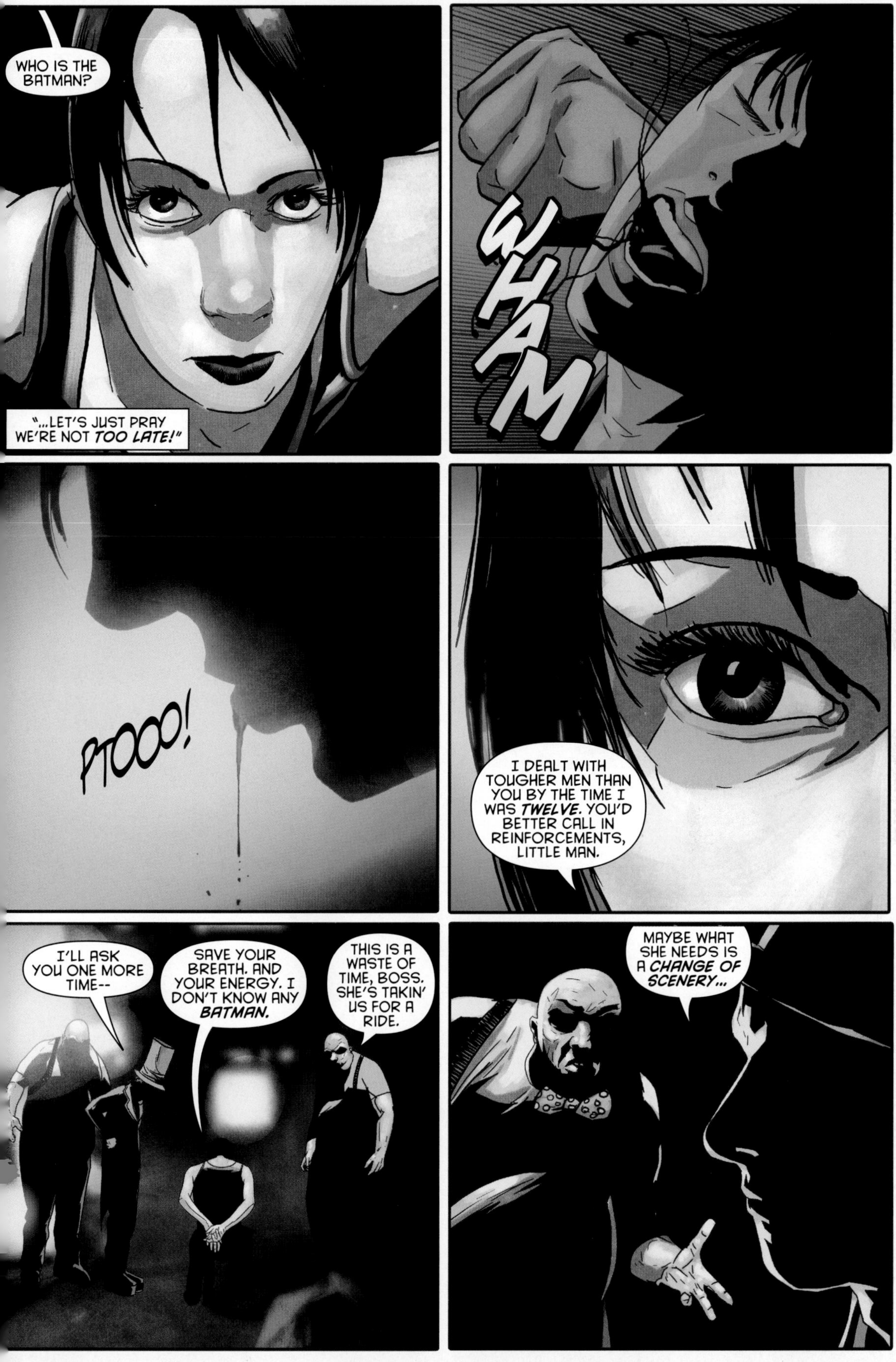
WHO IS THE BATMAN?
"...LET'S JUST PRAY WE'RE NOT TOO LATE!"
WHAM
PTOOO!
I DEALT WITH TOUGHER MEN THAN YOU BY THE TIME I WAS TWELVE. YOU'D BETTER CALL IN REINFORCEMENTS, LITTLE MAN.
I'LL ASK YOU ONE MORE TIME--
SAVE YOUR BREATH. AND YOUR ENERGY. I DON'T KNOW ANY BATMAN.
THIS IS A WASTE OF TIME, BOSS. SHE'S TAKIN' US FOR A RIDE.
MAYBE WHAT SHE NEEDS IS A CHANGE OF SCENERY...

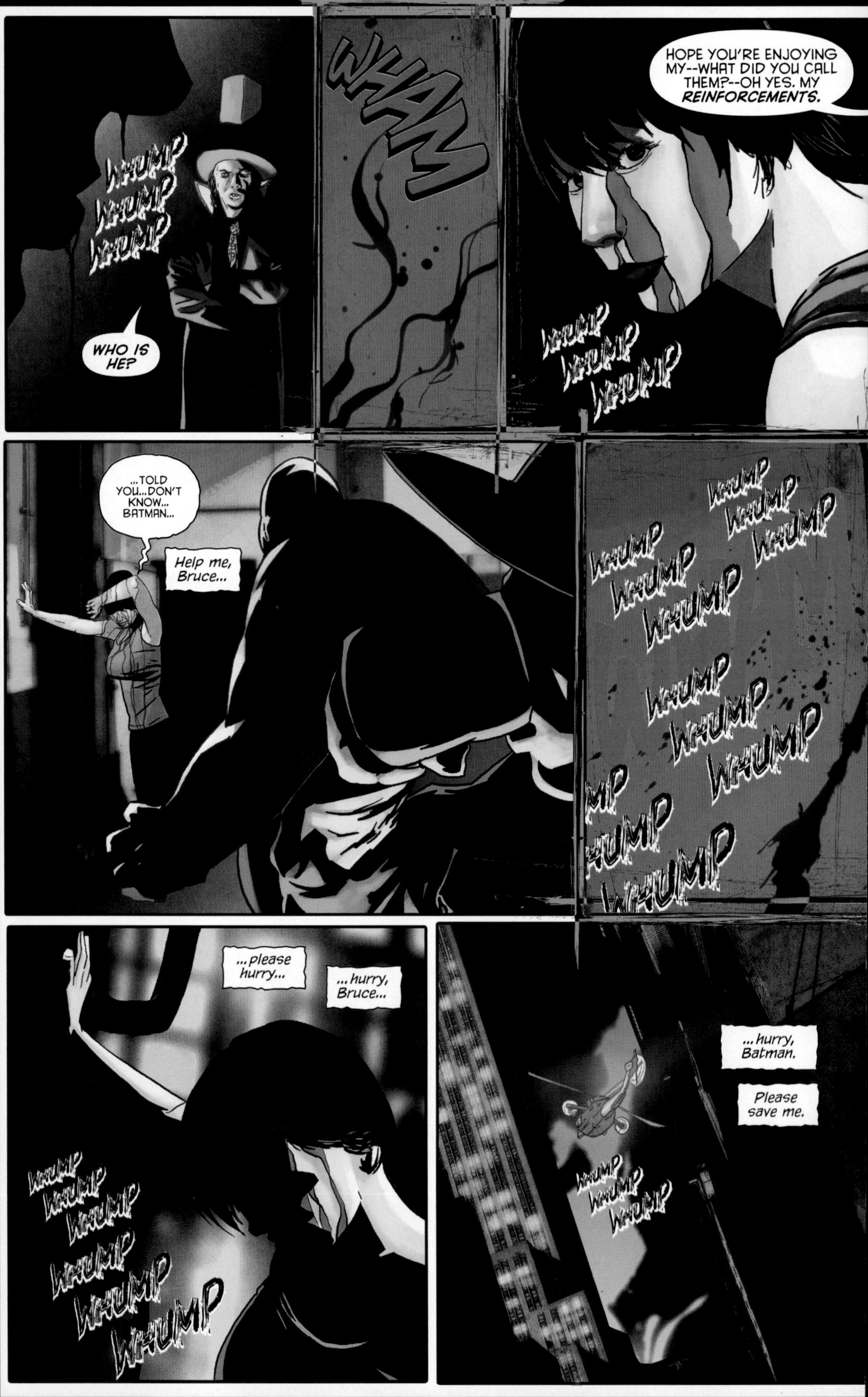
WHUMP
WHUMP
WHUMP
WHO IS HE?
WHAM
HOPE YOU'RE ENJOYING MY--WHAT DID YOU CALL THEM?--OH YES. MY *REINFORCEMENTS.*
WHUMP
WHUMP
WHUMP
...TOLD YOU...DON'T KNOW... BATMAN...
Help me, Bruce...
WHUMP WHUMP WHUMP
WHUMP WHUMP WHUMP
WHUMP WHUMP WHUMP WHUMP
...please hurry...
...hurry, Bruce...
WHUMP WHUMP WHUMP WHUMP WHUMP WHUMP
...hurry, Batman.
Please save me.
WHUMP
WHUMP
WHUMP

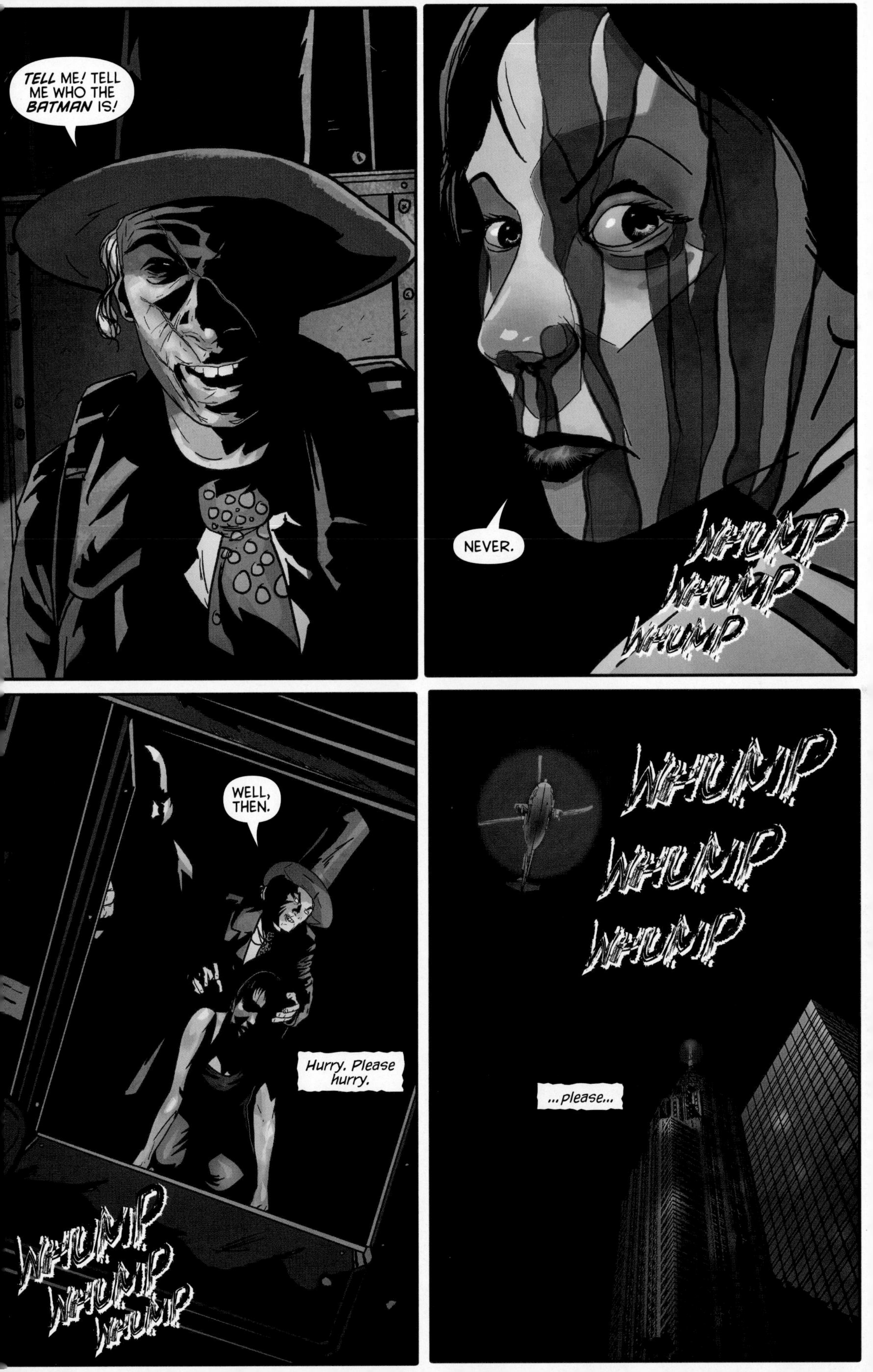
TELL ME! TELL ME WHO THE BATMAN IS!
NEVER.
WHUMP
WHUMP
WHUMP
WELL, THEN.
Hurry. Please hurry.
WHUMP
WHUMP
WHUMP
WHUMP
WHUMP
WHUMP
...please...

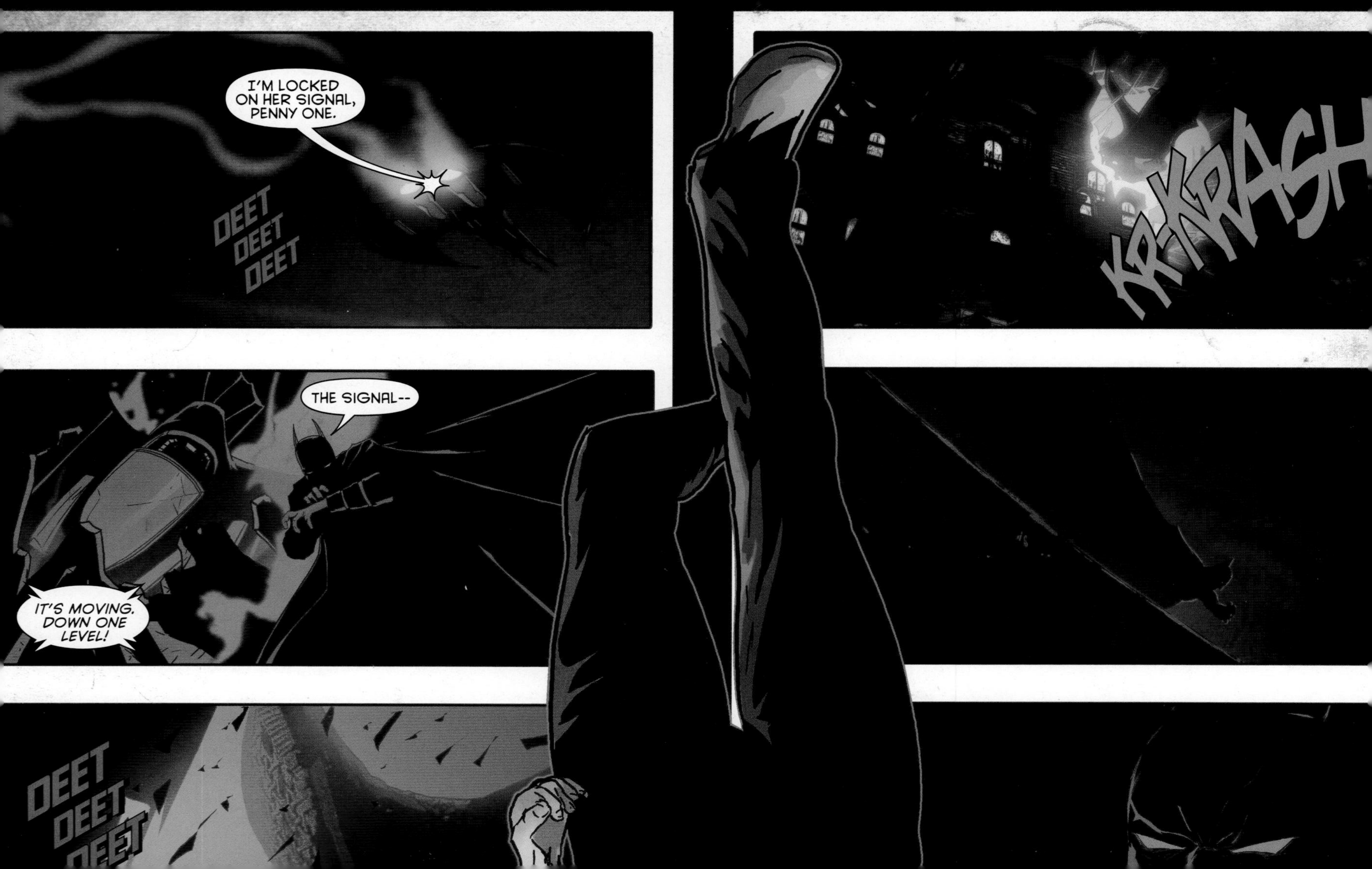
I'M LOCKED ON HER SIGNAL, PENNY ONE.
DEET DEET DEET
KR-KRASH
THE SIGNAL--
IT'S MOVING. DOWN ONE LEVEL!
DEET DEET DEET

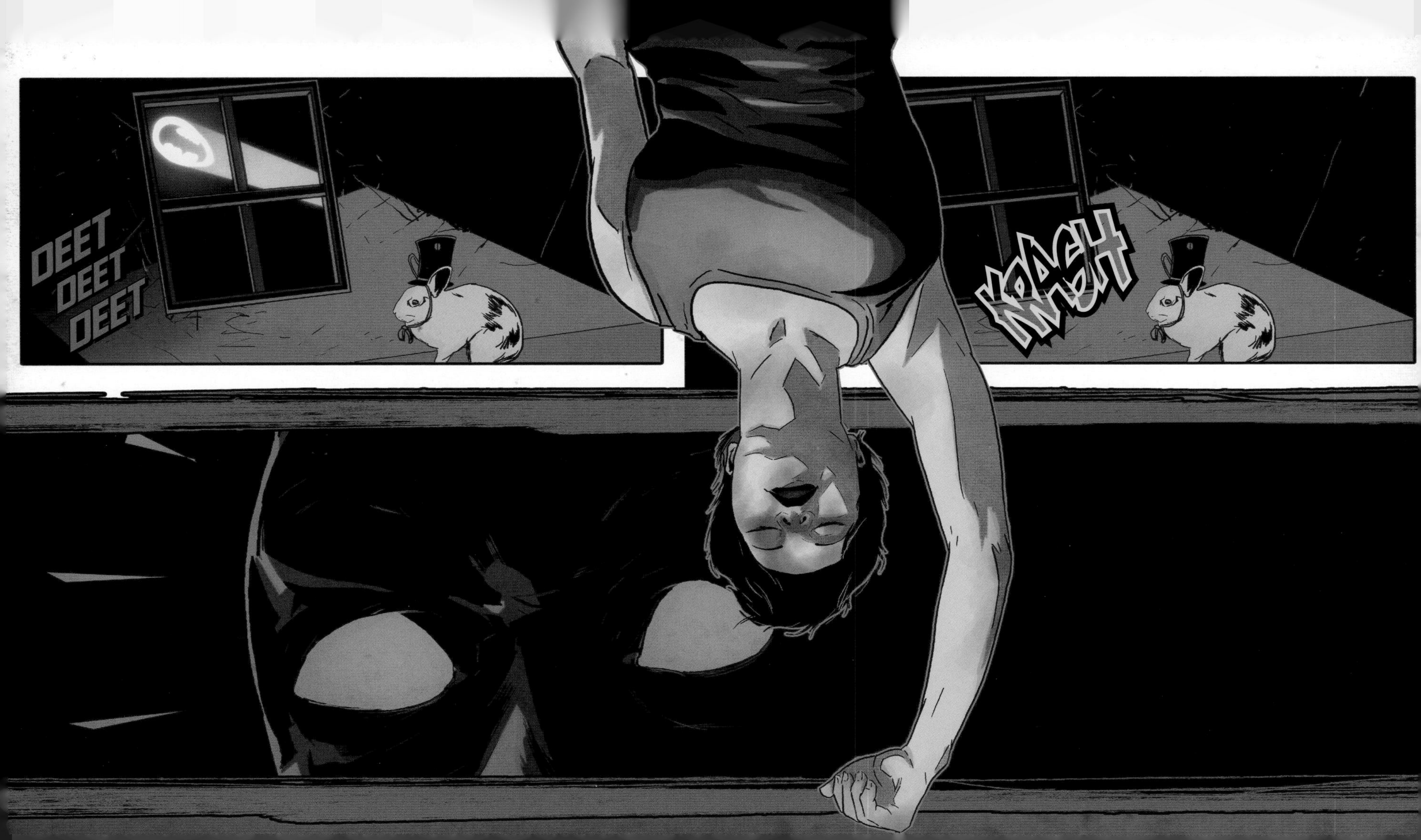
DEET
DEET
DEET
KRASH

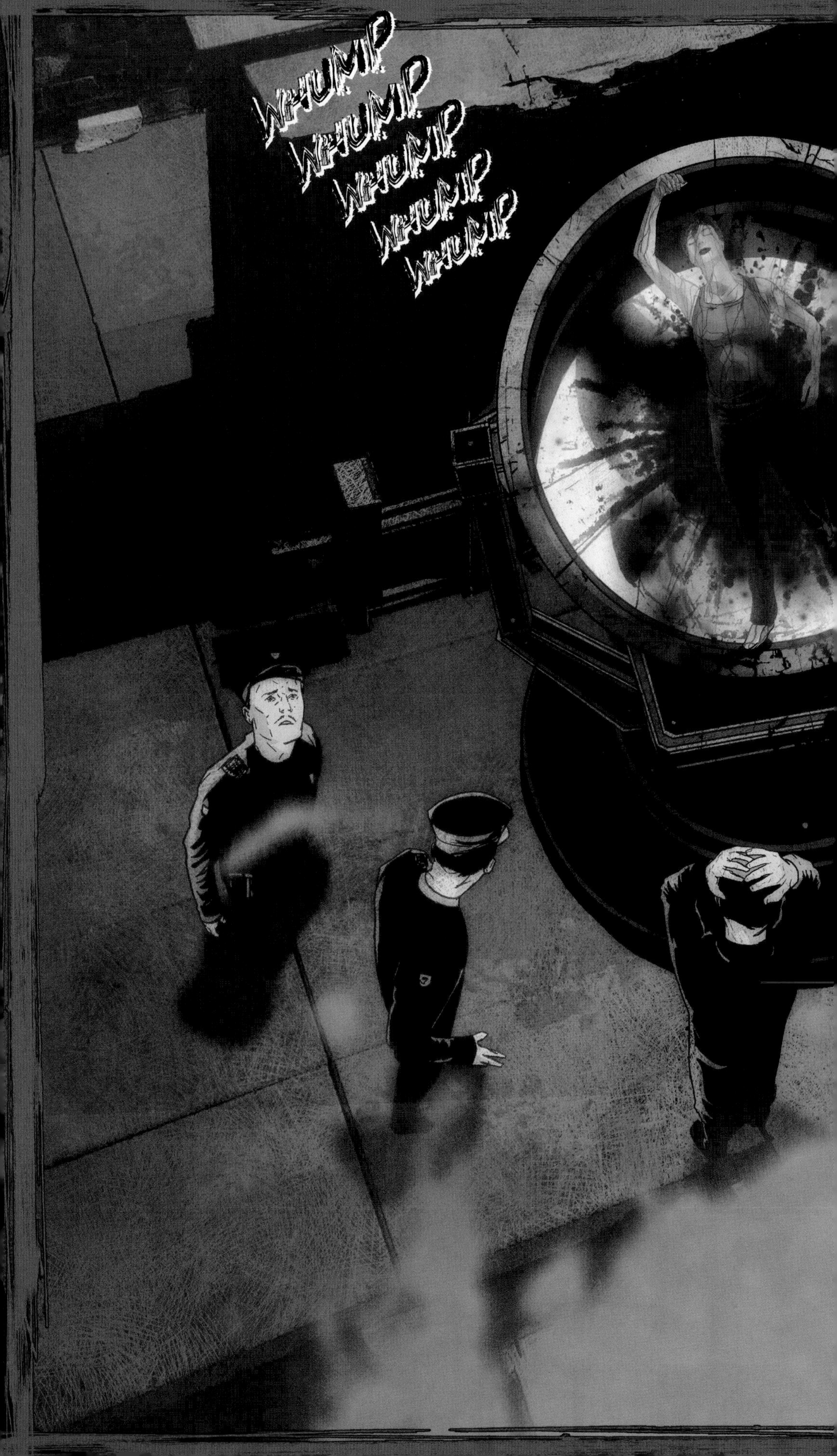
WHUMP
WHUMP
WHUMP
WHUMP
WHUMP
WHUMP

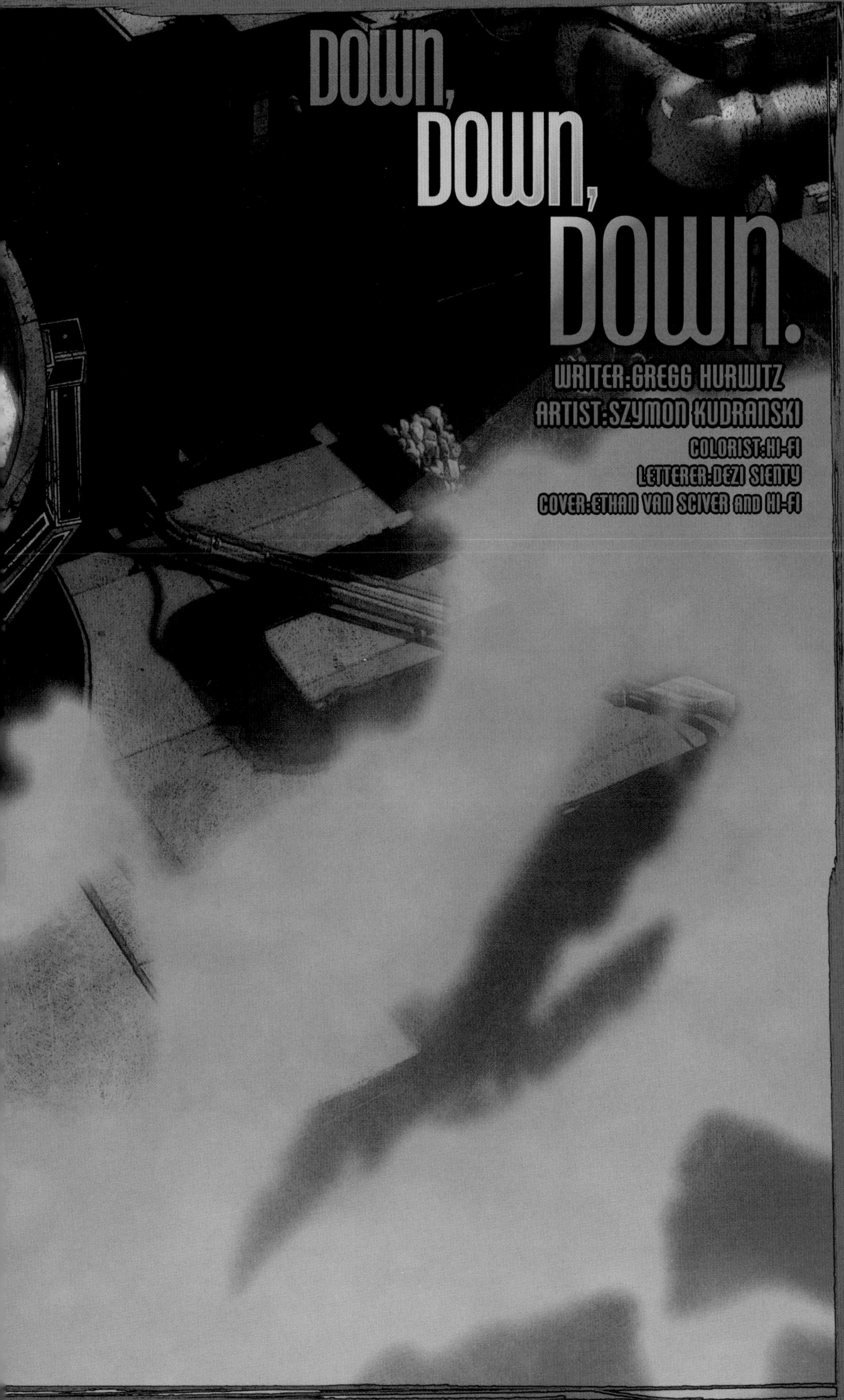
DOWN,
DOWN,
DOWN.
WRITER:GREGG HURWITZ
ARTIST:SZYMON KUDRANSKI
COLORIST:HI-FI
LETTERER:DEZI SIENTY
COVER:ETHAN VAN SCIVER AND HI-FI

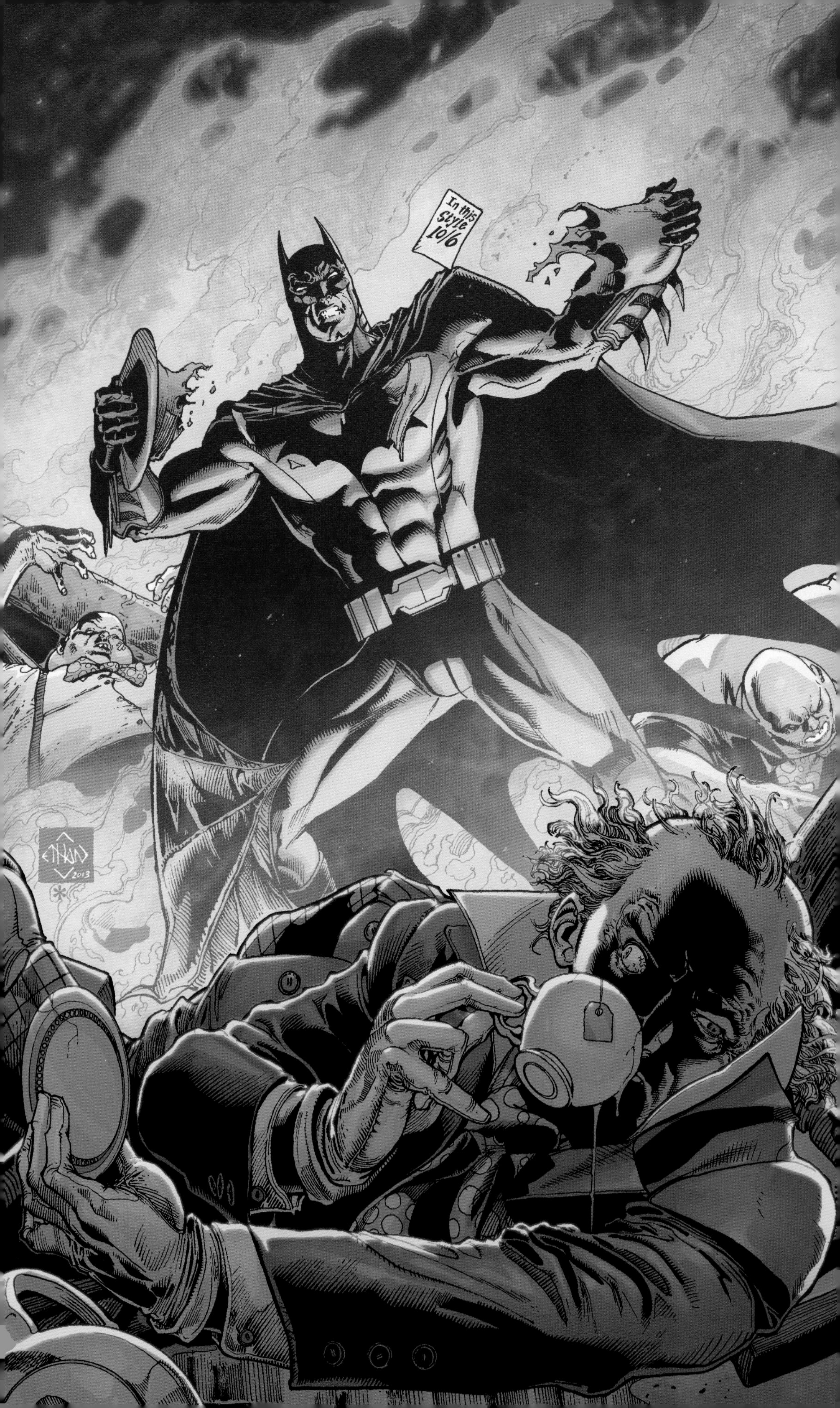
In this Style 10/6

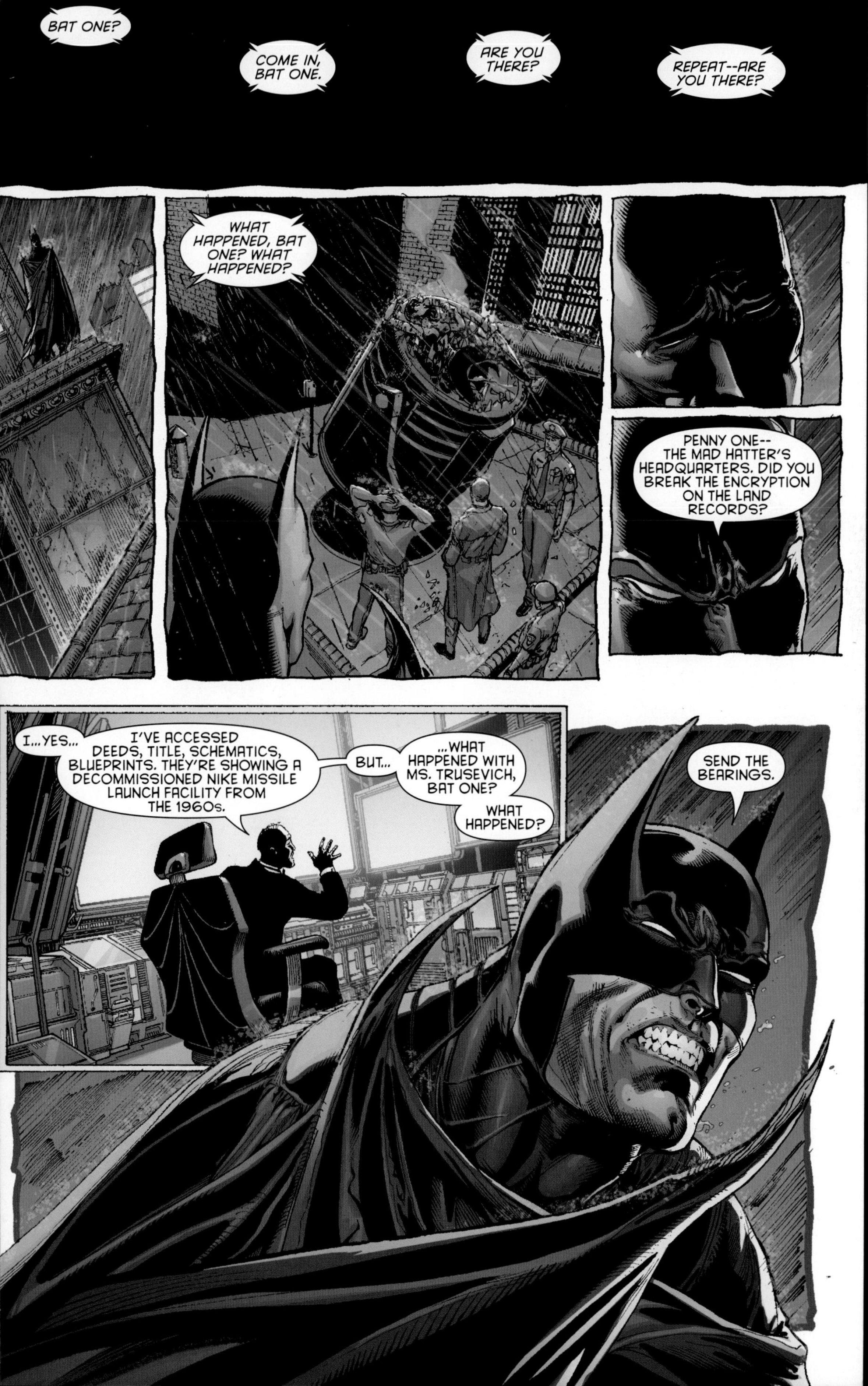
BAT ONE?
COME IN, BAT ONE.
ARE YOU THERE?
REPEAT--ARE YOU THERE?
WHAT HAPPENED, BAT ONE? WHAT HAPPENED?
PENNY ONE-- THE MAD HATTER'S HEADQUARTERS. DID YOU BREAK THE ENCRYPTION ON THE LAND RECORDS?
I...YES...
I'VE ACCESSED DEEDS, TITLE, SCHEMATICS, BLUEPRINTS. THEY'RE SHOWING A DECOMMISSIONED NIKE MISSILE LAUNCH FACILITY FROM THE 1960s.
BUT...
...WHAT HAPPENED WITH MS. TRUSEVICH, BAT ONE?
WHAT HAPPENED?
SEND THE BEARINGS.

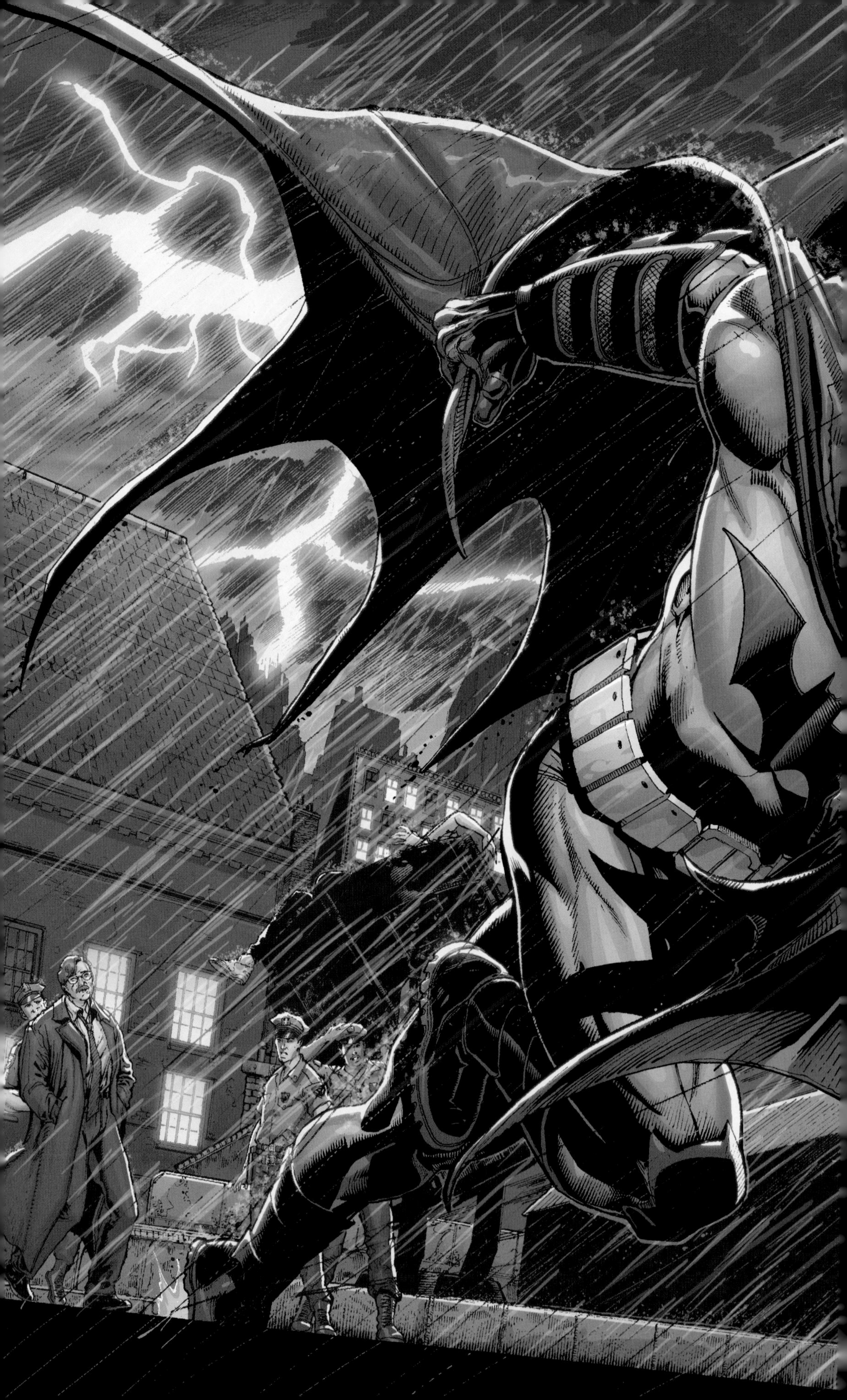

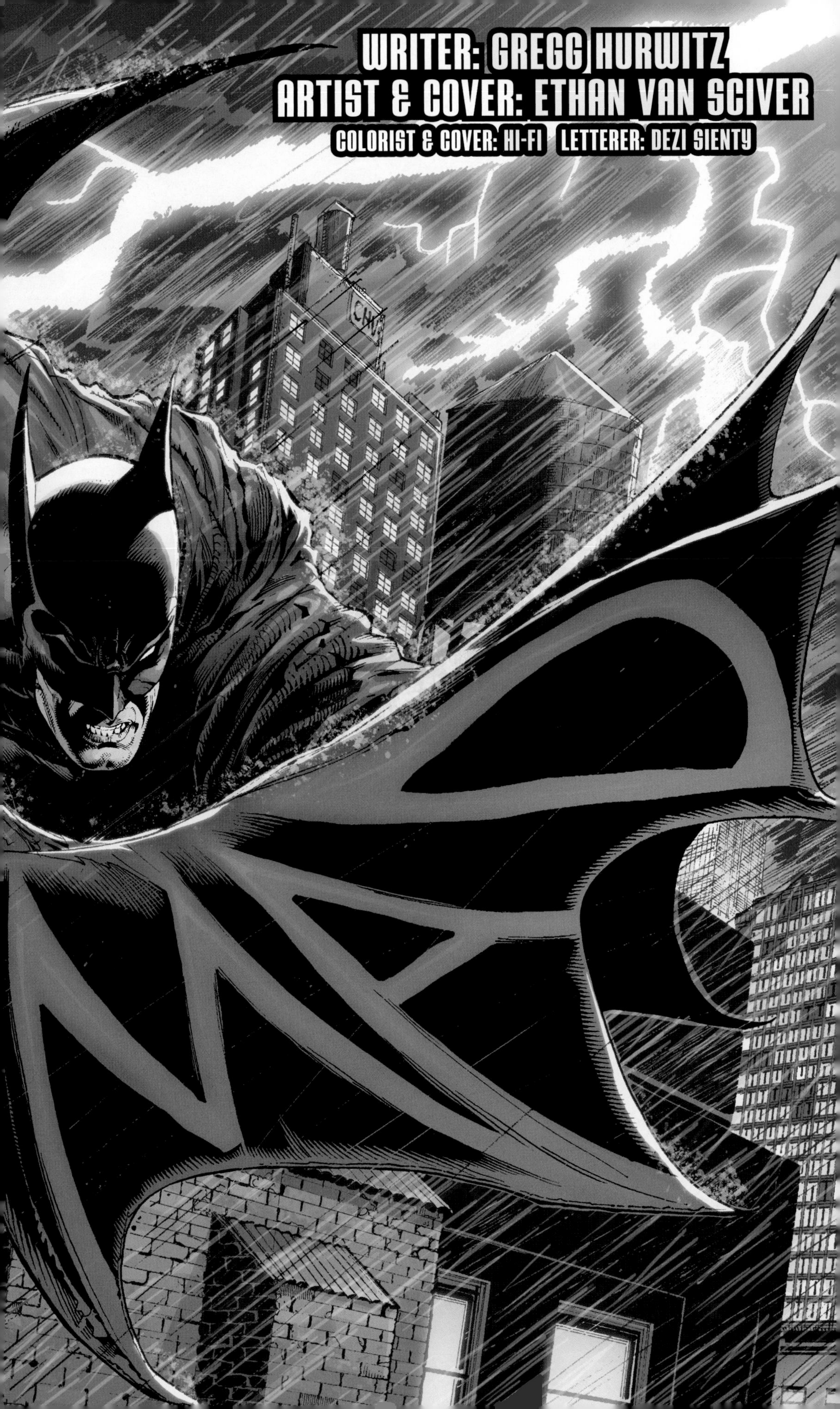
WRITER: GREGG HURWITZ
ARTIST & COVER: ETHAN VAN SCIVER
COLORIST & COVER: HI-FI LETTERER: DEZI SIENTY

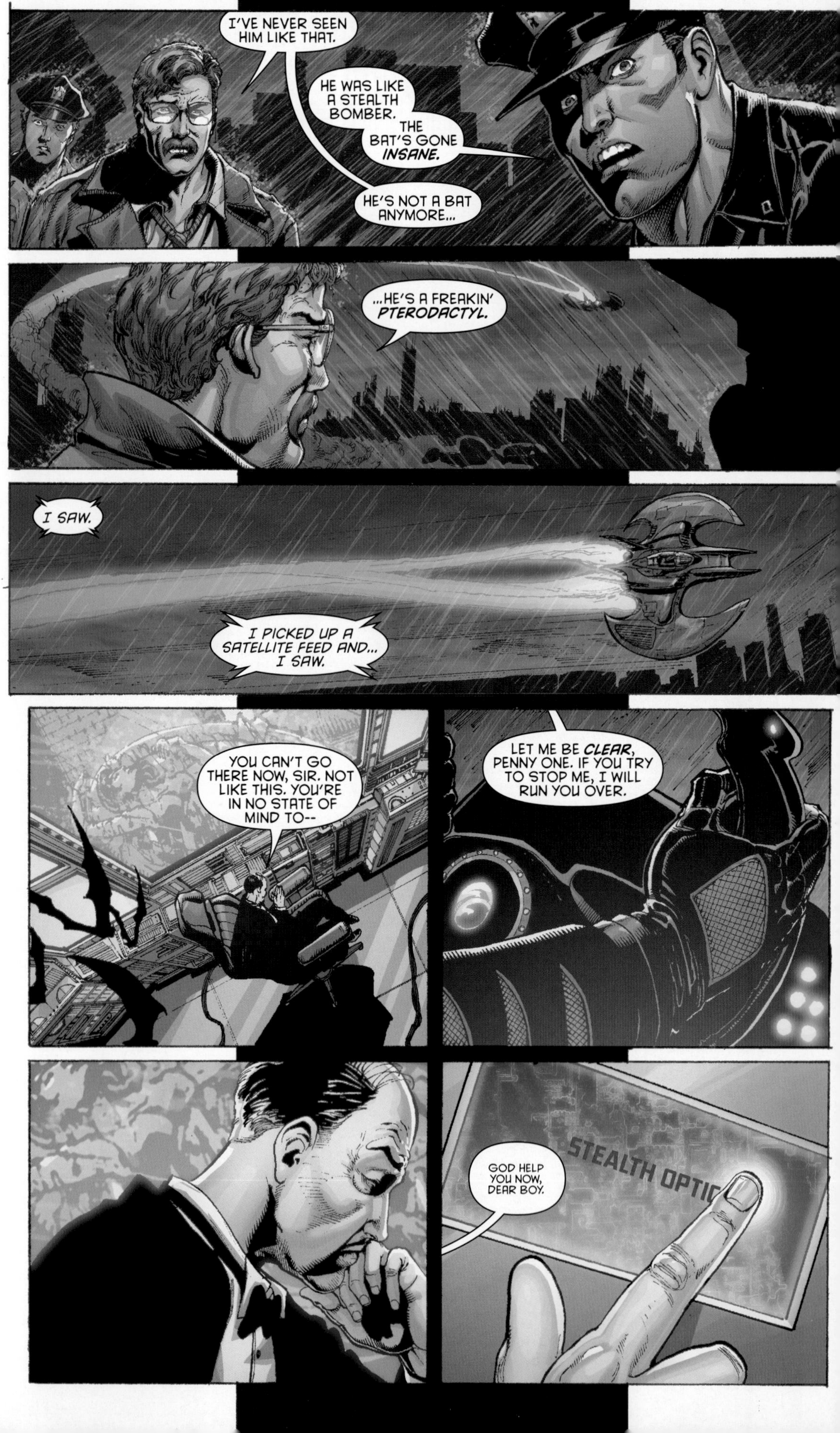
I'VE NEVER SEEN HIM LIKE THAT.
HE WAS LIKE A STEALTH BOMBER.
THE BAT'S GONE *INSANE.*
HE'S NOT A BAT ANYMORE...
...HE'S A FREAKIN' *PTERODACTYL.*
I SAW.
I PICKED UP A SATELLITE FEED AND... I SAW.
YOU CAN'T GO THERE NOW, SIR. NOT LIKE THIS. YOU'RE IN NO STATE OF MIND TO--
LET ME BE *CLEAR*, PENNY ONE. IF YOU TRY TO STOP ME, I WILL RUN YOU OVER.
STEALTH OPTIC
GOD HELP YOU NOW, DEAR BOY.

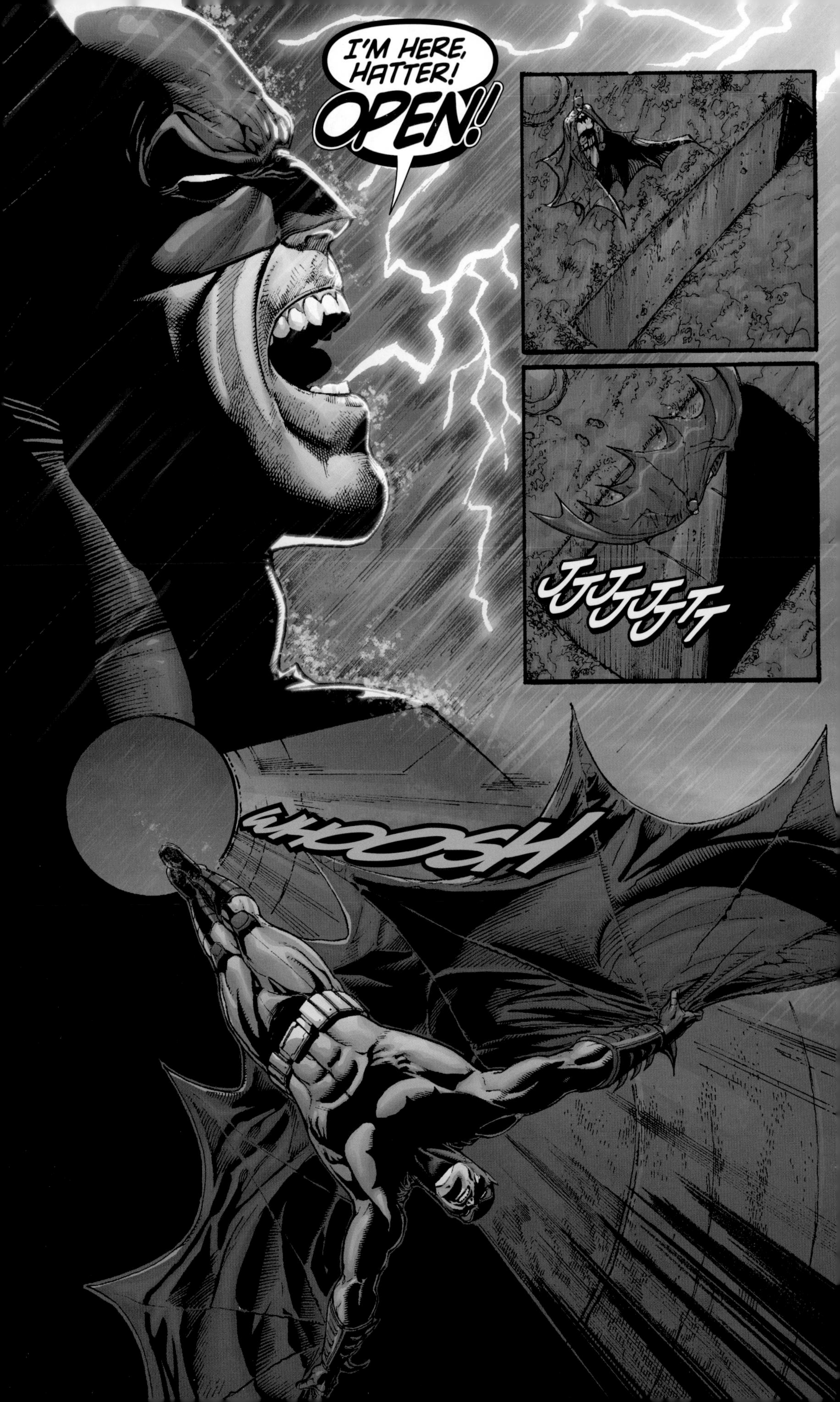

I'M HERE, HATTER! OPEN!
JJJJJJJTT
WHOOSH

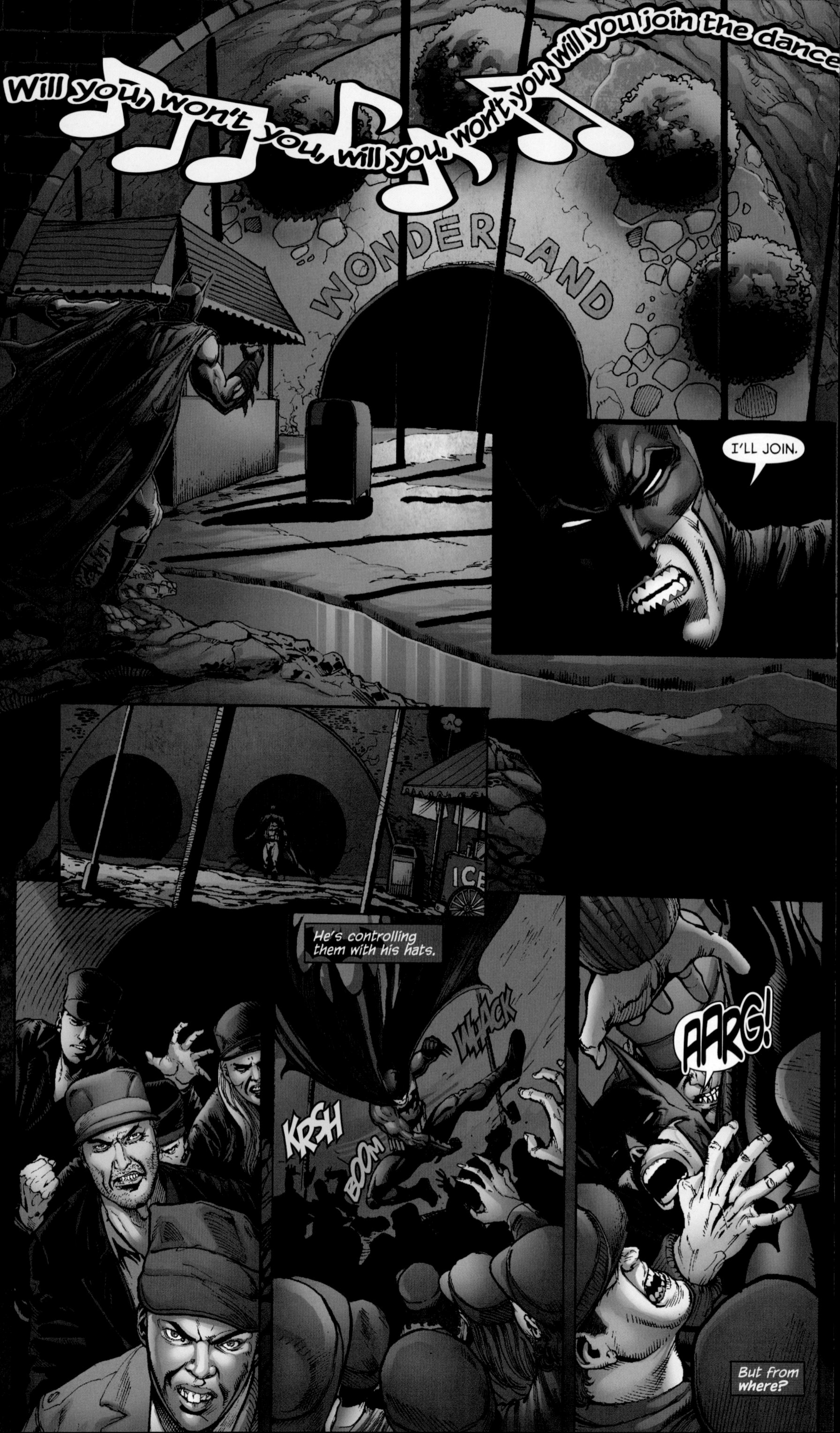
Will you, won't you, will you, won't you, will you join the dance
WONDERLAND
I'LL JOIN.
ICE
He's controlling them with his hats.
WHACK
KRSH
BOOM
AARG!
But from where?

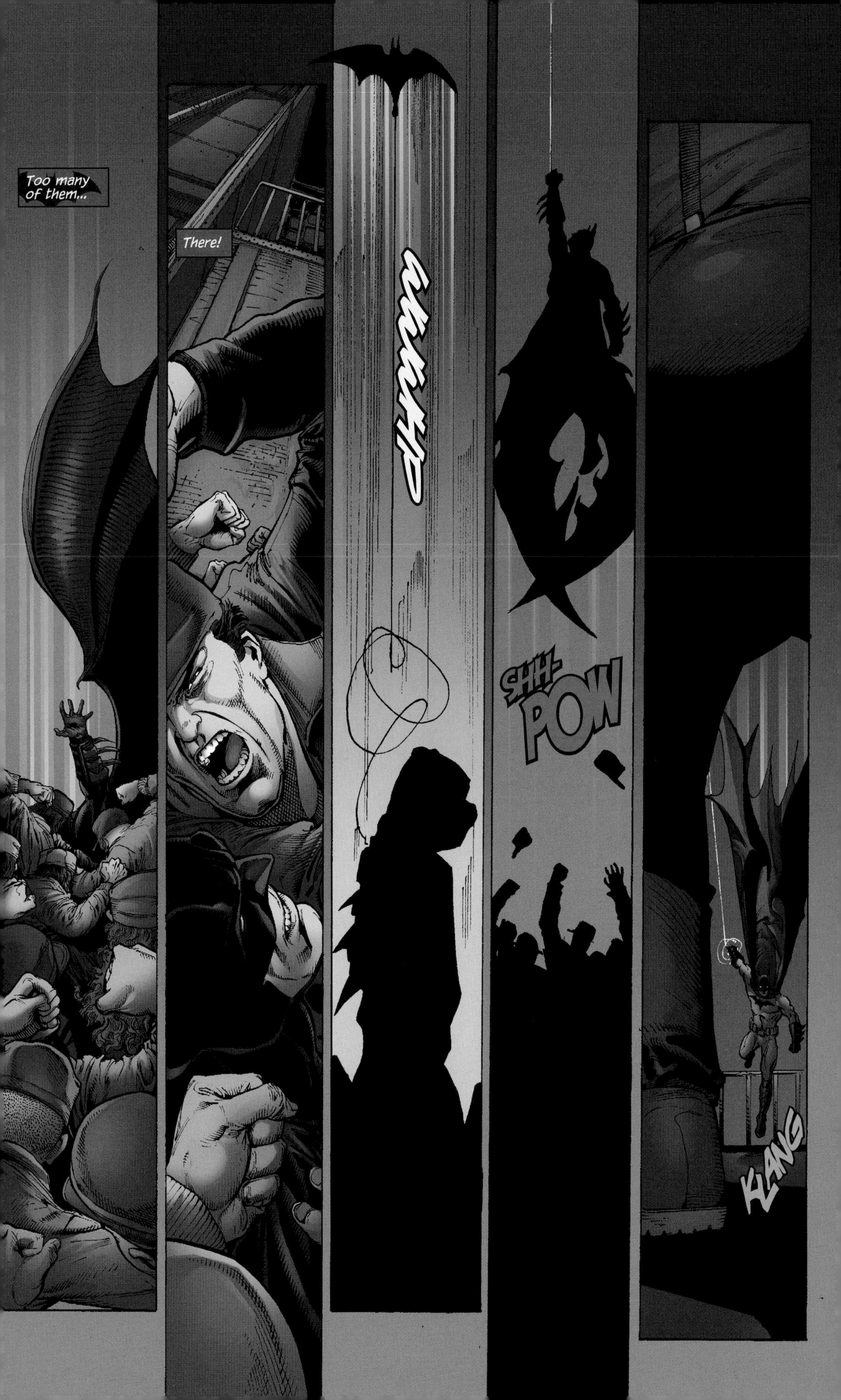

Too many of them...
There!
WHUMP
SHH-POW
KLANG

LISTEN, BATMAN, I ONLY--

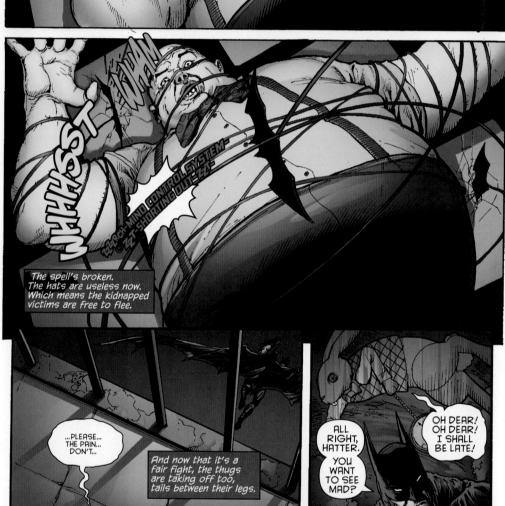

WHHHSST

WHAM

TETCH MIND CONTROL SYSTEM-- --ZZT-SHORTING OUT-ZZT

The spell's broken. The hats are useless now. Which means the kidnapped victims are free to flee.

...PLEASE... THE PAIN... DON'T...

And now that it's a fair fight, the thugs are taking off too, tails between their legs.

ALL RIGHT, HATTER. YOU WANT TO SEE MAD?

OH DEAR! OH DEAR! I SHALL BE LATE!

Which means it's down to me...

...and him.

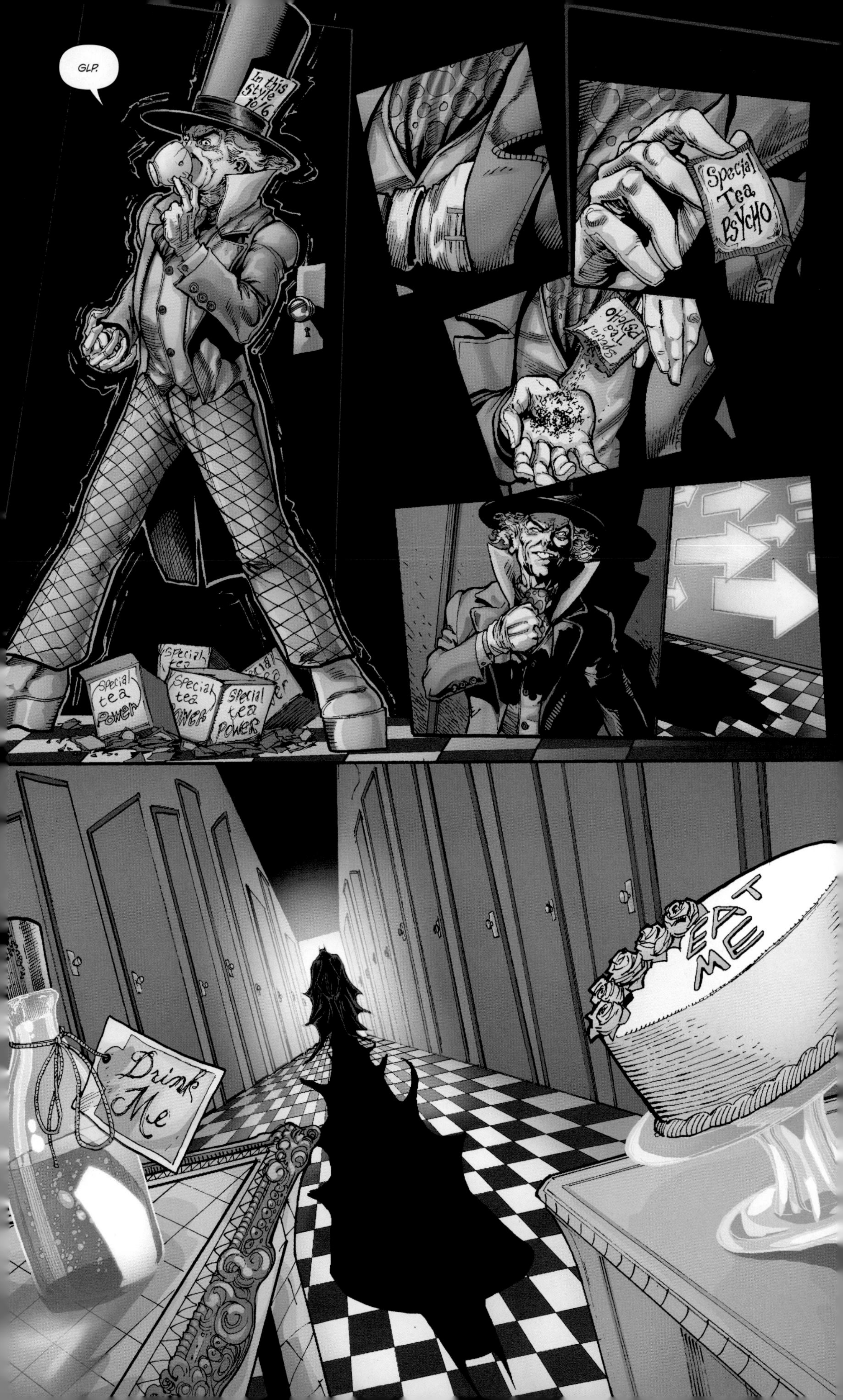
GLP.
In this Style 10/6
Special Tea PSYCHO
Special tea POWER
Special tea POWER
Special tea POWER
Drink Me
EAT ME

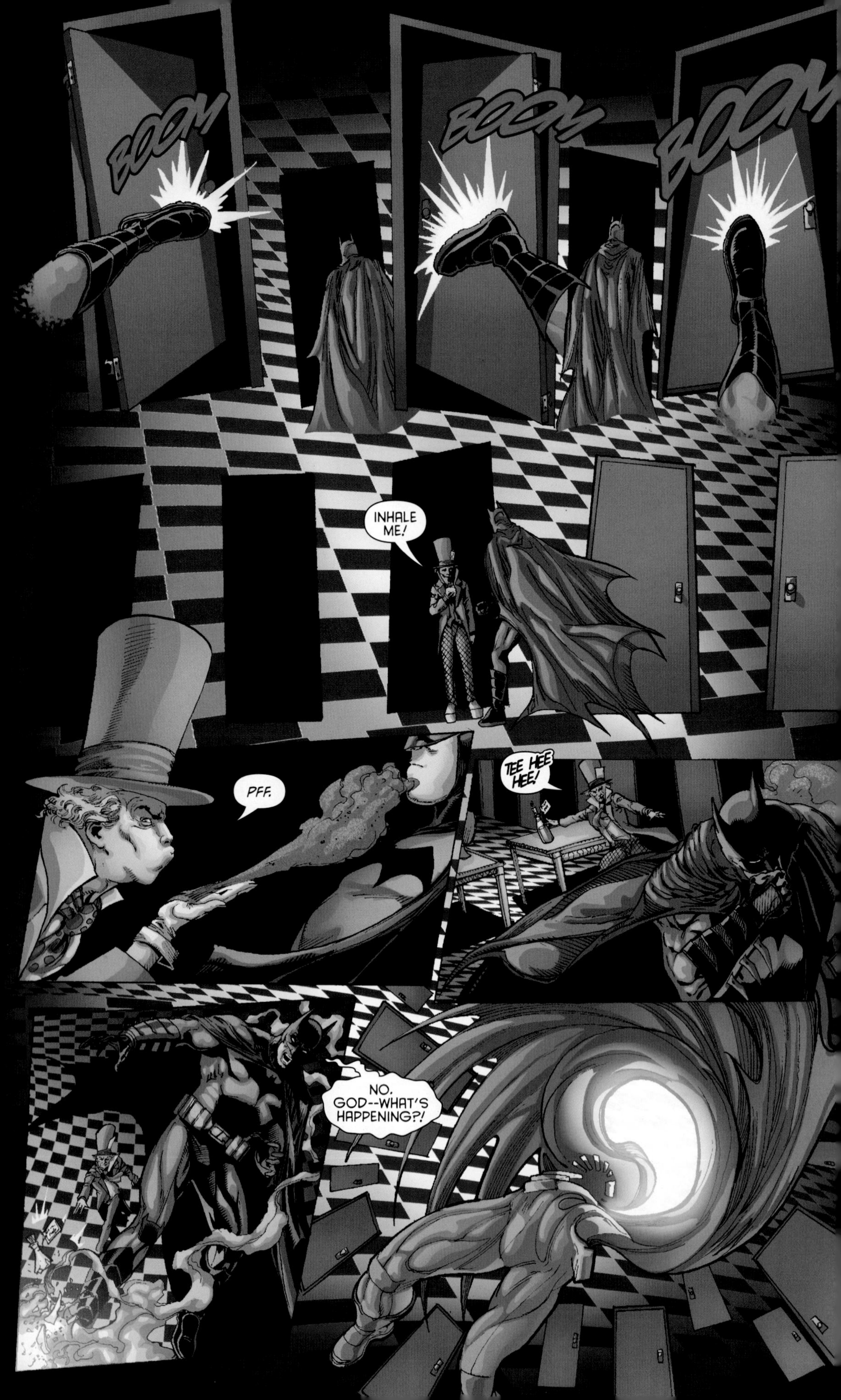
BOOM
BOOM
BOOM
INHALE ME!
PFF.
TEE HEE HEE!
NO. GOD--WHAT'S HAPPENING?!

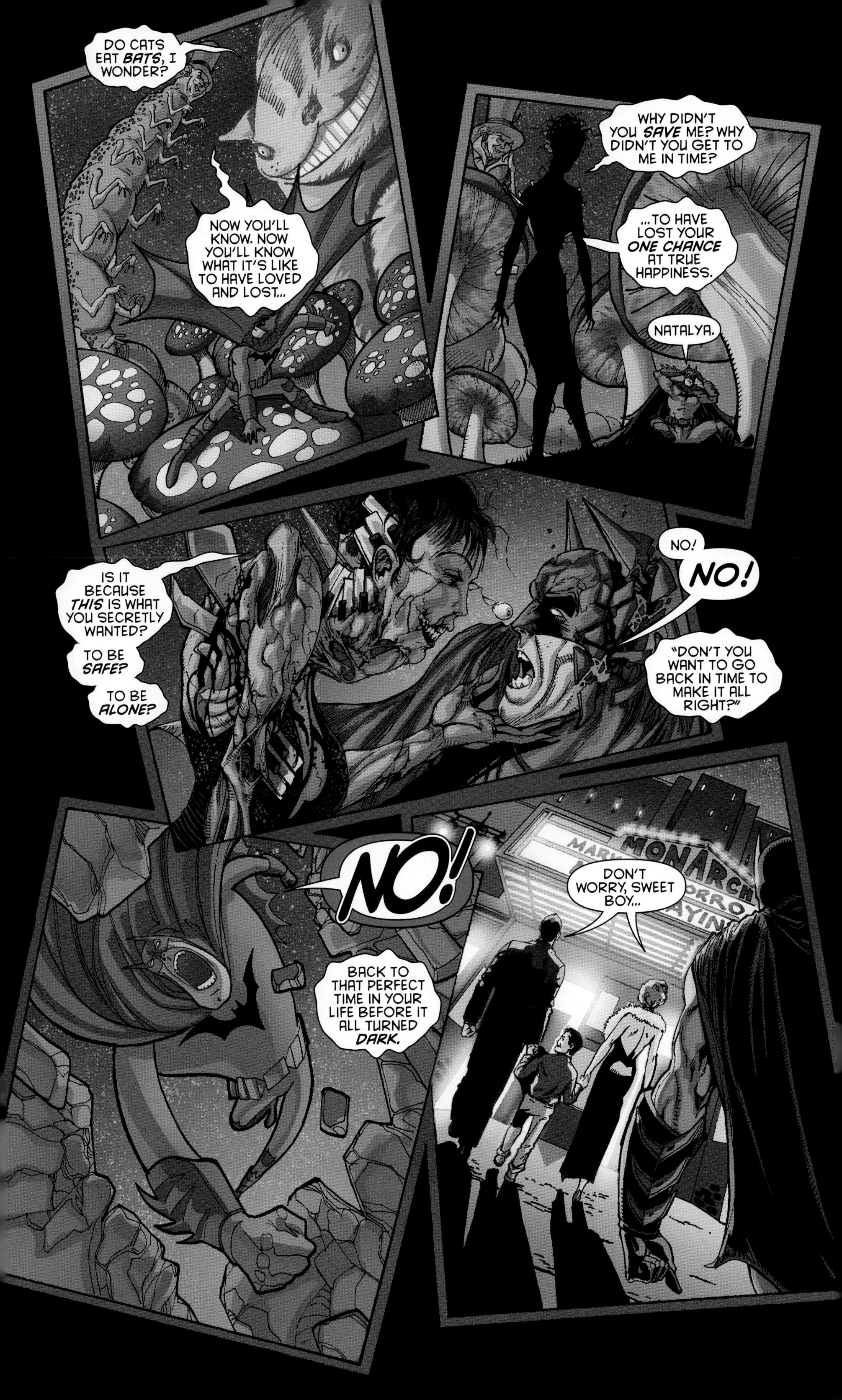
DO CATS EAT BATS, I WONDER?
NOW YOU'LL KNOW. NOW YOU'LL KNOW WHAT IT'S LIKE TO HAVE LOVED AND LOST...
WHY DIDN'T YOU SAVE ME? WHY DIDN'T YOU GET TO ME IN TIME?
...TO HAVE LOST YOUR ONE CHANCE AT TRUE HAPPINESS.
NATALYA.
IS IT BECAUSE THIS IS WHAT YOU SECRETLY WANTED?
TO BE SAFE?
TO BE ALONE?
NO!
NO!
"DON'T YOU WANT TO GO BACK IN TIME TO MAKE IT ALL RIGHT?"
NO!
BACK TO THAT PERFECT TIME IN YOUR LIFE BEFORE IT ALL TURNED DARK.
MONARCH
DON'T WORRY, SWEET BOY...

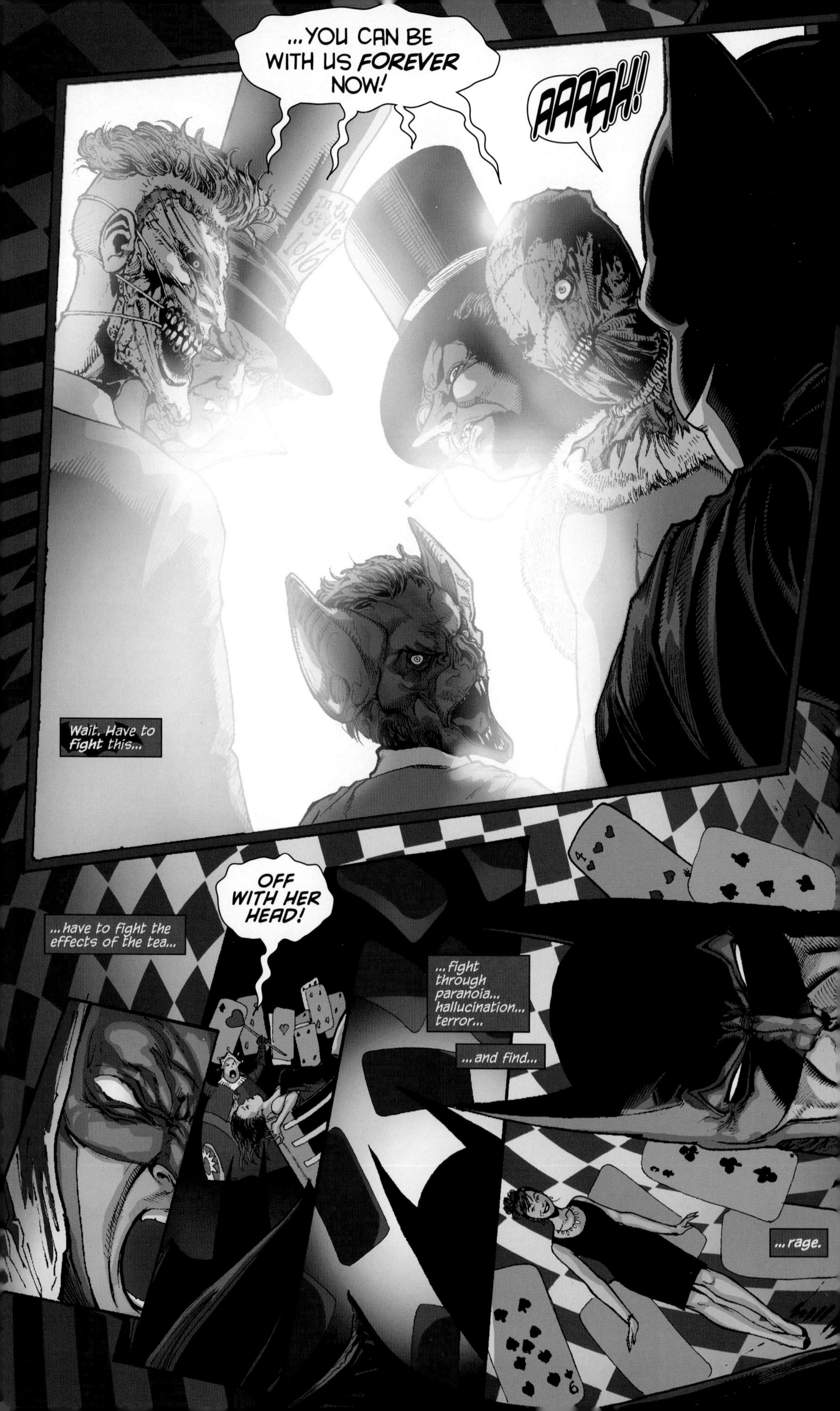
...YOU CAN BE WITH US FOREVER NOW!
AAAAH!
In the style 10/6
Wait. Have to fight this...
...have to fight the effects of the tea...
OFF WITH HER HEAD!
...fight through paranoia... hallucination... terror...
...and find...
...rage.

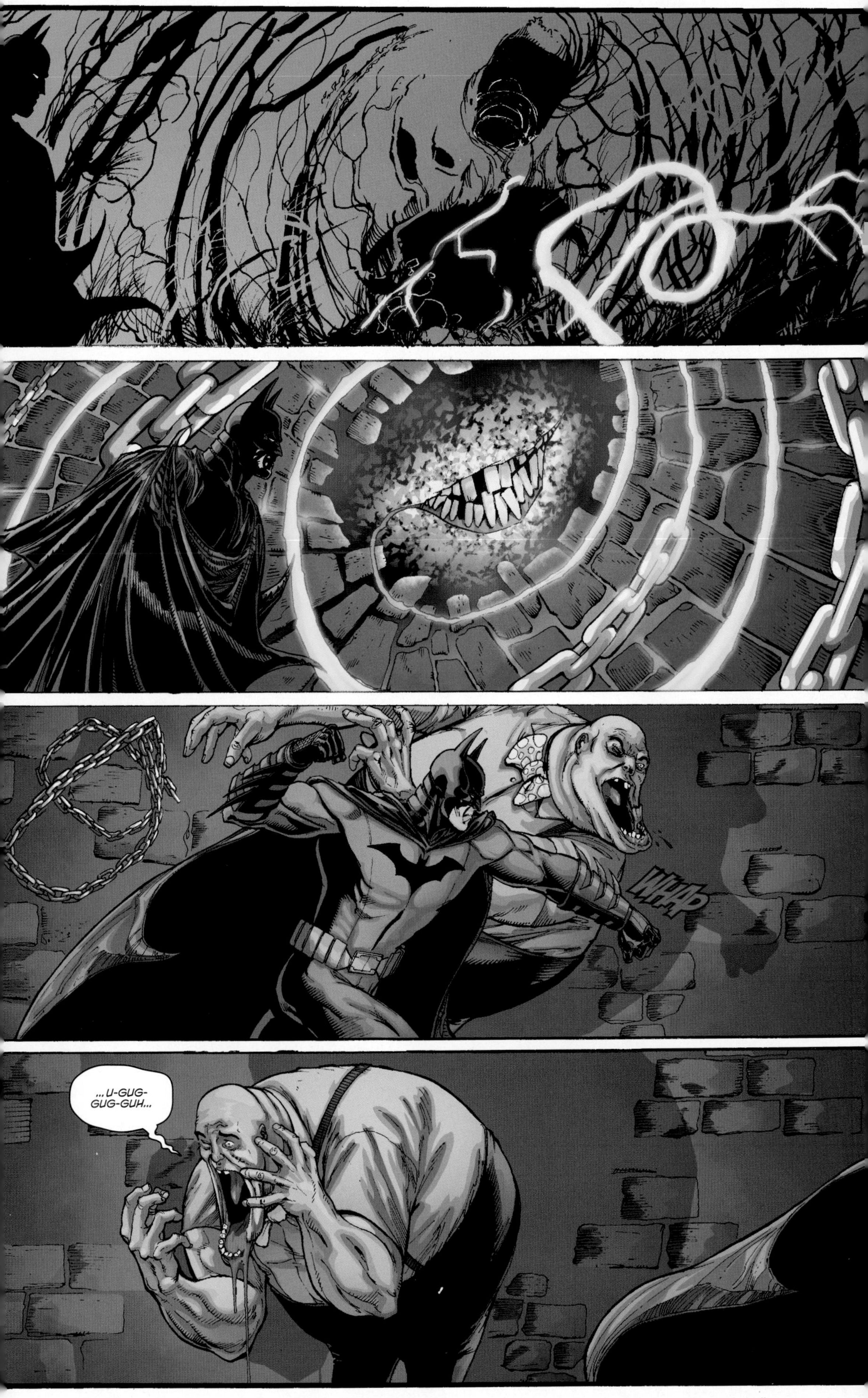
WHAP
...U-GUG-
GUG-GUH...

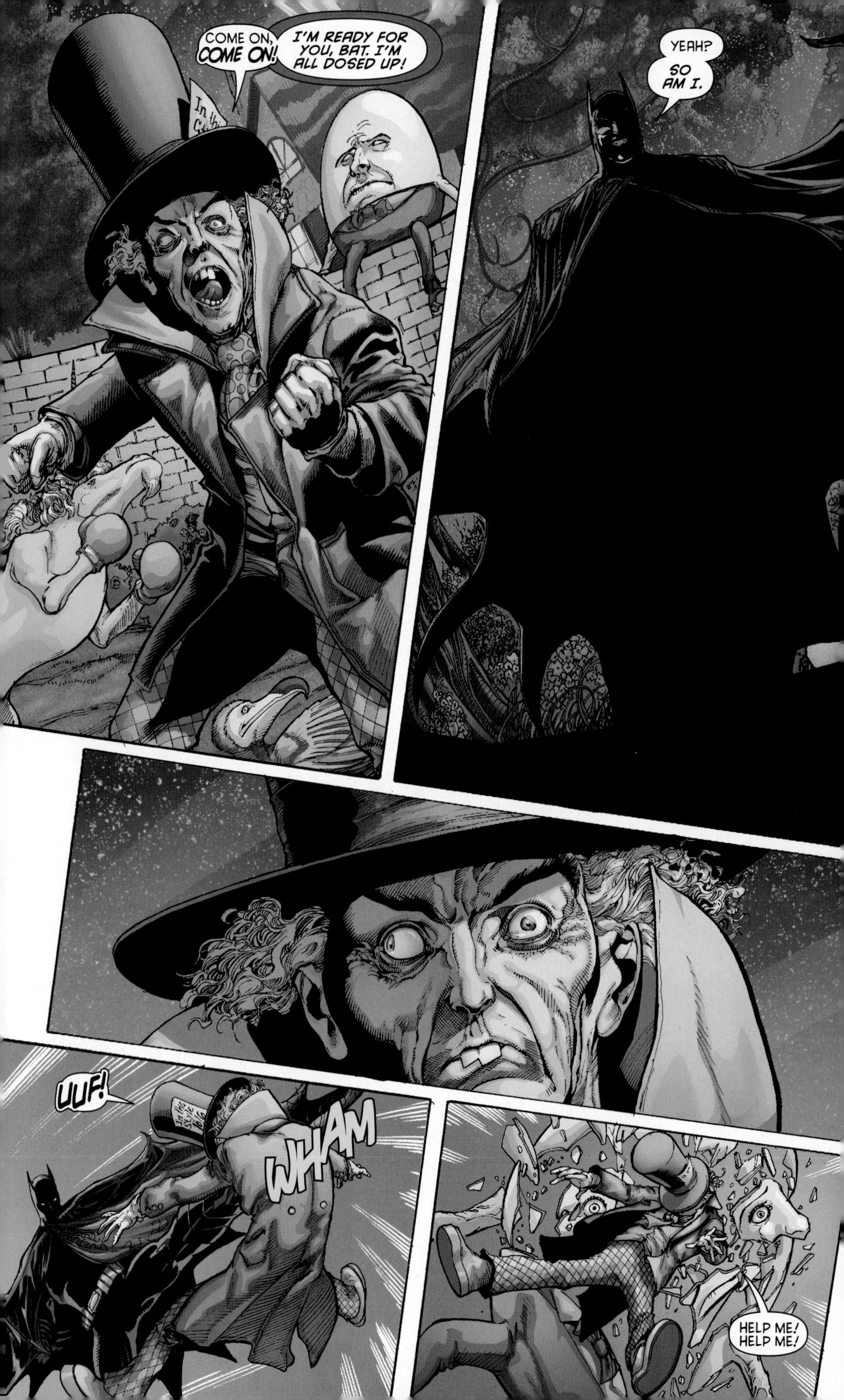
COME ON, COME ON!
I'M READY FOR YOU, BAT. I'M ALL DOSED UP!
YEAH?
SO AM I.
UUF!
WHAM
HELP ME! HELP ME!

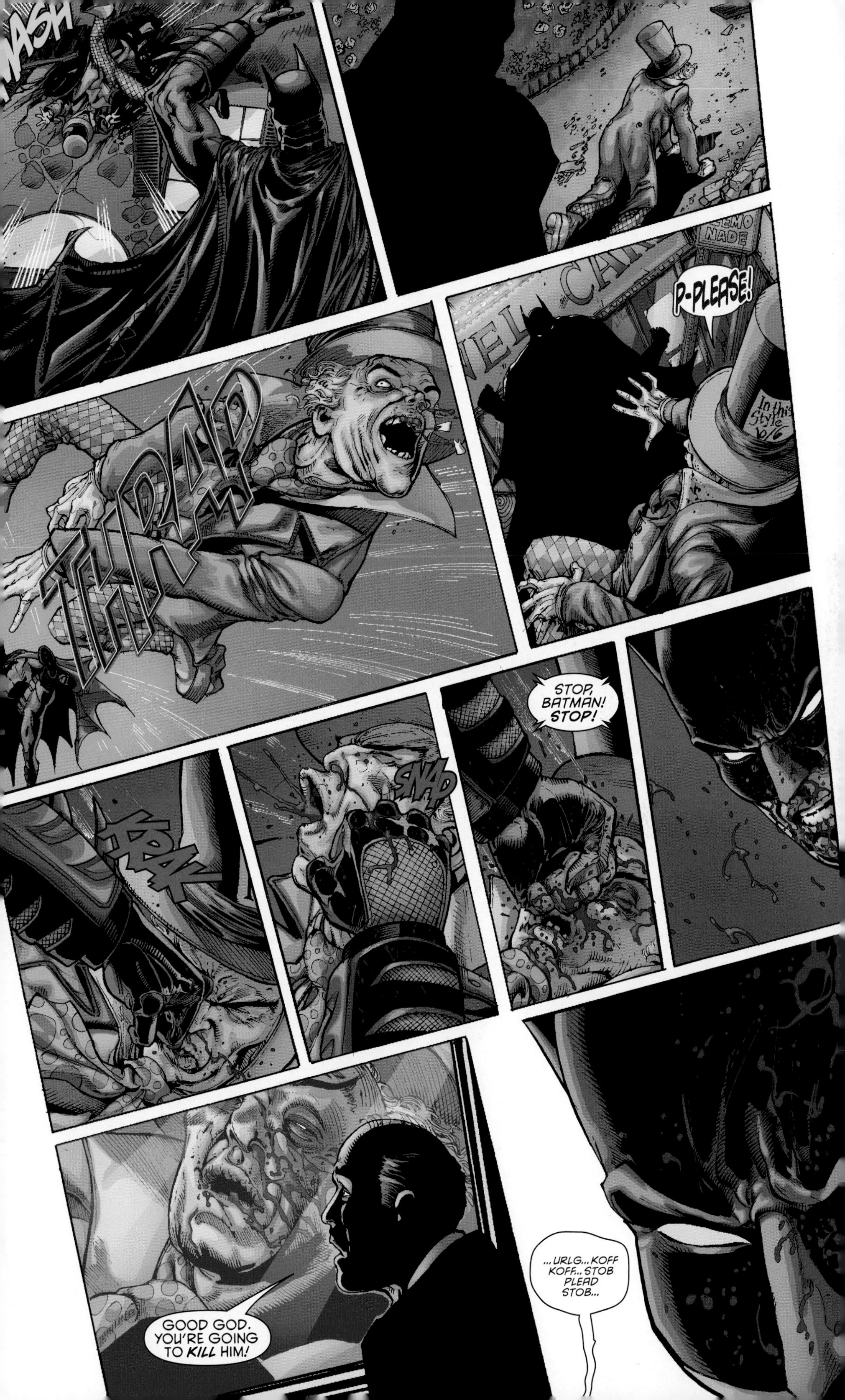

ASH
P-PLEASE!
THRAP
STOP, BATMAN! STOP!
KRAK
SNAP
GOOD GOD. YOU'RE GOING TO KILL HIM!
...URLG... KOFF KOFF... STOB PLEAD STOB...

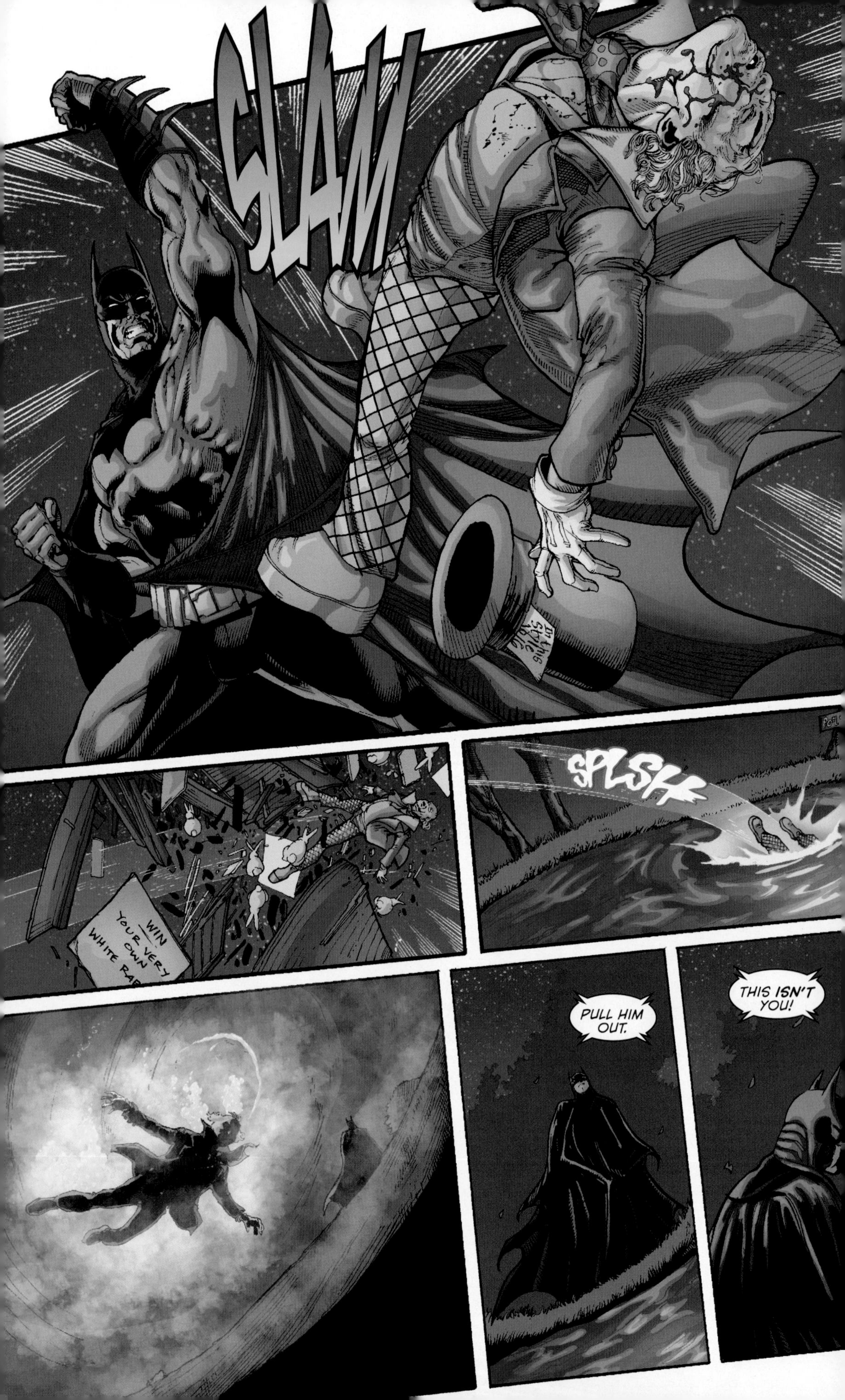
SLAM
WIN YOUR VERY OWN WHITE RAB
SPLSH
PULL HIM OUT.
THIS ISN'T YOU!

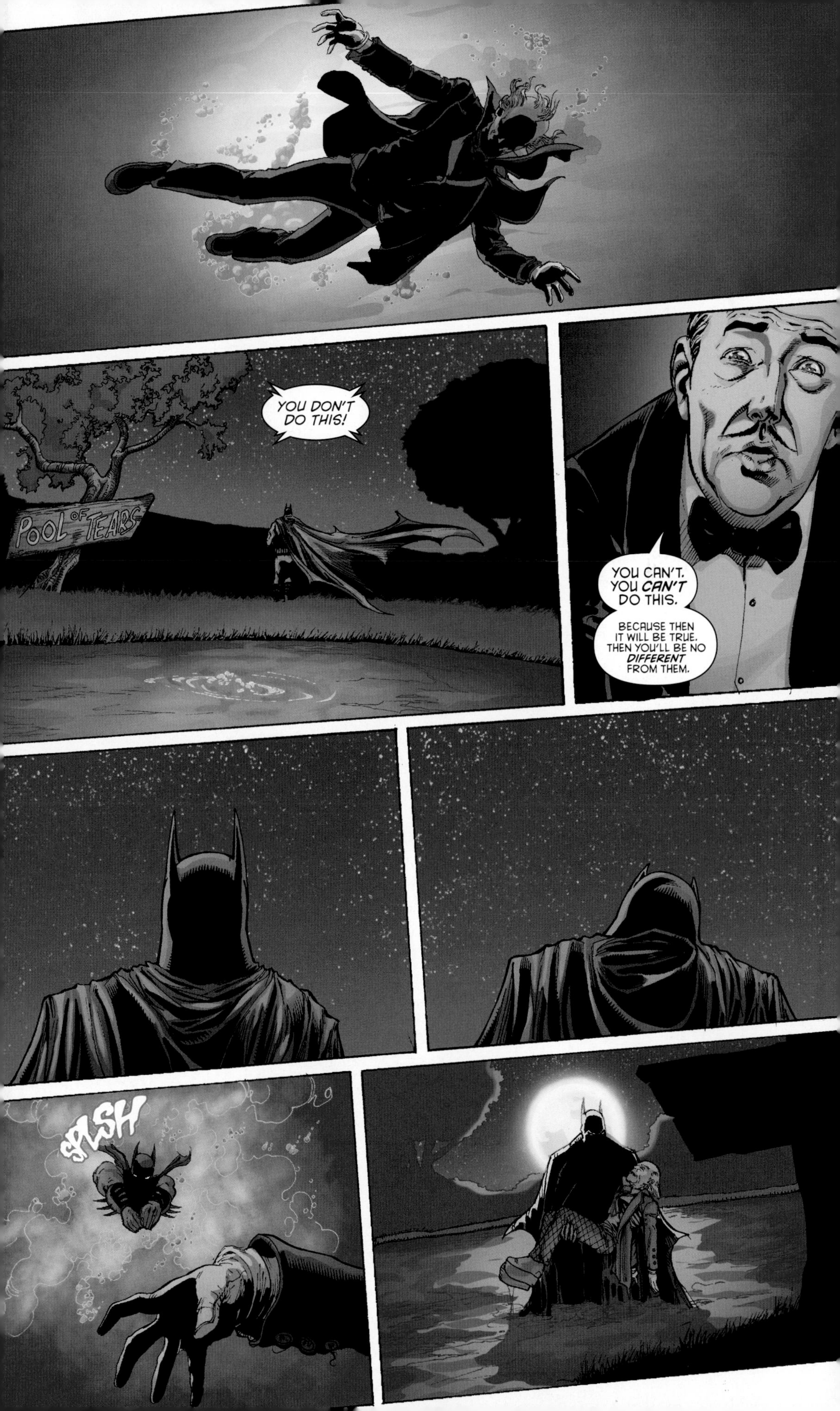
YOU DON'T DO THIS!
POOL OF TEARS
YOU CAN'T. YOU CAN'T DO THIS.
BECAUSE THEN IT WILL BE TRUE. THEN YOU'LL BE NO DIFFERENT FROM THEM.
SPLSH

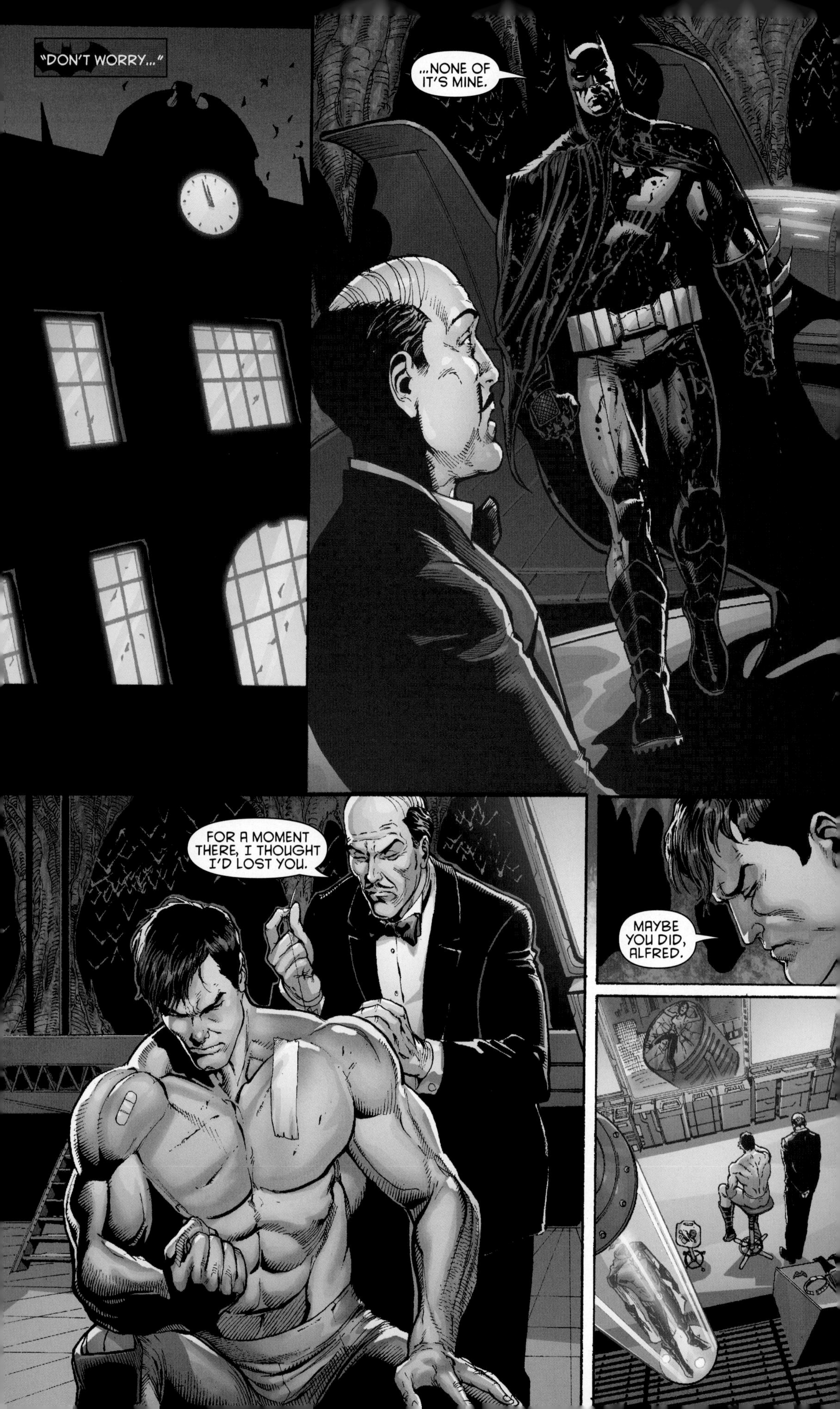
"DON'T WORRY..."
...NONE OF IT'S MINE.
FOR A MOMENT THERE, I THOUGHT I'D LOST YOU.
MAYBE YOU DID, ALFRED.

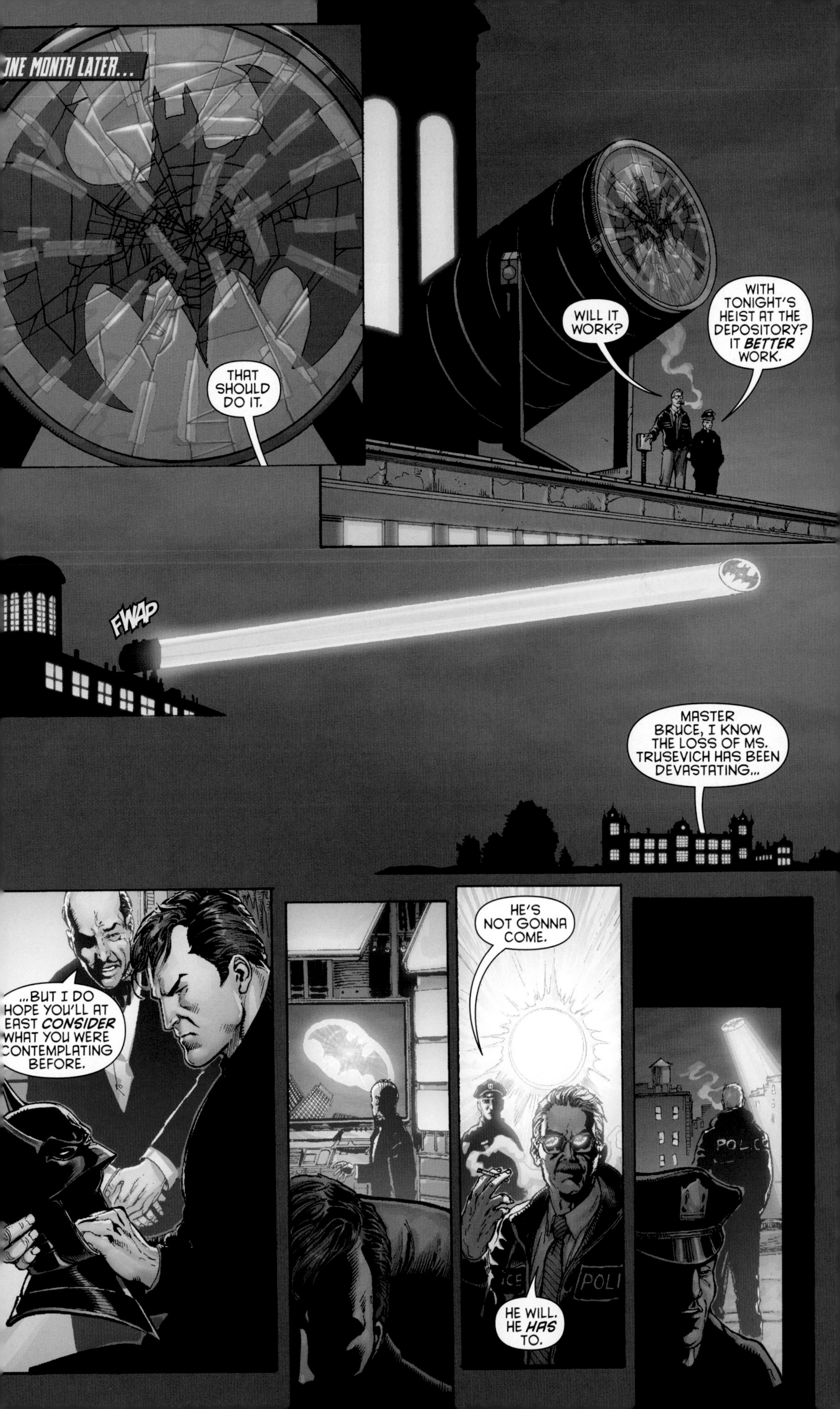

ONE MONTH LATER...
THAT SHOULD DO IT.
WILL IT WORK?
WITH TONIGHT'S HEIST AT THE DEPOSITORY? IT BETTER WORK.
FWAP
MASTER BRUCE, I KNOW THE LOSS OF MS. TRUSEVICH HAS BEEN DEVASTATING...
...BUT I DO HOPE YOU'LL AT LEAST CONSIDER WHAT YOU WERE CONTEMPLATING BEFORE.
HE'S NOT GONNA COME.
HE WILL. HE HAS TO.

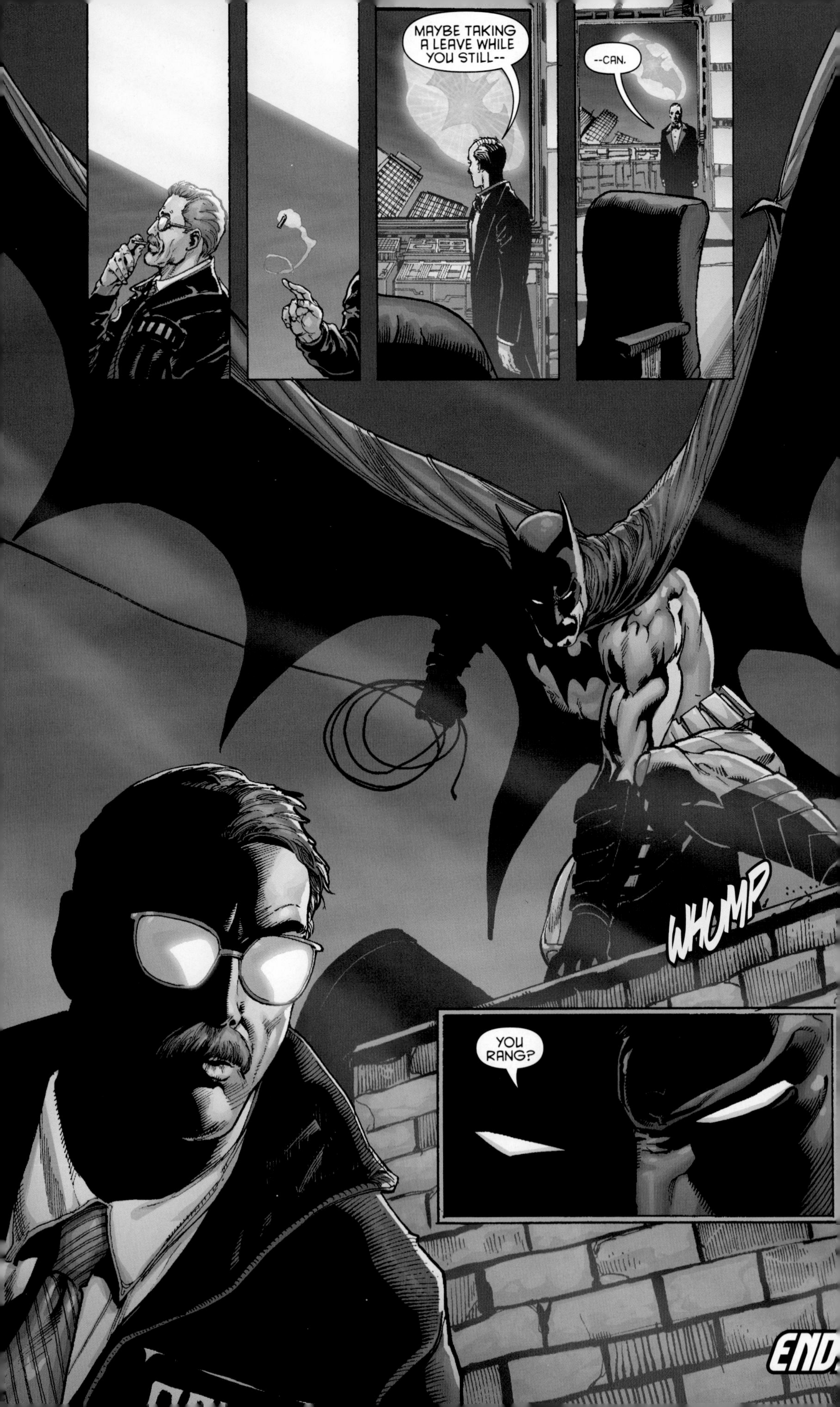

MAYBE TAKING A LEAVE WHILE YOU STILL--
--CAN.
WHUMP
YOU RANG?
END.

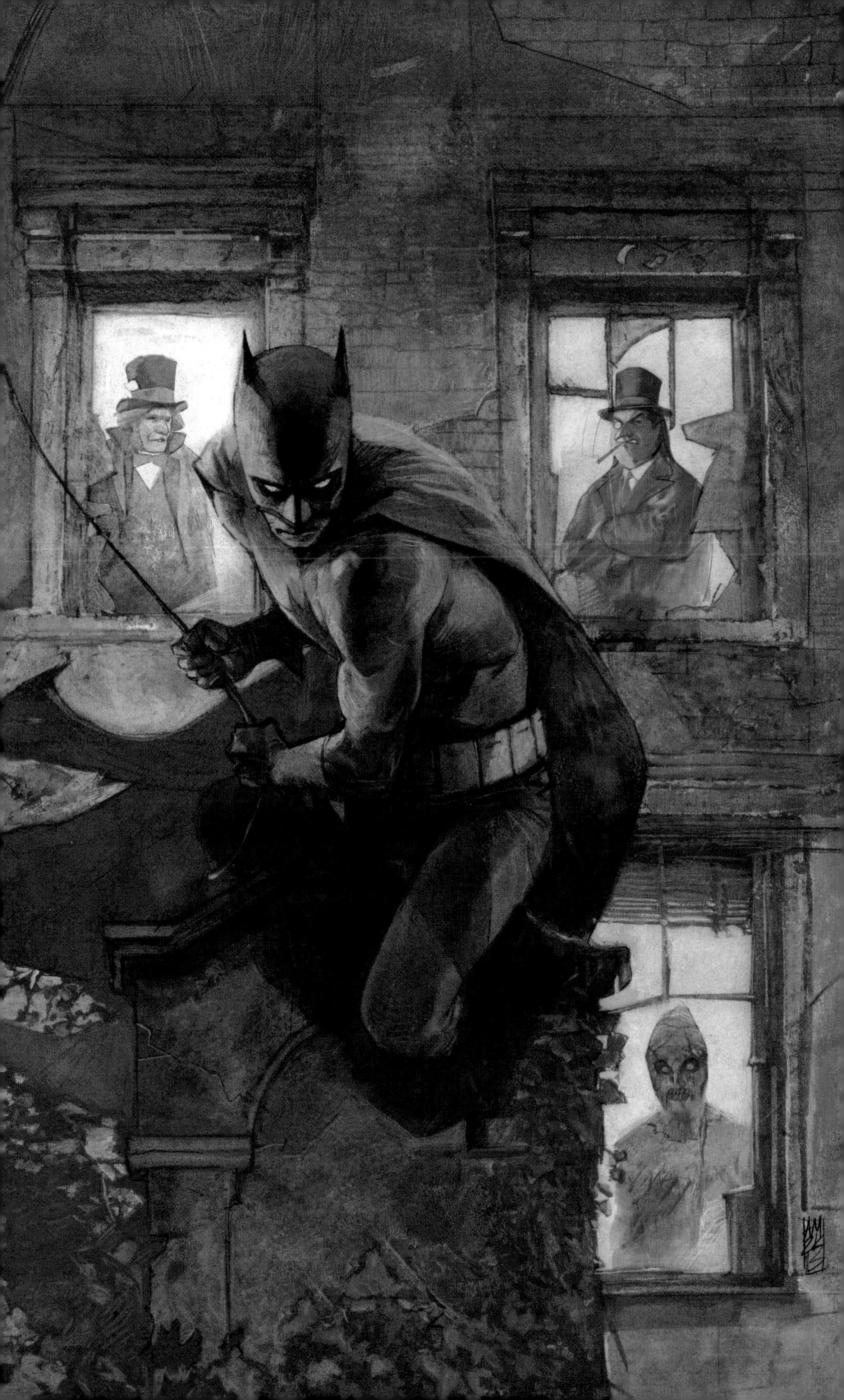

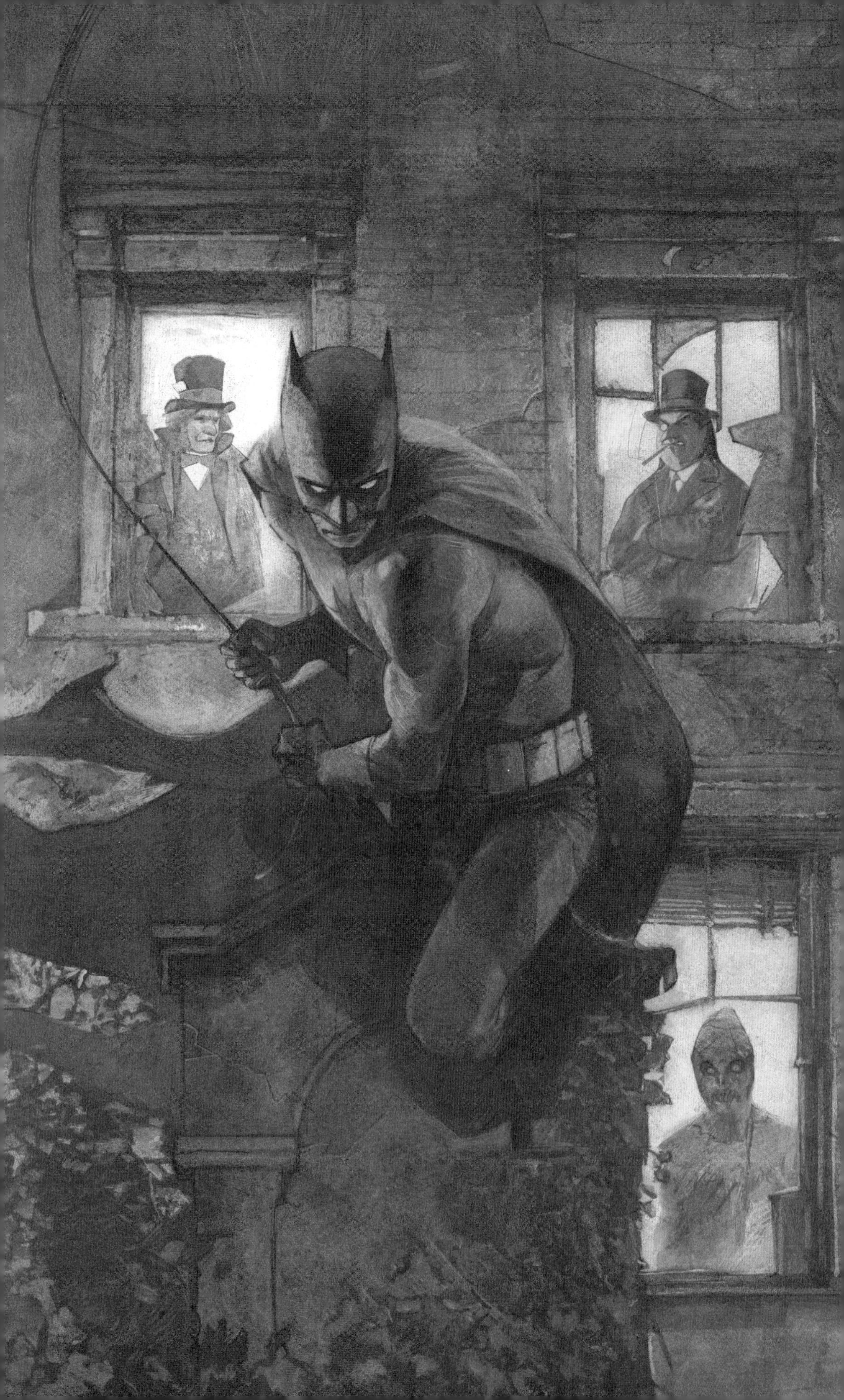

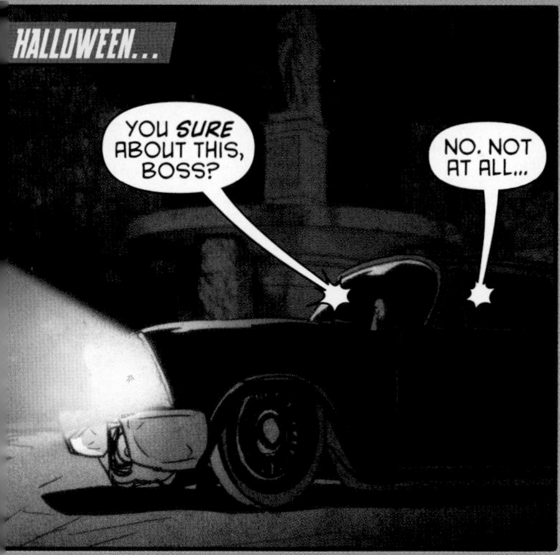
HALLOWEEN...
YOU SURE ABOUT THIS, BOSS?
NO. NOT AT ALL...

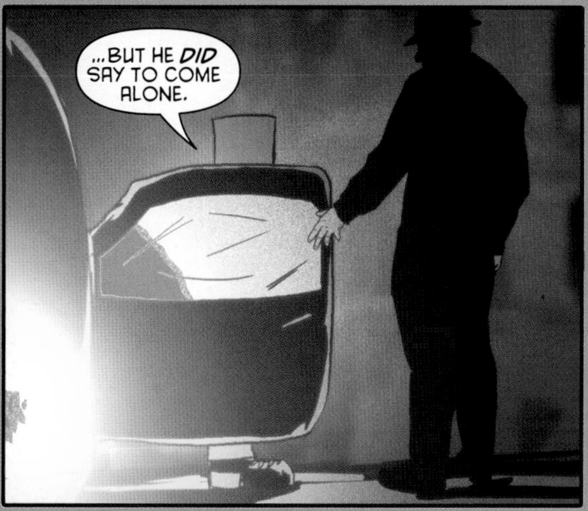
...BUT HE DID SAY TO COME ALONE.

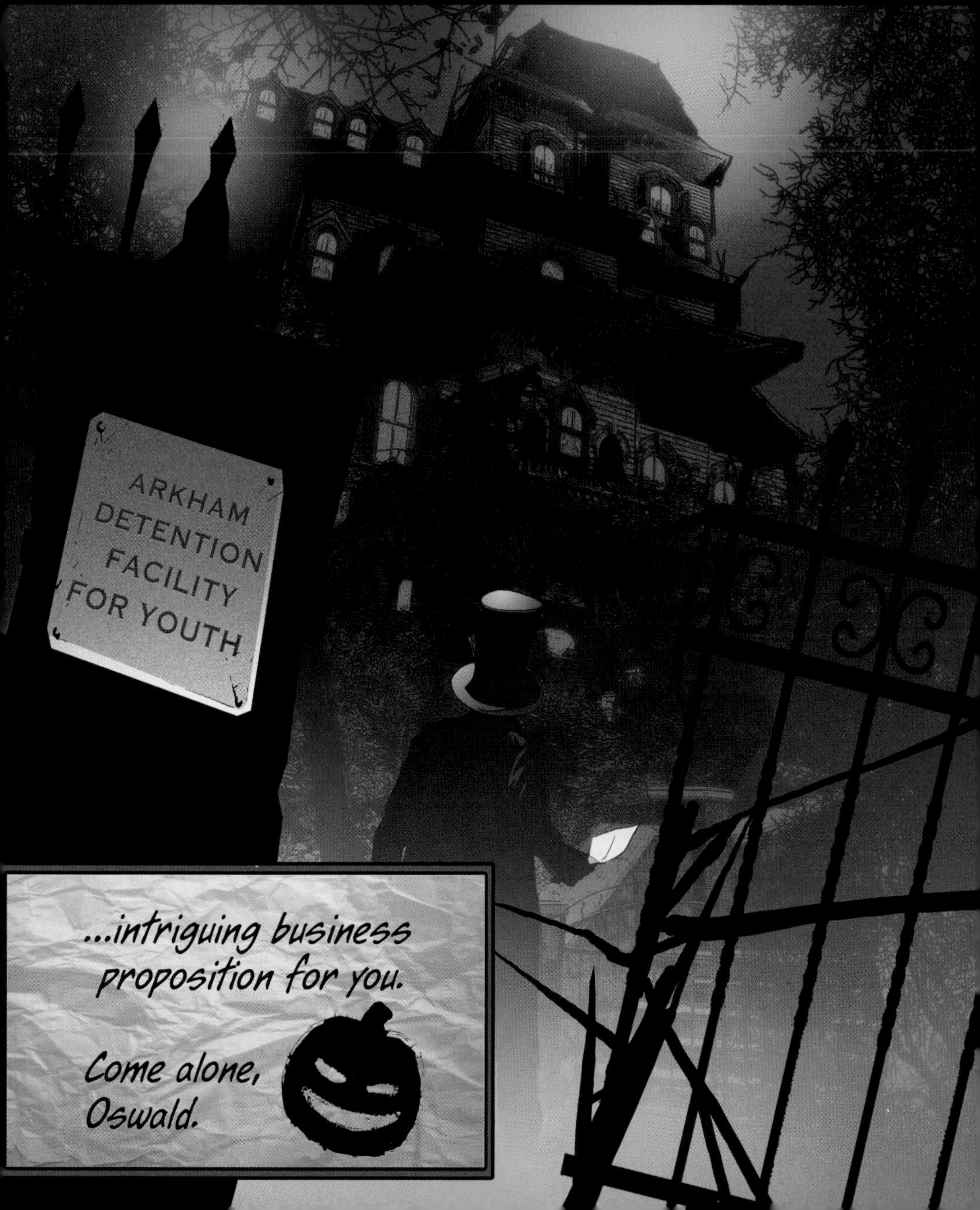
ARKHAM DETENTION FACILITY FOR YOUTH
...intriguing business proposition for you.
Come alone, Oswald.

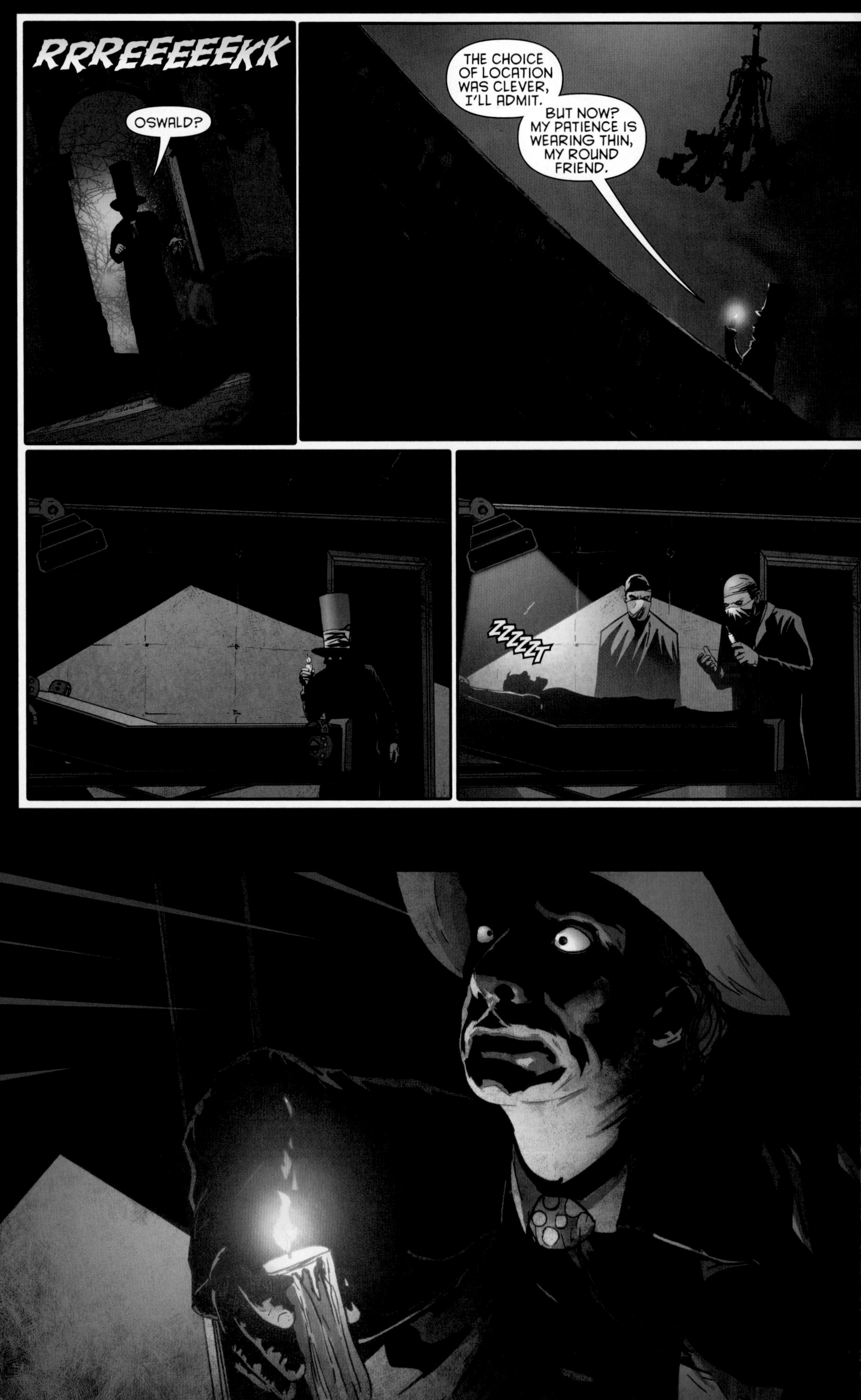
RRREEEEEEKK
OSWALD?
THE CHOICE OF LOCATION WAS CLEVER, I'LL ADMIT.
BUT NOW? MY PATIENCE IS WEARING THIN, MY ROUND FRIEND.
ZZZZZZT

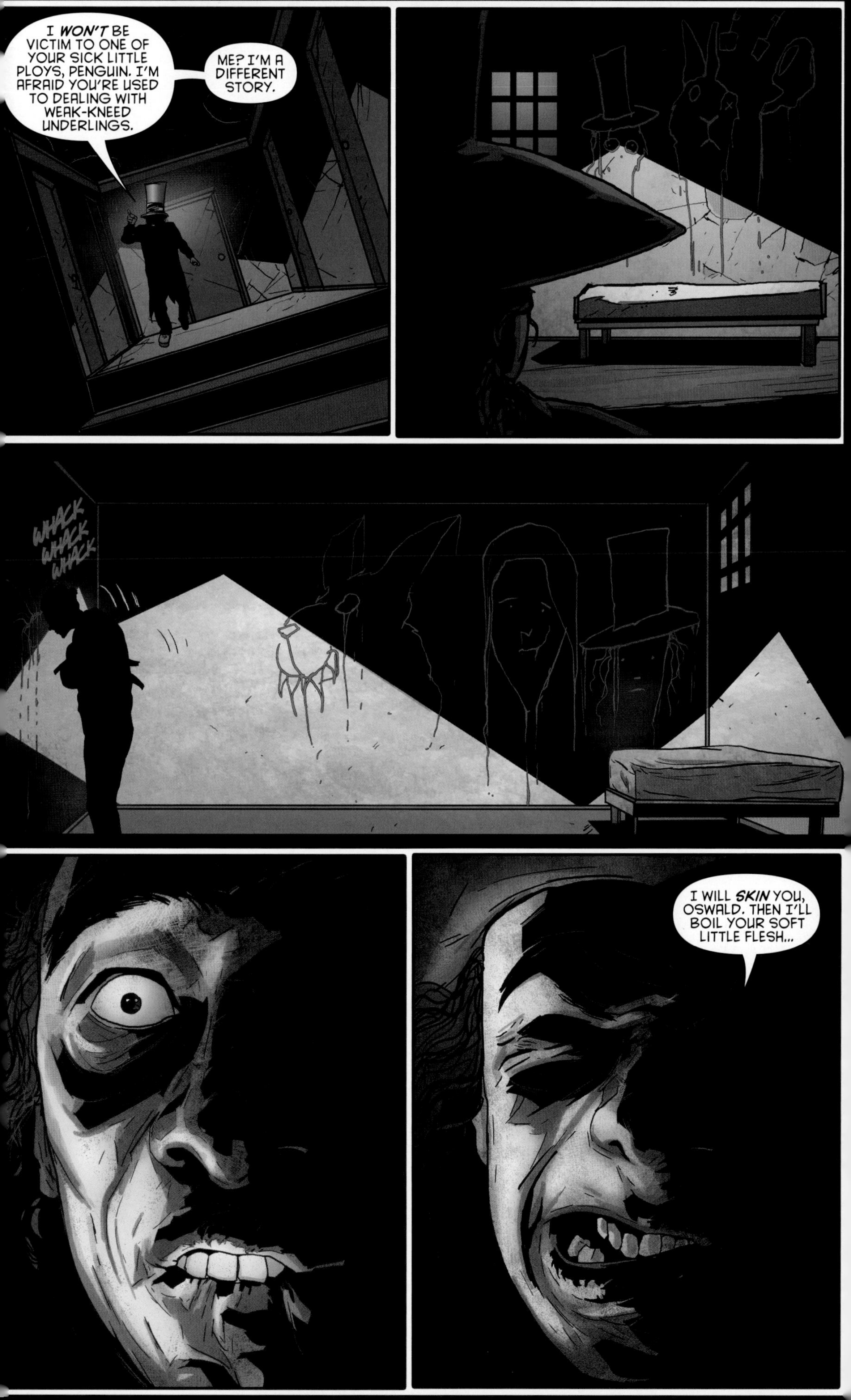

I *WON'T* BE VICTIM TO ONE OF YOUR SICK LITTLE PLOYS, PENGUIN. I'M AFRAID YOU'RE USED TO DEALING WITH WEAK-KNEED UNDERLINGS.
ME? I'M A DIFFERENT STORY.
WHACK WHACK WHACK
I WILL *SKIN* YOU, OSWALD. THEN I'LL BOIL YOUR SOFT LITTLE FLESH...

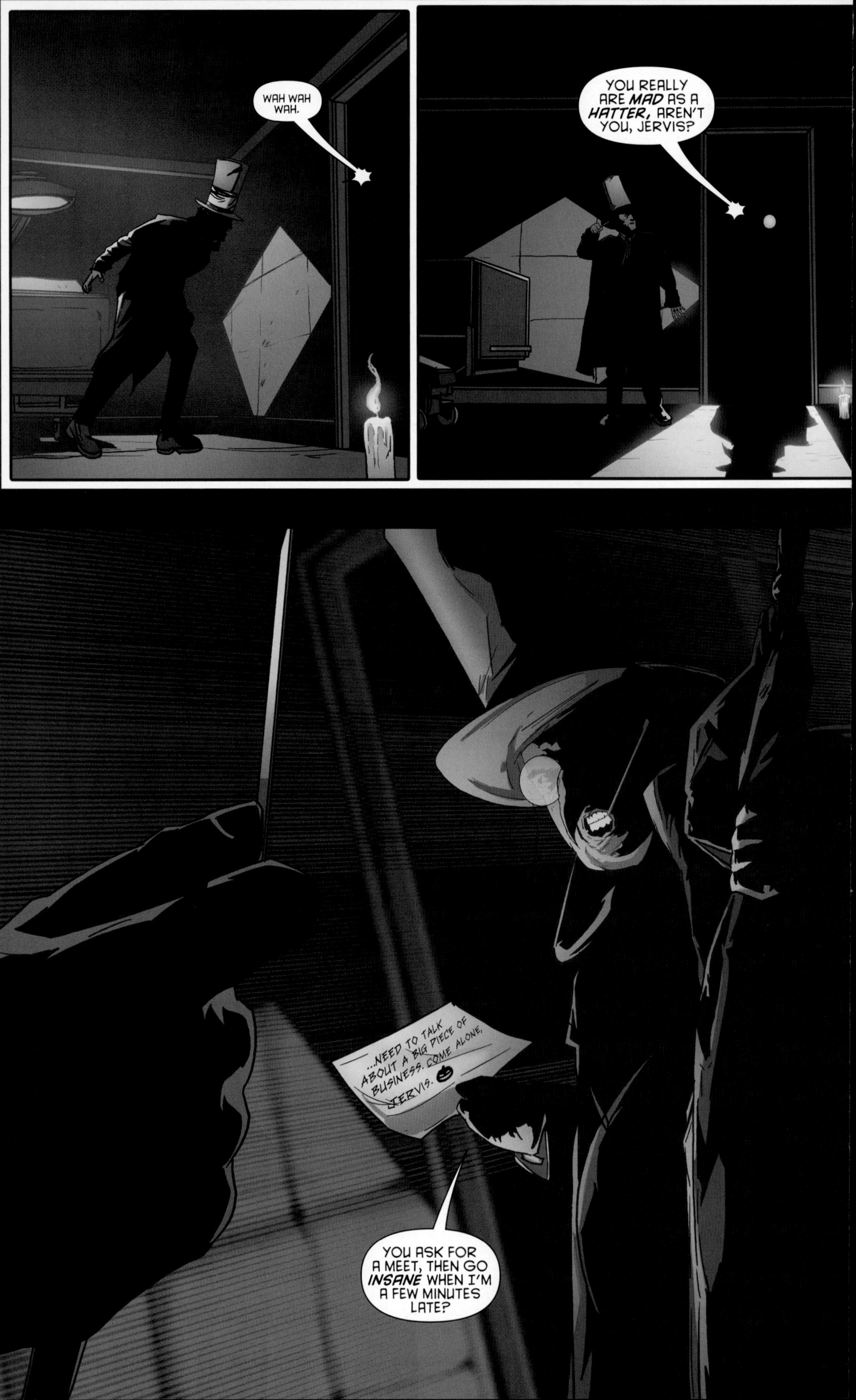
WAH WAH WAH.
YOU REALLY ARE MAD AS A HATTER, AREN'T YOU, JERVIS?
...NEED TO TALK ABOUT A BIG PIECE OF BUSINESS. COME ALONE, JERVIS.
YOU ASK FOR A MEET, THEN GO INSANE WHEN I'M A FEW MINUTES LATE?

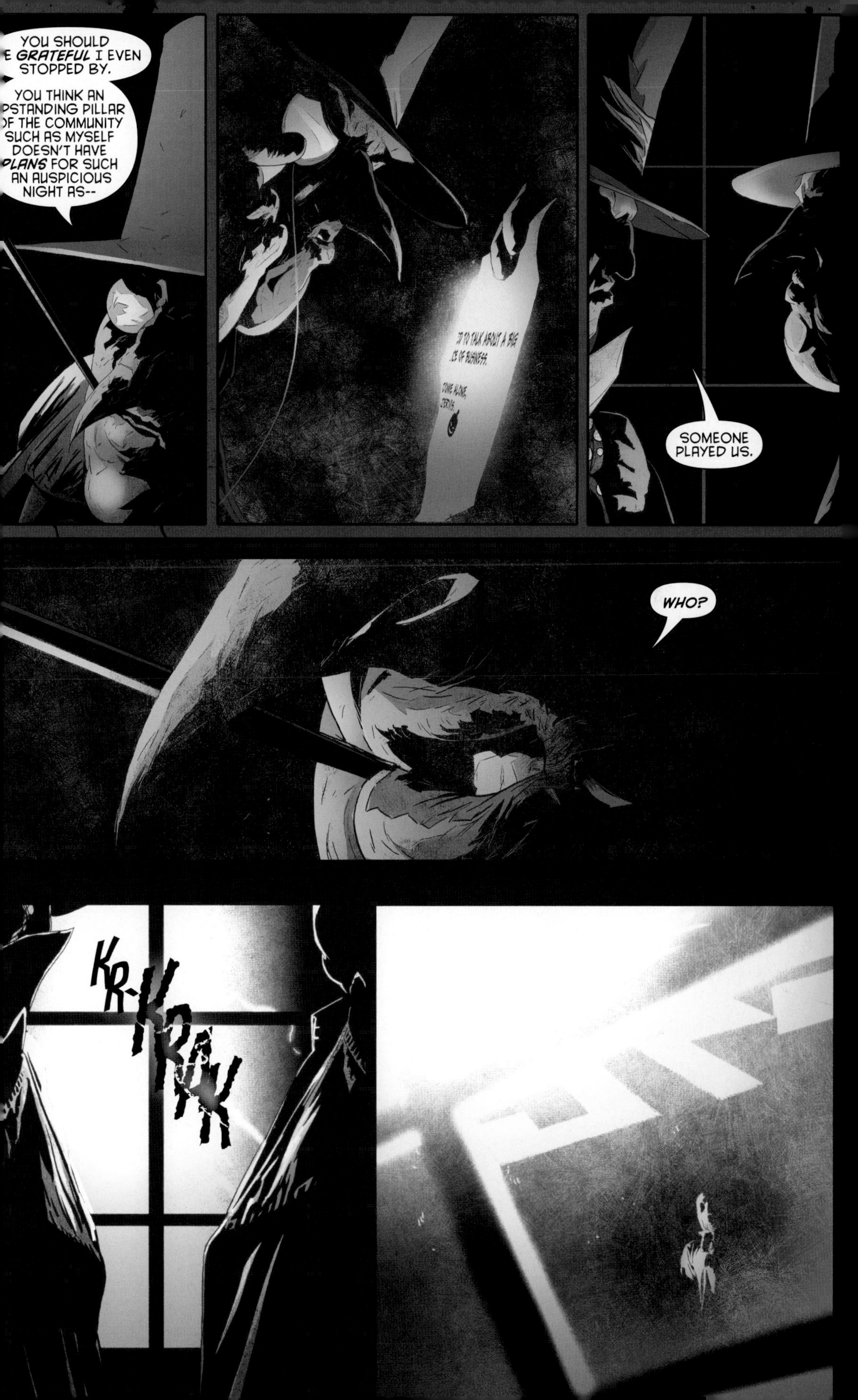
YOU SHOULD E GRATEFUL I EVEN STOPPED BY.
YOU THINK AN PSTANDING PILLAR OF THE COMMUNITY SUCH AS MYSELF DOESN'T HAVE PLANS FOR SUCH AN AUSPICIOUS NIGHT AS--
TO TALK ABOUT A BIG
OF BUSINESS.
COME ALONE,
CERTIS.
SOMEONE PLAYED US.
WHO?
KR-KRAK

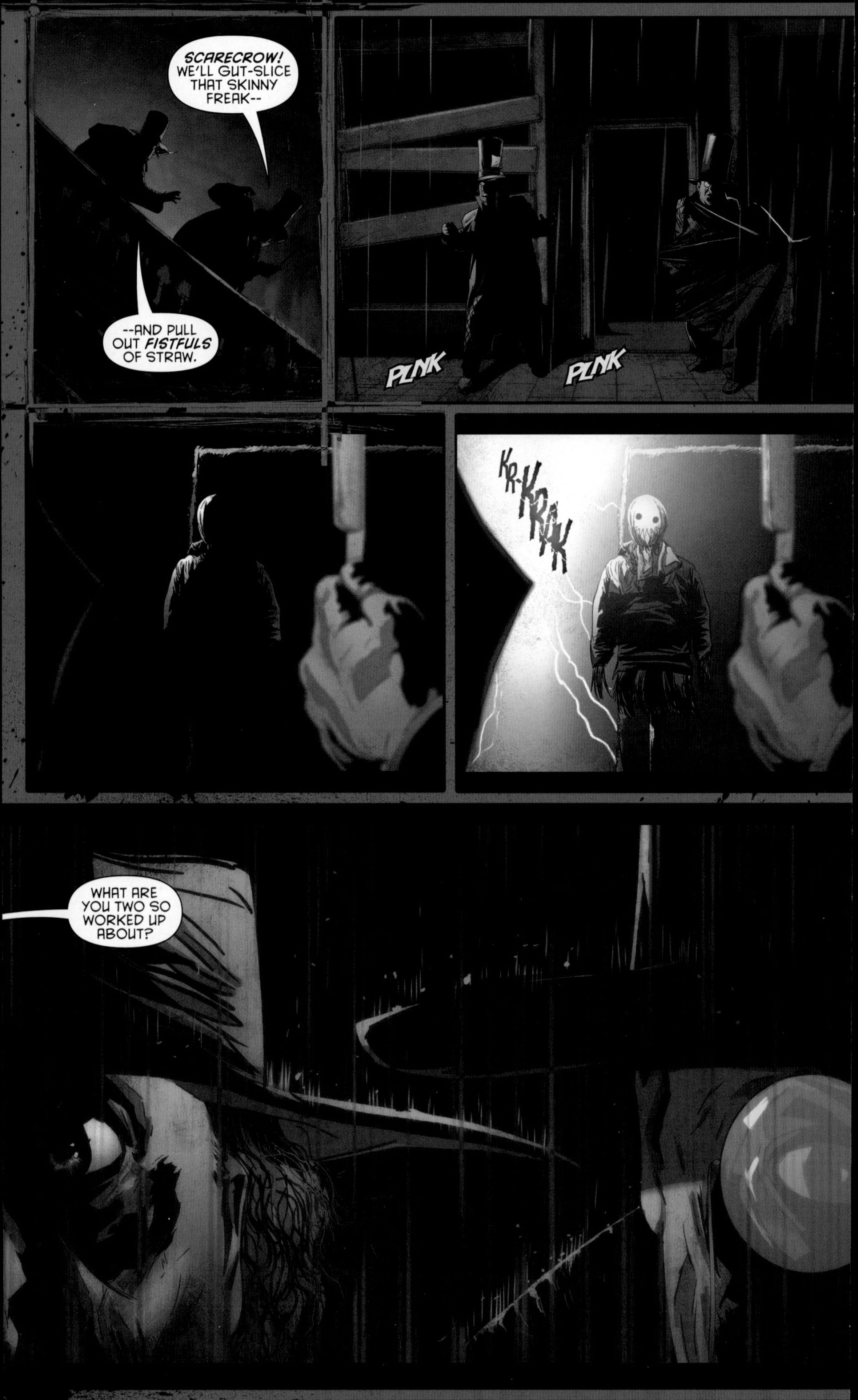
SCARECROW! WE'LL GUT-SLICE THAT SKINNY FREAK--
--AND PULL OUT FISTFULS OF STRAW.
PLNK
PLNK
KR-KRAK
WHAT ARE YOU TWO SO WORKED UP ABOUT?

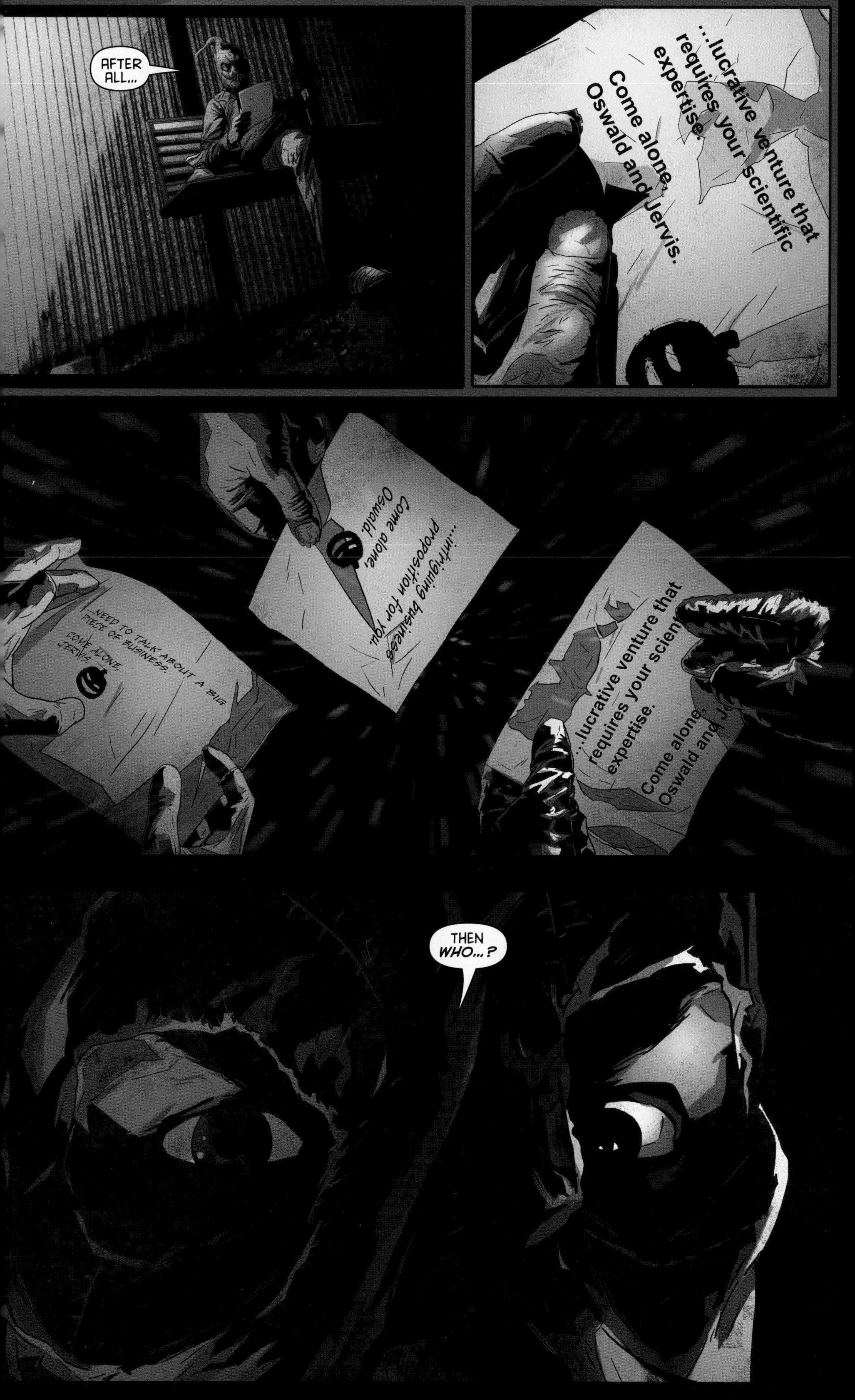
AFTER ALL...
...lucrative venture that requires your scientific expertise.
Come alone, Oswald and Jervis.
...intriguing business proposition for you.
Come alone, Oswald.
...NEED TO TALK ABOUT A BIG PIECE OF BUSINESS.
COME ALONE, JERVIS.
...lucrative venture that requires your scient
expertise.
Come alone, Oswald and J
THEN WHO...?

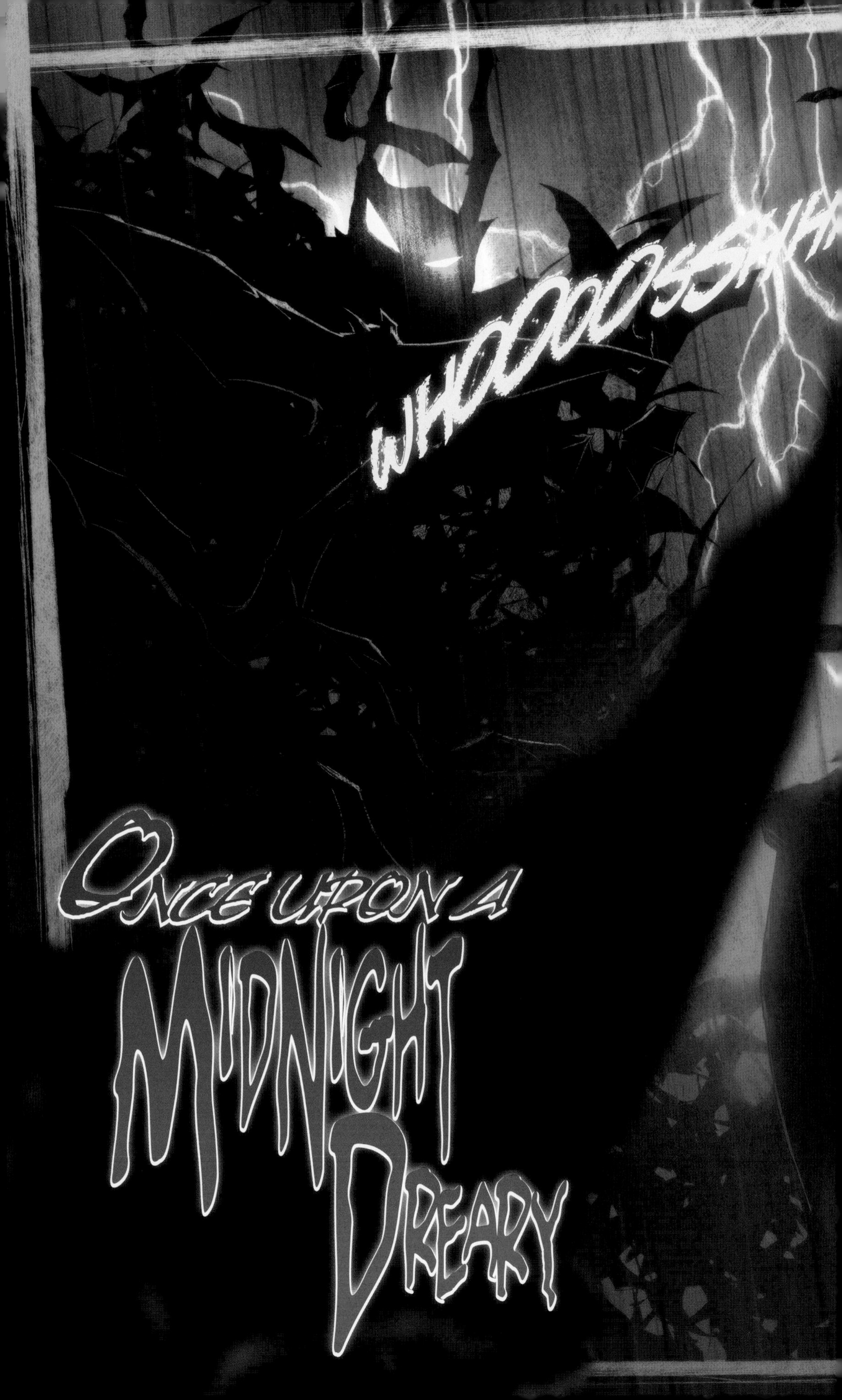
WHOOOOSSHH
ONCE UPON A
MIDNIGHT
DREARY

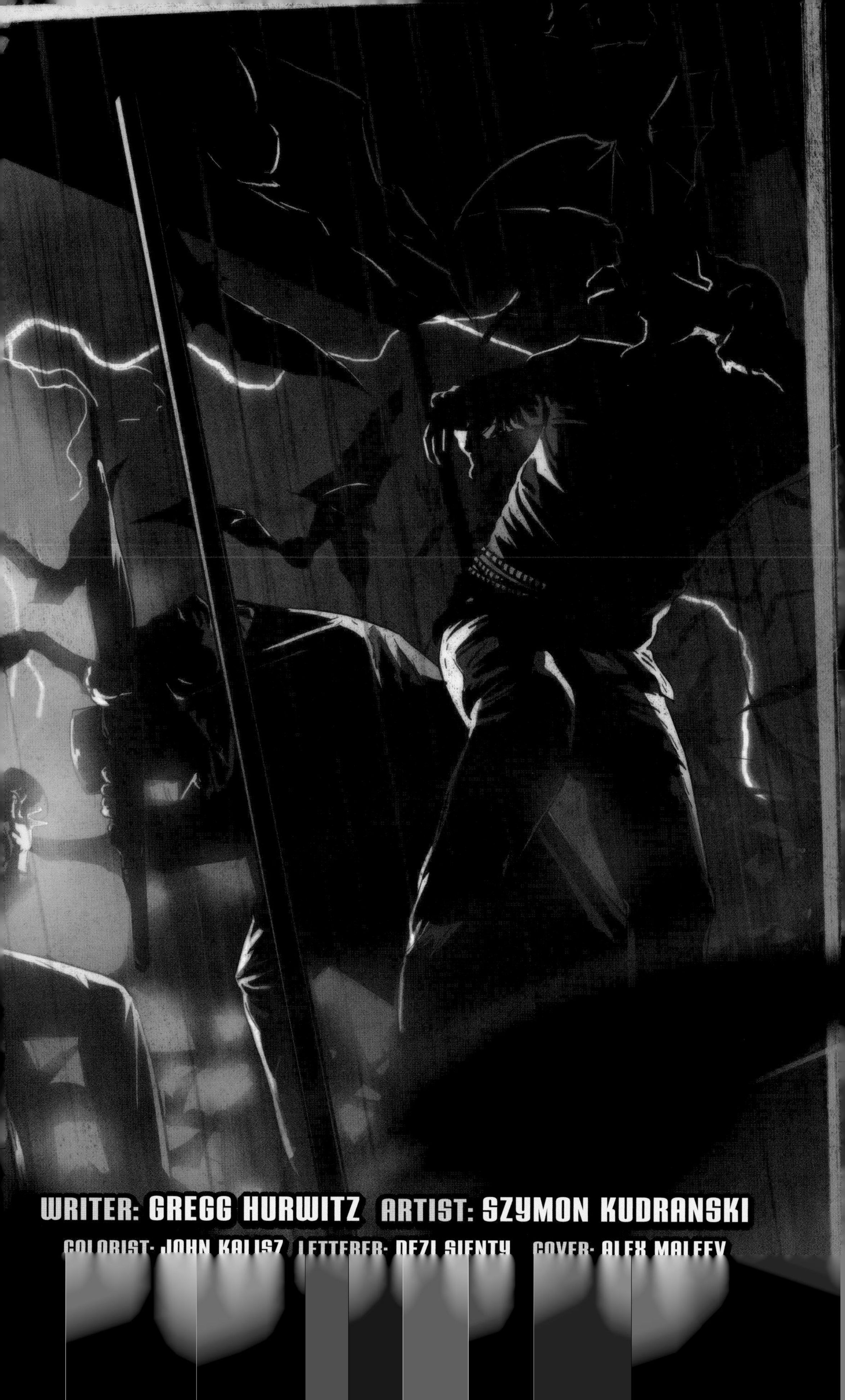
WRITER: GREGG HURWITZ ARTIST: SZYMON KUDRANSKI
COLORIST: JOHN KALISZ LETTERER: DEZI SIENTY COVER: ALEX MALEEV

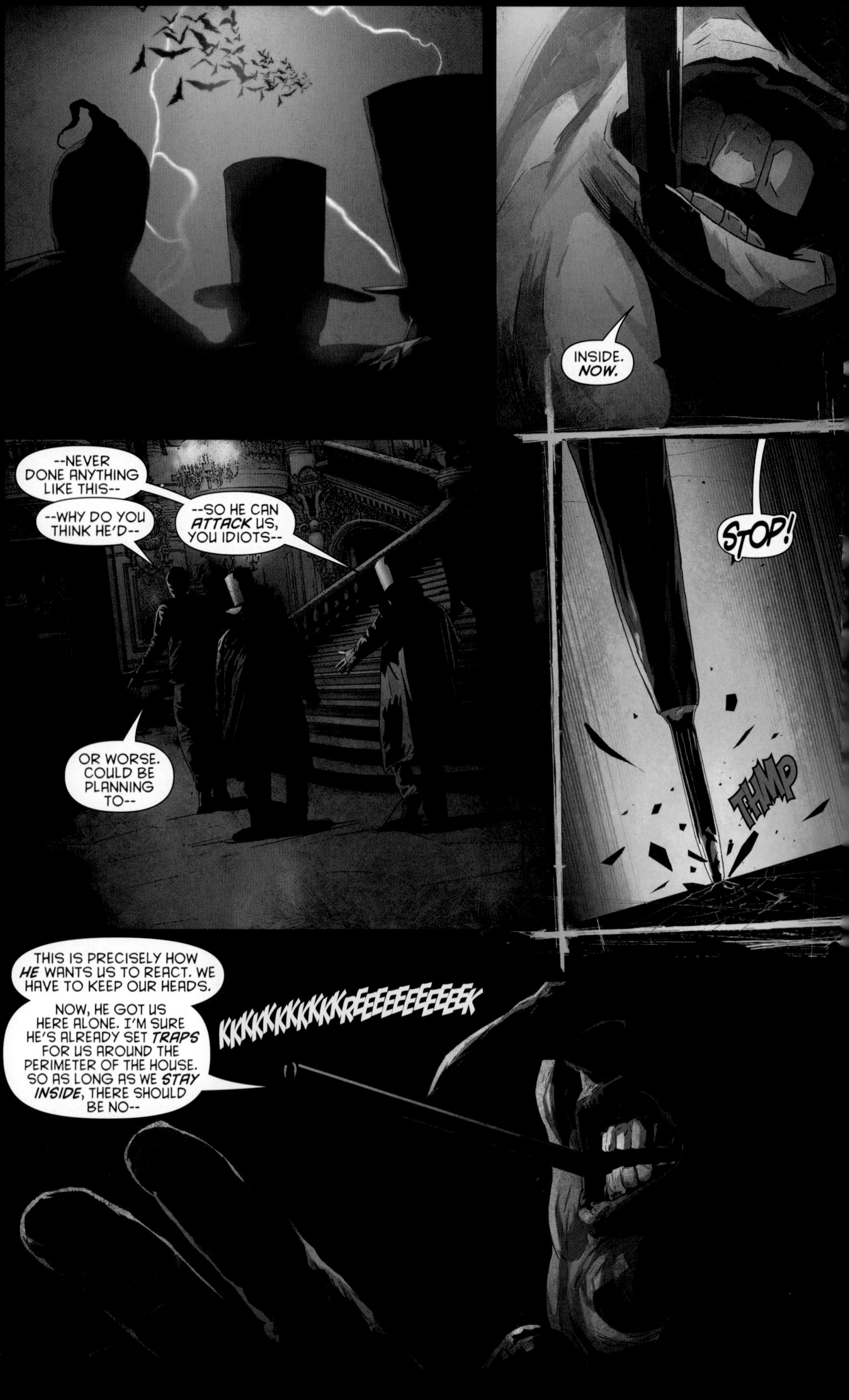
INSIDE. NOW.
--NEVER DONE ANYTHING LIKE THIS--
--WHY DO YOU THINK HE'D--
--SO HE CAN ATTACK US, YOU IDIOTS--
OR WORSE. COULD BE PLANNING TO--
STOP!
THMP
THIS IS PRECISELY HOW HE WANTS US TO REACT. WE HAVE TO KEEP OUR HEADS.
NOW, HE GOT US HERE ALONE. I'M SURE HE'S ALREADY SET TRAPS FOR US AROUND THE PERIMETER OF THE HOUSE. SO AS LONG AS WE STAY INSIDE, THERE SHOULD BE NO--
KKKKKKKKKKREEEEEEEEEEEK

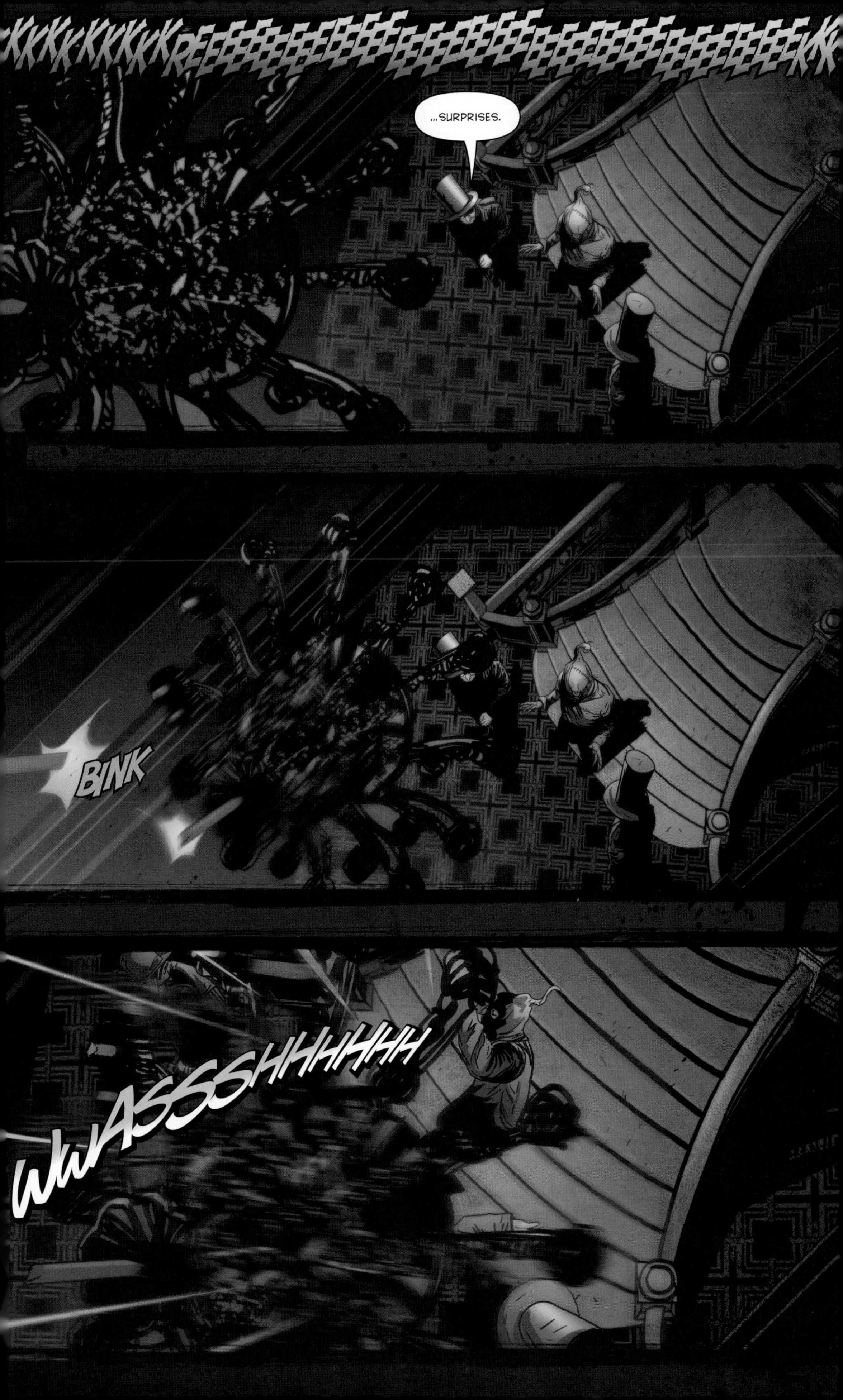

KKKK-KKKKKREEEEEEEEEEEEEEEEEEEEEEEEEEEEEEEEEEEEEEEEEKK
...SURPRISES.
BINK
WWASSSHHHHHH

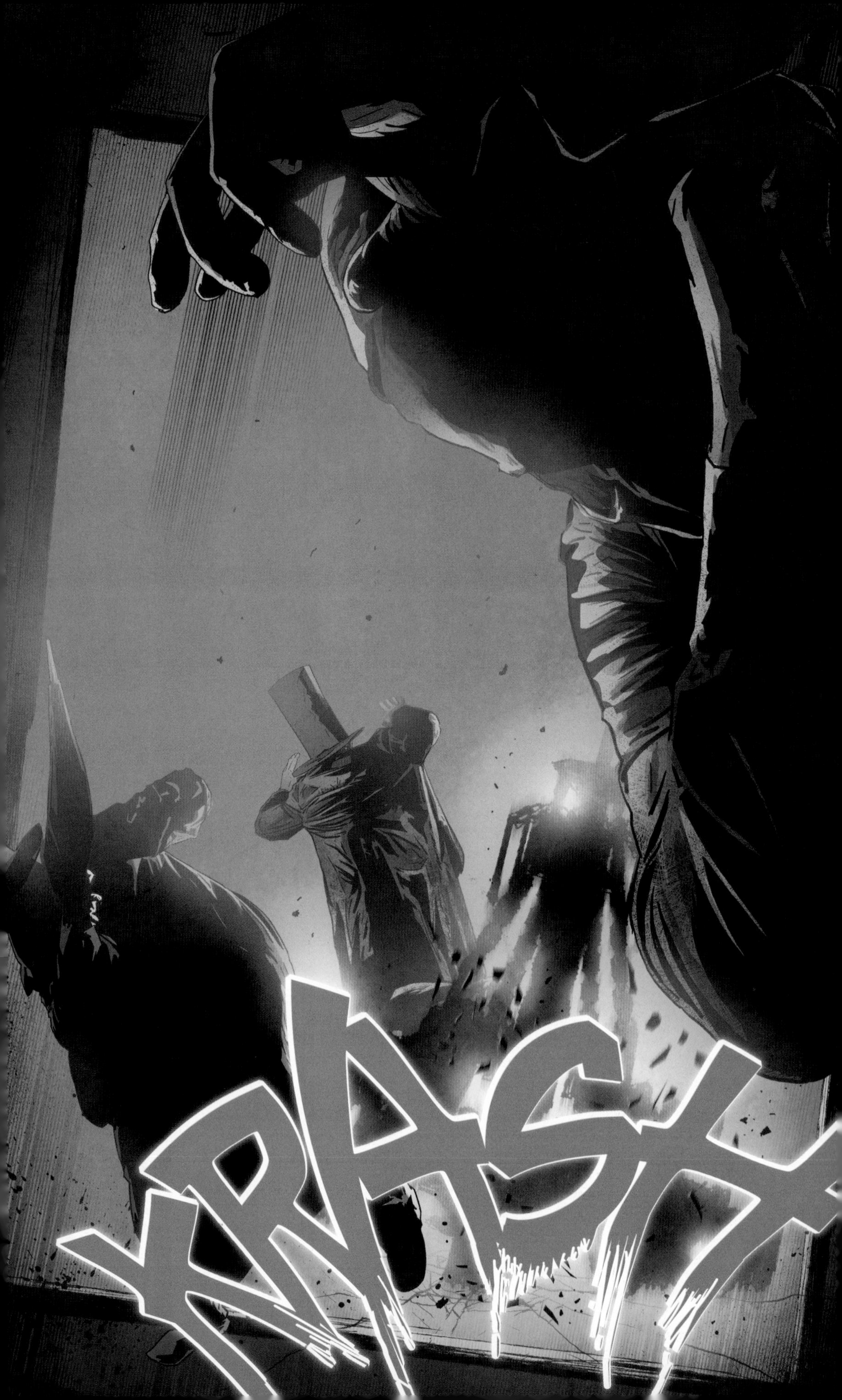
KRASH

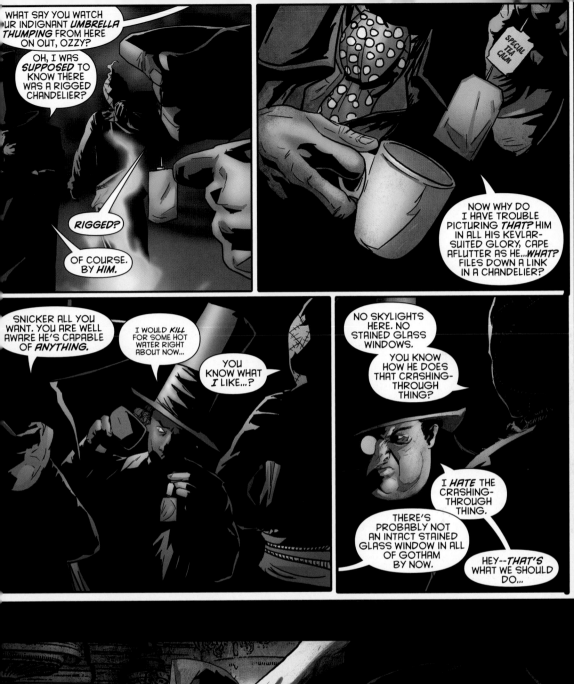

WHAT SAY YOU WATCH UR INDIGNANT *UMBRELLA THUMPING* FROM HERE ON OUT, OZZY?

OH, I WAS *SUPPOSED* TO KNOW THERE WAS A RIGGED CHANDELIER?

*RIGGED?*

OF COURSE. BY *HIM.*

SPECIAL TEA CALM

NOW WHY DO I HAVE TROUBLE PICTURING *THAT?* HIM IN ALL HIS KEVLAR-SUITED GLORY, CAPE AFLUTTER AS HE...*WHAT?* FILES DOWN A LINK IN A CHANDELIER?

SNICKER ALL YOU WANT. YOU ARE WELL AWARE HE'S CAPABLE OF *ANYTHING.*

I WOULD *KILL* FOR SOME HOT WATER RIGHT ABOUT NOW...

YOU KNOW WHAT *I* LIKE...?

NO SKYLIGHTS HERE. NO STAINED GLASS WINDOWS.

YOU KNOW HOW HE DOES THAT CRASHING-THROUGH THING?

I *HATE* THE CRASHING-THROUGH THING.

THERE'S PROBABLY NOT AN INTACT STAINED GLASS WINDOW IN ALL OF GOTHAM BY NOW.

HEY--*THAT'S* WHAT WE SHOULD DO...

...OPEN A STAINED GLASS WINDOW REPAIR BUSINESS.

WE'D MAKE A *MINT.*

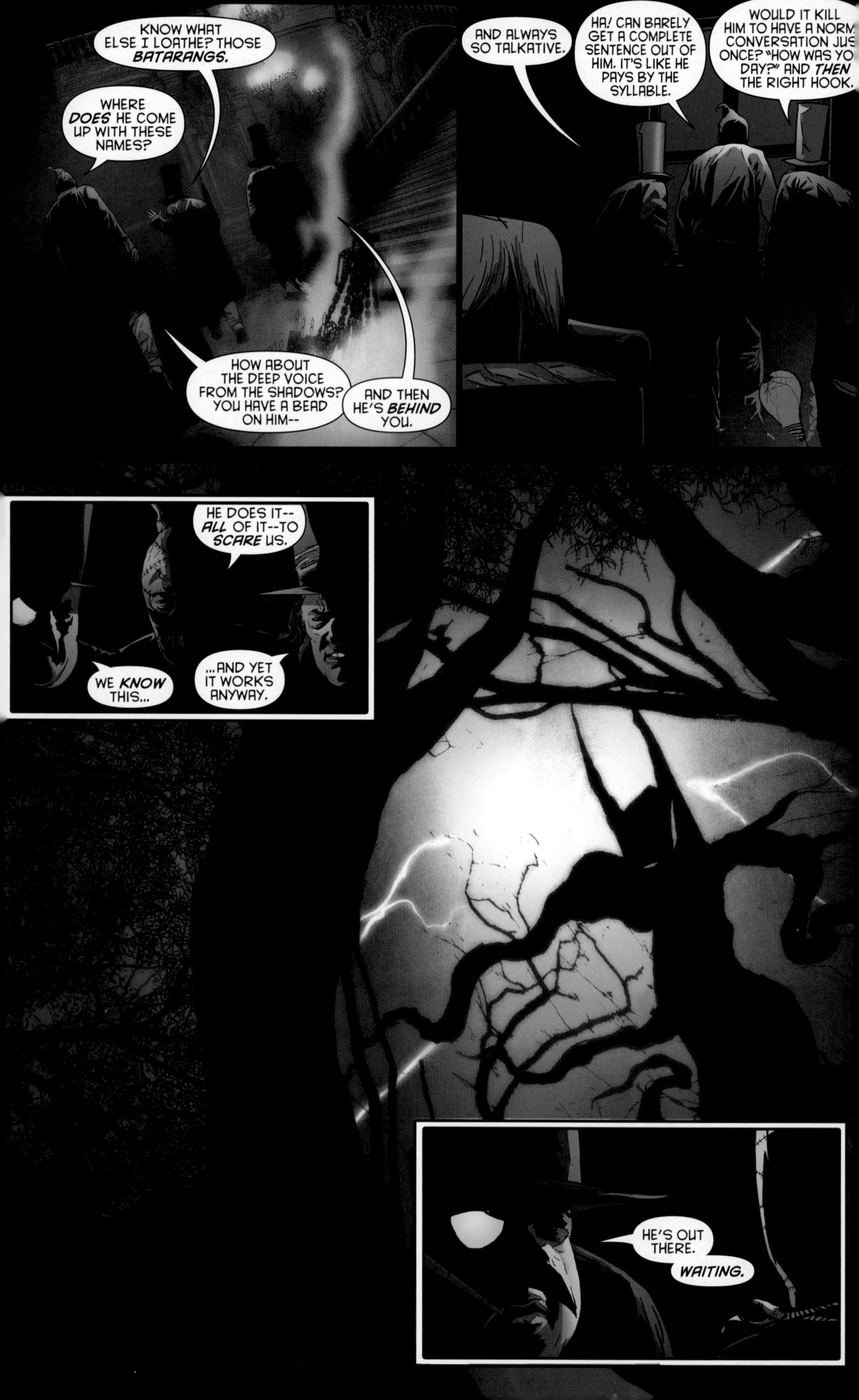
KNOW WHAT ELSE I LOATHE? THOSE BATARANGS.
WHERE DOES HE COME UP WITH THESE NAMES?
HOW ABOUT THE DEEP VOICE FROM THE SHADOWS? YOU HAVE A BEAD ON HIM--
AND THEN HE'S BEHIND YOU.
AND ALWAYS SO TALKATIVE.
HA! CAN BARELY GET A COMPLETE SENTENCE OUT OF HIM. IT'S LIKE HE PAYS BY THE SYLLABLE.
WOULD IT KILL HIM TO HAVE A NORM CONVERSATION JUS ONCE? "HOW WAS YO DAY?" AND THEN THE RIGHT HOOK.
HE DOES IT--ALL OF IT--TO SCARE US.
WE KNOW THIS...
...AND YET IT WORKS ANYWAY.
HE'S OUT THERE.
WAITING.

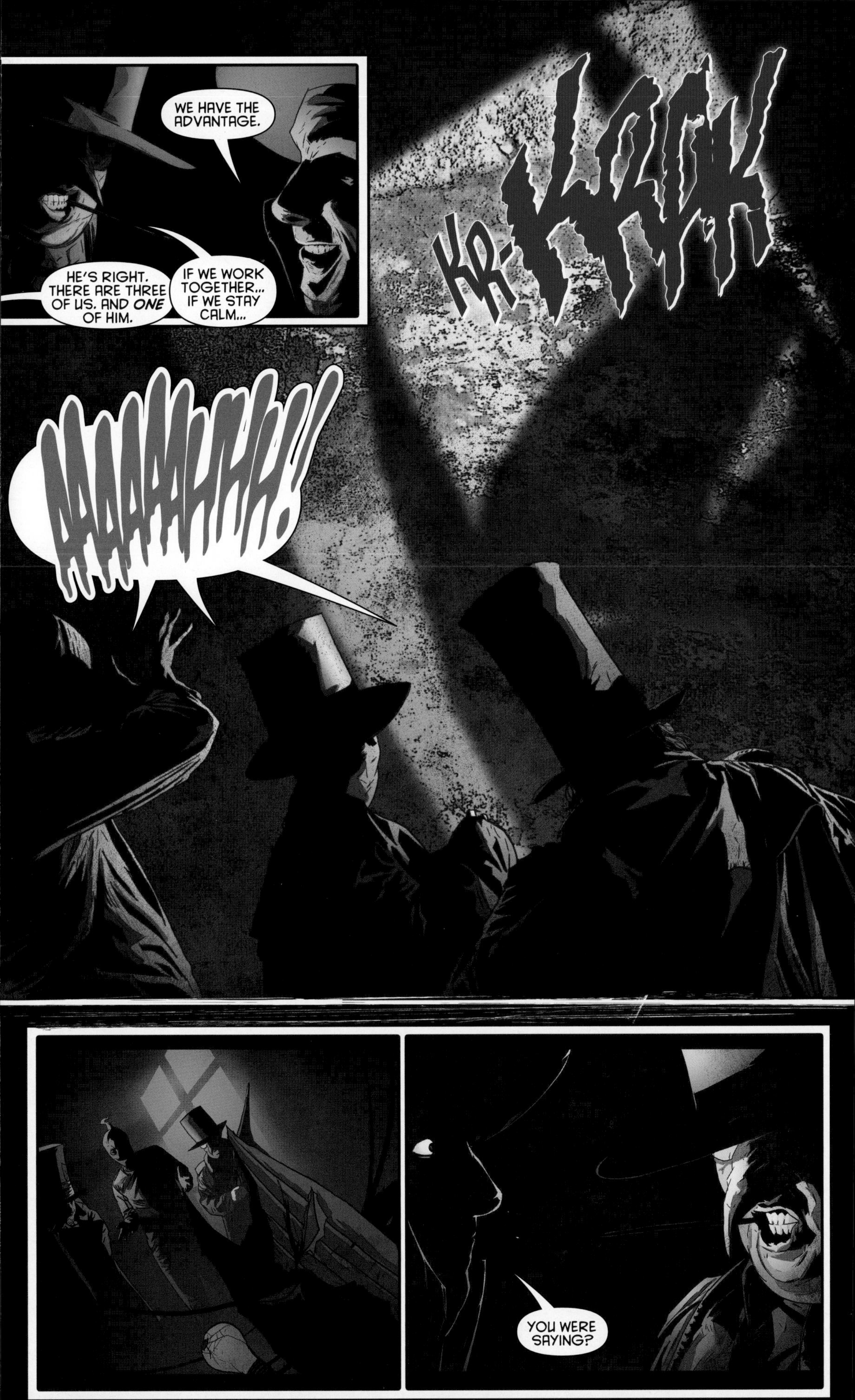
WE HAVE THE ADVANTAGE.
HE'S RIGHT. THERE ARE THREE OF US. AND *ONE* OF HIM.
IF WE WORK TOGETHER... IF WE STAY CALM...
KR-KRACK
AAAAAHHH!!
YOU WERE SAYING?

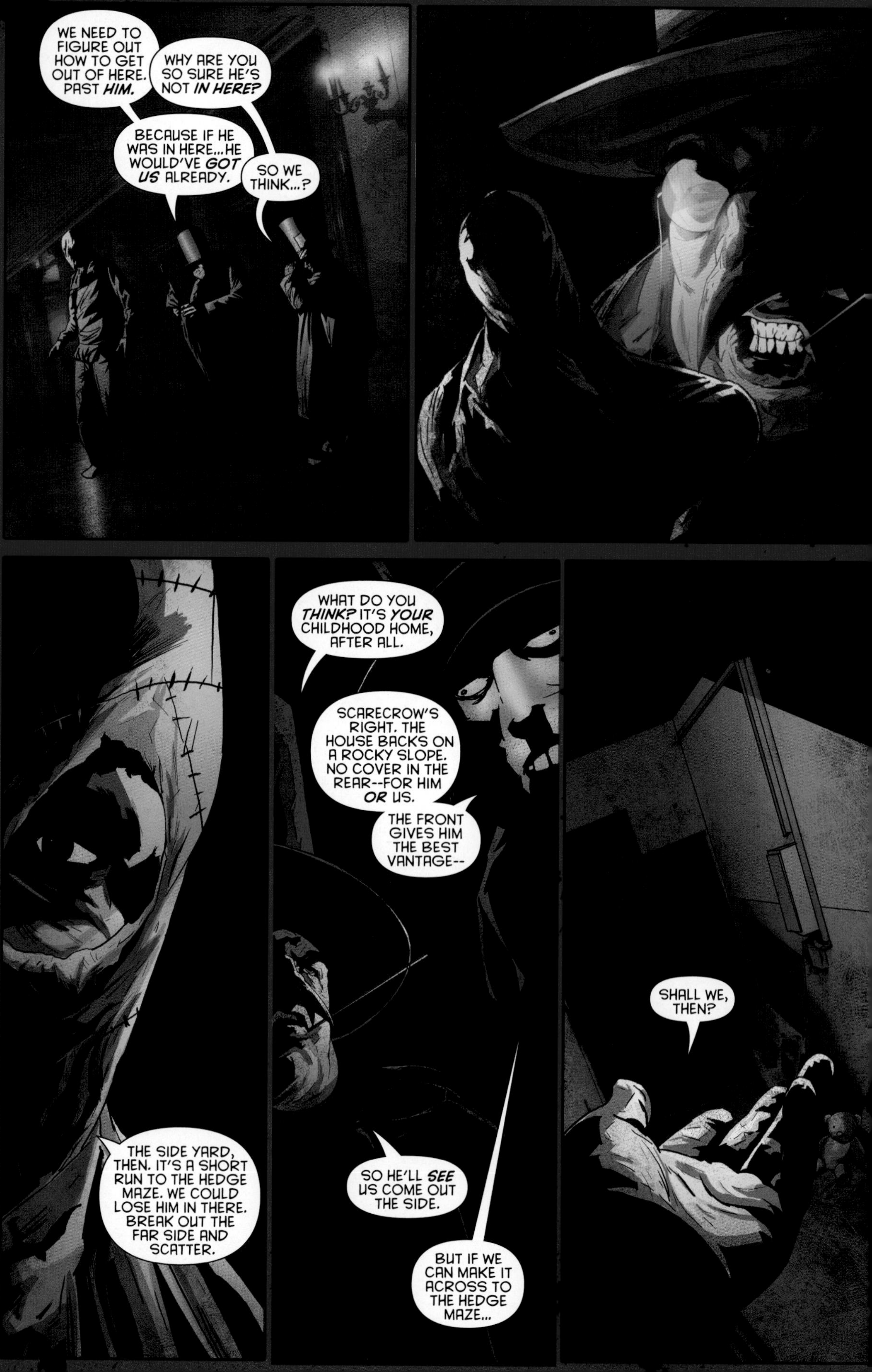
WE NEED TO FIGURE OUT HOW TO GET OUT OF HERE. PAST *HIM.*
WHY ARE YOU SO SURE HE'S NOT *IN HERE?*
BECAUSE IF HE WAS IN HERE...HE WOULD'VE *GOT US* ALREADY.
SO WE THINK...?
THE SIDE YARD, THEN. IT'S A SHORT RUN TO THE HEDGE MAZE. WE COULD LOSE HIM IN THERE. BREAK OUT THE FAR SIDE AND SCATTER.
WHAT DO YOU *THINK?* IT'S *YOUR* CHILDHOOD HOME, AFTER ALL.
SCARECROW'S RIGHT. THE HOUSE BACKS ON A ROCKY SLOPE. NO COVER IN THE REAR--FOR HIM *OR* US.
THE FRONT GIVES HIM THE BEST VANTAGE--
SO HE'LL *SEE* US COME OUT THE SIDE.
BUT IF WE CAN MAKE IT ACROSS TO THE HEDGE MAZE...
SHALL WE, THEN?

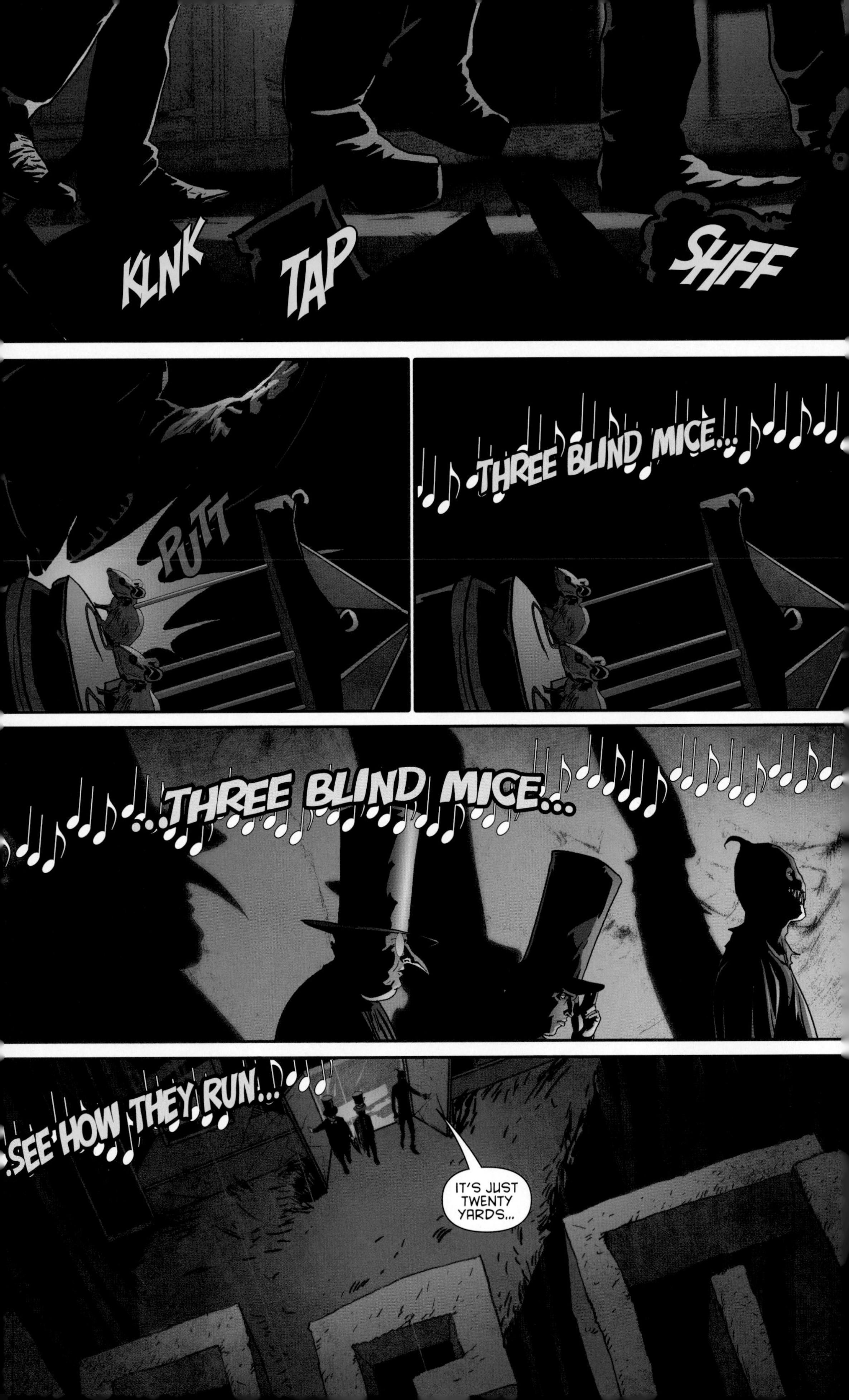
KLNK
TAP
SHFF
PUTT
THREE BLIND MICE...
THREE BLIND MICE...
SEE HOW THEY RUN...
IT'S JUST TWENTY YARDS...

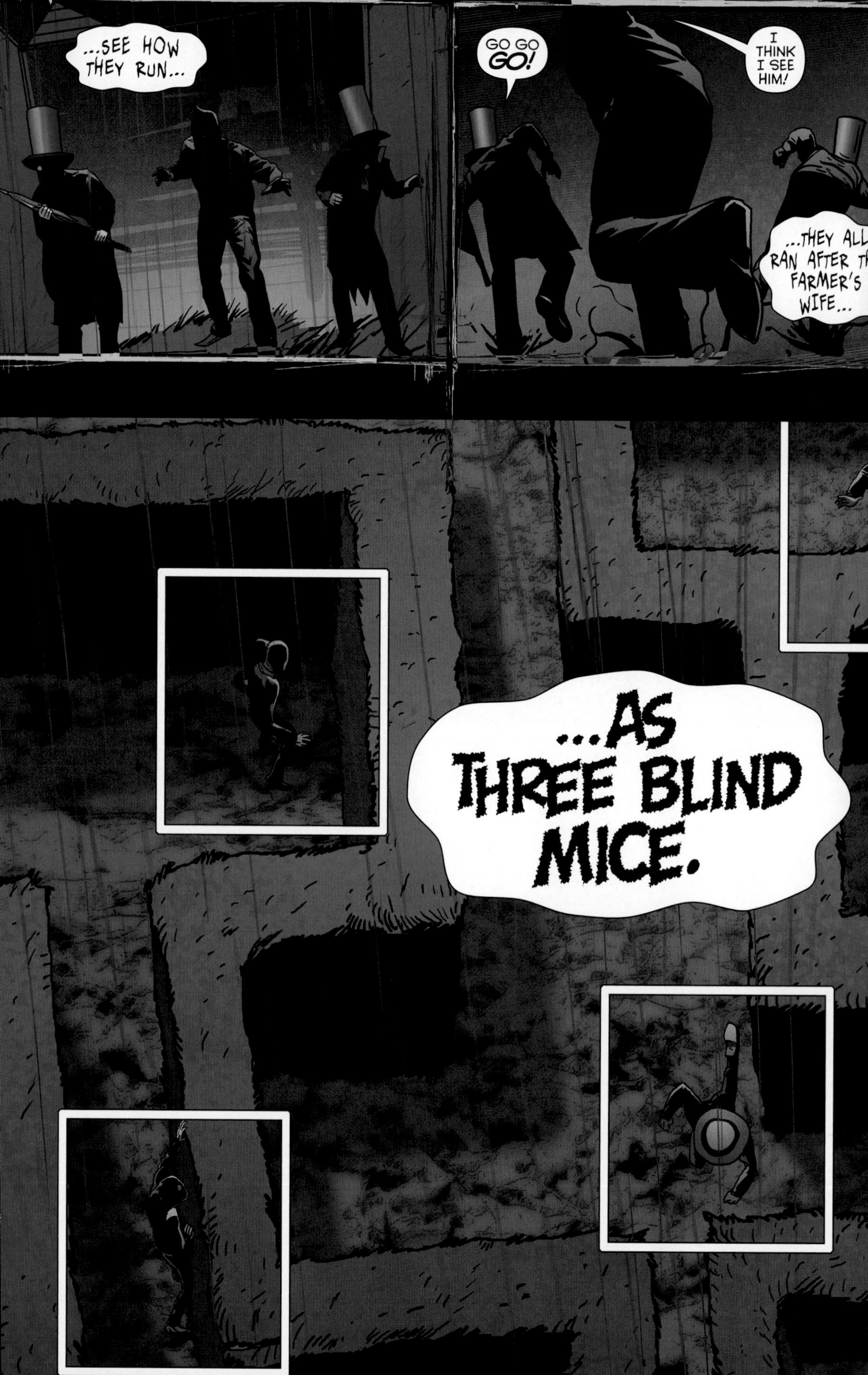
...SEE HOW THEY RUN...
GO GO GO!
I THINK I SEE HIM!
...THEY ALL RAN AFTER TH FARMER'S WIFE...
...AS THREE BLIND MICE.

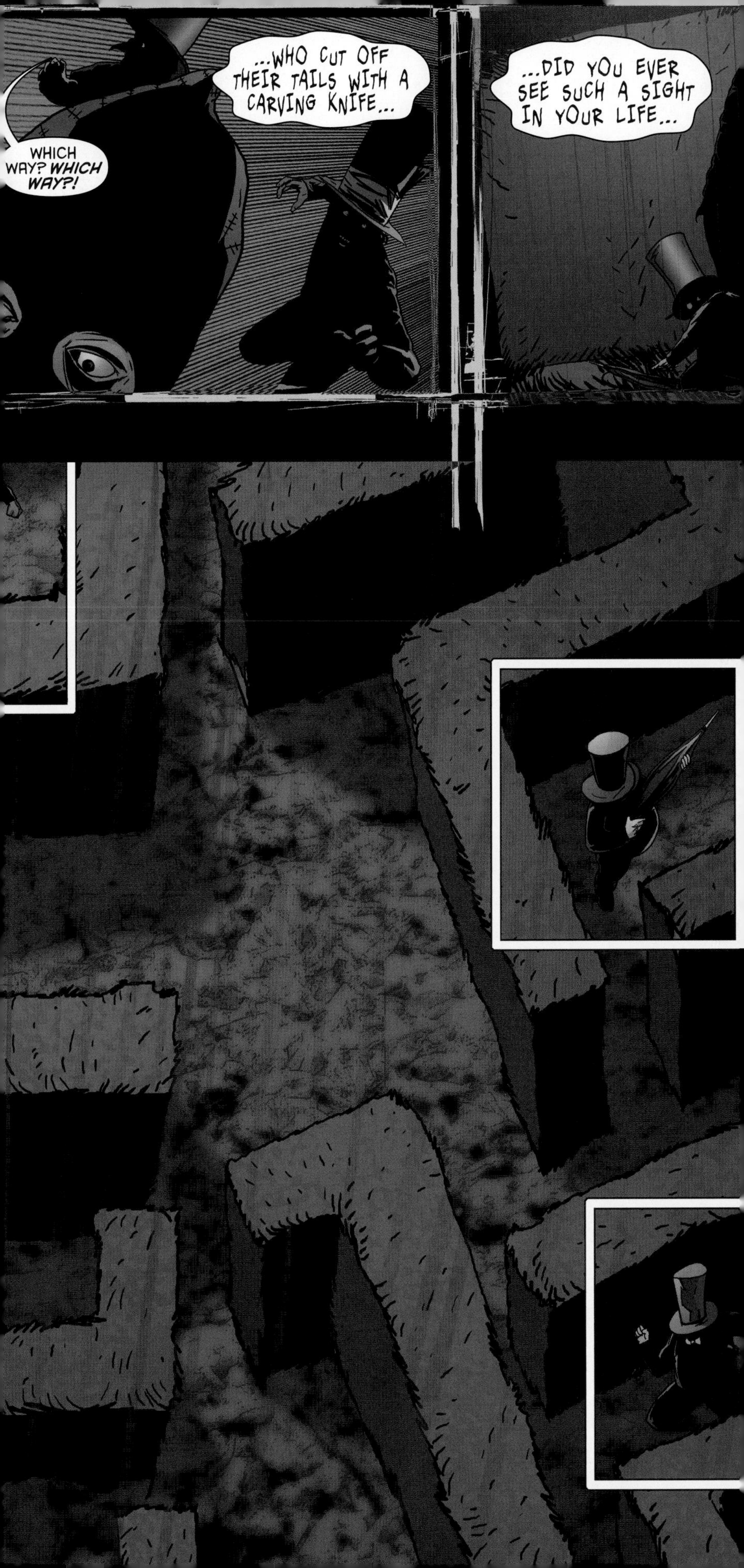
...WHO CUT OFF THEIR TAILS WITH A CARVING KNIFE...
WHICH WAY? WHICH WAY?!
...DID YOU EVER SEE SUCH A SIGHT IN YOUR LIFE...

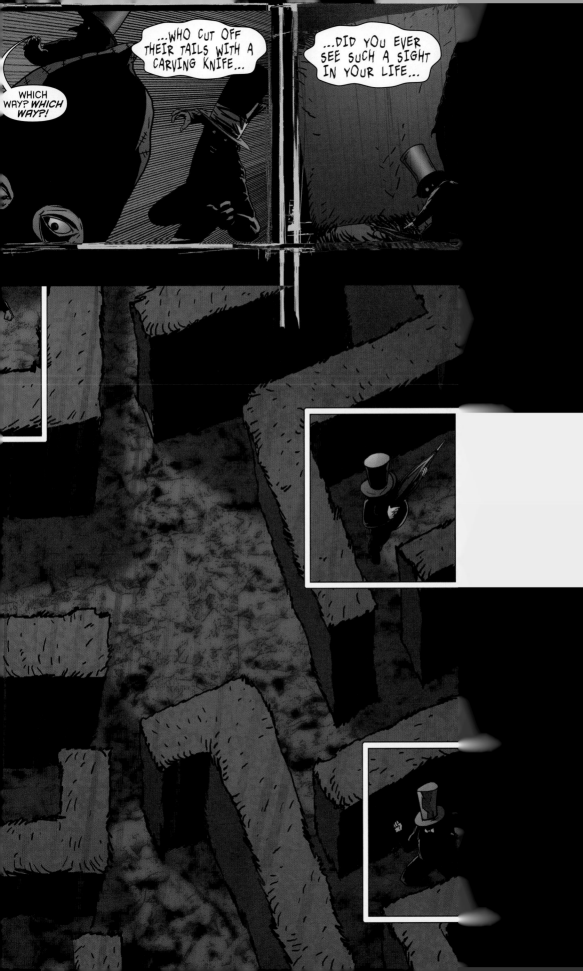

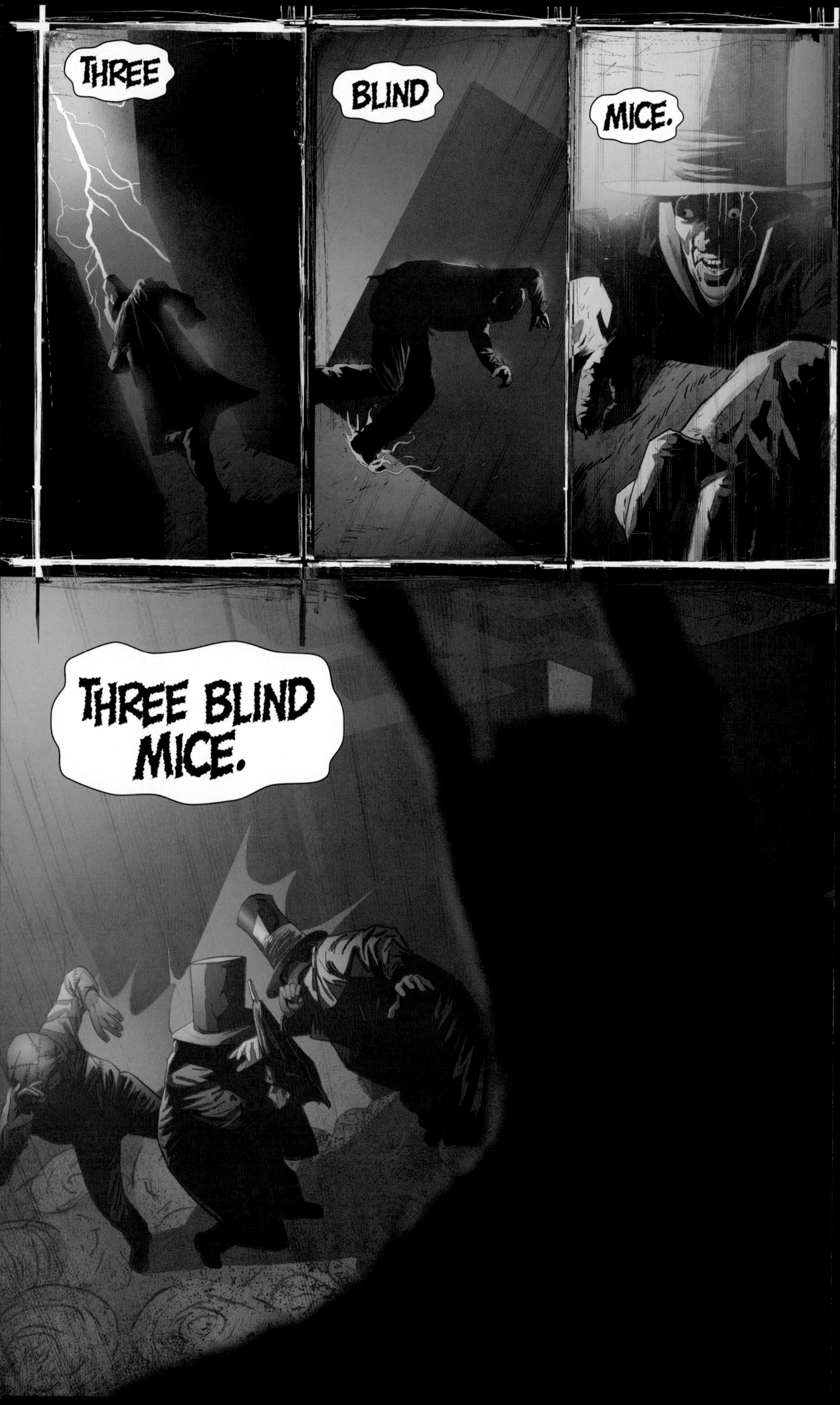
THREE
BLIND
MICE.
THREE BLIND MICE.

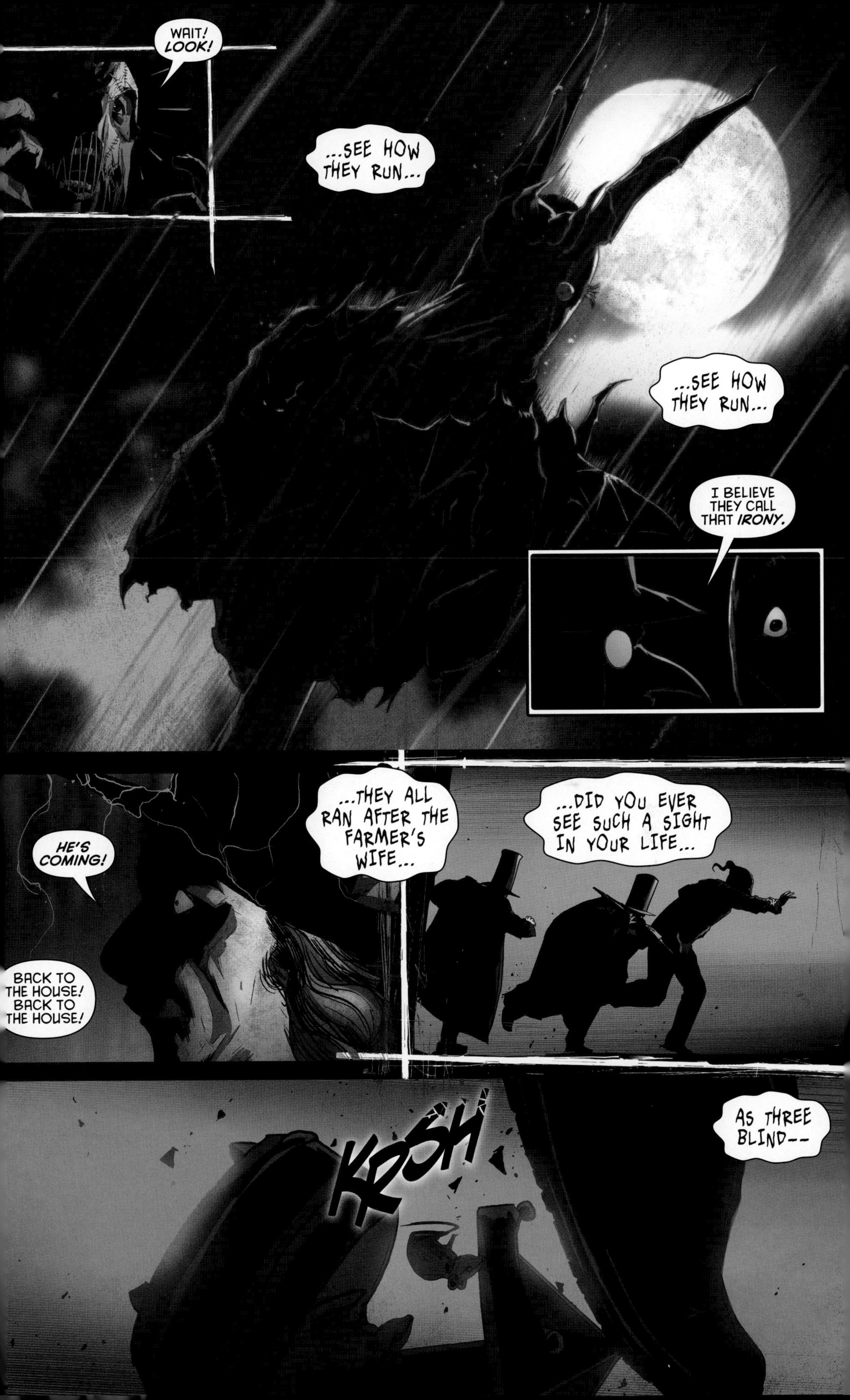
WAIT! LOOK!
...SEE HOW THEY RUN...
...SEE HOW THEY RUN...
I BELIEVE THEY CALL THAT IRONY.
HE'S COMING!
BACK TO THE HOUSE! BACK TO THE HOUSE!
...THEY ALL RAN AFTER THE FARMER'S WIFE...
...DID YOU EVER SEE SUCH A SIGHT IN YOUR LIFE...
KRSH
AS THREE BLIND--

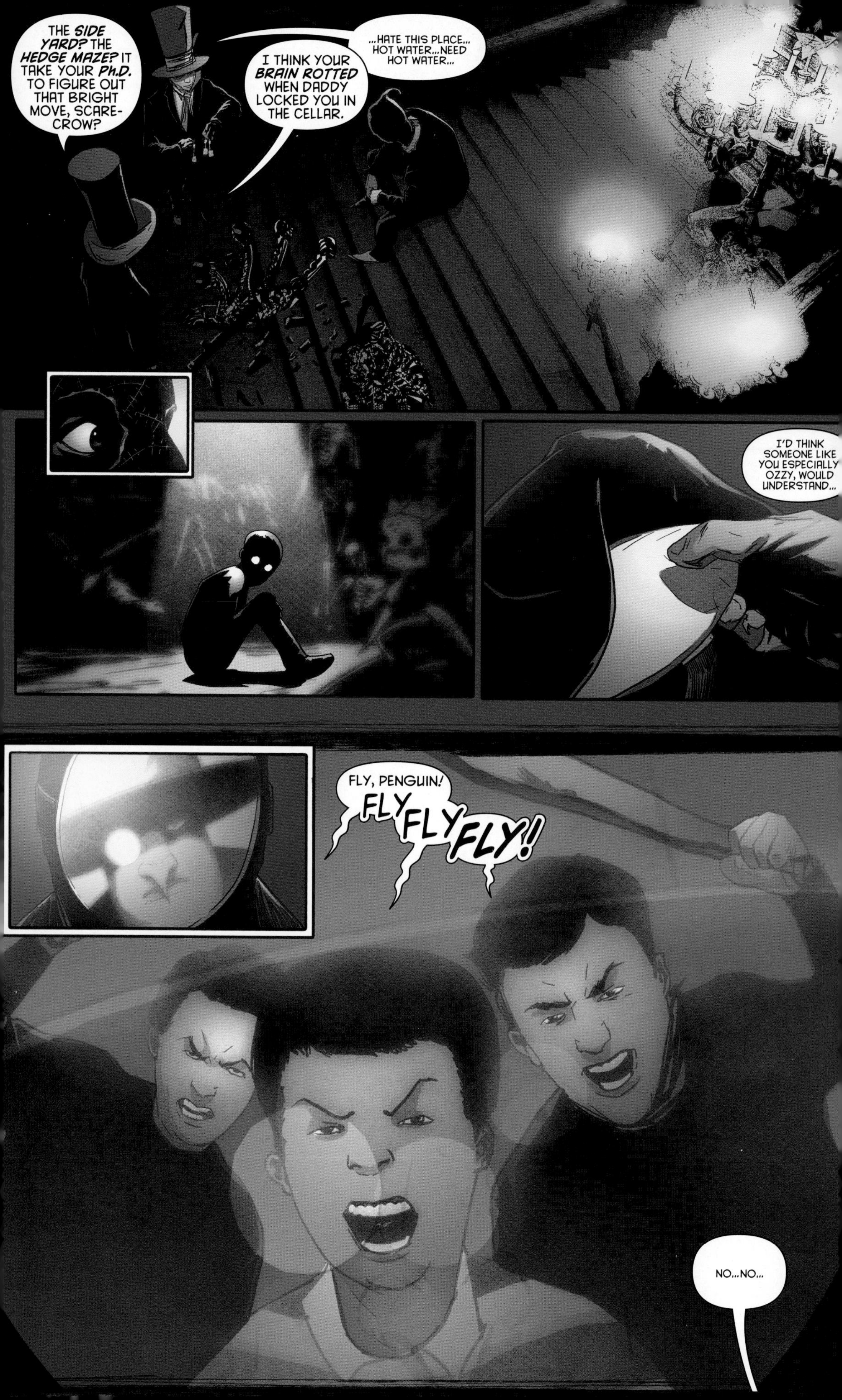

THE SIDE YARD? THE HEDGE MAZE? IT TAKE YOUR Ph.D. TO FIGURE OUT THAT BRIGHT MOVE, SCARECROW?
I THINK YOUR BRAIN ROTTED WHEN DADDY LOCKED YOU IN THE CELLAR.
...HATE THIS PLACE... HOT WATER...NEED HOT WATER...
I'D THINK SOMEONE LIKE YOU ESPECIALLY OZZY, WOULD UNDERSTAND...
FLY, PENGUIN!
FLY FLY FLY!
NO...NO...

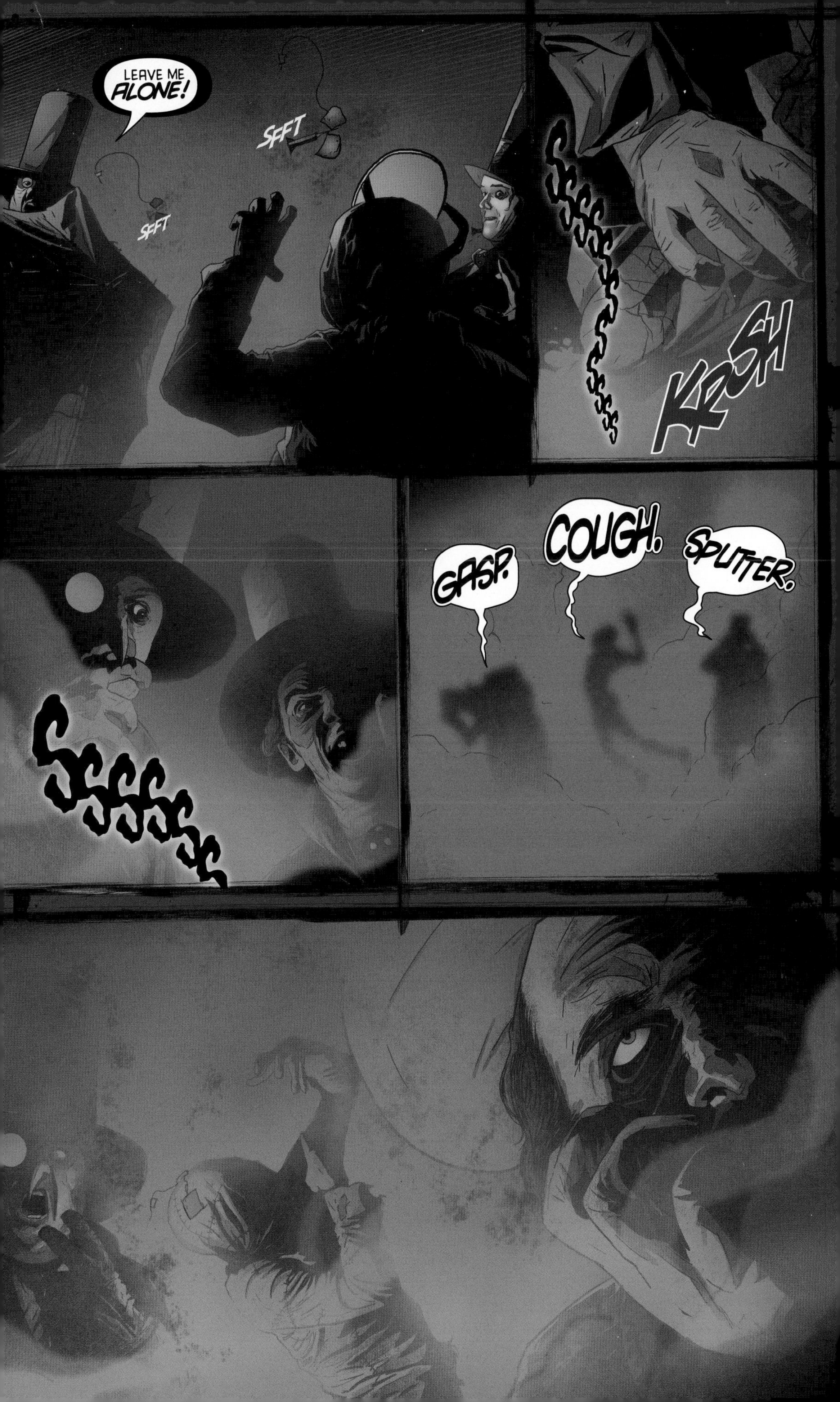
LEAVE ME ALONE!
SFFT
SFFT
SSSSSSSSSSSSS
KRSH
SSSSSSS
GASP.
COUGH.
SPUTTER.

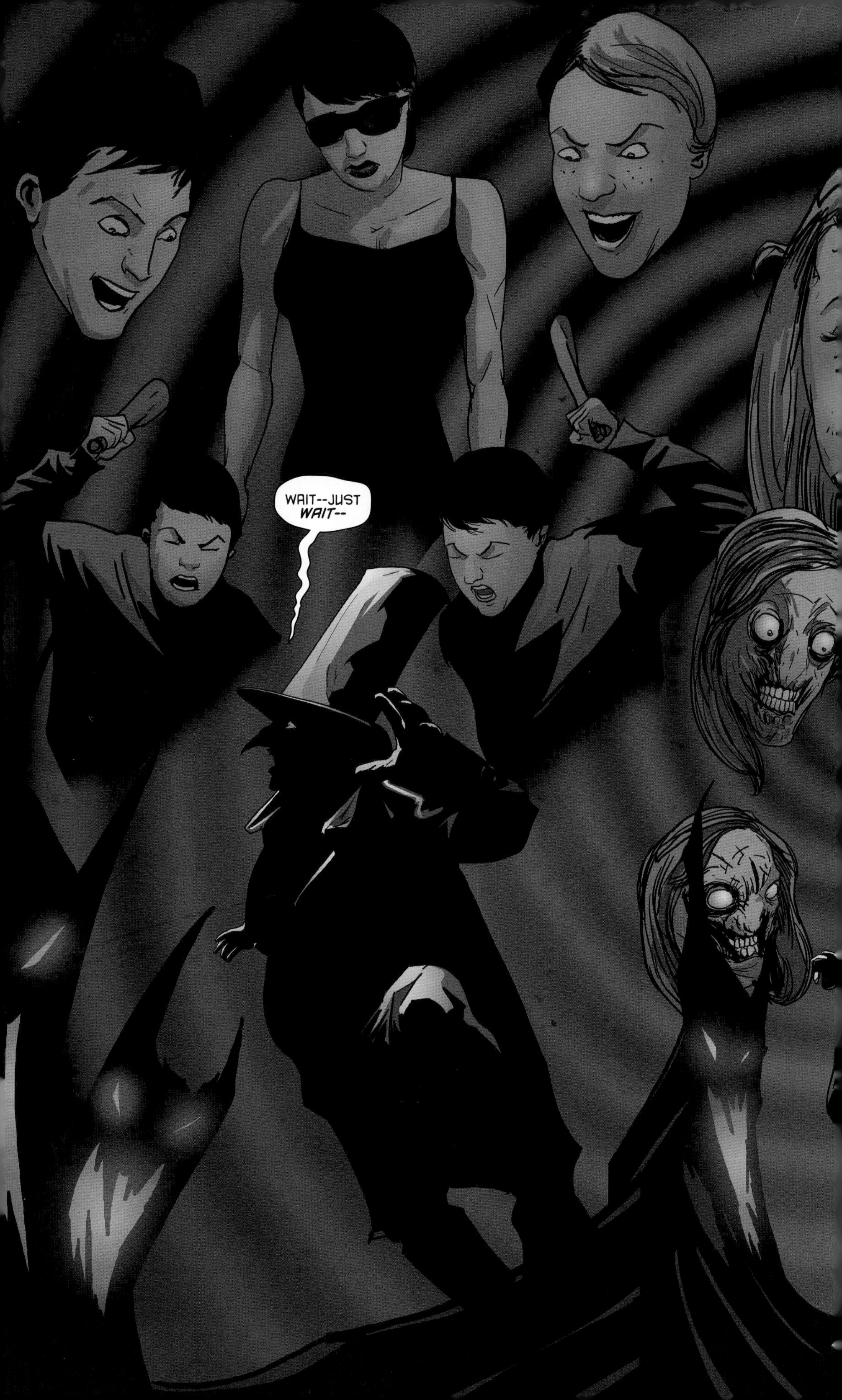
WAIT--JUST *WAIT*--

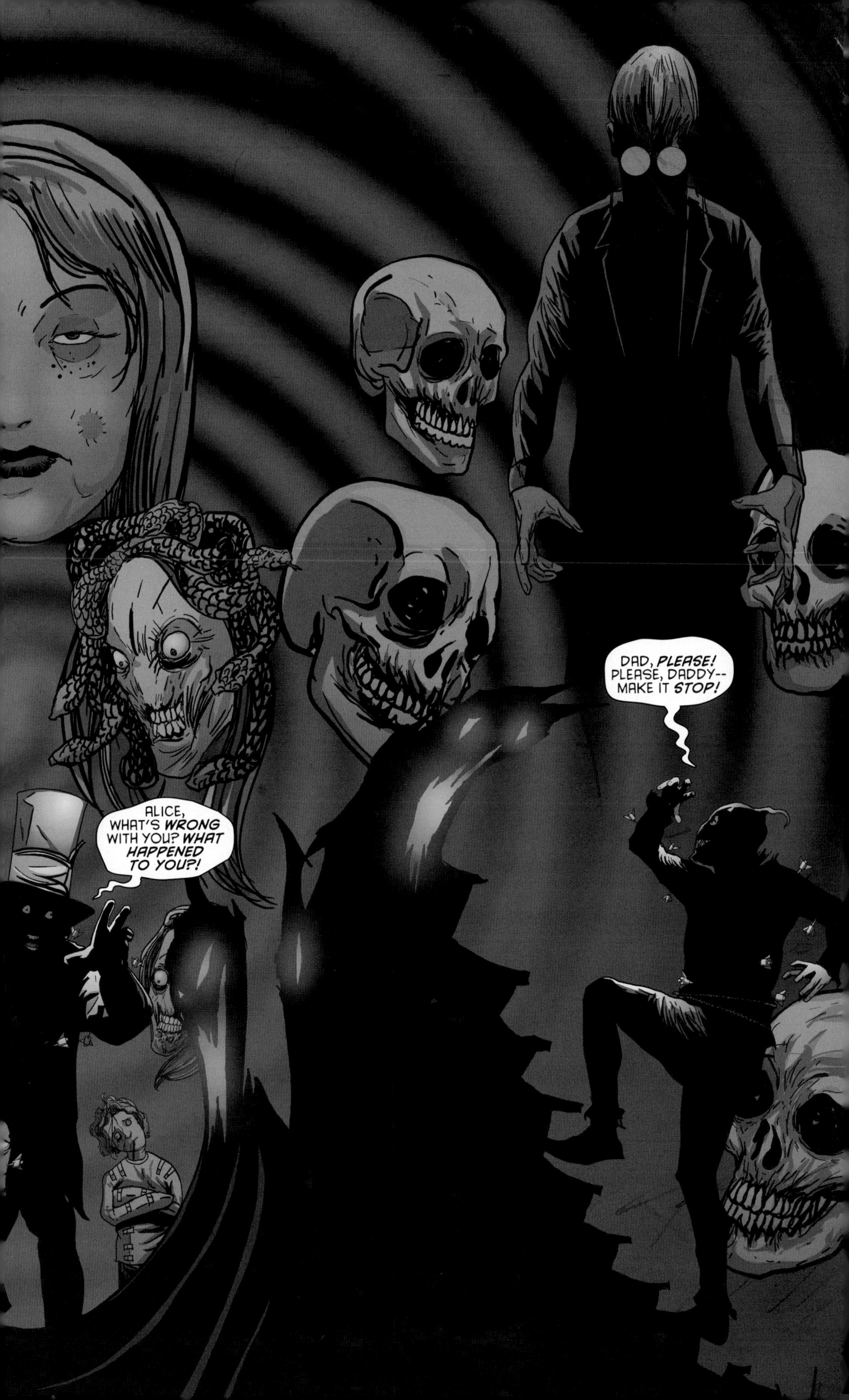
DAD, PLEASE! PLEASE, DADDY-- MAKE IT STOP!
ALICE, WHAT'S WRONG WITH YOU? WHAT HAPPENED TO YOU?!

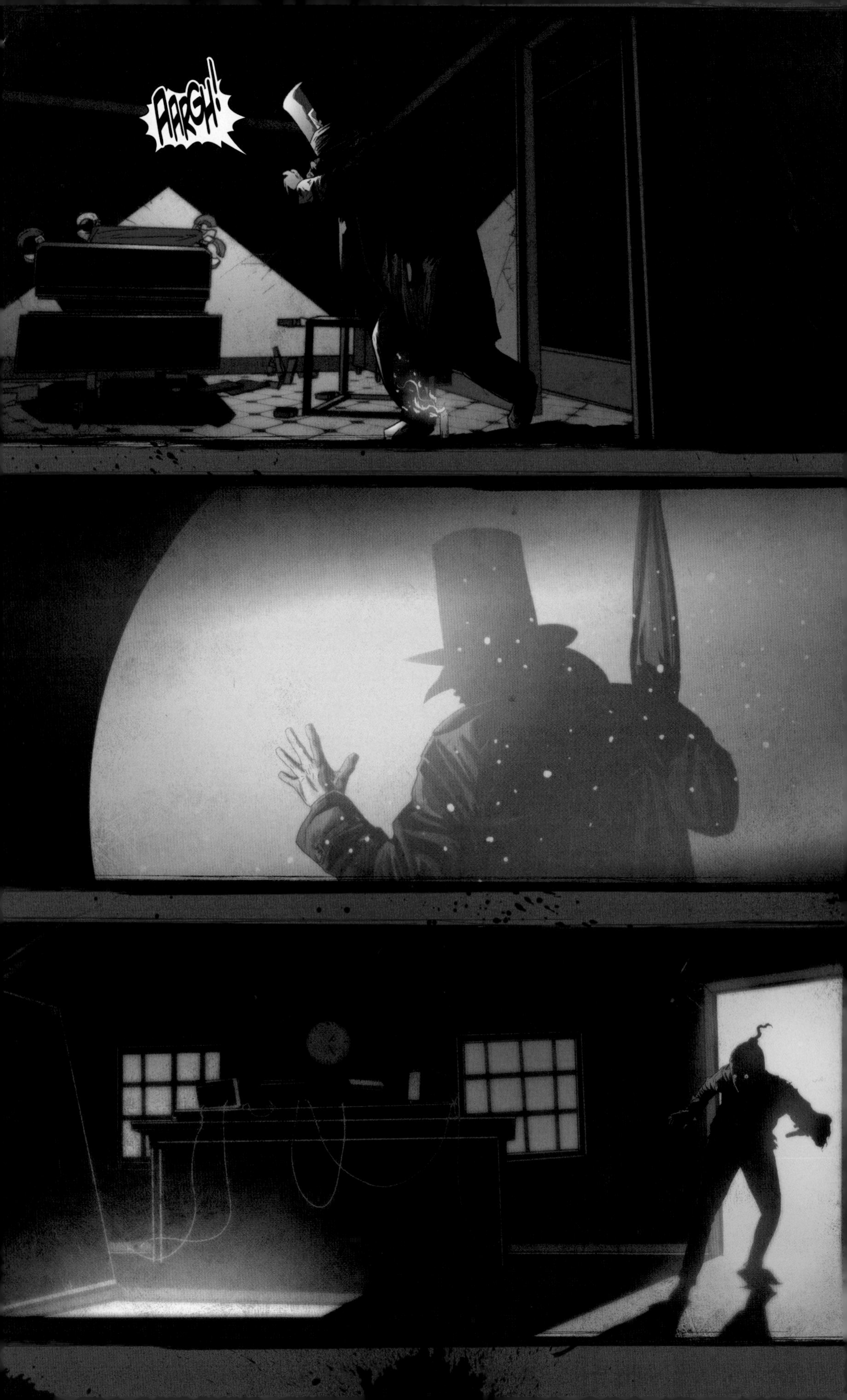
AARGH!

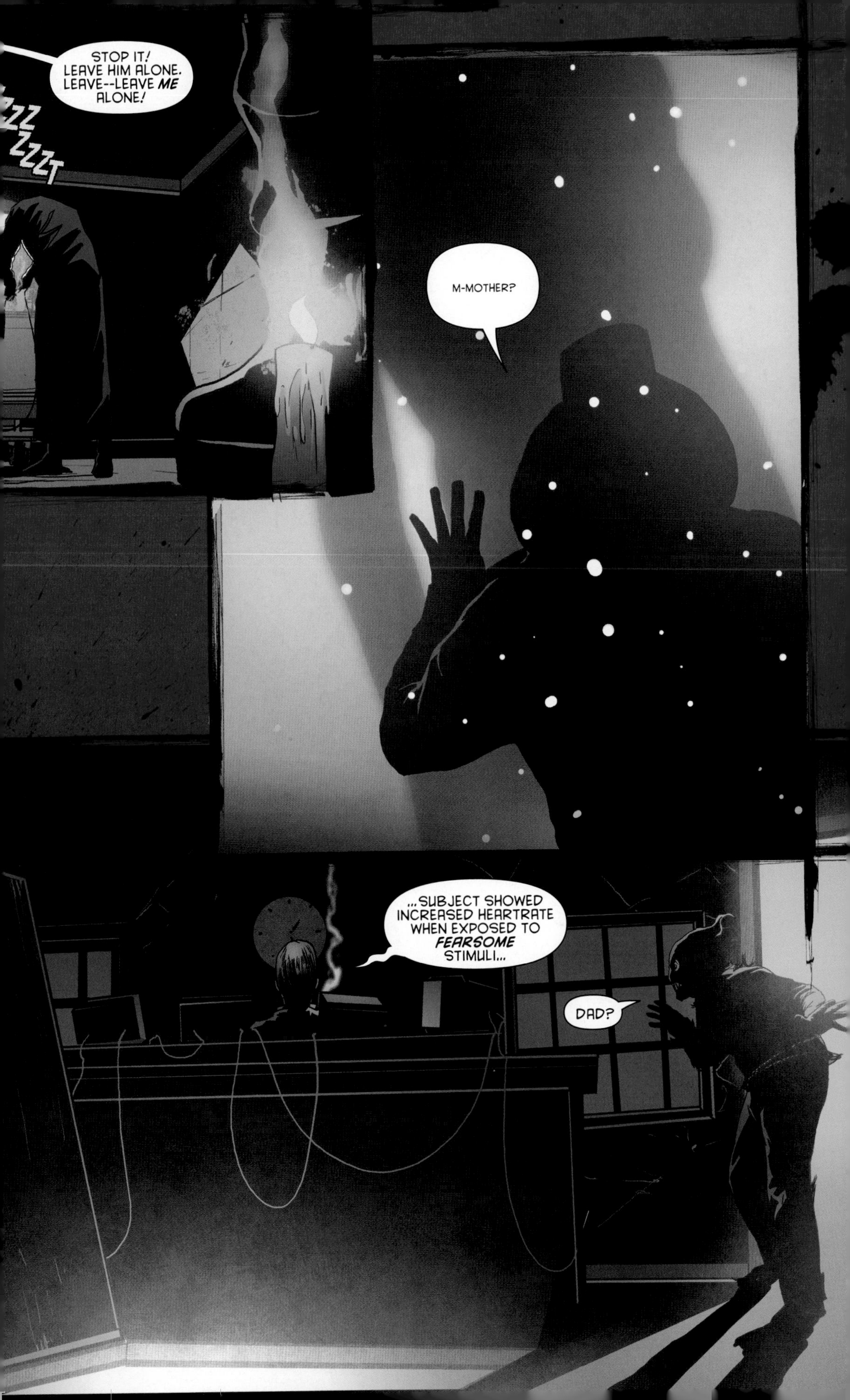
STOP IT! LEAVE HIM ALONE. LEAVE--LEAVE *ME* ALONE!
ZZZ ZZZT
M-MOTHER?
...SUBJECT SHOWED INCREASED HEARTRATE WHEN EXPOSED TO *FEARSOME* STIMULI...
DAD?

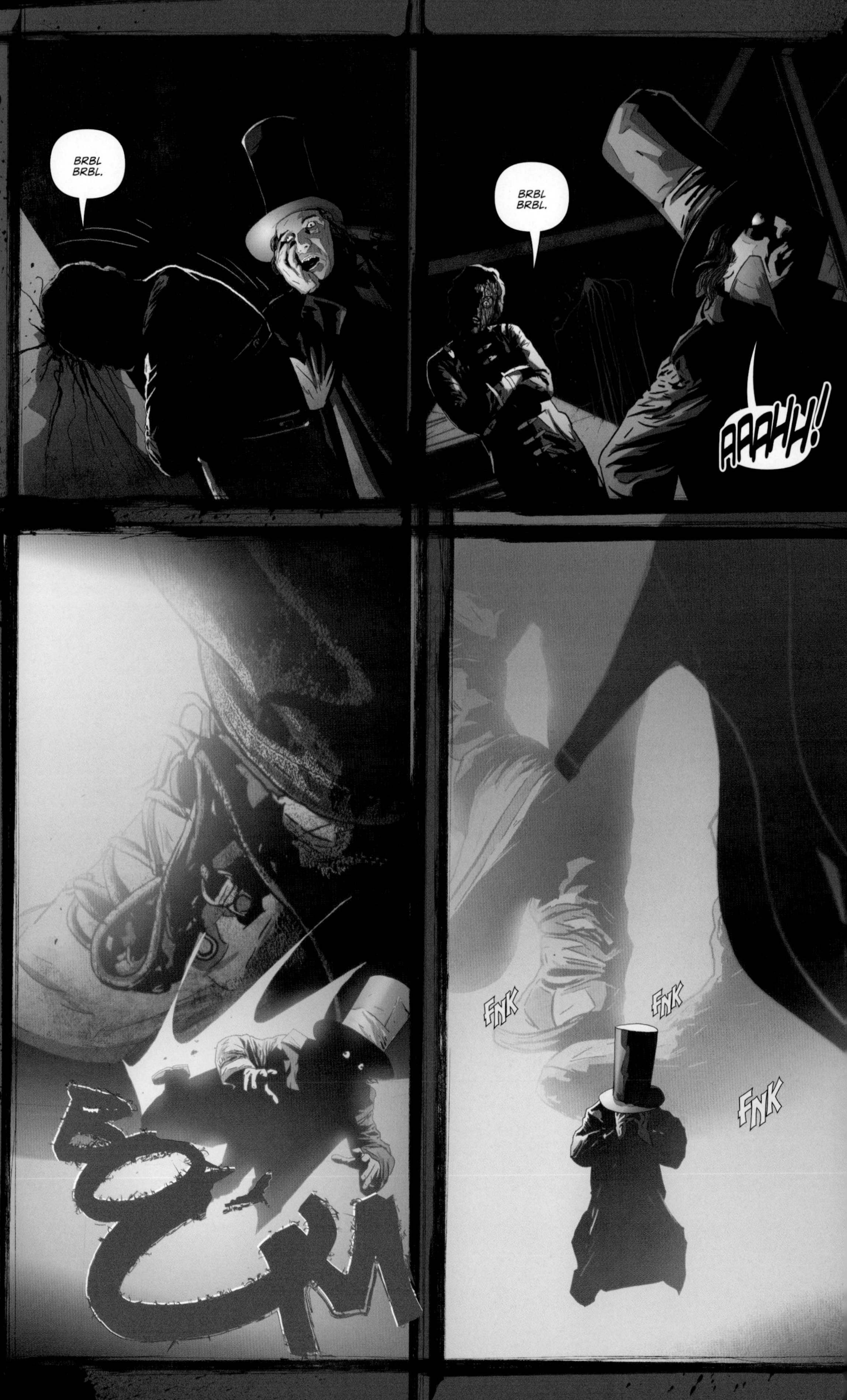
BRBL BRBL.
BRBL BRBL.
AAAHH!
BOOM
FNK
FNK
FNK

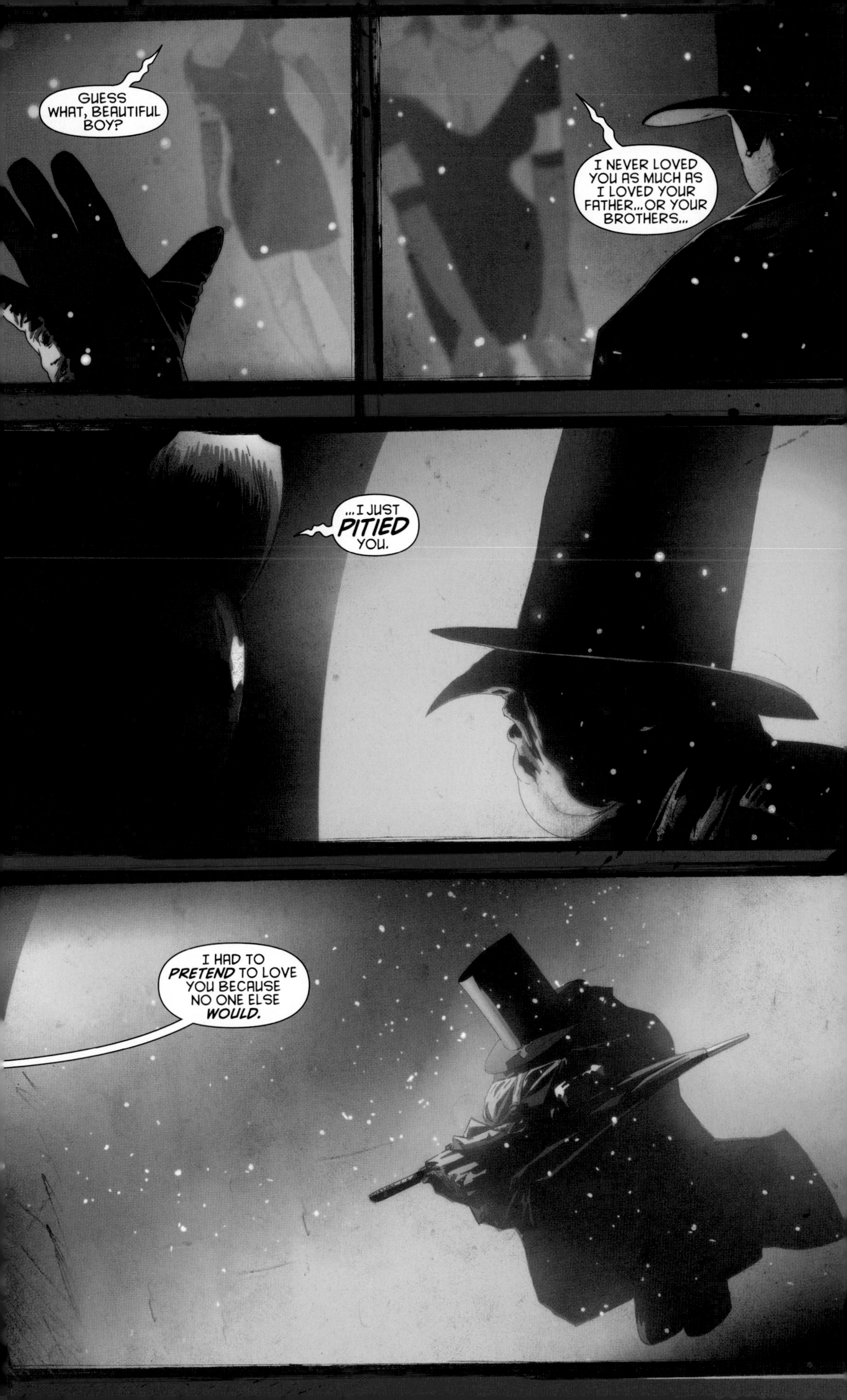
GUESS WHAT, BEAUTIFUL BOY?
I NEVER LOVED YOU AS MUCH AS I LOVED YOUR FATHER...OR YOUR BROTHERS...
...I JUST PITIED YOU.
I HAD TO PRETEND TO LOVE YOU BECAUSE NO ONE ELSE WOULD.

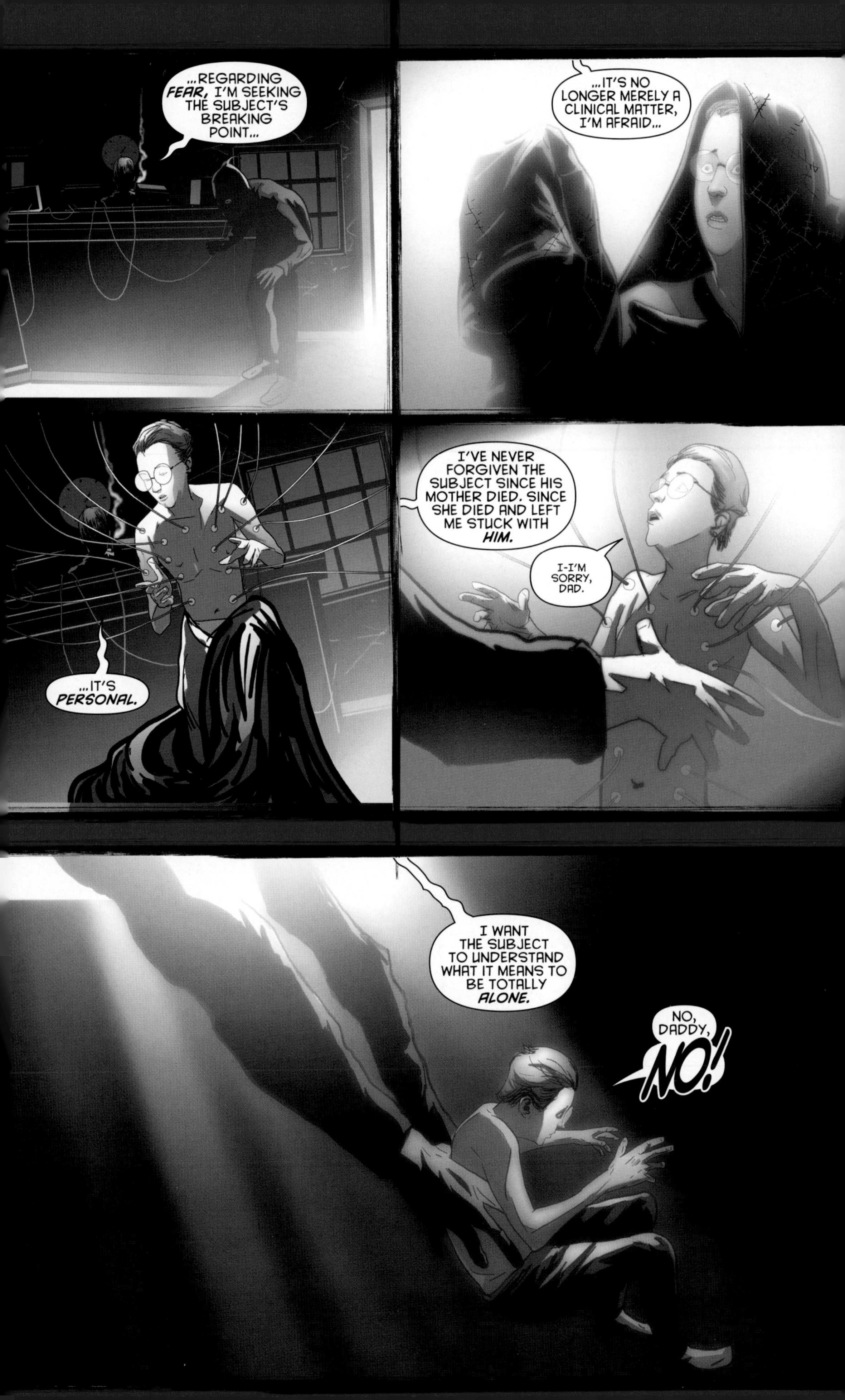
...REGARDING FEAR, I'M SEEKING THE SUBJECT'S BREAKING POINT...
...IT'S NO LONGER MERELY A CLINICAL MATTER, I'M AFRAID...
...IT'S PERSONAL.
I'VE NEVER FORGIVEN THE SUBJECT SINCE HIS MOTHER DIED. SINCE SHE DIED AND LEFT ME STUCK WITH HIM.
I-I'M SORRY, DAD.
I WANT THE SUBJECT TO UNDERSTAND WHAT IT MEANS TO BE TOTALLY ALONE.
NO, DADDY, NO!

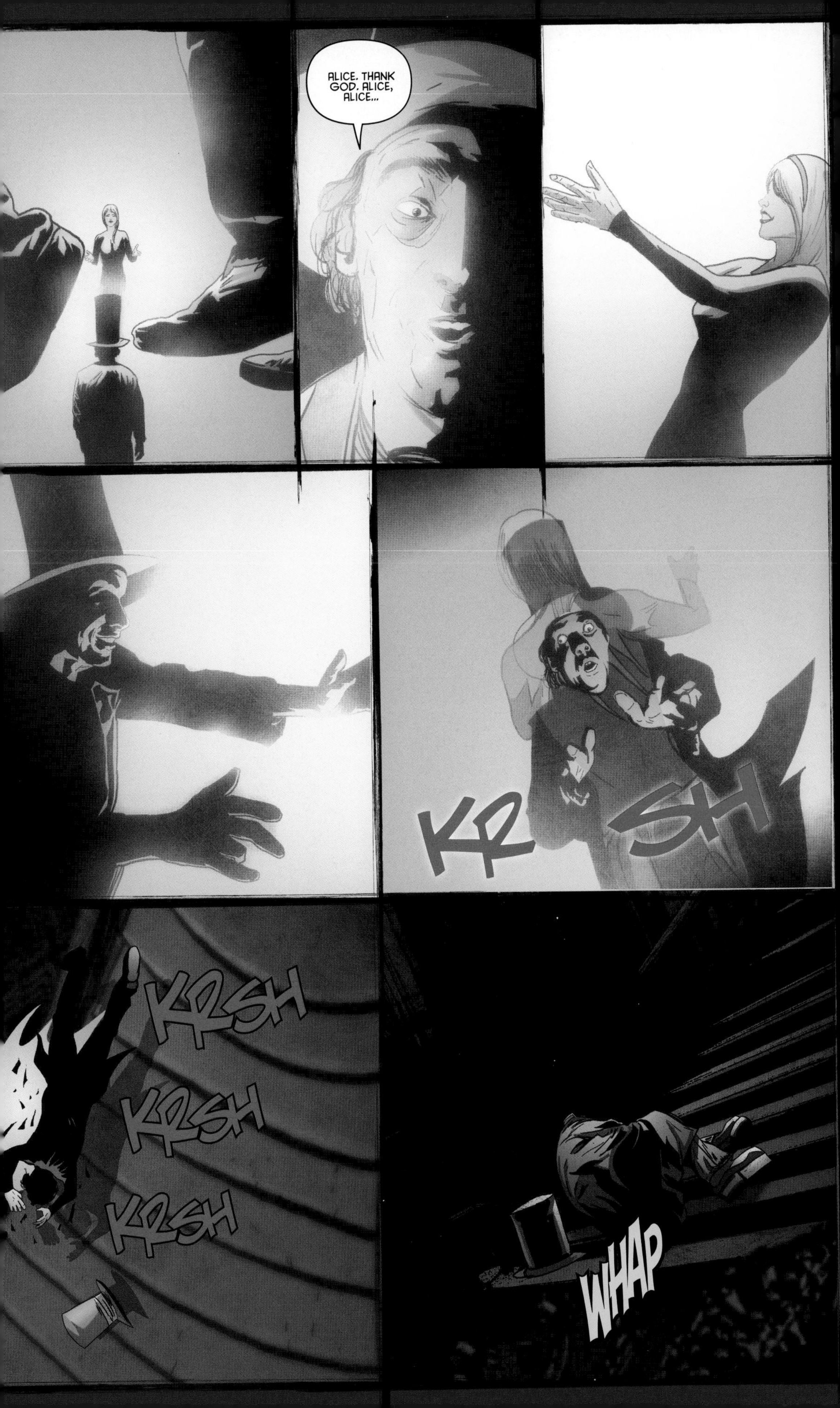
ALICE. THANK GOD. ALICE, ALICE...
KR SH
KRSH
KRSH
KRSH
WHAP

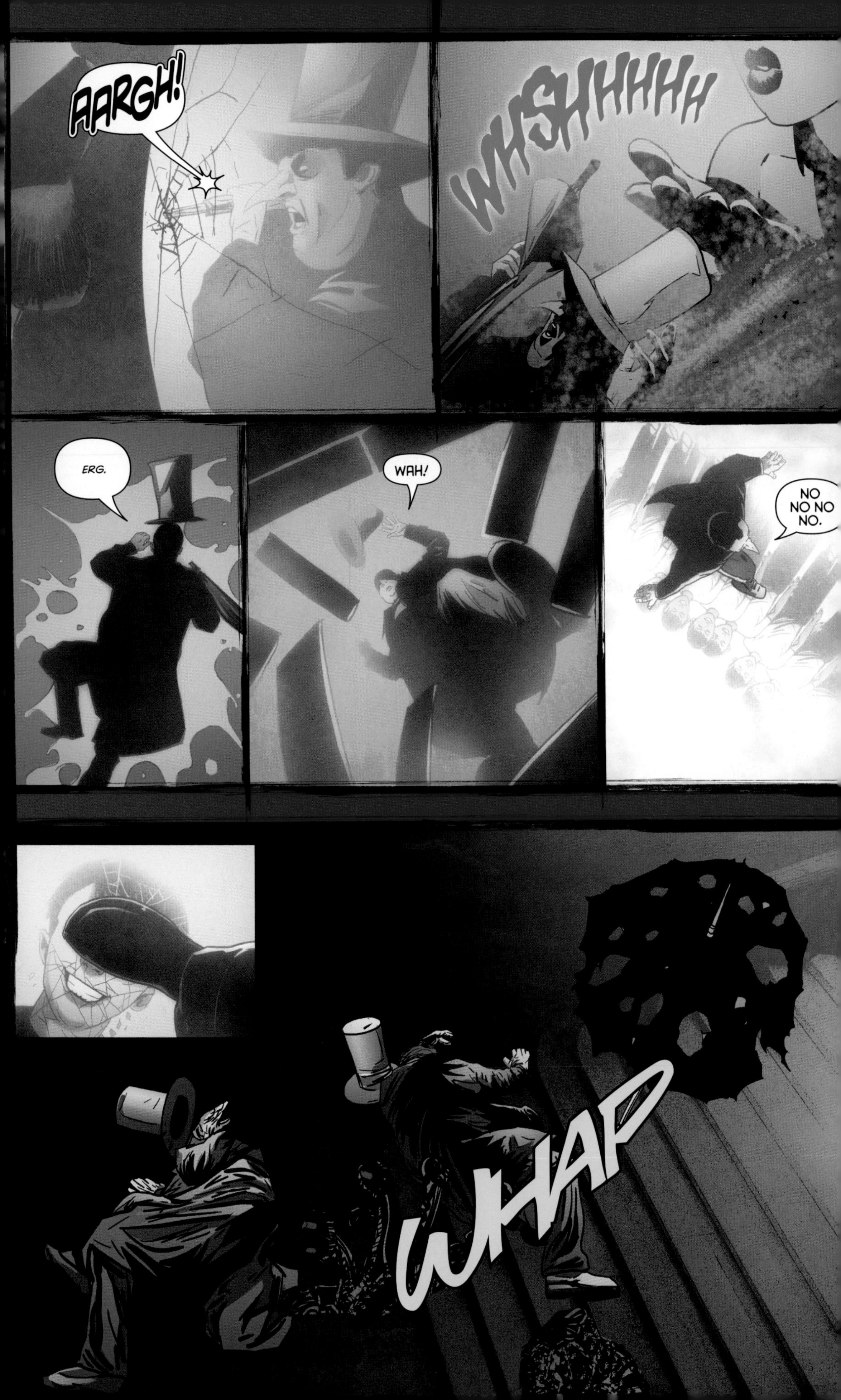
AARGH!
WHSHHHHH
ERG.
WAH!
NO NO NO NO.
WHAP

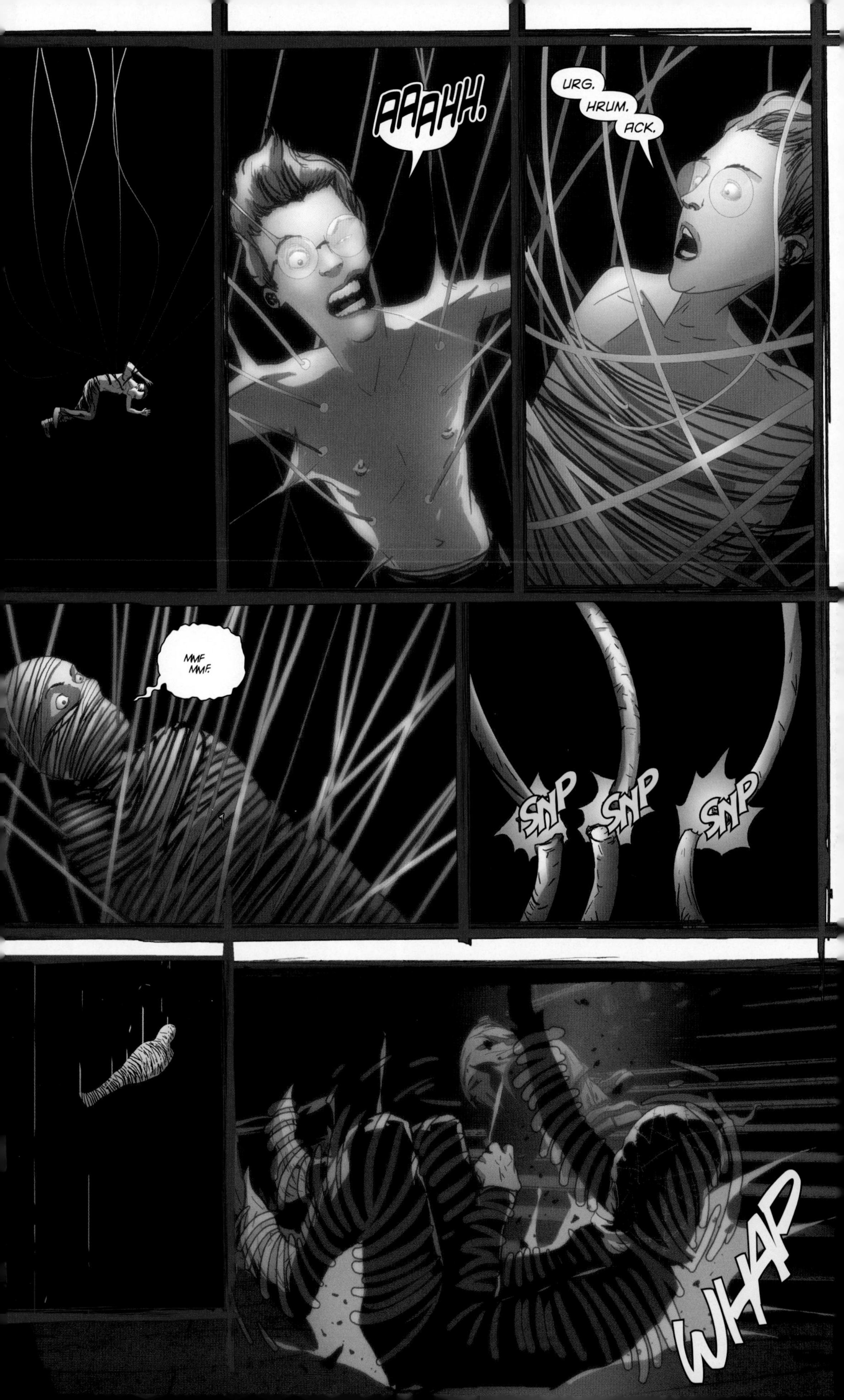
AAAHH.
URG.
HRUM.
ACK.
MMF MMF.
SNP
SNP
SNP
WHAP

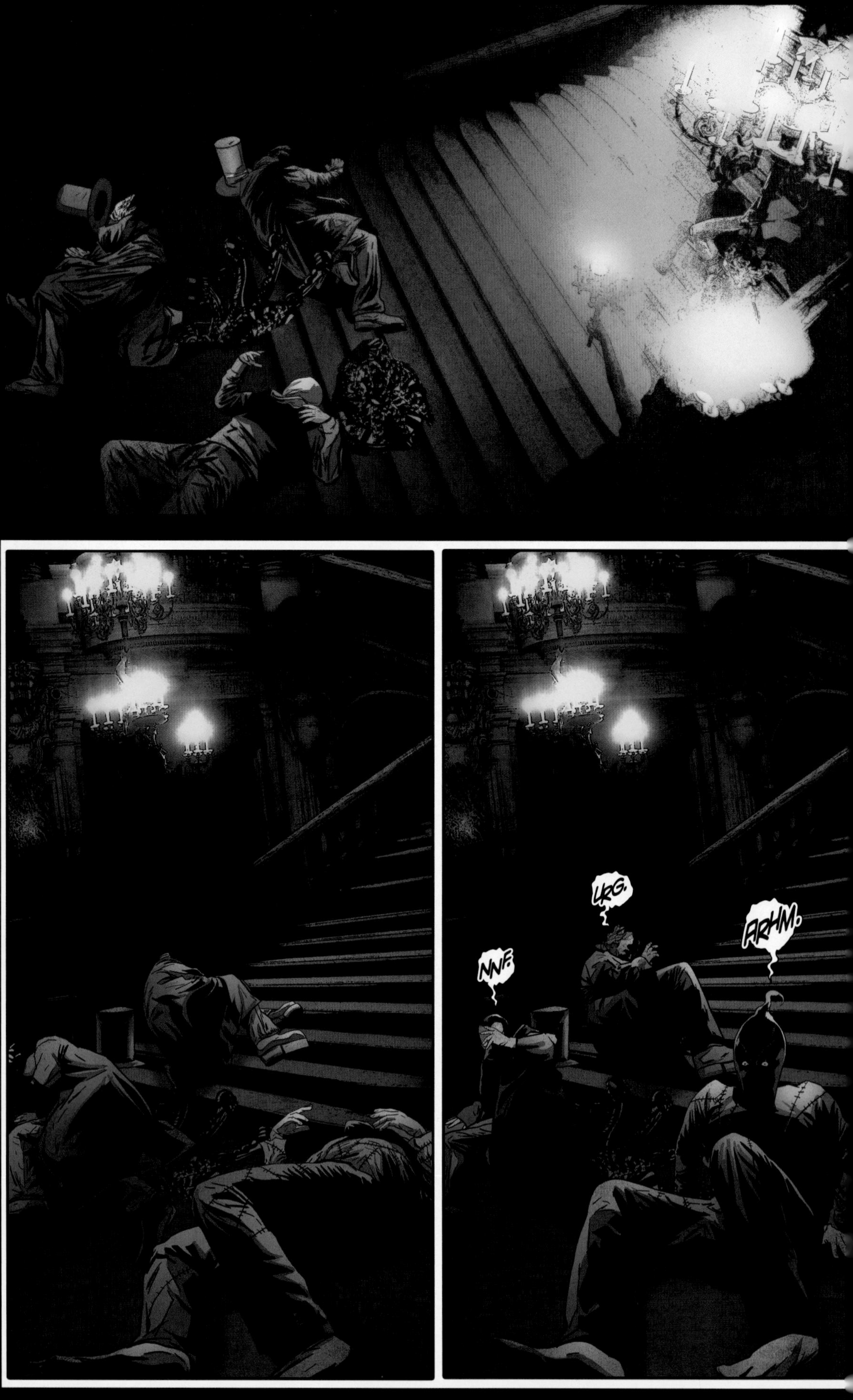
NNF.
URG.
ARHM.

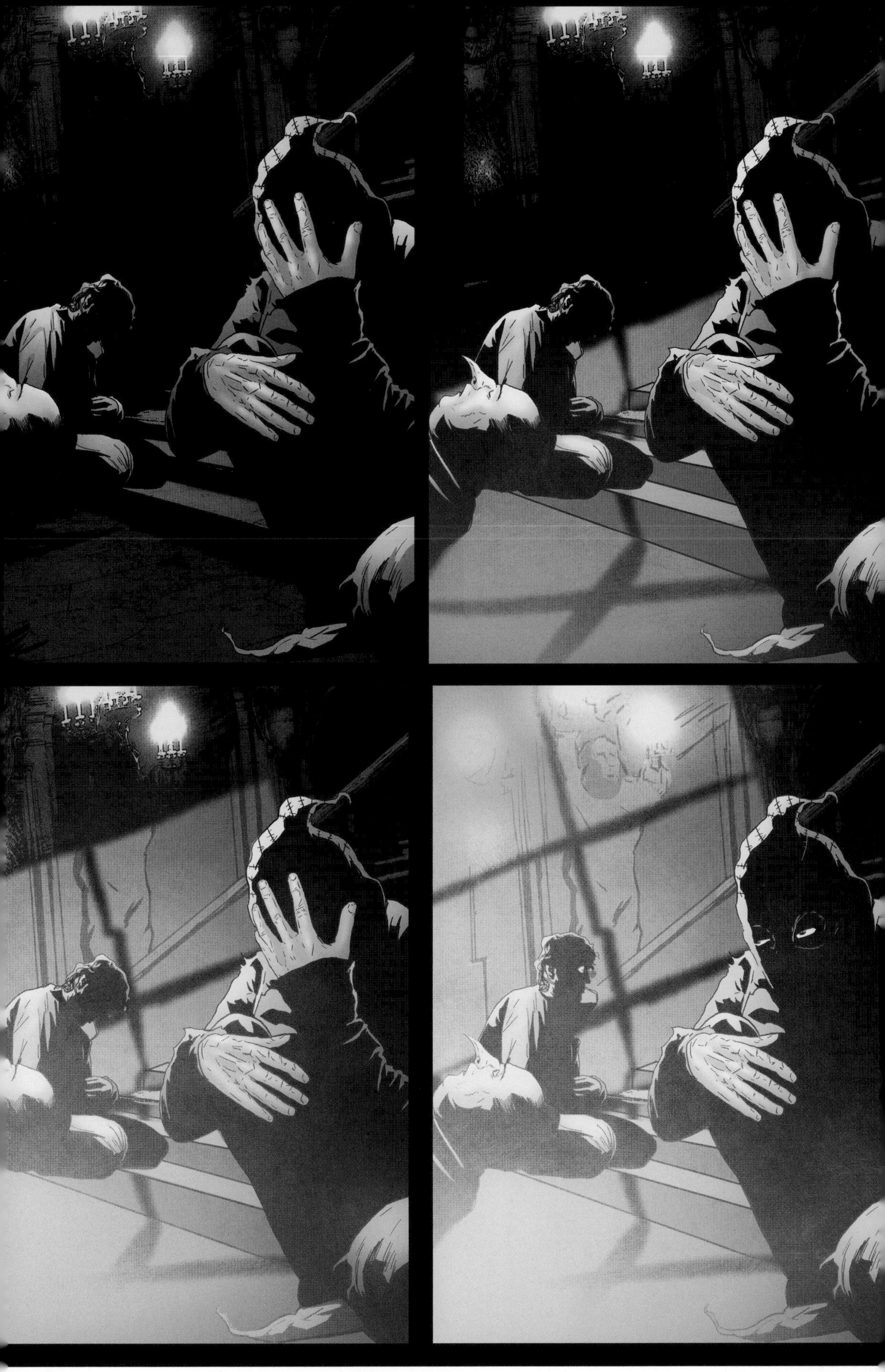

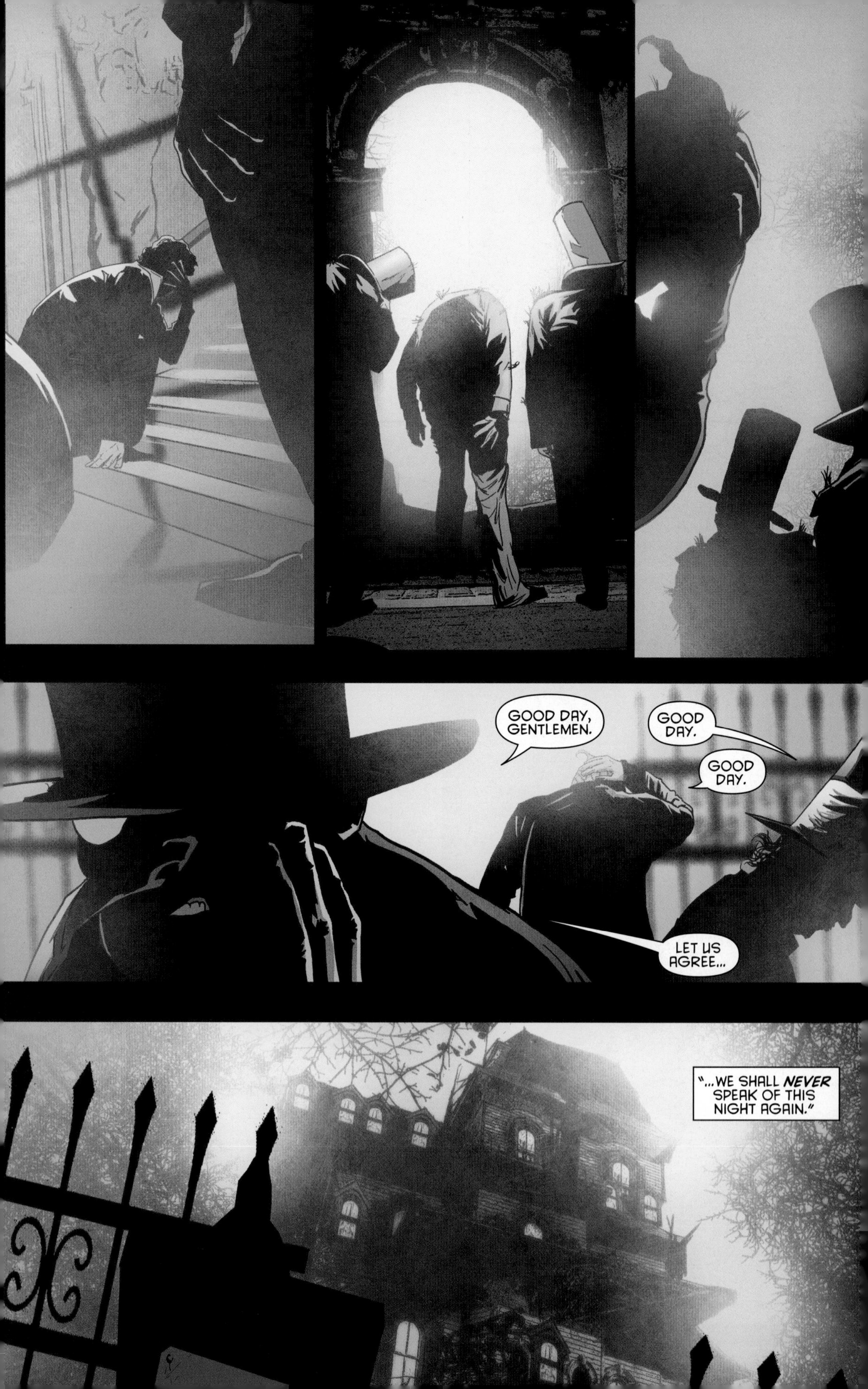
GOOD DAY, GENTLEMEN.
GOOD DAY.
GOOD DAY.
LET US AGREE...
"...WE SHALL NEVER SPEAK OF THIS NIGHT AGAIN."

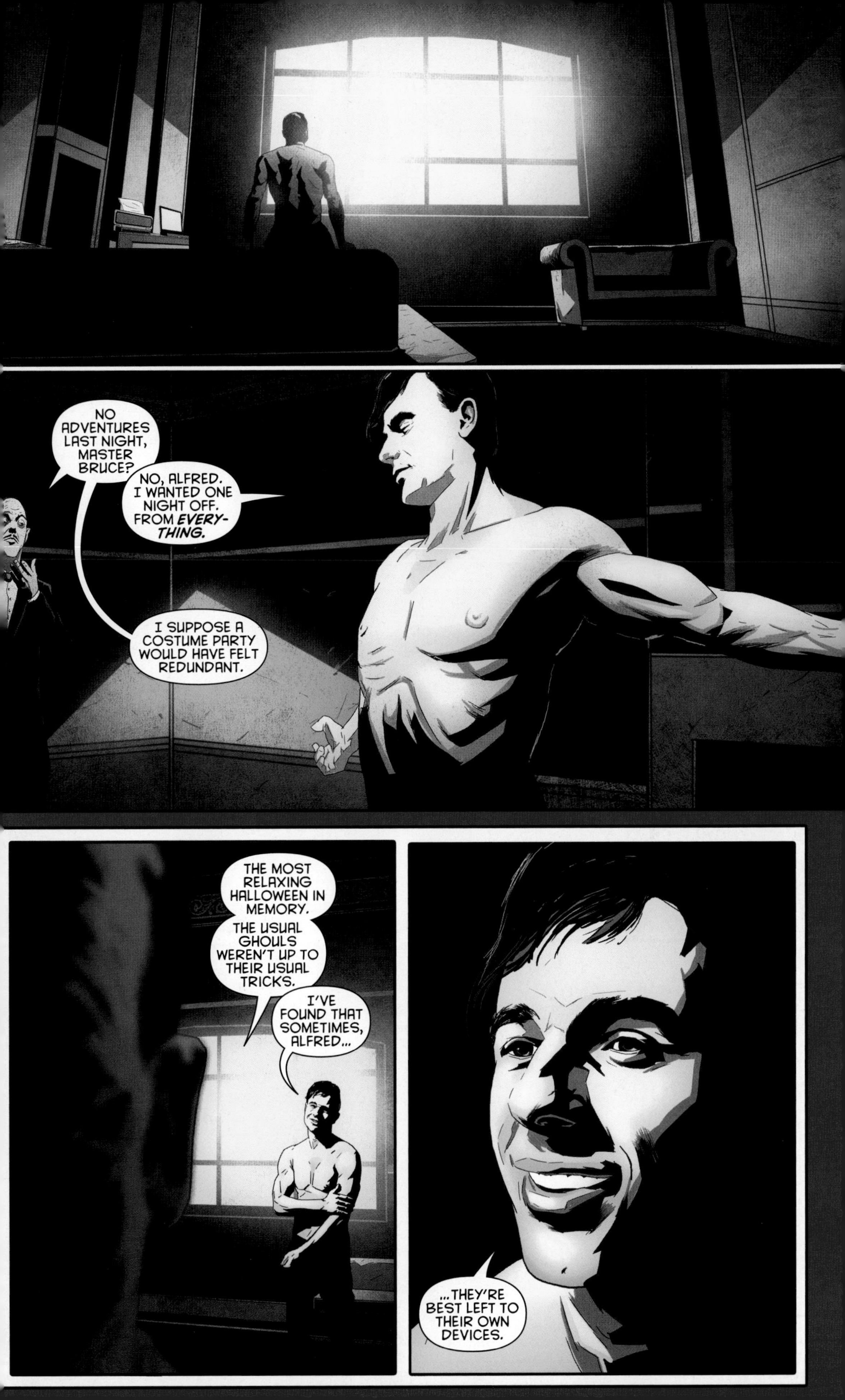
NO ADVENTURES LAST NIGHT, MASTER BRUCE?
NO, ALFRED. I WANTED ONE NIGHT OFF. FROM *EVERYTHING.*
I SUPPOSE A COSTUME PARTY WOULD HAVE FELT REDUNDANT.
THE MOST RELAXING HALLOWEEN IN MEMORY.
THE USUAL GHOULS WEREN'T UP TO THEIR USUAL TRICKS.
I'VE FOUND THAT SOMETIMES, ALFRED...
...THEY'RE BEST LEFT TO THEIR OWN DEVICES.

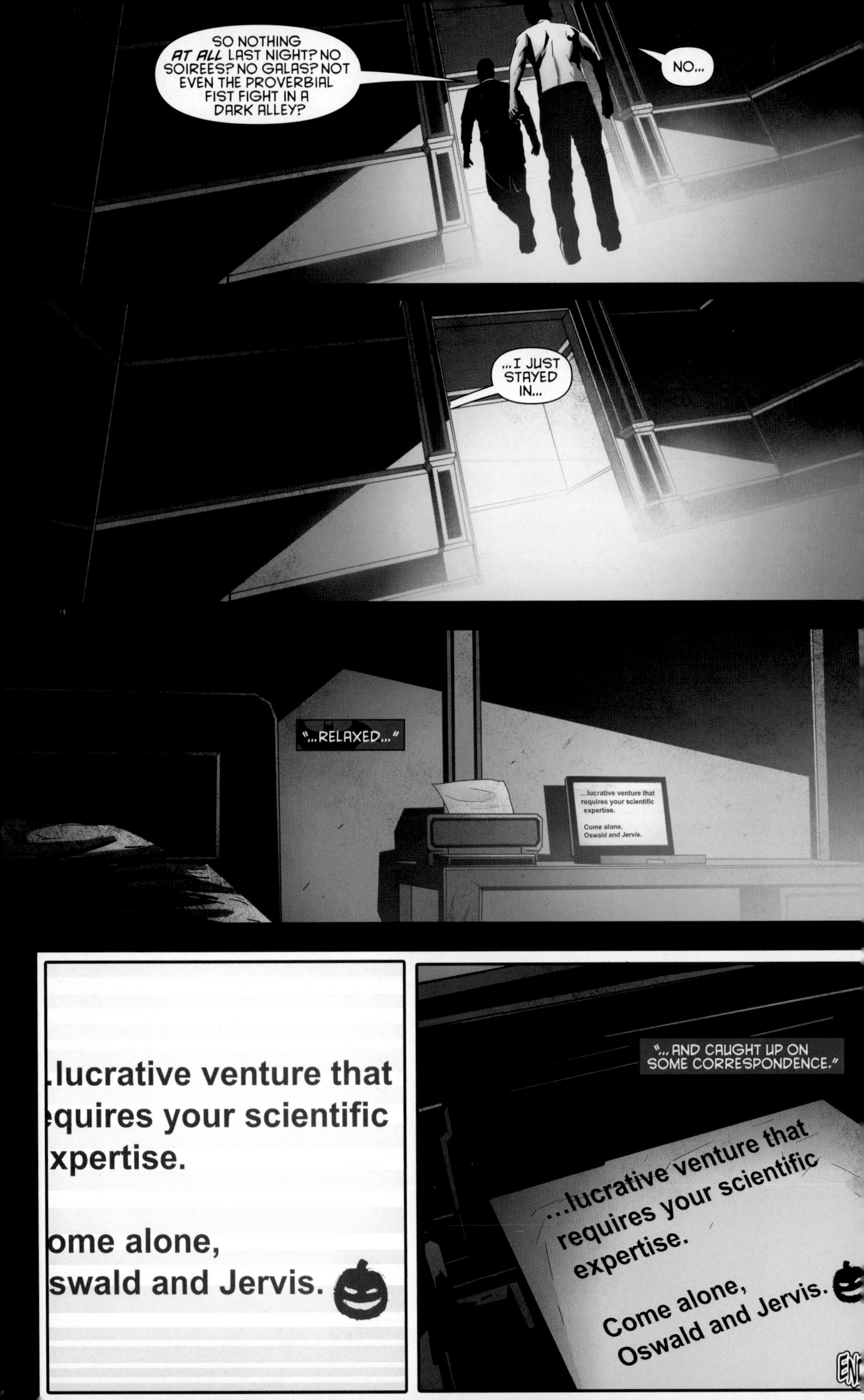

SO NOTHING *AT ALL* LAST NIGHT? NO SOIREES? NO GALAS? NOT EVEN THE PROVERBIAL FIST FIGHT IN A DARK ALLEY?
NO...
...I JUST STAYED IN...
"...RELAXED..."
...lucrative venture that requires your scientific expertise.
Come alone, Oswald and Jervis.
"... AND CAUGHT UP ON SOME CORRESPONDENCE."
...lucrative venture that requires your scientific expertise.
Come alone, Oswald and Jervis.